Making the Heartland Quilt

Making the Heartland Quilt

A Geographical History

of Settlement and Migration

in Early-Nineteenth-Century Illinois

DOUGLAS K. MEYER

Southern Illinois University Press
Carbondale and Edwardsville

Copyright © 2000 by the Board of Trustees,
Southern Illinois University
Printed in the United States of America

03 02 01 00   4 3 2 1

Library of Congress Cataloging-in-Publication Data
Meyer, Douglas K.
   Making the heartland quilt : a geographical history of
settlement and migration in early-nineteenth-century Illinois /
Douglas K. Meyer.
      p.   cm.
   Includes bibliographical references and index.
   1. Land settlement patterns—Illinois—History—19th century.
2. Human geography—Illinois.   3. Migration, Internal—
Illinois—History—19th century.   4. Illinois—Geography.
5. Illinois—History—1778–1865.   I. Title.
F545.M55   2000
977.3′03—dc21   99-41235
ISBN-8093-2289-7 (cloth : alk. paper)   CIP

The paper used in this publication meets the minimum
requirements of American National Standard for Information
Sciences—Permanence of Paper for Printed Library Materials,
ANSI Z39.48-1992. ♾

Contents

Illustrations

TABLES

Preface

The advantages of the western country consist in the great fertility of
the soil, . . . the cheapness of lands, and the newness of the country,
which affords room and opportunity for enterprise. These, together
with its commercial advantages, the total exemption from all taxes and
political burthens, and the comparatively small portion of labour
requisite to procure the necessaries of life, certainly render this a
desirable home.
— Hall, 1828

Immigrants spread across transAppalachia in the late eighteenth and early nineteenth centuries. Perceived New West advantages in the Old Northwest sparked
a surge in geographic mobility, known as the Great Migration. The directional-
biases of immigrants affected shifting settlement frontiers and the diffusion of
cultural traditions. Westward movement emerged as the dominant American migration theme. Historians have employed the framework for explaining settlement expansions and cultural changes between the Atlantic and Pacific shores
(Billington 1967; Merk 1978; Turner 1920). Parker contends that rather fixed, homogeneous immigrant zones arrayed east-west in the Old Northwest (1975, 12–13).
"Any reconstruction of a regional character must be partly imaginary, particularly
at a hundred years' distance, and a tracing of its origins must involve a degree of
plausible myth" (11).

Analysis of unpublished county birthplace data for 1850 unmasks diverse immigrant patterns across Illinois. There is little attempt to narrate a history of individuals or groups who participated in the settlement of a particular place or area.
Local libraries and genealogical societies, newspapers, diaries, scrapbooks, family
genealogies, household attics, and personal recollections furnish the stuff for a
historical or genealogical approach to the immigrant landscape. The most readily
available late-1800s historical sources of birthplace data are county histories,
county atlases, and county biographies, known as "mugbooks." A genealogical approach to immigrant patterns functions at the micro-scale of individual families,
rural townships, urban places, and intracounty movements. Additional sources of

county-scale birthplace data are the membership rolls of state old settlers associations, but coverage is limited (Rose 1983, 1985b).

Genealogical sources of birthplace data are of minimal utility at the intrastate level of geographic analysis. These sources of birthplace data are not universally available for all counties. Historical references are not of comparable publication date, scope, accuracy, or quality. As sources of birthplace data, county atlases, histories, and mugbooks reveal another implicit problem: they are at least one to three generations removed from the major migration flows that impressed Illinois during the Great Migration. Thus, the immigrant birthplace data for the closing frontier period of the state would be underrepresented. Birthplace data aggregated from such genealogical sources tend to create a socially biased sample. This approach is advantageous if an elitist perspective towards community development represents the focus of an immigrant study. An account of important people in a particular rural area or urban place is only valuable for understanding their role in shaping the post-pioneer period.

Census enumerators in 1850 recorded place of birth for the first time. Unfortunately, birthplace data were not published at the township or county level but by aggregate state totals. Microfilm copies of the 1850 United States manuscript schedules provided the unpublished county birthplace data that are the immigrant data base for this study of Illinois' immigrant fabric (*Seventh Census Population Schedules, 1850*). Township birthplace data are limited because of the failure to implement the township political system statewide. Native-born place of birth origins are limited to state of birth and not county or urban center. Foreign-born origins specified only country of birth and not province or urban place.

Native- and foreign-born birthplace fields were used as surrogates for county migration fields. Place of birth data were collected for all adult males twenty years old and over. Two important factors influenced the sampling method: (1) the role of the adult male in the decision-making process of selecting the destination and (2) the impracticality of copying and tabulating the data for the 851,470 Illinois residents in 1850. The adult male birthplace data for 1850 included 196,896 immigrants: 152,591 native-born (77.5 percent) and 44,305 foreign-born (22.5 percent). Unpublished 1850 United States manuscript schedules proffer the only comprehensive birthplace data source that is equivalent in reliability and areal availability. They are the only practical migration data source for documenting the benchmark immigrant structures arrayed in Illinois' ninety-nine counties at the time of first effective settlement.

Interpretations of nineteenth-century population origins have often consisted of implicit, rather than explicit, immigrant patterns. Historical geographers' studies of immigrant patterns have been exceptions: Ohio (Wilhelm 1982; Rose 1988a), Indiana (Rose 1983, 1985a, 1986a, 1986c, 1991), Illinois (Meyer 1976a, 1976b, 1976c, 1980, 1984), Michigan (Rose 1986b, 1987a, 1987b), Missouri (Gerlach 1986), Texas

(Jordan 1967, 1969), Oregon (Bowen 1972), and Middle West (Hart 1972; Hudson 1984a, 1986, 1988; Rose 1988c). My historical-geographical approach in analyzing immigrant diversity in Illinois is more comprehensive in scope and in context. My purpose in writing the book is twofold. First, historians have called for greater elaborations of essential immigrant patterns in rural landscapes during the formative settlement periods (Conzen 1980; Swierenga 1981). Second, geographers' speculations of midwestern population origins, cultural borders, culture regions, and regional way stations demand reexamination for midcontinental Illinois (Hart 1972; Hudson 1988; Jordan and Rowntree 1979; Mitchell 1978; Zelinsky 1973).

My book, *Making the Heartland Quilt,* documents the clustering and dispersion patterns of thirty-three immigrant groups and the emergence of discrete culture regions and regional way stations in Illinois. Historically and geographically, the state mirrors both regional and national settlement developments. I argue that Illinois symbolizes a prototypal midwestern "historic test-strip" of the diverse population origins that unfolded during the Great Migration. I posit that a synthesis of the native-born county migration fields requires redrawing Zelinsky's subculture regions and cultural borders for Illinois (1973). Mitchell infers that replicated regional way stations interconnected within a westward-diffusing American culture region system (1978). I hypothesize that Upland Southerners, New Englanders, Midlanders and Midwesterners, and foreigners formed culturally mixed regional way stations in Illinois that interrelated in expanding continental urban-transport and culture region systems.

Distinctive immigrant spatial orderings emerged in Illinois by 1850. Without systematic mapping of states and large regions, the extent, persistence, and influence of America's immigrant diversity remains lost, hidden, and little understood. Immigrant distribution maps mirror the collective processes modifying the actions and behaviors of individuals, families, and groups who settle a region. Borchert stresses the essential value of maps for a geographical study of settlement systems (1987). Maps increase the clarity and order of geographic movements, networks, and structures. Thirty-three immigrant maps are cartographic diagrams of clusterings and dispersions that are interwoven in evolving regional settlement networks. My findings are communicated cartographically with over sixty maps that depict an immigrant "lumpy stew." Immigrant region maps, culture region maps, a regional way station map, and supportive thematic maps stand as a kind of mini-settlement and immigrant atlas at the closing of the frontier in Illinois.

Diverse immigrant groups were attracted to early Illinois: Upland Southerners, New Englanders, Midlanders, Midwesterners, Germans, Irish, and English. Both cohesive and mixed settlements were established. Smaller immigrant groups from the Lowland South and other foreign countries usually intermixed but also formed enclaves among the larger immigrant groups. Balkanized immigrant islands meshed within the settlement framework. Cultural diversity was enhanced because of Illinois' midcontinental location, its water and land routeway linkages, and its lengthy north-south axis. The barrier effect of Lake Michigan contributed to the convergence and mixing of immigrant structures. First effective immigrant imprints during the frontier period persist as important influences on settlement, cultural, social, political, and economic spatial orderings (Zelinsky 1973, 13–14). Immigrant patterns reinforced the evolving historical-cultural record of ordinary people responding to the lure of transplanting and penetrating deeper into the continent. Illinois epitomizes midwestern dichotomies: northern versus southern; native-born versus foreign-born; rural versus urban; agriculture versus manufacturing. Today's regional characteristics and problems reflect the diverse immigrant structures interwoven during the Great Migration.

Spatial processes—migration, cultural, economic, settlement, urban, and transportation—engender change (growth versus decline) or prevent change (stability versus stagnation). Change-producing mechanisms shaped uniform, mixed, segmented, segregated, and dichotomous immigrant patterns. Distinctive south-north and east-west immigrant polarities emerged. A number of migration factors explain the settlement theme of cultural mixing in pivotal settlement areas. First, place images of attractive settlement areas possess greater legibility and imageability in immigrants' mental maps. Second, alluring migration clusters display greater connectivity between immigrants' origins and destinations. Larger migration flows relate to accessibility of transport modes and improvements, fewer intervening obstacles, and relative unattractiveness of alternative destinations at the time of migration. Third, successive linkages occurred over time within expanding national and regional urban-transport and culture region systems. During the Great Migration, immigrants increasingly traveled fixed, interconnecting routes.

Attempting to sort out fiction from fact in the immigrant patterns of Illinois is a difficult, unfinished task. Varied immigrant distributions represent elemental structures of developing regional landscapes. Instead of viewing immigrant structures as static, isolated, closed systems at the time of first effective settlement, I explore them as dynamic, interconnected, open systems. Interacting processes within open systems mold immigrant patterns. Illinois is indeed more than two states: metro-Chicago and downstate.

Immigrants ebbed and flowed across vast stretches of variant landscapes from the Atlantic seaboard to the Mississippi Valley (Friis 1974). Macro- and micro-scale migration streams were place-specific at their endpoints. In the Old Northwest, immigrant clusters revealed both cohesive and diverse immigrant compositions. Patterns of convergence and divergence emerged as immigrants followed worn diffusion paths. Social networks developed chain and channelized migration patterns that shaped immigrant clusters. Sense of place served as an integrating mechanism that predisposed the migration decision-making process. Social networks functioned as important motivating and organizing factors that spatially sorted immigrants. Mainstream migration flows from Upland South, New England, and Midland hearth areas and interior areas of transAppalachia dispersed westward and northwestward to Illinois within expanding continental diffusion networks. Intertwined within American urban-transportation and culture region systems, regional culture groups configured processions of immigrant diversity on a featureless plain. Infilling of Germans, Irish, English, and smaller foreign groups, such as Swiss and Swedes, intensified the diversity of the emerging immigrant mosaic.

In this book, I analyze the immigrant patterns of twenty-three native-born and ten foreign-born adult male groups who peopled Illinois by 1850. The following geographical questions are explored: What was the extent and configuration of each immigrant group's distributional patterns? Were there significant similarities and differences between immigrant groups' principal migration clusters? What processes shaped the intrastate immigrant patterns of the native- and foreign-born groups? Migration flows caught up in "Illinois fever" were not directionless or placeless. Immigrants knew their routes and destinations as they transformed midwestern settlement landscapes.

Meinig views "the United States as a gigantic geographic growth with a continually changing geographic character, structure, and system" (1986, xv). The settlement of midcontinental Illinois was affected by an expanding continental America. Geographical concepts serve as integrative themes: places and regions; patterns and structures; routeways and corridors; circulations and networks; urban hierarchies and hinterlands; cores and peripheries; cultural borders and divides; cultural uniformity and mixtures; change and persistence; and regional and national systems. Migration concepts decode spatial processes: cohesion and diversity; ethnicity and enclave; immigrant region, culture region, and regional way station; migration cluster and dispersion; information fields and social networks; chain and channelized migration; migration push and pull factors; and migration stream and stepwise migration.

I have organized this investigation of the historical geography of early processes and patterns of settlement and migration in Illinois as follows. Chapter 1 interprets place images that served as essential elements of "Illinois fever." Early-nineteenth-century emigrant guides and gazetteers contributed to shaping immigrants' cognitive maps. Historical and geographical processes affecting the progression of settlement patterns are explored in chapter 2. Chapter 3 probes emerging regional overland circulation linkages and urban networks. Five early road maps from the Illinois State Historical Library Map Collection document expanding urban-transport infrastructures (Carey and Lea 1822; Knight 1828; Young 1839; Morse and Breese 1844; Cowperthwait 1850). The impact of flatboats and steamboats on riverine movement-settlement corridors are assessed in chapter 4. Chapter 5 analyzes sequential settlement frontiers for six time periods: 1800, 1810, 1820, 1830, 1840, and 1850.

Twenty-three native-born immigrant regions are examined in chapters 6, 7, and 8. Chapter 6 focuses on the regional culture group that initially settled Illinois, the Upland Southerners. Yankees from New England and New England extended (New York and Upper Middle West) are analyzed in chapter 7. Chapter 8 investigates Midlanders and Midwesterners, a regional culture group that included settlers from Middle Atlantic states, particularly the southeast Pennsylvania hearth area and Midland extended (Lower Middle West). In each chapter, the largest state contributors are discussed first, then the smaller states. Chapter 9 dissects ten foreign-born immigrant regions by examining the largest country contributors, then the smaller countries. Each chapter concludes with a delimitation of a discrete culture region. The conclusion, chapter 10, reevaluates population origins, cultural borders, culture regions, and regional way stations in the Prairie State.

I thank the undergraduate assistants who read the 1850 manuscript schedules and tabulated data in the 1970s. Faculty Research Council grants at Eastern Illinois University supported purchasing microfilm copies of the manuscript schedules, research assistants, and archival research. Presidential Summer Research Awards ensured completion of data analysis, papers for professional meetings, and publishable computer maps. Reference librarians at Booth Library at Eastern Illinois University, the Illinois Historical Survey at the University of Illinois Library at Champaign-Urbana, the Chicago Historical Society Library, and the Illinois State Historical Library in Springfield aided me in numerous ways.

I appreciate the encouragement of John Jakle, Bob Bastian, Keith Sculle, and David Meyer and the criticisms of the anonymous referees who reviewed the manuscript. I especially recognize Mike Conzen's perceptive notion that Illinois is an archetypal "historic test-strip" of midwestern cultural origins. I am indebted to Jim Stratton of the geology/geography department at Eastern Illinois University and Charles Blaich of Wabash College in Indiana, formerly of the psychology department at Eastern Illinois University, for exposing me to the "Macintosh world." Finally, I dedicate the book to my wife, Joann, and my children, Karen Meyer Freeman and Todd Meyer. The book reflects their patience, understanding, and support over many years.

Various topics and themes relating to the settlement history and migration patterns of Illinois have been presented at professional meetings at the international, national, regional, and state levels for over a quarter century. Portions of the immigrant research have appeared in substantially different form in the following articles: "Native-Born Immigrant Cluster on the Illinois Frontier," *Proceedings*, Association of American Geographers, 8 (1976): 41–44; "Southern Illinois Migration

Fields: The Shawnee Hills in 1850," *Professional Geographer* 28 (1976): 151–60; "Immigrant Clusters in the Illinois Military Tract," *Pioneer America* 12 (1980): 97–112; "Foreign Immigrants in Illinois, 1850," *Illinois History Teacher* 5 (1998): 5–28 (coauthored with Robert Ashley); "Illinois Culture Regions at Mid-Nineteenth Century," *Bulletin of the Illinois Geographical Society* 18 (1976): 3–13; and "Types of Farming on the Illinois Frontier," *Bulletin of the Illinois Geographical Society* 21 (1979): 9–17. This book represents a culmination of a historical, geographic exploration to unravel the geographical history of settlement and migration in the Prairie State during the early nineteenth century.

Making the Heartland Quilt

1

Frontier Illinois Place Images

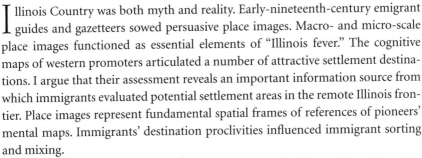

The state of Illinois has probably the finest body of
fertile land of any state in the Union, and the opportunities for speculation are numerous—property will continue
to advance—admirable farms and town lots may be purchased with a certainty of realising large profits. The country
here is beautiful.

    —Peck 1837

I llinois Country was both myth and reality. Early-nineteenth-century emigrant
guides and gazetteers sowed persuasive place images. Macro- and micro-scale
place images functioned as essential elements of "Illinois fever." The cognitive
maps of western promoters articulated a number of attractive settlement destinations. I argue that their assessment reveals an important information source from
which immigrants evaluated potential settlement areas in the remote Illinois frontier. Place images represent fundamental spatial frames of references of pioneers'
mental maps. Immigrants' destination proclivities influenced immigrant sorting
and mixing.

    Real and imagined frontier place images intertwined in the continental interior.
Allen contends that geographical movements of a colonizing frontier society often
reflected inadequate and inaccurate objectives, directions, and geographical information (1976). Jakle stresses that geographical perceptions, behavioral experiences, and geographic mobility were deeply rooted in a sense of place (1977).
Pioneers spatially organized the tangible and intangible frontier world by men-
tally and emotionally creating spatial frames of references (Downs and Stea 1977,
99–145).

    Jakle argues that on the transAppalachian frontier, pioneers viewed places in a
time-space framework. In a geographical context, places possess locational attributes, areal extent, and perceived boundaries. In a temporal context, places reveal
"a sequence of openings and closings, and function for set durations of time"
(1990, 83). Attractive settlement destinations as place images focused pioneers'

conscious and unconscious behavioral predispositions. Belief, attitude, intentionality, and icon embrace the primary components of a place image (84). Settlers believed their destination existed. They were driven by affective orientation towards their perceived new home nested in a distinctive place image. The pioneers' willingness to uproot from place of origin to a new place of destination reveals the intentionality of beliefs and attitudes woven into their ongoing behavior. Beliefs and attitudes associated with place attach themselves to intentional objects in the landscape or icons. Place as icon symbolizes the satisfactions and dissatisfactions tied to or expected in a place. Alluring destinations formed the basis of a family's hopes, dreams, and future prosperity perceived in a new environmental location or place image.

I argue that immigrants' cognitive mapping attempted to make sense out of locational attributes, physical habitats, and settlement developments in the insular Illinois frontier. Correspondence in spatial information emerged between the attributes and arrangements of the mental maps shared by like-minded mobile immigrants. My argument focuses on immigrants' essential behavioral requirement to live in a socially cohesive context and desire to seek and identify similar or better place environments. Such a constructive place strategy permitted immigrants to implant, modify, and persist in the remote wilderness.

A backwoods colonization culture rapidly expanded a hunting-agricultural strategy across transAppalachia in the late eighteenth and early nineteenth centuries. Widespread transformation to market-oriented farming hinged on efficient, effective urban-transport networks. The suitability of adaptive Midland–Upland South pioneer culture offered immigrants the benefits of rapid, successive movements across the woodland environment into the heart of North America (Jordan and Kaups 1989). Immigrants replicated pioneer culture settlement islands in the forested habitat. Mainline migration flows formed cultural fusion settlement areas in the continental interior. Within the evolving American culture region system, regional way stations (Mitchell 1978) and landscape formation zones (Pillsbury 1987) emerged as developmental sources of distinctive American regional cultures and place landscapes. Settlements and movement pathways provided a progression of sequential places and route maps for pioneers traversing the interior.

Immigrants' social networks integrated origins and destinations as mutually shared cognitive place images. American frontiersmen arriving in Illinois Country developed flexible route maps via overland and water pathways. Wilderness fears were lessened with easily visualized places. I contend that sustainability of place images represented a prerequisite quality of landmark settlement areas. Distinctive destinations endured temporally and expanded spatially through successive immigrant infillings in a developing regional settlement framework. Pivotal settlement areas in expanding frontiers were entwined in mental maps. Legibility and imageability were essential qualities of attractive destinations. American pioneers colonized slowly across early Illinois Country. Western boosters propagandized place images that areally shifted during the Great Migration. Shifting migration streams and gateway channels altered regional settlement structures in Illinois in the 1830s and 1840s. Persistence of "siren" place images amplified pioneers' hopes and dreams. Authenticity and lore linked in immigrants' mental maps.

Early-Nineteenth-Century Illinois Boosters

Early emigrant guides and gazetteers for the territory and new state of Illinois championed macro-scale place images. The borderlands of navigable waterways and their tributaries formed fundamental settlement preference types. They functioned as penetration corridors, accessible settlement areas, optimum habitat choices, and trade and communication linkages in an expanding, integrated settlement frontier (fig. 1.1). The American Bottom opposite St. Louis evolved as an alluring destination.

Samuel R. Brown recognized the fundamental advantages of riverine movement-settlement corridors in advocating the American Bottom and other watercourses in the Territory of Illinois:

> No state or territory in North America can boast of superior facilities of internal navigation. Nearly 1,000 miles, or, in other words, two-thirds of its frontier is washed by the Wabash, Ohio, and Mississippi. The placid Illinois traverses this territory in a southwestern direction, nearly 400 miles. . . . The large tract of country through which the Illinois river and its branches meander, is said not to be exceeded in beauty, levelness, richness and fertility of soil, by any tract of land, of equal extent, in the United States. . . . [T]he Kaskaskia . . . the finest country I have ever seen . . . is suited to the growth of Indian corn, wheat, rye, oats, barley, hemp, tobacco. . . . The climate is too cold for cotton, as a staple, or for sugar. . . . The great American bottom of the Mississippi begins at the mouth of the Kaskaskia river, extending nearly to the mouth of the Illinois river. . . . No land can be more fertile. Some of it has been in cultivation one hundred and twenty years, and still no deterioration has yet manifested itself—it is unquestionably the Delta of America. . . . The banks of the Kaskaskia and Illinois in some places present a sublime and picturesque scenery. (1817, 17–23)

Federal land districts and military bounty lands were also promoted as potential destinations in emigrant guides. Legal documentation of land ownership was clearly supported with the governmental surveying of the land. Military tracts had been originally set aside in New York, Ohio, Tennessee, and Kentucky for Revolutionary War veterans, only to fall prey to speculators. Van Zandt focused on the detailed surveyors' reports of the new Military Bounty Lands between

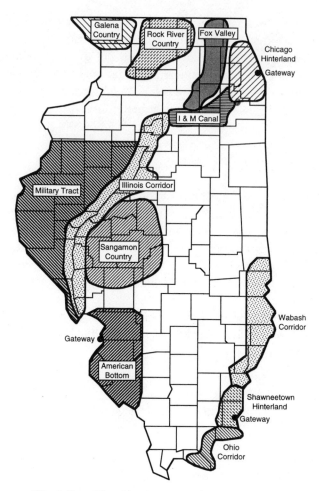

FIG. 1.1. Illinois Fever Place Images

the Mississippi and Illinois Rivers in the Illinois Territory (1818). Brief habitat synopses of the three federal land districts operating at the time were included in his guidebook for intrusive, hungry land seekers. The hinterlands of the land offices of Shawneetown, Kaskaskia, and Edwardsville served as early frontier settlement foci.

Other smaller riverine corridors in central and southern Illinois were also advocated by western promoters. Bisected by the Illinois Valley, the Military Tract and Sangamon Country contested ten to fifteen years later as "siren" settlement areas. Dana alludes to the alluring nature of Sangamon Country: "The tract drained by the Sangamo and its tributaries, seems to display as enchanting a rural scenery as could be painted by the fairest fancy of a poet or a writer of romance. The extent of this beautiful country is not yet ascertained by actual survey: but by hunters and military rangers, who have traversed the region. . . . The Sangamo country occupies a central position, extends within a few miles of Vandalia, the metropolis of the state of Illinois" (1819, 146).

The Emigrant's Guide, or *Pocket Geography of the Western States and Territories* offered more detailed information (1818, 223–49). When migration escalated, it became standard in gazetteers to provide helpful details concerning emerging counties and towns. Given the early settlement history of the territory, places in proximity to the entrepôt of St. Louis were prominent. "Madison County . . . is the most northerly county on the Mississippi. This county comprehends a part of the American bottom. In general its surface is uneven, affords some prairie, and is allowed to be fertile. . . . The Goshen settlement is situated between the mouth of Wood river and St. Louis, and may be said to extend as far east as Edwardsville. . . . Belleville . . . is situated in the centre of the noted Turkey Hill settlement, 4 miles east of the bluff which bounds the American Bottom, 6 miles from Silver creek, and 18 miles south-east of St. Louis" (238–39).

Other key places in the territory of Illinois linked with earlier French settlements and Wabash and Ohio Valley corridors.

> Kaskaskia, the present seat of government for the territory, and of justice for this county [Randolph], is situated on the east edge of the American Bottom . . . this flourishing town sunk down to a paltry French village. But within a few years it has given flattering symptoms of resuscitation. . . . There is a weekly paper called the "Illinois Herald," printed in this town which is the only paper printed in the territory. . . . White County, situated immediately north of Gallatin, is bounded on the east by the Great Wabash. This is a very rich county, affording some excellent prairie, and several fine mill seats. The Little Wabash runs through it. Its seat of justice is Carmi. (240–41, 245)

A Gazetteer Model

The flow of the Great Migration substantially increased to Illinois and its sister Mississippi Valley state of Missouri. Lewis C. Beck, an early influential western promoter, provided an important organizational change in his emigrant gazetteer of Illinois and Missouri (1823). He expanded the available geographical information, established an improved new format, and dictated higher standards of authenticity. His gazetteer model of three segments along with information was later borrowed by Peck (1836), Mitchell (1837), and other writers. Beck devoted 155 pages to describing Illinois, the most comprehensive early guidebook of the state. The first section pertained to a general geographical and statistical view of Illinois. The second section described the political structure of the state with a general view of the counties. Beck's county descriptions were in many cases more inclusive than those in Peck's highly respected later Illinois gazetteers. The final segment, over half the pages, addressed a detailed, alphabetically arranged topographical view of the towns, villages, settlements, rivers, creeks, lakes, prairies, and forts in the state. Buck noted the unusual value of Beck's gazetteer with its explicit community information in the early statehood period (1914, 94).

An incipient settlement stage penetrated the watercourses of southwest and southeast Illinois and the lower Illinois Valley in west-central Illinois in the 1820s. Beck allocated the largest proportion of his gazetteer pages to the place data most desired by immigrants: counties, urban places, loosely clustered settlements, navigable streams, and the ecological niches of rivers and creeks (1823). The importance of site, situation, accessibility, riverine corridors, and flatboating were geographic imperatives of destinations. These attributes of the land intertwined in Beck's and later western promoters' geographical evaluations of favorable locations. An example of each place image category follows:

> Edwards County raises a surplus quantity of produce, the principal part of which is shipped down the Wabash. Like the other counties lying on this stream, it possesses the advantage of a water conveyance to the different parts of the valley of the Mississippi. The Wabash, for several months in the year, is navigable for 200 or 300 miles. This, together with the Little Wabash, which is also navigable for a short distance, affords the inhabitants of this county every facility for transporting their produce. (Beck 1823, 64–65)

> Golconda, (formerly Lusk's ferry,) a small post town, and the seat of justice of Pope county. It is situated on the right bank of the Ohio river, about eighty miles above its junction with the Mississippi, and twenty below the mouth of Cumberland river. . . . Here is a ferry across the Ohio, which affords a direct communication by roads with different parts of Kentucky and Tennessee. (116)

> Marine settlement, a very flourishing settlement of Madison county. It is situated on a beautiful prairie, near a branch of Silver creek. . . . The settlement was commenced in 1819 . . . and is now one of the most flourishing in the state. It is healthy and well watered; the lands are gently undulating, and the soil very fertile. . . . Marine settlement is about 12 miles east of Edwardsville, on the mail route between St. Louis and Vandalia. (126)

> Big Muddy river . . . a considerable stream in the southwestern part of the state. It rises between the waters of the Kaskaskia and Little Wabash, and running a southern and southwestern course through the counties of Jefferson, Franklin, Jackson and Union, empties into the Mississippi. . . . Being fed by Little Muddy river, Beacoup creek, and several other smaller streams, it is rendered boatable for 40 or 50 miles through a fine prairie country. (92)

Tributaries that were navigable for flatboats were prized micro-scale movement-settlement corridors. Road conditions, limited linkages, and haulage costs of overland transportation meant that economic development of inland settlement islands generally lagged behind areas bordering steamboat channels. Upland areas peripheral to creeks that flowed into the trunk arteries and the larger and smaller tributaries were highly favored ecological niches for settlement. High spring runoff made the lower portions of various creeks navigable for flatboats in some years. Flatboats reduced frontier isolation and greatly influenced the momentum of interior settlement and agricultural growth. "Shoal creek, a beautiful stream, running in a southerly direction through the counties of Bond and Washington, and emptying into the Kaskaskia. . . . It is formed by the union of the east and west fork, and is navigable for small craft a considerable distance" (Beck 1823, 156). Pioneers intent on farming slowly dispersed inland across central and northern Illinois prior to the Black Hawk War of 1832. By early statehood, the settlement landscape was spatially ordered into primary destinations that persisted into the late 1830s and 1840s. Commercial agriculture and market center activities promoted population increases.

Early New West Image Builder

Timothy Flint, a seminal source of early-nineteenth-century Mississippi Valley place images, described the land, navigable waterways, attractive destinations, and cultural imprints (1828). Climate, terrain, soil, and vegetative similarities were addressed in this classic historical geography of early expanding continental America. Flint noted that Illinois "has the same climate with Missouri, being much more nearly assimilated in this respect to that state, than to Indiana, or Ohio. . . . It embraces between five and six degrees of latitude. The southern parts will bring cotton, in favorable years, for domestic use. While the climate of the northern parts is not much unlike that of New York and Albany" (2:127). Environmental affinity was important to farmers who desired to maintain crop and livestock traditions (Steckel 1983). Flint stressed, "The people of the West . . . are cultivators of the soil" (1:201).

Sangamon Country received special attention as an Edenic destination: "All, who have visited this fine tract of country, admire the beauty of the landscape, which nature has here formed in her primeval freshness. So beautiful a tract of country was early selected by immigrants from New England, New York, and North Carolina. . . . It now constitutes a county, and is thickly settled by thriving farmers. . . . This fine tract of country is nearly central to the state" (Flint 1828, 2:120). Northerners and southerners understood the importance of its accessibility to the Illinois, Mississippi, and Ohio Rivers (fig. 1.1).

Flint commented on emerging cultural imprints in the West. "The north has given to us, and the south has not kept back. The puritan and the planter, the German and the Irishman, the Briton and the Frenchman, each with their peculiar prejudices and local attachments, and all the complicated and inwoven tissue of sentiments, feelings and thoughts, that country, and kindred, and home, indelibly combine with the web of our youthful existence, have here set down beside each other" (1:206–7). Flint observed differences in immigrants' cultural character in the Old Northwest states. "The people of Ohio and Indiana, for example, have a character somewhat distinct from that of the other western states. That of the former, especially, is modelled, as a very fair sample of the New England and New Jersey patterns. In the latter this character is blended, not merged with the manners, opinions and dialect of Kentucky. Illinois, though a free state, has a clear preponderance of Kentucky nationality" (1:208). Illinois achieved diverse immigrant veneers that exceeded Flint's imagination.

The Premier Illinois Image Maker

Illinois sustained a phenomenal immigrant influx during the 1830s and 1840s. *A Guide for Emigrants* (Peck 1831), *A New Guide for Emigrants to the West* (Peck 1836), *A Gazetteer of Illinois* (Peck 1837), and *Illinois in 1837* (Mitchell 1837) were among the best migrant gazetteers. The most influential writer was John Mason Peck, born in 1789 in Litchfield, Connecticut. In 1811, Peck moved to Green County, New York, and two years later was ordained a Baptist minister. Being appointed a missionary to the West, he moved to St. Louis in 1817 (Babcock 1965, xiii). Four years after Illinois statehood, he relocated across the Mississippi River to live the remainder of his life at Rock Spring in St. Clair County, about eighteen miles from St. Louis (xiv). An astute observer of the land and frontier society, Peck carefully compiled voluminous amounts of materials for his books (Buck 1914, 12, 114, 129; Babcock 1965).

Peck's role as an Illinois image builder for almost two decades reflects his stature, reliability, and influence. The historical significance and geographical value of Peck's booster literature is well illustrated in his *Gazetteer of Illinois*. The subtitle illustrates the plethora of micro-scale migration stimuli in the gazetteer: *A General View of the State, a General View of Each County, and a Particular Description of Each Town, Settlement, Stream, Prairie, Bottom, Bluff, Etc.; Alphabetically Arranged.* Peck embraced the standardized three segments formalized by Beck in his gazetteer of Illinois and Missouri: a general narrative about the state, a description of each county, and detailed place image information. Micro-scale information accounted for over half of the material.

Peck emphasized his carefulness in compiling the geographical characteristics of places and the reasons for his authoritativeness:

> In complying with the call for a new edition, it became necessary to make an entire revision of the work and add much new matter—so rapid had been the changes and the progress of this state in three years. Ten new counties have been organized . . . and

a large addition to the descriptive list of names in part third. No state in the "Great West" has attracted ... an emigrating population from all parts of the United States, and several kingdoms of Europe. Consequently, the call for correct information of all portions of the state has become pressing. ... Accuracy of description, or a registry of facts and things as they actually exist in every part of the state, has been a paramount object. (1837, v–xi)

Besides traveling extensively in the state, Peck added topographical and historical details acquired from state political officers, legislators of both houses, and the perusal of public documents, state records, and journals. For several weeks during the winter of 1832–33, Peck interviewed prominent persons at the state capital of Vandalia. "The course of the author was, to spend two or three hours each evening with gentlemen from a county, who were well acquainted with every part, and write a brief sketch of the same. These were drawn off in proper order the next day, and, in many instances, submitted to the same persons for inspection and revision. All the items for one county were thus finished before entering upon a survey of another" (1837, viii).

Peck personifies an influential image disseminator of the 1830s and 1840s. Much of his work was copied by others, such as S. Augustus Mitchell. Peck observed that about three-fourths of Mitchell's *Illinois in 1837* "were unwarrantably and illegally taken from" his *New Guide for Emigrants to the West* and *A Gazetteer of Illinois* (1839, 10). Western boosters' prose was lucid, informative, authoritative, colorful, and picturesque. As a promoter, Peck projected visual images that were intrinsic to the formation of immigrants' place consciousness. Buck asserts that "among the gazetteers and guide-books, the various works of John Mason Peck occupy first place" (1914, 12).

He employed Edenic, visual descriptors of hope: "beautiful groves of timber, and rich, undulating, and dry prairies; richest quality; an undulating surface, a rich, deep, black, sandy, calcareous soil; a beautiful situated village; the most extensive and fertile-tract; a soil of exhaustless fertility; deer very numerous; and beef the finest in the world." His stamp of future success for a place included a few replicated phrases: "must eventually become a rich and populous county ... some of the finest lands in the state are in this county ... one of the best inland agricultural counties in the state ... one of the finest agricultural districts in the United States" (1837, 91–313).

Immigrants evaluated Illinois' place images from a survivalist and materialist perspective, not an eastern idealist or humanitarian viewpoint. Neither were immigrant farmers western promoters who wrote books; however, they did write letters and visit relatives and friends in their connected social networks. Promotional literature linked images of place and landscape that symbolized immigrants' beliefs, attitudes, values, and dreams. Physical and cultural place images in early gazetteers represented implicit messages of present and future place and regional development in Illinois. The potentials for opportunities, success, and prosperity at destinations were important stimuli causing immigrants to migrate. The nature and diversity of macro- and micro-scale place images were interwoven in peoples' consciousness.

Macro-Scale Migration Stimuli

Because of competing regional settlement frontiers, Peck adapted "Illinois fever" place images to mesh with dynamic settlement changes. By the late 1830s, a number of settlement areas received praise as Edenic landscapes of hope, fertility, and success. Four alluring destinations emerged as macro-scale migration stimuli or pull factors. After the Black Hawk War of 1832, the siren's impulse quickened for the American Bottom, Sangamon Country, the Military Tract, and Rock River Country (fig. 1.1).

The American Bottom linked with earlier French and American intrusions. Its appeal persisted as the premier place image during the territorial and early statehood period. Interpersonal contacts within social networks spawned chain and channelized migration flows. Contiguous to St. Louis, the American Bottom and its uplands' verge containing the Goshen and Turkey Hill settlements witnessed rapid population growth. Peck wrote concerning the American Bottom in southwest Illinois:

> A name it received when it constituted the western boundary of the United States, and which it has retained ever since. It commences at the mouth of the Kaskaskia river, five miles below the town of Kaskaskia, and extends northwardly along the Mississippi to the bluffs at Alton, a distance of ninety miles. Its average width is five miles, and contains about 450 square miles. . . . The soil of the American bottom is inexhaustibly rich. About the French towns it has been cultivated, and produced corn in succession for more than a century. . . . Seventy-five bushels of corn to the acre is an ordinary crop. The roots and worms of the soil, the acorns and other fruits from the trees . . . accelerate the growth of swine. Horses and cattle find exhaustless supplies of grass in the prairies. (1837, 5–7)

Earlier, Flint painted the Sangamon Country in west-central Illinois in glowing terms (1828). Mitchell perpetuated the alluring place image:

> The country traversed by the Sangamon river and its branches is a region seldom equalled in fertility. It is high and undulating, well watered with creeks and springs, and is beautifully interspersed with timber and prairie. . . . At the present time, the borders of the prairie are covered with hundreds of smiling farms, and the interior is animated with thousands of domestic animals; the rough and unseemly cabin is giving place to comfortable framed or brick tenements; and plenty everywhere smiles upon the laboures of the husbandman. . . . The Sangamon country is one of the finest stock districts in the Western states, the summer range for cattle is inexhaustible, and

the amount of excellent hay that may be made every season from the rich prairies almost without limit. Horses, cattle, sheep, and hogs, can be raised here with but little trouble and expense, compared with the eastern states. . . . And the richness and flavour of the beef thus fattened, has been much esteemed at St. Louis and New Orleans, and generally reckoned of the finest quality. (1837, 25–26)

Western boosterism promoted a mesopotamian wedge in west-central Illinois as an earthly paradise. Known as the Military Tract, Mitchell wrote of the land between the Illinois and Mississippi Rivers:

Taking all the Bounty Tract together . . . there is no region of country in the west more eligibly situated for all the purposes of agriculture and commerce. The lands everywhere, with but few exceptions, are of the best quality, and in a manner surrounded by a sheet of navigable waters; and the country exhibits a climate of great variety for the space occupied; whereby its productions are varied, and the means of traffic greatly increased and facilitated. Lands of excellent quality may yet be had at the government price of $1.25 per acre, in desirable parts of the country, so that means of wealth, or at least of a comfortable competence, are still within the reach of the poor as well as the opulent. (1837, 21)

A deluge of immigrants was arriving in northern Illinois by way of gateway Chicago after the mid-1830s. Mitchell vividly described the Rock River Country as a large, promising habitat:

That portion of Illinois, situated in the northern part of the state, watered by Rock river and its branches, is known by the appellation of the Rock River Country. It is a fertile agricultural region, combining all the advantages of a rich and fruitful soil, a healthy and temperate climate, a fine navigable river, and clear perennial streams, affording excellent mill-seats, together with many of the most useful and important minerals. . . . Easy access to market will always insure to the farmer the rewards of industry; and a rich agricultural community ever promotes the steadiest and purest prosperity to all other classes. Mechanics are always demanded by the wants of an improving country; and the lack of competition in a new country, guaranties to such as emigrate the best of prices and the best of pay. The boundless resources of the great resources of the great west spread out their harvest for the sickle of the young and the enterprizing. (1837, 22–25)

By the early 1840s, these captivating settlement areas mushroomed in population. Immigrants sought the potential prosperity available from a commercial agricultural economy focus. Increasing density and complexity of the regional urban-transport networks and improving integration with the national system reinforced the maturing regions' competitive settlement and economic edge. Immigrants' locational-biases channelized toward these attractive destinations.

Micro-Scale Migration Stimuli

Distinctive micro-scale place images were entwined within the macro-scale migration stimuli. Micro-scale migration stimuli influenced immigrants' patterns of regularities and irregularities. Examples from Peck's *Gazetteer of Illinois* address the potential impact of up-to-date information concerning counties, small prairies, immigrant settlements, and urban places. The main strand of my argument is that the perceived opportunities of micro-scale places offered migration stimuli.

> Some of the finest lands in the state are in this county [Putnam]; beautiful groves of timber, and rich, undulating, and dry prairies. There are a number of large settlements of industrious and thrifty farmers, amongst which are Bureau Grove, Ox Bow Prairie, Knox's settlement, Spoon river settlement, and Strawn's settlement. Population about 4,800. There are many fine springs in the county, and excellent mill seats on the streams. (Peck 1837, 128)

> Allison's Prairie, in Lawrence county, five miles northeast from Lawrenceville. It is ten miles long, and five broad. The eastern part towards the Wabash, contains some wet land and purgatory swamps, but the principal part is a dry, sandy, and very rich soil, covered with well cultivated farms. Few tracts in Illinois are better adapted to corn than this. The population equals 200 families. This prairie was settled in 1816 and '17, by emigrants from Ohio and Kentucky. (146)

> Irish Settlement in Randolph county, six miles northeast of Kaskaskia, on Plum Creek. (227)

> Weigle's Settlement, in Adams county, has 600 or 700 industrious Germans, of the society of Dunkards, and is watered by the West fork of McKee's creek. (310)

> Ford's Ferry, in Gallatin county, on the Ohio, twenty miles below Shawneetown, and twenty-five miles south of Equality. It is on the great road [Nashville-Saline Trail] from the southern parts of Kentucky and Tennessee to Illinois and Missouri. (201)

Nodes and their hinterlands in the emerging regional urban networks served as primary destinations. Descriptions of a hamlet, a village, and a town integrate a sense of urban images and functions that Peck perceived as important in a dynamic urban-frontier system.

> Prairie du Rocher, an ancient French village, in Randolph county, on the American bottom, near the Rocky bluffs, from which it derives its name, fourteen miles northwest of Kaskaskia. It is a low, unhealthy situation, along a small creek of the same name. . . . The houses are built in the French style, the streets very narrow, and the inhabitants preserve more of the simplicity of character and habits peculiar to early times, than any village in Illinois. It has its village lots, common fields, and commons. (Peck 1837, 276)

Charleston, the seat of justice for Coles county, is situated on the border of the Grand prairie, two and a half miles from, and on the west side of, the Embarras river, on section eleven, township twelve north, nine east. The surface around is tolerably level, the soil fertile, and the settlements already considerable, will soon be extensive. It has three stores, three groceries, and about twenty five families. It was laid out in 1831. (178)

Jacksonville is one of the largest inland towns in the state, and the seat of justice for Morgan county. It is situated on elevated ground, in the midst of a most delightful prairie.... Situated near the centre of the county, and in the midst of one of the finest tracts of land, densely populated with industrious and enterprising farmers, with the advantages of good water, health, and good society, Jacksonville must continue to prosper, and doubtless will attract many emigrants who are seeking an agreeable home in the "far west." (228–29)

Place image stereotypes formed salient pull factors. Standardized landscape elements were woven into successful guidebooks. Two categories of place images emerged: *physical landscape elements* (climate, soil fertility, wet or dry land, groves and prairies, slope, springs, rivers and creeks, navigability of rivers, mill sites) and *human landscape elements* (crops, livestock, number of farm families, ethnic origins, religious groups or denominations, population numbers, roads, variety and number of businesses in urban places).

Information fields included macro- and micro-scale migration stimuli. Immigrants shared their experiences with relatives and friends through letters and personal visits intertwined in social networks. Successful immigrants were informal western boosters. The process of chain migration inscribed migration clusters. Social networks molded channelized migration patterns among family, friends, and inhabitants from place-specific origins, such as rural areas, villages, and towns, to place-specific destinations. Morris Birkbeck observed: "We are seldom out of sight ... of family groups, behind and before us, some with a view to a particular spot, close to a brother perhaps, or a friend, who has gone before, and reported well of the country" (1818b, 31–32).

Farmers, artisans, professionals, and merchants striving to improve their quality of life and measures of worth controlled the transformation of Illinois by 1850, not romanticists nor footloose backwoods frontiersmen. Peck projected place images of hope, comfort, and well-being:

This State is advancing rapidly in population, and when her public works, which are progressing with all possible speed, are completed, and in successful operation, she will be the admiration of the "far West." It being by far the richest State in soil in the Union, of course it holds out the greatest prospect of advantage to farmers. Here, too, there is plenty of room for farmers, there being vast quantities of first rate land lying in every direction uncultivated, which may be had very cheap, and one acre of it will produce at least three times as much as the same amount of land in most of the eastern States! . . . Indeed, Illinois may with propriety be called the "Canaan" of America! (1837, 328)

Southern Illinois Enigma

Illinois boosterism failed to advocate any macro-scale place images as attractive settlement areas south of the proposed National Road, except for the American Bottom in southwest Illinois (fig. 1.1). Was this an intentional omission of southern Illinois? Did western champions perceive the region as an uninviting environmental landscape? Did they perceive limited agricultural opportunities and materialistic rewards for marketplace-oriented farmers? Did propagandists view Illinoisan glacial drift south of the Shelbyville Moraine as potentially less fertile, in contrast to Wisconsin glacial drift to the north? Did boosters familiar with southern Illinois assume limited availability of land for immigrant infilling because of its earlier settlement by Upland Southerners? Did advocates of the "Garden State of the West" write with a cultural bias toward New Englanders and Midlanders?

Earlier settlement areas in southern Illinois required less stimulus from western promoters because of Upland Southerners' settlement timing. Upland Southerners explored, penetrated, and settled the American Bottom and the Shawnee Hills of southern Illinois by the end of the eighteenth century (Buck 1967; Meyer 1976c). Woodland frontiersmen dispersed rapidly northward across southern Illinois astride waterway corridors and evolving overland routeways in the decade prior to statehood in 1818 (Buck 1967). By the 1820s and early 1830s, they had spread northward into the southern fringe of central Illinois (Boggess 1968; Meyer 1976b, 1976c, 1980, 1984). Both cohesive and mixed migration clusters of Upland Southerners from particular population source areas implanted in the Shawnee Hills area of southern Illinois (Meyer 1976c). The processes of chain and channelized migration linked families, friends, and immigrant groups from particular origins. Operating for over a generation, the routeways, migration clusters, urban nodes, and social networks were etched and duplicated in southern Illinois.

New waves of Upland Southerners did not require convincing about transplanting to southern Illinois. Immigrants migrated within a spreading Upland South diffusion network. An expanding circulation system connected the transAppalachia with the Lower Middle West or Ohio movement-settlement corridor. By the early nineteenth century, a procession of Upland Southerners sequentially planted their subculture settlements deeper into the interior of eastern United States (Jordan and Kaups 1989; Mitchell 1978; Zelinsky 1973). The subculture areas became spatially integrated over time into a dynamic, efficient network of routes, nodes, and replicated regional way stations within an American culture region system (Mitchell 1978). Spreading northward in southern Illinois by the early 1830s by way of the water and land routeways was a traditional Upland South cultural landscape. Illinois proponents, therefore, did not promote new, large destination areas in southern Illinois as potentially attractive to large-scale population intrusions by Midlanders, Midwesterners, Yankees, and foreigners.

Other reasons for not stressing southern Illinois linked with latitude-specific movements and environmental affinities. A conspicuous latitudinal-bias migration filtered across the eastern United States. Darby observed that "[t]he stream of migration is S. W. The inhabitants of the New-England states remove to Ohio; those of New-York, New-Jersey, and Pennsylvania, to Ohio, Indiana, and Illinois; those of Maryland and Virginia, to Tennessee and Missouri; and those of the Carolinas and Georgia, to Mississippi, Louisiana, and Alabama. Many exceptions to this course daily occur, but this is the usual course" (1818, 121). Flint, commenting on Mississippi Valley climate, noted: "It is very obvious, why climate in this valley should so accurately correspond to latitude. It is an immense basin, spreading from north to south" (1828, 1:47). Three years later, Peck asserted, "The climate of the Valley of the Mississippi corresponds . . . more exactly with the latitude, than that of the Atlantic States does; this is owing to the uniformity of the Valley, and its freedom from mountains and other natural causes affecting climate" (1831, 39–40).

Midcontinental Illinois was arrayed across latitudinal zones. "The state of Illinois, extending as it does through five and a half degrees of latitude, has considerable variation in its climate. It has no mountains, and though undulating, it cannot be called hilly. Its extensive prairies, and level surface, give greater scope to the winds, especially in winter" (Peck 1836, 61). The climate of Illinois and Wisconsin was thought similar to that between Montreal and Boston (Flint 1828, 1:49; Peck 1831, 37–38). Yet Illinois was perceived in the familiar climatic belt between 41 degrees and 37 degrees: "In this climate lie Missouri, Illinois, Indiana, Ohio, Western Pennsylvania and Virginia, and the larger part of Kentucky" (Peck 1831, 38). Peck discerned a climatic polarity because of its north-south axis: "There is considerable difference between the northern and southern parts of the State in the severity of its winters" (1831, 41).

Western promoters focused on a comparative eastern seaboard and transAppalachia climatic view.

> Louisiana, Mississippi and the lower half of Arkansas, lie between the latitudes of 30° and 35°, and correspond with Georgia and South Carolina. Their difference of climate is not material. The northern half of Arkansas, Tennessee and Kentucky, lie west from North Carolina and the southern portion of Virginia. The climate varies from those states only as they are less elevated than the mountainous parts of Virginia and Carolina. Hence, the emigrant from the southern Atlantic states, unless he comes from a mountainous region, will experience no great change of climate, by emigrating to the Lower Mississippi Valley. Missouri, Illinois, Indiana and Ohio, lie parallel

with the northern half of Virginia, Maryland, Delaware, Pennsylvania, New Jersey, and so much of New York and New England as lies south of the 42° of north latitude. (Peck 1836, 57–58)

Peck asserted that "the New Englander and New Yorker north of the mountains of West Point, should bear in mind that his migration is not to the West but South West; and as necessarily brings him into a warmer climate. . . . The settlers from Virginia to Kentucky, or those from Maryland and Pennsylvania to Ohio, or further west, have never complained of hotter summers than they had found in the land from whence they came" (1836, 59). He stressed that "emigrants from New England and the northern part of New York state, must not expect to find the same climate in the West, at 38 or 40 degrees; but let them remove to the same parallel of latitude in the West, to Wisconsin, or the northern part of Illinois, and they will probably find a climate far more uniform than the land of their birth" (66–67). The Census Bureau superintendent noted that "[m]en seldom change their climate because to do so they must change their habits; the almost universal law of internal emigration is, that it moves west on the same parallel of latitude" (*Eighth Census, 1860*, xxxv).

In the antebellum southern frontier, Lynch argued that "as a rule, home seekers migrating to frontier country preferred to go where the seasons were similar to those with which they were familiar. To locate where winters were colder and longer, or where summers were hotter and longer, meant not only getting used to new and irritating conditions but also that the pioneers must learn to produce new crops or old crops under new rules and by new methods. The latter was a handicap which could be overcome only through several years of experimentation and intelligent observation" (1943, 305–6). Owsley stressed the impact of environmental attributes on destination selection: "The agricultural immigrant far more than the herdsman has a tendency to seek out a country as nearly as possible like the one in which he formerly lived, in the matter of soil, rainfall, temperature, and appearance—that is having similar topography, streams, trees, and grasses. The similarity of appearance is of great importance for both psychological and practical reasons" (1945, 164–65).

Immigrants' settlement predilections stressed replicating old communities in new ones. "A settler simply could never be entirely happy and at home unless he was surrounded by a landscape much like the one where he had spent his earlier years" (Owsley 1945, 165). "The basic and sound assumption of the farmer . . . is that he can continue in the new country to grow the field crops, fruits, and vegetables, the tillage, habits, and marketing of which are part of his mental furniture" (166). Farmers' survival meshed in accepted habitats. "The farmers making new homes in the West were, in the majority of cases, not in search of the richest lands of the public domain, but merely the richest of the particular type of land to which they were accustomed back in the East. Perhaps in most cases they were content with land almost identical with that left behind except that the new land was fresh" (168).

Steckel explored the hypothesis that "latitude-specific investments in seeds and human capital induced migrants to move along east-west lines" (1983, 14). Frontier perpetuation of agricultural skills and cultural traditions was desirable because "[a] farmer contemplating a move sought, other things being equal, a location that maximized the return on previous investments in human capital; namely, a place where the climate, soil, and terrain were familiar" (24). People acquire skills and acclimatize themselves to particular habitats that duplicate and maintain human comfort and the home economy for family well-being (27–28). Steckel concluded that east-west mobility "was attributable to an important extent to farmers who used seeds, particularly corn, that were adapted to a given latitude, and to farmers who acquired latitude-specific skills. Farmers who moved too far north or too far south sacrificed crop yields, animal productivity, human comfort, and output in the home economy" (31). Latitude-specific movements ensured the safest alternative to the old community and compatible options.

Westward-bias, geographical clustering, and habitat affinity were deep-rooted predispositions of immigrants. Sparks observed that community social ties caused pioneers "who sought the new country for a home to locate in the immediate vicinity. Security and the enjoyment of social intercourse were more frequently the incentives for these selections than the fertility of the soil or other advantages. Immigrants dispersed due west from their former homes, and were sure to select, as nearly as possible, a new one in the same parallel" (1872, 20). Sparks noted that pioneers "sought as nearly as possible just such a country as that from which they came" (331). "With the North Carolinian, good spring-water, and pine-knots for his fire, were the 'sine qua non.' These secured, he went to work with the assiduity and perseverance of a beaver to build his house and open his fields" (20).

Peck clearly stated Americans' latitude-specific shift: "The march of emigration from the Atlantic border has been nearly in a line due west. Tennessee was settled by Carolinians, and Kentucky by Virginians. Ohio received the basis of its population from the states in the same parallel, and hence partakes of all the varieties from Maryland to New England. Michigan is substantially a child of New York. The planters of the south have gone to Mississippi, Louisiana, and the southern part of Arkansas. Kentucky and Tennessee have spread their sons and daughters over Indiana, Illinois and Missouri" (1836, 103). Given latitude-bias mobility and Upland South channelized flows, there were limited reasons for emphasizing macro-scale destinations in southern Illinois. Micro-scale place images for southern Illinois were just as Edenic and numerous as for central and northern Illinois in Peck's voluminous appendix.

The persistence of Illinois' "paradise-garden myth" was linked with a number of factors: a four-hundred-mile north-south axis; the barrier affect of Lake Michigan; greater heartland centrality; accessible, converging, penetrating waterways—rivers, lakes, and canals; effective road and network development; settlement timing; large amounts of cheap, fertile land; and numerous magnet destinations. The evolving "historic test-strip" typified a quintessential midwestern development and cultural diversity. As Peck argued 150 years ago: "The state of Illinois has probably the finest body of fertile land of any state in the Union, and the opportunities for speculation are numerous—property will continue to advance—admirable farms and town lots may be purchased with a certainty of realising large profits. The country here is beautiful" (1837, 132). The Great Migration responded by forming mesmeric destinations. Dynamic settlement areas developed powerful migration flows, urban-transport hierarchies, and marketplace economies by 1850.

From an agricultural perspective, the "Canaan of the West" was "pre-eminently Illinois, whose extremely fertile prairies recompense the farmer at less trouble than he would be obliged to incur elsewhere, in order to attain the same results. Her virgin soil, adapted by nature for immediate culture, only awaits the plough and the seed, in order to mature within a few months golden ears of the most beautiful Indian corn" (Gerhard 1857, 289). "Illinois is the paradise of the farmer" (307). Perceived place images affected immigrants' destinations.

2

Historical and Geographical Settlement Conditions

The bulk of the population is settled upon the Mississippi, Kaskaskia and its branches. There are a few detached settlements on the Wabash, and some of the streams entering the west bank; and detached ones on the Ohio. Those on the Illinois are small, insulated, and sometimes 50 miles apart.
   —Brown 1817

Historical and geographical processes operating at local, regional, national, and international scales shaped Illinois' settlement structure. Numerous factors—geographical, cultural, political, settlement, and economic—integrated population infillings linked with boom-and-bust economic cycles during the late eighteenth and early nineteenth centuries. Regional shifts in population and economic growth occurred between the Revolutionary War and the Civil War. In an expanding continental America, the Old Northwest transformed into the Midwest (Parker 1975). Large amounts of fertile land, steamboat riverine movement-settlement corridors, and central location in the interior perpetuated "Illinois fever." Illinois metamorphosed from an insular, subsistent frontier to riparian, commercial-settlement corridors tied to regional, national, and world economic systems.

Late-Eighteenth-Century Settlement Conditions

Settlers slowly penetrated peripheral frontiers in the interior. Returning soldiers from George Rogers Clark's foray against the French at Kaskaskia and Vincennes in 1778–79 spread the word of the fertile lands of Illinois Country. Veterans of Clark's campaign who settled the American Bottom primarily emigrated from Virginia and Maryland (Moses 1889, 1:227). A few opted to reside within the remnant French villages. The vast majority of the woodland frontiersmen established dispersed farmsteads. Other veterans established in 1779 the first nucleated settlement at Bellefontaine in the uplands, about one mile south of present day Waterloo in Monroe County (Alvord 1920, 358–59). About 150 backwoods pioneers arrived in Illinois Country prior to the Ordinance of 1787 (408).

A pivotal American point of attachment and typical Virginian settlement originated in 1786 at New Design in Monroe County (Boggess 1968, 91–92). The colonizing pathfinder was James Lemen, a Virginian from Berkeley County (now in West Virginia). He had settled for a time in the vicinity of Wheeling, West Virginia. His family traveled the Ohio River by flatboats, upstream on the Mississippi River to Kaskaskia, and inland to their wilderness settlement. Lemen intended to implant a "new design" about four miles south of earlier settled Bellefontaine (*Combined History of Randolph, Monroe and Perry Counties, Illinois* 1883, 330). Having fought in the Revolutionary War, this anti-slavery, Scotch-Irish Presbyterian was prominent in local politics and served as justice of the peace and judge of the county court.

His youngest son, James Lemen, Jr., and two brothers relocated in Ridge Prairie, which extended from present-day Belleville in St. Clair County to Madison County (fig. 2.1). He served as a delegate from St. Clair County to the state constitutional convention and later in the House and Senate of Illinois. As the dominant personality in the early colonizing days of the New Design settlement, James Lemen helped sway immigrants to settle within the security and social net of the expanding, loose settlement cluster. The fission of the socially cohesive Lemen kinship network represented a commonplace duplication with each generation's familiarity with the backwoods frontier. Within the American Bottom, New Design emerged as the most attractive and largest settlement of woodland frontiersmen prior to 1800 in Illinois Country. It developed as a major source for splinter kinship colonies on the frontier's verge.

The military background of many early frontiersmen and the need for a defensive site among hostile Amerindians warranted tiny, nucleated settlement outposts. Elevated upland locations in proximity to the Mississippi and Kaskaskia Rivers were initially selected by these hardy backwoods pioneers (Moses 1889, 1:227). Blockhouses were essential Amerindian defense artifacts for the survival of these settlement clusters. In the 1790s, settlers from New Design spread southward toward the Kaskaskia River and into Randolph County and northward, coalescing with the smaller Bellefontaine settlement. Led by a Baptist minister, the largest colony of 154 settlers arrived in 1797 from Hardy County, Virginia (now West Virginia), on the south branch of the Potomac (Boggess 1968, 92). They traveled by flatboats downstream on the Ohio River to Fort Massac and made the tedious overland journey to Kaskaskia, then inland to New Design (*Combined History of Randolph, Monroe and Perry Counties, Illinois* 1883, 77).

Early American Bottom settlements exemplify prototypical processes and patterns of a penetrating pioneer society. Movements between origins and destina-

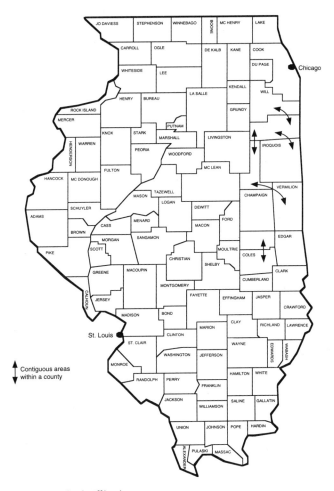

FIG. 2.1. Counties in Illinois, 1850

tions of extended family groups and small colonies of relatives, friends, and
neighbors were essential to a probing, backwoods society's survival and success.
Social networks spawned chain migration patterns to particular destinations. Pioneer groups from particular population sources, but of like-minded cultural
backgrounds, formed numerous entwined social networks that engendered channelized migration patterns. Upland Southerners emigrated, owing to their slavery
opposition and desire for cheap land (Boggess 1968, 92).

In the initial colonizing process, isolated farmsteads were scattered three to ten
miles between dwellings in remote woodland frontiers. Settlement diffusion fostered sequential settlement patterns. Settlement structure, however, reflected a
predominance of loose family or clan settlement clusters where farmsteads were
dispersed less than a mile apart (Jordan and Kaups 1989, 123). The inherent nature

of propinquity supports the notion that small, socially cohesive units were primary dispersal seeds of the westward-moving settlement frontier. The processes of social fission and chain and channelized migration were elemental mechanisms in the diffusion and replication of loosely clustered settlements. Ostergren argues that kinship was an integral motivating factor that intensified the role of socially cohesive communities on the American frontier (1982, 318).

The American Bottom and its bordering uplands were the first quintessential settlement area in Illinois Country (fig. 1.1). Yet routine Amerindian hostilities between 1783 and 1795, slow cessions of Amerindian lands, ineffectual governmental control, dispute over French lands grants, slowness of land surveys, and lack of public land for sale retarded settlement for almost three decades (Boggess 1968, 40–98). The growth in numbers and population density owing to immigrant infilling of the older, attractive settlement cores and the lateral expansion of their settlement peripheries were minimal on this remote American frontier. Settlement patterns were elemental and changed minimally prior to the War of 1812.

Settlement Conditions from 1800 to 1809

The years 1793 to 1808 marked a period of unparalleled prosperity that was linked to international trade and shipping (North 1961, 46–58). Economic hard times characterized the subsequent period between 1808 and the War of 1812 (Taylor 1931, 471). Preceding 1812, the vortex of geographic mobility was directed toward the interior margins of eastern and central Tennessee, eastern and central Kentucky, western Pennsylvania, eastern and southern Ohio, and southern Indiana. Areas contiguous to the movement-settlement corridors of the Ohio-Mississippi Rivers gradually emerged as farming country. Deep in midcontinent, a frontier outpost had been inaugurated by the late 1790s adjacent to the Mississippi River. The American Bottom unfolded as the core of this tiny American settlement enclave.

Between 1800 and 1808, Illinois Country was incorporated within the western portion of the Old Northwest, known as Indiana Territory. Settlement of the American Bottom at the outer margin of the American frontier was delayed owing to repeated Amerindian difficulties, the morass of French land titles, and ineffectual territorial government from Vincennes, the Indiana Territory capital on the Wabash River. The Louisiana Purchase of 1803 altered the relative location of the American settlements in Illinois Country. They ceased to be situated on the western verge of the fledgling Union. With its new centrality in the continental interior, the American Bottom acquired the settlement advantages of commercial exchange downstream and across the Mississippi River without restraints (Howard 1972, 73). The American Bottom's settlement and economic advancements were concomitant with proximity to the mercantile entrepôt of St. Louis and its far-flung continental enterprises (Wade 1958).

The federal government acquired from the Amerindians in 1803 the Saline Creek salt springs near Shawneetown on the Ohio River (Pooley 1968, 317). Shawneetown grew slowly as a gateway, although it was on a primary trunk route connecting central Kentucky, St. Louis, and the American Bottom (Boggess 1968, 125). Taylor argues that Ohio Valley settlers in the New West prior to the War of 1812 were increasingly ambitious farmers with great optimism and exaggerated wealth expectations (1931). In the boom times preceding the Louisiana Purchase, farmers perceived the Mississippi River's bordering frontiers as potential new "Canaans." Fertile riverine corridors compensated farmers' hard work with bountiful harvests. Whether by flatboat or keelboat, yeoman farmers delivered their agricultural surpluses to market, but prices were frequently very low. Their economic problems were a function "of transportation, of communication, and of imperfect marketing and financial organization" (505).

Woodland pioneers were slow to modify their habitat affinities for the forested fringes of the rivers and creeks. Interior interstream divides were extensive, empty, inaccessible tracts of wilderness. Alvord suggests that prior to 1810, the settlers were already "paying more attention to the prairie territory" bordering the American Bottom (1920, 415). Between 1806 and 1810, the population increased from about four thousand to some twelve thousand. The first decade of the nineteenth century witnessed an almost fourfold immigrant increase, in contrast to the extremely slow growth of the antecedent century of French settlement (Alvord 1920, 415). In 1809, Illinois was established as a territory that included Illinois, Wisconsin, and northeast Minnesota.

Settlement Conditions from 1810 to 1819

The years 1810 to 1814 were not a particularly prosperous economic period. After the War of 1812, the advent of peace in 1815 spawned an economic surge until the severe depression of 1819 (North 1961). During the Illinois territorial period from 1809 to 1818, immigrants were constrained by Amerindian cessions and land questions (Alvord 1920, 428–50; Boggess 1968, 99–111; Buck 1967, 40–60). By statehood, these settlement restraints had been substantially removed. Settlers who arrived prior to governmental land sales obtained squatters' rights of preemption in 1813. For pioneers who settled in the previous three decades in Illinois Country, fears of losing their land and site improvements were lessened. Assurance of clear, secure land titles and the removal of disputes over conflicting French land claims eliminated major settlement retardants. By statehood, progress was made with Amerindian cessions. Still, the powerful Kickapoo tribe claimed and held virtually all of central Illinois east of the Illinois River. The celebrated Sangamon Country experienced the penetration of frontiersmen in its southern margins (Boggess 1968, 110–11; Buck 1967, 43–45). In 1819, the Kickapoo ceded their land

and transferred west of the Mississippi River. Not until the early 1830s were the remaining Amerindian lands north and south of the canal cession ceded over as government land.

The final settlement hurdle during the territorial period was the extremely slow pace of surveying and selling public lands. Government land offices were established at Kaskaskia in 1804, Shawneetown in 1812, and Edwardsville in 1816 (Boggess 1968, 103–6; Buck 1967, 45–60). Kaskaskia's land sales were delayed for a decade while disputed French claims were extricated (fig. 2.2). Public sales at Kaskaskia and Edwardsville distributed little of the best land because of private claims and preemption rights. Acreage sales from the land offices in 1817 and 1818 suggest a shift in destinations (Boggess 1968, 105). In 1817, almost 300,000 acres were purchased: 23 percent at Shawneetown, 29 percent at Kaskaskia, and 48 percent at Edwardsville. In 1818, the year of statehood, almost 460,000 acres were sold: 47 percent at Shawneetown, 26 percent at Kaskaskia, and 27 percent at Edwardsville.

Buck compiled a map delineating the location of private land holdings at the time of statehood (1967, 56–57). He cautions that the distribution patterns were not a definitive index of settlement progress. As in most early frontiers, speculators purchased considerable acreage for speculation rather than for settlement. Numerous pioneers also squatted land belonging to the federal government. Bordering the Mississippi River, the largest contiguous tract of private land holdings originated in the uplands of Madison and St. Clair Counties (55–58). A contiguous ribbon of purchased land penetrated northward from Kaskaskia in the American Bottom. The Wabash Valley corridor was punctuated with numerous small, adjacent blocks of land. The largest tract superimposed the English settlement in Edwards County, about two and a half townships. Smaller blocks of land formed in the hinterland of Shawneetown and the lower Ohio Valley where speculators envisioned vital commercial nodes.

Upland Southerners tended to create tiny, dispersed settlements. First, land was especially valued adjacent to streams. Within the mixed deciduous forests of southern Illinois, the drier valley slopes and bordering uplands were preferred over the flood-disposed valleys. By 1818, colonizing settlements dispersed along the following streams: Kaskaskia River and its Silver and Shoal Creek tributaries, Big Muddy River in Jackson County, Cache River in Union County, Saline River in Gallatin County, and Little Wabash River paralleling the Wabash River. Second, in the inaccessible interstream areas, frontiersmen prized land in proximity to the early traversing trails. Private holdings were dispersed astride southeast-northwest roads: Shawneetown-Goshen, Shawneetown-Kaskaskia, and Golconda-Kaskaskia. Portions of the east-west Vincennes-Kaskaskia Road crossed north of the survey line. Widely scattered, small land tracts abutted this old French trail as pioneers colonized the frontier's edge. Third, as arriving settlers purchased their

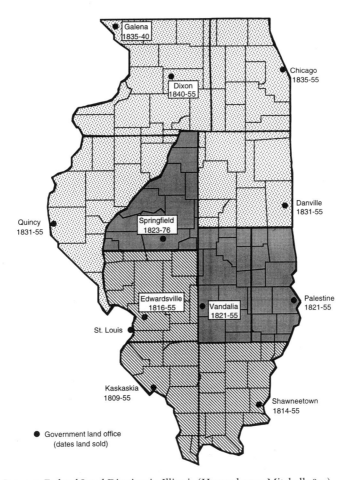

FIG. 2.2. Federal Land Districts in Illinois (Howard 1972; Mitchell 1837)

property units in half, quarter, and eighth sections, the rectangular survey and the subsequent checkerboard field patterns nurtured a new agricultural order (Cronon 1991, 102).

Early roads served as social-economic lifelines. Proximity to roads provided access to potential market centers for early colonizing pioneers. For over two decades, the American Bottom in southwest Illinois exhibited the perseverance of slow but constant immigrant influx. Initially, dispersed and nucleated settlements formed as narrow colonization ribbons of south-north points of attachment along streams. Later, contiguous blocks of private land holdings straddled the two primary south-north roads: Kaskaskia to Cahokia in the American Bottom and Kaskaskia to Goshen paralleling the upland bluffs. The terminal nodes were linked with the mercantile center of St. Louis.

In a political context, early settlement growth lagged because of repeated Amerindian hostilities associated with the War of 1812 (Alvord 1920, 428–54; Boggess 1968, 71–133). Buck contends that migration to Illinois Country finally witnessed a real boom with the dawn of peace in 1815 and the initiating of public land sales in 1814 (1967, 97). By the end of the second decade, premier land locations in earlier-settled Kentucky, Ohio, and Indiana were either infilled by pioneers or acquired by speculators. Buck estimates that Illinois Country increased in population from about fifteen thousand in 1815 to almost forty thousand by the end of 1818 (97). In the next two years, about fifteen thousand settlers were added. Consequently, the Great Migration deflected to the new, Edenic land fevers bordering the Mississippi, Missouri, and Illinois Rivers. Settlers were so new that almost half had not lived in Illinois for three years (97).

By 1820, the best of times appeared on the distant horizon for immigrants settling Illinois Country. Yet, the primitive duresses of frontier life persisted as the worst of times prior to the Black Hawk War of 1832. Boggess stresses the persistence of fundamental social, economic, political, and locational limitations in a remote frontier (1968, 98). Amerindian hostilities and removal, secure land titles, unsettled slavery issues, physical separation and psychological isolation from the eastern seaboard and older settlements in transAppalachia, and distance from commercial markets were key problems. In addition, the continued allure and greater accessibility of areas in Kentucky, Ohio, and Indiana adjacent to the Ohio Valley corridor; the real and perceived dangers and costs of migration; a dearth of a humanized landscape in sparsely populated areas; minimal urban-transport structure; and extensive outliers of the prairie peninsula in the northern margins of southern Illinois served as settlement obstacles.

After the continental military struggle ended in 1815, a transitional frontier settlement period ensued. Early statehood witnessed a surge in the process of colonization. New dispersed farmstead settlements, settlement clusters, small colonies, and urban nodes at ferry crossings and at road junctures formed across southern Illinois. Immigrant destinations emerged in the interstices of the settlement framework, in proximity to early roads, astride stream valleys, in woodland uplands, and in small local prairies. Minimal accessibility to markets and inland remoteness generally characterized settlement locations. But the evolution of new dispersed and clustered settlements epitomizes the process of colonization expansion.

Another theme related to the interior settlement of southern Illinois reveals the initial contacts, reactions, and adaptations of a backwoods pioneer culture when faced with the task of transplanting into a prairie habitat. McManis argues that the early nineteenth century was a "trial and error" period where pioneers utilized the smaller prairies and sought solutions for the problems discovered in the process (1964, 89). The local prairies varied from a few square miles to a few acres. The larger prairies were situated in the interstream divides and surrounded and separated by widespread forests (9). Tiny, isolated prairies and parkland edges bordering the larger prairies engendered favorable evaluations from the early woodland pioneers. By 1820, the small prairies were positively evaluated in terms of three essential habitat elements: "the fertility of the soil, the ease of establishing a homestead, and the luxurious pasturage" (90).

Settlement Conditions from 1820 to 1829

Earlier obstacles to migration and settlement endured to the Black Hawk War of 1832 (Boggess 1968, 134–35, 153–64; Pease 1918, 9–12, 150–72; Pooley 1968, 321–29). Amerindian hostilities and disputed land claims across northern Illinois persisted as settlement hindrances. Final Amerindian land cessions occurred in 1833. Minimal pioneer flows were associated with the unsettled slavery issue, which lingered until 1824. Its resolution served as only one of many positive pull factors. Transportation remained an overriding problem to settlement and commercial activities. Steamboat travel improved and commenced on the Illinois River in 1828. The Illinois Valley corridor connected newer settlements with the more established American Bottom. Land travel survived in a state of extreme slowness, high costs, and difficulty. Crude road linkages in earlier-settled southern Illinois converged on St. Louis.

Problems related to the public sale of governmental lands persisted as a settlement impediment (Boggess 1968, 136–45). The remaining constraints were reduced or removed: the price of governmental lands declined to $1.25 per acre, land was made available for purchase in smaller fractions of a section (smallest amount: eighty acres), preemption rights were offered to squatters who settled prior to 1830, and state salt spring reservations decreased in size. Land holdings of absentee owners and speculators were recurring detrimental settlement factors. In addition, many acres of land were removed from the public domain for sale. The federal government granted Illinois considerable tracts of land for schools and internal improvements, particularly the canal corridor.

Illinois' population slowly increased from 1820 to 1825 by adding about 18,000 to some 73,000 (Boggess 1968, 187–88). By 1830, the population substantially increased by almost 85,000 to about 157,000. Overall economic growth during the 1820s was slow in the eastern United States, with minor recessions in 1824 and 1827 (North 1961, 67–68, 192). Few economic incentives encouraged settling distant Illinois Country. In the 1820s, "Indiana fever" predominated in the Old Northwest, whereas in the 1830s and 1840s, "Illinois fever" developed a hegemony.

Federal Land District Sales: 1820s

In addition to Kaskaskia, Shawneetown, and Edwardsville, three new land office districts were established during this transitional settlement period: Vandalia in

Fayette County in 1821; Palestine in Crawford County in 1821; and Springfield in Sangamon County in 1823 (fig. 2.2). Though one must keep in mind the role of speculators and squatters on the frontier, an analysis of public land sales in the 1820s offers clues to regional migration and settlement shifts. The number of acres of public land sold from the federal land offices were abysmally slow during most of the 1820s (fig. 2.3). Fluctuating yearly acreage sales at the individual land offices mark the ebbs, flows, and changing preferences of immigrants' destinations.

Minimal immigrant influx in 1820 was directed toward the older, established and better-known settlement districts associated with the three earliest land offices of Edwardsville, Shawneetown, and Kaskaskia (fig. 2.4). The Edwardsville land office dominated land sales in 1821. Yet the new capital and land office of Vandalia jumped in land sales. The middle Kaskaskia Valley in the interior borderlands of central and southern Illinois was perceived favorably. The new capital was centrally located within the northward-moving interior settlement frontier. But the attractiveness of the Vandalia land office district to pioneers during most of the 1820s was minimal, given its physical remoteness and limited connectivity within the slowly expanding state road network.

Land sales were cut almost in half in 1822, which suggests a weakening in the slow transplanting of immigrants. A new land office was located north of Shawneetown on the east side of southern Illinois. Palestine dominated land sales in 1822. A distinct migration shift gradually emerged during the 1820s as immigrants' choices of destinations expanded northward astride the accessible Wabash Valley corridor bordering Indiana. In southwest Illinois, Edwardsville in the upland Goshen area sold respectable amounts of land, but the other land offices' acreage sales were minimal.

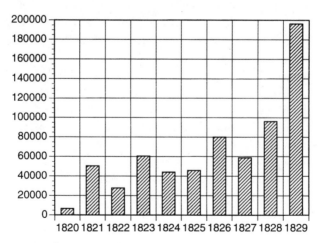

FIG. 2.3. Total Acres Sold from Federal Land Districts in Illinois: 1820s (Pease 1918, 176)

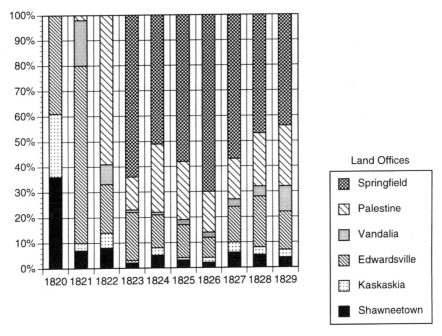

FIG. 2.4. Federal Land District Sales in Illinois: 1820s (Pease 1918, 176)

Acreage sold more than doubled in 1823 (fig. 2.3). The new land office of Spring-field in the heart of Sangamon Country dominated land sales, supplanting Palestine, the previous year's leader (fig. 2.4). When new land offices opened, immigrants often altered their selected destinations and surged to the perceived "siren" settlement area. The allure of the settlement district in proximity to St. Louis endured, thus suggesting that not all the good land had been previously purchased. A lull in the immigrant flows developed as land sales substantially declined to similar levels in 1824 and 1825. The majority of the land sales were at the Springfield land office. By 1823, a pivotal settlement theme emerged as immigrants' place and directional proclivities thrust northward with probing colonizations deep into the borderlands in west-central, east-central, and southern Illinois.

Immigrants' predilections for untouched destinations inaugurated mesmeric settlement areas in the Springfield and Palestine land offices' hinterlands. With the addition of Edwardsville, about 83 to 90 percent of the total acreage sales of public land occurred at these three land offices between 1823 and 1829 (fig. 2.4). Public land sales showed steady increases, but still not a substantial sales volume in comparison with the 1830s. Between 1826 and 1829, 1827 represented a hiatus in land sales, whereas 1829 reflected a doubling. In the last half of the 1820s, Sangamon Country was the premier settlement area in Illinois. It was accessible via the

Mississippi and Illinois Rivers and a northward-thrusting trail from St. Louis and Edwardsville, which linked with the southern Illinois road network. It developed as a more powerful place image than the American Bottom, the middle Kaskaskia Valley, and the middle Wabash Valley. Sangamon Country was fashionable, famous, and Edenic. Beck wrote, "[E]ver since its first settlement, [Sangamon Country] has been justly esteemed the most desirable tract in the state; and it consequently has been settled with a rapidity heretofore unequalled" (1823, 83).

But the American Bottom, with its abutting Goshen and Turkey Hill settlements in southwest Illinois, reflected an immigrant pool of restless pioneers. It epitomized the persistence of an old, popular migration destination. The Edwardsville land district possessed four essential locational and environmental qualities for the sustainability of its attractiveness: accessibility via the Mississippi River, linchpin terminus of the early road network, extensive tracts of fertile, mixed forested and prairie lands, and proximity to the market and production of St. Louis. The generational vigor of this mesmeric destination was accentuated by the social networks operating between numerous origins and destinations.

Land sales in 1829 from the six land offices hint at a distinctive temporal-spatial change in migration and settlement patterns (fig. 2.4). Immigrants' destinations were now focused on four land offices rather than three. The inclusion of Vandalia with Springfield, Palestine, and Edwardsville meant that almost 93 percent of the acreage sold transpired at these land offices in 1829. The interior area peripheral to the state capital on the middle Kaskaskia River grew slowly but persisted as an increasingly attractive destination. By the late 1820s, the National Road was on the distant eastern horizon with travelers reaching Vandalia in 1839 (Hardin 1967, 16). Accessibility of the land office district improved as Vandalia unfolded as a mid-state road hub connecting central and southern Illinois by the late 1830s.

This narrow time span of public land sales reveals subtle crosscurrents of inter- and intrastate immigrant shifts. The evolving regional frontiers of Illinois were fluid and dynamic immigrant environments. Immigrants who had arrived earlier left their remote, dispersed family or kinship unit settlements in southern Illinois. The settlement types functioned as adaptive staging areas that furnished an important stimulus to the strength of immigrants' shifts to the latest destinations. The inherent character of frontiersmen prompted repeated stepwise migrations. Distinctive cultural traits of hunter-farmers offer clues to their willingness to uproot: they possessed individualism, nuclear family or small kinfolk units, locational instability, dependence upon nonagricultural pursuits, a settlement pattern comprising dispersed farmstead enclaves in the forests, open-range livestock, and a small number of simple, efficient, and interchangeable log house and barn plans (Jordan and Kaups 1989, 3–4). The backwoods pioneers' cultural artifacts and lifeways imprinted landscape elements that were more ephemeral, flexible, and easily relocated.

Peck stresses the hunter-farmer's desire to be located in the frontier margins: "It is quite immaterial whether he ever becomes the owner of the soil. . . . He builds his cabin, gathers around him a few other families of similar taste and habits, and occupies till the range is somewhat subdued, and hunting a little precarious, or, which more frequently the case, till neighbors crowd around, roads, bridges and fields annoy him, and he lacks elbow-room. The pre-emption law enables him to dispose of his cabin and cornfield, to the next class of emigrants, and, to employ his own figures, he 'breaks for the high timber,' . . . 'clears out for the New Purchase,' or migrates to Arkansas or Texas, to work the same process over" (1836, 114–15). Frequent lifetime searchings by woodland frontiersmen for isolated frontier niches were commonplace to a way of life that cherished extreme levels of personal freedom (Jordan and Kaups 1989, 3). The settlement preferences of backwoods pioneers with their dependency on hunting and "patch agriculture" generally placed these pathfinders at the cutting edge of frontiers.

Yeoman farmers' motivations and lifeways were interwoven with dreams of becoming successful, prosperous, and upward, socially mobile, landed citizens. They were not propelled by an innate geographic mobility. Yet real and perceived greater opportunities that included cheaper, larger tracts of more fertile land were only a move away. Peck notes the more permanent landscape impresses of this so-called second-class settlement frontier wave: "The next class of emigrants purchase the lands, add 'field to field,' clear out the roads, throw rough bridges over the streams, put up hewn log houses, with glass windows, and brick or stone chimneys, occasionally plant orchards, build mills, school houses, court houses, etc., and exhibit the picture and forms of plain, frugal, civilized life" (1836, 115).

A sizable proportion of the hunter-farmers and yeoman farmers were stayers and not constant movers. Peck concluded that sequential settlement frontiers were like revolving doors as settlers moved in and out: "Migration has become almost a habit in the west. Hundreds of men can be found, not fifty years of age, who have settled for the fourth, fifth, or sixth time on a new spot. To sell out and remove only a few hundred miles, makes up a portion of the variety of backwoods life and manners" (1836, 116). The process of stepwise mobility was not generally as intense and frequent for the yeoman farmer, who became increasingly preoccupied with accessibility to markets, farmstead improvements, and net worth.

During the 1820s, the earlier captivating settlement islands in proximity to the three original land offices (Kaskaskia, Shawneetown, and Edwardsville) supplied preadapted pioneer settlers. Hunter-farmers and yeoman farmers relocated in a stepwise custom to the recently opened land office districts of Vandalia, Palestine, and Springfield. They caught the fever for Sangamon Country, the middle Kaskaskia Valley, and the middle Wabash Valley. The frontier of settlement hurdled northward, especially invigorated by new settlers who circumvented the isolated empty lands of extreme southern Illinois. The land offices at Kaskaskia and

Shawneetown experienced a trickling of acreage sales as immigrants infilled the large, isolated tracts of land still available in these southern tier settlement areas.

Settlement Conditions from 1830 to 1839

The intensity of the migration flows gyrated greatly in the 1830s owing to political, social, and economic mechanisms: the Black Hawk War of 1832; the speculative land boom from 1835 to 1839 of the public domain across central and northern Illinois, particularly west-central; conjectural "paper towns," about five hundred of them between 1835 and 1837; panics of 1834 and 1837; severe economic depression from 1839 to 1843; and increasing debate over the slavery issue. Agricultural stagnation persisted throughout much of the 1830s. Farmers' hard times coincided with worn-out lands; crop failures; price declines for agricultural cash crops; increasing land prices in the older seaboard areas of New England, the Middle Atlantic, and the southern states; the competitive edge of cheaper western agricultural products moving through the Erie Canal; and continued availability in Illinois of large amounts of cheap, fertile lands.

Transportation influenced settlement and economic growth in the interior. Improvements in steam power and ship design of river and lake vessels and expansion of the steamboat network with greater penetration toward the headwaters of the Ohio, Mississippi, and Missouri Rivers and their navigable tributaries were important transport changes. The establishment of a network of communication and transport lines radiating from gateway lake ports, such as Chicago, and pivotal river nodes, such as Peoria, and the expansion of trunk, feeder, and bridge lines within the regional and national road and waterways networks improved accessibility and circulation. Completion of bridging canals in Ohio linking the Great Lakes and the Ohio Valley corridor and increasing dominance of the northern gateway corridor of the Great Lakes–Erie Canal precipitated shifts in the movements of commerce (Hunter 1949; North 1961, 1974; Pease 1918, 173–93; Pooley 1968, 330–51, 559–74).

During the 1830s, population almost tripled, as during the previous decade. But this time, the increase was a frenzied addition of almost 320,000 to the total population of 157,445 in 1830. Although natural increase was important, migration explains the majority of the population growth in the Old Northwest prior to 1840 (Vedder and Gallaway 1975, 161). Illinois' population momentum over other state fevers of the Old Northwest is substantiated in its greater net migration of 245,868 individuals out of a 1840 population of 476,183 (163). Illinois' centrality and accessibility enhanced convergence of the primary migration flows in the interior. Feverish land speculations; a surge in small, cohesive kinship groups; myriad immigrant colonies; and continued squatting on government land prior to the completed surveying of the frontier were all too common.

Federal Land District Sales: 1830 to 1839

Two new government land offices were added in 1831. Quincy in Adams County served the Military Tract of west-central Illinois, and Danville in Vermilion County promoted the Grand Prairie of east-central Illinois (fig. 2.2). By 1835, two additional land offices were established in Galena in Jo Daviess County and Chicago in Cook County. The Chicago land office district comprised the northeast section of northern Illinois. The Galena land office closed in 1840 and was replaced by the more centrally located and accessible Dixon on the Rock River in Lee County. The Galena-Dixon land office district circumscribed the northwest quadrant of northern Illinois. The opening of the final land offices reflect a shift in migration streams' destinations and an astonishing increase in population between 1835 and 1839.

Between 1830 and 1834, land sales at the eight federal land district offices were not as volatile as in the 1820s (figs. 2.3, 2.5). Total acreage sales were considerably greater from year to year and increased at an astonishing rate after the Panic of 1834. The last half of the decade, from 1835 to 1839, land sales at the ten government offices increased at a mercurial rate. Total acreage sold oscillated greatly with the intense land speculation precipitated by eastern entrepreneurs, colonies, and a rapid increase in settlers via the gateway movement corridors. Public land sales suggest significant regional changes in patterns of migration and settlement between 1830 and 1839 (fig. 2.6). Variant regional patterns in land sales hint at the vitality of destination permutations. Rapid increases in migration flows in the 1830s fluctuated in short two- to three-year cycles, from a mix of older destination

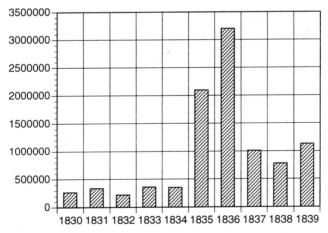

FIG. 2.5. Total Acres Sold from Federal Land Districts in Illinois: 1830s (Pease 1918, 177)

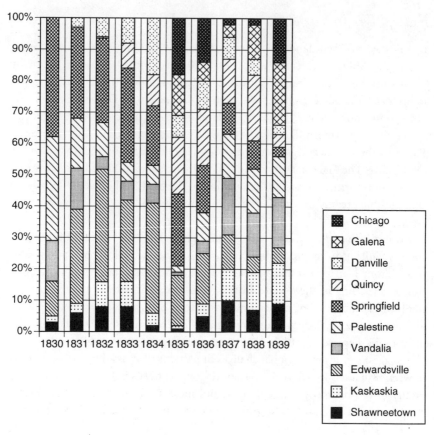

Fig. 2.6. Federal Land District Sales in Illinois: 1830s (Pease 1918, 177)

areas in southern and central Illinois with newer destinations in central and northern Illinois.

The years 1830 to 1834 were a transitional period, since land sales and regional patterns perpetuated in the late 1820s. This five-year land sales period divides into two slightly different trends. Between 1830 and 1831, the number-one land sales office shifted between Springfield and Edwardsville. The Springfield federal land district persisted as an attractive settlement island, because it included the northern half of Sangamon Country, hinterlands of Jacksonville and Springfield, and eastern margins of the middle Illinois Valley. By contrast, the Edwardsville federal land district sustained its mesmeric status with the northern portion of the American Bottom and Goshen area contiguous with Alton, eastern margins of the lower Illinois Valley corridor, and southern verge of Sangamon Country. The Palestine and Vandalia federal land districts received renewed interests from arriving pioneers. The accessible Wabash Valley corridor and the paralleling Little Wabash and Embarras tributaries were alluring ecological niches. The Kaskaskia Valley settlement corridor infilled, given its flatboating capabilities.

Regional land sales between 1832 and 1834 reveal the continued rivalry between the land offices of Springfield and Edwardsville. The "siren" pendulum oscillated between the two premier settlement districts. What made this three-year cycle different was the development of a widespread increase in land sales at virtually all federal land offices. Renewed immigrant interests in the older settlement areas associated with southern Illinois was substantial. About three to four times as much acreage was sold in these federal land districts between 1830 and 1834, in contrast to the entire 1820s. Most of the acreage in these southern Illinois federal land districts had still not been sold by 1834.

The eastern verge of central and southern Illinois received considerable attention from immigrants between 1832 and 1834. The federal land district of Palestine was slightly favored by settlers over interior Vandalia (fig. 2.6). Even the east-central Illinois land office of Danville within the heart of the Grand Prairie witnessed increased land sales. Danville was third in land sales volume in 1834. Quincy's land sales in the Military Tract rose from minuscule levels. Squatters had preempted the public domain bordering the Mississippi and Illinois Rivers and their tributaries in the southern portions of the bounty lands prior to federal surveying and land sales.

The late 1830s were characterized by a number of key divergences in sales trends and regional patterns. Land sales increased a phenomenal sixfold between 1834 and 1835 and then increased another 50 percent by 1836 before the net effect of the Panic of 1837 (fig. 2.5). Ten federal land districts now existed from which immigrants could select their final destinations. No federal land offices dominated in sales volume as they had in the past (figs. 2.4, 2.6). In fact, not a single land office between 1835 and 1839 garnered as much as one-quarter of the total land sales in a year, whereas in the early 1830s, 35 to 38 percent sales domination was common. During the 1820s, with fewer land offices, it was not uncommon for 50 to 70 percent of the total acreage sales to occur at one federal land district. Sangamon Country surrounding Springfield reigned supreme in seven out of the ten years during the 1820s.

The last half of the decade, in contrast to the first half, was as distinctive in migration and settlement history because of the massive acreage sales volume, extreme fluctuation in annual land sales, and sales patterns. Two slightly different patterns in land sales emerged. Between 1835 and 1836, federal land districts in central and northern Illinois dominated land sales. In west-central Illinois, the Military Tract and Sangamon Country competed for land sales leadership and alternated their status. In both years, Quincy's and Springfield's land sales surpassed the total state acreage sold in 1834, about 350,000 acres. With the opening of the

Chicago and the Galena land offices, the federal land districts on opposite sides of northern Illinois witnessed an instantaneous surge in land sales.

Edwardsville was an anomaly among the five older land offices, since it had comparable acreage sales with the newer land offices. Its land district had sustainability because of its proximity to gateway St. Louis and its smaller, upstream Illinois counterpart of Alton in Madison County. The Goshen and Turkey Hill settlements in the American Bottom, the eastern periphery of the lower Illinois Valley, and the southern fringe of Sangamon Country marked a number of attractive destinations. Southern Illinois land offices of Kaskaskia, Shawneetown, and Vandalia sold small percentages of the total land sales in 1835 and 1836. Yet they either surpassed or almost equalled the total acreage sold between 1820 and 1834.

The late 1830s experienced a cataclysmic decline in acreage sold across Illinois (fig. 2.5). Land sales in the last three years were not equivalent to the total acreage purchased in 1836. The economic panics of 1837 and 1839 dramatically restrained the momentum of migration. The 1837–39 period must be interpreted in comparison with previous trends in land sales and regional patterns (figs. 2.3–2.6). Each year far exceeded the total acreage sold in the entire 1820s period. Collectively, the three years exceeded land sales volume for the 1830–34 period. And the individual years represented total land sales two to five times greater than for any year between 1830 and 1834.

Between 1837 and 1839, regional land sales leadership oscillated from south-central to west-central to northwest Illinois federal land districts (fig. 2.6). Vandalia's total acreage sales had grown substantially from the previous fifteen years. Immigrants found the converging, integrating road network that linked this transitional southern and central Illinois area considerably improved. Quincy's sales percentages reflect growth and then a considerable falloff. The Quincy federal land district coincided with the Military Tract between the Mississippi and Illinois Rivers; thus, it was highly accessible by the waterway channels and was an increasing focus of the road network in west-central Illinois. Galena's land sales depict a rapid ascendancy in volume to its leadership position. In each year, the acreage sold more than doubled, reflecting the Rock River Valley's increasing attractiveness and popularity of the lead mining center's hinterland. The Chicago land office in northeast Illinois witnessed plummeting land sales but then rebounded (fig. 2.6). Sangamon Country in west-central Illinois lost some of its luster as a destination as the prime agricultural tracts had been purchased earlier as in the Military Tract. In addition, this older federal land district was not as accessible to settlers pouring through the northern point of entry of Chicago. Acreage sales at Springfield held their own initially and then sharply declined.

Stretching across the northern portion of southern Illinois between the Mississippi and Wabash Rivers, three federal land districts persisted in attracting immigrants. The older Edwardsville land office had witnessed the purchase of the choicest agricultural land. Acreage sales were substantially less in the final two years. By contrast, land sales at Palestine were significantly greater than in any period since the 1820s, just like Vandalia's sales, as noted previously. The renewed immigrant appeal of Kaskaskia and Shawneetown federal land districts attests to an incredible quantity of vacant land that had been bypassed. Acreage purchased between 1820 and 1835 was diminutive in comparison with the late 1830s. Even though economic hard times prevailed during much of the 1830s, land sales reflect a powerful "Illinois fever" impulse and delineate those settlement areas embracing the greatest population increases by 1840.

Settlement Conditions from 1840 to 1849

The underlying settlement stage across Illinois by 1840 forged pivotal immigrant destinations intertwined within the state's settlement, urban, economic, and transport infrastructure. Population grew to 851,470 in 1850, or an increase of 375,287 during the 1840s, but this was an increase of only 56,549 over the population increase of the 1830s. Why was there a decline in the population growth rate of 79 percent of the 1840s in comparison with the 202 percent of the 1830s? The explanation relates to regional shifts in net migration trends in the Middle West, given the fundamental westward aberration of American movements deeper into the continent. Relative location within the heartland, availability of navigable arteries, the demise of the internal improvement system, economic conditions, and the impact of a railway network were processes that impacted the oscillation of migration streams.

Illinois' northern neighbors of Wisconsin and Michigan exhibited spectacular population growth rates during the 1840s. Wisconsin witnessed extraordinary growth pains as it led all Old Northwest states in net migration (Vedder and Gallaway 1975, 162–64). It deflected migration flows, particularly Yankees and Germans, employing the northern gateway corridor from Illinois. Wisconsin and Michigan replicated as "daughter states" of New York. Although natural increase accounted for 54 percent of the population increase by 1850, Illinois' net migration was still second to Wisconsin in the Old Northwest. Ohio emerged as a net population exporter after 1840 and mushroomed after 1850 as a source of human resources involved in stepwise migration. Indiana followed in the 1850s with a negative net migration. In half a century, Ohio transformed "from being a raw frontier state to being a mature 'older' area which was losing population to newer areas to the west" (Vedder and Gallaway 1975, 164). Vedder and Gallaway found that "Illinois' net migration was greatest in the 1850s. Interestingly, the peak in net migration in both Indiana and Illinois came twenty years later than the state directly to the east" (164).

Relative location in midcontinent and large amounts of cheap, fertile, surveyed land contributed to the sustainability of Illinois' attractiveness. Accessible river

trunk lines; increasing steamboat activity on the inland channels, traversing navigable tributaries; and profitability of flatboats on numerous smaller tributaries
were dynamic transportation processes stimulating commercial agricultural pursuits. Unparalleled steamboat and flatboat access were inseparable from the settlement and economic growth of most of Illinois prior to 1830. The Mississippi River
trunk system attached the state to the southern marketplace focal point of New
Orleans by way of St. Louis. Further developments of the steamboats' inland system in the next two decades revealed lateral inland settlement extension from the
navigable channels. Hunter argues that this peripheral settlement expansion man-
ifested an "upward climb from a plane of relative self-sufficiency to one of economic interdependence" (1949, 32).

During the 1840s, an extraordinary settlement and economic adaptation
emerged. It modified the directional-biases of the spatial linkages of west-central
Illinois situated astride the Mississippi and Illinois Rivers between rival entrepôts
of St. Louis and Chicago. Construction of the Illinois and Michigan Canal and
earlier eastern Midwest canals altered the organizational ties of Illinois and the
entire Lower Middle West from a southern nexus economy to a northeast orientation of agricultural exports and imported goods (Taaffe and Gauthier 1973,
52–57). The resultant competitive economic struggle enhanced and sustained the
magnetism of western and northern Illinois.

Settlers who were profit-motivated agriculturalists recognized that both internal and external markets significantly increased the value of the land's economic
potential and their own materialistic gains (Parker 1975, 22). Parker contends that
in the generation prior to the Civil War, an extensive transfer of marketplace-
oriented farmers to more suitable regions included grain and meat producers
from Pennsylvania and the Ohio Valley corridor and dairy farmers from New
England and New York to the Upper Middle West. Primary settlement-economic
connections integrated the lakeport regional node of Chicago, its northeast
Illinois hinterland, and the upper and middle Illinois Valley corridor with the
northern commercial gateway's seaboard terminus, the national node of New
York City (6–7, 24–25).

Diversion of freight traffic from the southern commercial gateway quickened
with the Erie Canal and Ohio's feeder canals. By 1850, the entire Great Lakes region
emerged tributary to New York. Upper Middle West settlement and economic advancements were rapid. Cheap water access to the eastern seaboard escalated New
York to the premier Atlantic port (Hunter 1949, 483). Hunter argues that for steamboat interests, the critical decade of the fifties "was marked by depression and mis-
fortune and by the beginning of the trend which within a few years was to relegate
steamboats to a minor role in the economic life of the West" (481).

The disintegration of steamboating and southern commercial orientation resulted from several fundamental factors: internal commerce flows shifted to alter-

native channels; railroads short-circuited a significant proportion of the freight traffic between the larger river cities; geographical alignment of the rivers was counter to America's economic expansion and linkages; and individualistic steamboat operations were deficient (Hunter 1949, 481–519). Antebellum railroads marked reliable, flexible services; lower costs over greater distances; increased tonnage capacities; reduced shipping times; rapid expansion of trunk, feeder, and bridge lines; and the emergence of national and regional systems. Transport processes associated with the railroad hastened the competitive crisis that forced an auxiliary and nonessential role for steamboats in the expanding economic life of the eastern United States (Fishlow 1965; Fogel 1964; Hunter 1949; Meyer 1948; North 1961, 1974; Taylor 1951).

A deep-rooted "Illinois fever" persisted during the 1840s and 1850s. Rapid agricultural and manufacturing developments unfolded with the competitive struggle between steamboats and railroads in Illinois and the Midwest (Haites and Mak 1970–71, 1971; Haites, Mak, and Walton 1975; Hunter 1933–34, 1949; Lee 1917; Parker 1975; Putnam 1918; Walton 1987). Regional and local marketplace organizational frameworks fused through the commercial gateways that linked midcontinent with national seaboard and world systems. During the antebellum period, east-west penetrating rail lines and thickening of north-south rail lines brought the cessation of any remaining Illinois regional settlement frontiers of incipient agriculture and southern-oriented economy (Parker 1975, 27).

The Internal Improvement Act of 1837 was an attempt to commit the state to an incredible railroad building program of more than 1,300 miles and improved river and road travel. The Illinois and Michigan Canal had been previously authorized by the General Assembly. Sutton argues that an ambitious program to revolutionize transportation within Illinois was doomed to failure from the start (1965, 36–40). Two primary factors explain the internal improvements boondoggle. The legislature erred in bowing to jealous sectionalism that required that all the projects be initiated simultaneously. Years later, abandoned construction activity reminded locals and regions of their greed as these derelict artifacts epitomized the "state's supreme folly" (39). Symptoms of economic depression, including frenzied land speculation, currency stringencies, and stagnating business activity in the state and nation, were clearly evident before the General Assembly enacted the internal improvements legislation. The Panic of 1837 was a national depression, followed by a worse one in 1839 (North 1961, 194). State debt became a lasting burden that intensified and perpetuated difficult economic times. Pease asserts that the mania for internal improvements was not relegated to state actions, but private enterprises developed their own alternatives (1918, 194–235).

Economic hard times persisted between 1837 and 1843. The Panic of 1837 triggered a universal economic slowdown. North drew a parallel to the 1839–43 period and a similar epoch ninety years later since "both were severe and prolonged drops in economic activity" (1961, 202). Extended, deep economic depressions were characterized by a precipitous decline in domestic and export prices; the cessation of capital imports; states defaulting on interest payments; and a sharp decline in domestic and foreign trade. By 1843, economic stagnation ran its course as price levels resumed normalcy and new economic expansions emerged (202–3). But the agricultural growing seasons of 1843 and 1844 in Illinois were extremely poor crop years that retarded regional and local economic turnarounds (Pooley 1968, 568–71).

A widespread return to economic prosperity in the nation marked the last half of the 1840s. North asserts that tremendous acquisition of territory, accelerated pace of industrialization, and evolution of an incipient manufacturing region in the Northeast brought a return to an active market economy (1961, 204–9). Rudimentary manufacturing activities developed in the regional nodes of Chicago and St. Louis and subregional nodes of Illinois. Finished goods were produced for local and regional agricultural markets. Economic recovery and expansion in the Northeast and West included the renewal of railroad construction, the expansion of manufacturing, rising manufactured goods prices, an increase in foreign immigration, rising farm prices, an increase in grain exports to Europe, a phenomenal increase in Erie Canal shipments, and increases in migration flows (206–7).

Although manufacturing growth in the Northeast was the key stimulus to economic expansion, North suggests that railroads accelerated and intensified economic activities (1961, 208). Railroads improved the accessibility of the Northeast and West to interregional and world export markets and procurable sources of manufactured goods. They brought a dramatic decline in transport costs that hastened the demise of the steamboat. Railroad expansions of the 1850s connected the patterns of exchange and economic activity of Illinois and the interior to an eastern focus. The increasing railroad density quickened a transformation from a predominantly subsistent agricultural economy to a commercial agricultural economy. By the late 1830s and 1840s, the Old Northwest, with its expanding waterway transport networks, fashioned a pattern of interregional trade based on market-oriented agricultural production that was more diversified than in the South. In time, the Midwest developed the most broadly based economy of any United States region (Meyer 1983, 1989; North 1974, 78–79). By 1900, midcontinental Illinois epitomized that delicate, balanced economy between agriculture and manufacturing.

Railroad corridors frequently paralleled earlier transport corridors such as the Illinois River, the Illinois and Michigan Canal, and the National Road. North contends that railroads were the initial large-scale enterprise in the eastern United States (1974, 109–10). As a sophisticated large-scale business organization, railroad expansions were closely analogous to evolving large-scale manufacturing organizations. Because railroads comprised numerous rival large-scale businesses, an incredible railroad density and network emerged in the heartland. By 1860, Illinois presaged widespread commercial agriculture spawned and captured by the web of rail lines.

Railroad expansions in the interior were dissimilar to Northeast settlement, economic, and social conditions. Meyer stresses the following episodes: sparser settlements, a dearth of large cities, hazardous banking and financing, a lack of local capital, sectional antagonisms, and caution of eastern capitalists (1948, 487). In a seminal study of the Old Northwest's sequential, annual railroad mileage growth, Paxson documented the vortex of railroad fever beginning in 1848 (1911). Within a decade, integrated border-to-border railroad networks modified social-economic life of the region. Between 1854 and 1856, a land grant railway linked the Prairie State. Extending southward from Galena and Chicago, linking at Centralia, and reaching Cairo, the Illinois Central Railroad resulted in the longest and most geographically prominent railway in the Old Northwest (Gates 1934). Its eastern branch traversed the least sparsely populated and lesser-developed Grand Prairie of east-central Illinois.

Midcontinental Illinois, with Lake Michigan to the north, engendered paralleling east-west rail lines. Three lines crisscrossed the state: Toledo, Wabash, and Western from Toledo, Terre Haute and Alton from Indianapolis, and Ohio and Mississippi from Cincinnati (Fishlow 1965, 174; Paxson 1911). They traversed the sparsely settled and least economically mature eastern half of Illinois that was peripheral to Indiana and the Wabash Valley corridor. These east-west trunk lines' objective was not development of local freight traffic but to provide competitive through service to the Mississippi River. They achieved their western goal by 1859. In 1857, the two southern trunk lines converged at St. Louis (Paxson 1911).

Fishlow (1965) examined the railroad's impact on transforming the antebellum economy by analyzing Paxson's (1911) annual railroad mileage maps. He concluded that the earliest Illinois railroads radiating from lakeside Chicago were an attempt to exploit wheat surpluses in the northern tier counties in the Fox and Rock River Valleys during the late 1840s and 1850s. They benefited from the opening of the Illinois and Michigan Canal as the Rock Island and Burlington rail lines paralleled the settlement-economic corridor (Fishlow 1965, 171–77). Another example of pursuing traffic opportunities occurred with the establishment of rail lines in the leading corn-growing counties of west-central and southwest Illinois. By 1853, a disproportionate number of total rail miles, 60 percent, concentrated in the wheat- and corn-growing counties. Early rail lines by 1850 aligned where marketplace agriculture had evolved in delicately balanced riparian corridors. Principal trunk roads and developing regional road networks for over half a century played a complementary role to trunk water passageways.

3

Evolution of Urban Road Networks

Population is rapidly increasing, and trade fluctuating from point to point; the courses of roads are consequently often changed, before a permanent route is adopted. Few roads, therefore, have become so fixed, as to their location, as to have been beaten by travel, and improved by art; and the traveller who ventures out in the spring, may expect to be obliged to wade through mire and water-ancle deep, knee deep, and peradventure deeper than that.
—Hall 1831

An expanding continental nation engineered east-west movement corridors in the nineteenth century (Vance 1990). Immigrant waves depended from the beginning on overcoming distance and improving spatial linkages (Sauer 1976, 45). Illinois Country was not immune from settlers' predispositions for improved connecting land-and-water circulation routes. Geographical value of an Illinois and Michigan canal was a reiterated agenda for decades. "The construction of a canal, thus opening a communication between the Mississippi River and the Atlantic states, is a work so easy, and of such immense importance both to the welfare of this country, and the advantage of the United States in general, that it cannot fail to meet with a very speedy accomplishment" (*The Emigrant's Guide, or Pocket Geography* 1818, 228–29). Early land routes were essential for settlement and economic growth. Corliss argues that "the secret of Illinois' remarkable progress is told in one word—transportation" (1937, foreword).

Immigrants followed fundamental movement laws. Frontier integrations shifted from isolation to accessible status, which spawned effective movements of people, goods, and communications. Circulation flows coalesce in networks of points and areas. Transport lines adapt to changing origins, destinations, costs, demands, technology, and settlement growth. Settlers' aspirations and activities transformed Illinois from local self-sufficiency to increasing marketplace-economic interdependence by the 1840s. Regional and national integrations were tied to navigable waterways. Improving road ties enhanced relationships between midcontinental Illinois, transAppalachia, and seaboard America. Expanding regional road structures were a prerequisite to frontier settlement and economic growth.

Steamboats engendered distinctive riparian movement-settlement corridors. Their heyday in the interior and Illinois occurred during the 1830s and 1840s. Waterborne transport processes replicated riverside nodes and channelized economic and regional growth structures. Washed by navigable channels, the featureless plains of Illinois evolved numerous movement corridors. The Illinois Valley corridor emerged as a quintessential riparian corridor. Prior to the spread of railroad networks in the 1850s, the expansion of regional road networks were closely integrated with the inflexible waterways and their riverside and lakeside nodes with their expanding tributary areas.

Commonplace points, lines, and areas represent integral elements of urban-transport networks (Abler, Adams, and Gould 1971, 236–97; Haggett 1966). Immigrant flows were dynamic point-to-point and area-to-area transfers between origins and destinations. Regional movements suggest the spread and replication of cultural traditions as a westward procession across the eastern United States (Hudson 1988; Mitchell 1978; Parker 1975; Swierenga 1989; Zelinsky 1973). Areal movements involving individuals, families, relatives, friends, groups, or colonies were in reality point-to-point movements to new areas. Place movements to magnetic settlement areas emerged as channelized migration flows. Attractive destinations, such as the American Bottom and Sangamon Country, were both point and area place images integrated in immigrants' mental maps (Abler, Adams, and Gould 1971, 241). Settlement cores and peripheries connected to interdependent riparian corridors and regional road networks.

Geographic mobility was not placeless nor directionless, since points or nodes were linked by lines or routes. Improving water and land routes served as fundamental determinants of transportation, settlement, economic, and urban infrastructures. Expanding circulation systems were essential for transforming frontier agriculture from subsistence to interdependent interregional, national, and world space-economies (Agnew 1987; Meinig 1986; Vance 1970; Wallerstein 1989). The early frontier urban road network of Illinois focused on elemental lines, points, and areas in southwest Illinois.

Early Interior Movement Corridors

Overland and waterway movement corridors traversed and intersected in the interior. Natural waterways (the Ohio, Mississippi, and Missouri Rivers and the Great Lakes), canals, and roads engendered distinctive networks. Transport systems connected the Midwest, transAppalachia, southern and eastern seaboards, and northwest Europe. Natural environs of the routeways and accoutrements of the transport corridors influenced the mental maps of a mobile society. Linkages and nodes formed integral elements of an expanding continental movement-settlement system (Taaffe and Gauthier 1973, 5). During the Great Migration, immigrants followed salient paths of diffusion (Friis 1974).

Prior to the Revolutionary War, immigrants had dispersed southwestward into the Great Valley astride the Great Wagon Road. Settlement infillings of the ridge and valley area and Virginia, the Carolinas, and Georgia piedmonts were extensive. Spreading northwestward, the Wilderness Road, which penetrated the Appalachian barrier through the Cumberland Gap, extended to the Bluegrass Region. Two branches of the Wilderness Road extended from central Kentucky to Illinois Country. From the Falls of the Ohio at Louisville, the Vincennes Trail reached the old French point of attachment of Vincennes on the Wabash River. The St. Louis Trace continued across south-central Illinois to the fur trading outpost. A branch bifurcated near modern-day Salem to the old French settlement of Kaskaskia. Another road extension from Lexington, Kentucky, linked with Shawneetown near the confluence of the Wabash-Ohio Rivers. Two early roads dispersed from the entry point: the Shawneetown-Kaskaskia Trail and the Goshen Road. Other frontiersmen utilizing the Great Wagon Road bypassed the Cumberland Gap and circumvented the Appalachian ranges as they dispersed to the Nashville Basin. Early population infilling of extreme southern Illinois was greatly influenced by the Nashville-Saline Trail from central Tennessee. This trunk line bifurcated at Princeton in western Kentucky and crossed the Ohio River at Golconda and Ford's Ferry. Northwest trails connected with Kaskaskia and St. Louis. Southern tributaries of the lower Ohio River—the Kentucky, Cumberland, and Tennessee Rivers—were alternative transport options.

Two old military roads emerged as important migration routes. Forbes Road from Harrisburg on the Susquehanna River and tied to Philadelphia dispersed pioneers from southeast Pennsylvania. Braddock's Road commenced at Cumberland, Maryland, on the Potomac River. Tied to Baltimore and Philadelphia, it evolved as the Cumberland Road in 1811. The first national pike connected Cumberland, Wheeling, and the capitals of Columbus, Indianapolis, and Vandalia in the Old Northwest states of Ohio, Indiana, and Illinois. The early destination nexus of the middle trunk route was located at the confluence of the Allegheny and Monongahela Rivers. With its upstream and downstream hinterland, Pittsburgh emerged as a pivotal interior gateway entrepôt. The Ohio River functioned as the pivotal movement corridor during the first quarter of the nineteenth century (Barnhart 1970; Buley 1950). Replicated settlement clusters emerged at favorable downstream terrace sites and inland astride tributary channels.

Parallel overland routes spread westward across northern Pennsylvania and upstate New York toward Lake Erie, where they coalesced as a peripheral lake road. An all-water route developed with the opening of the Erie Canal in 1825. With improved steam navigation on the Great Lakes and the bridging canals of

Ohio, Indiana, and Illinois, the northern movement corridor rose to prominence. The Great Lakes–Erie Canal trunk line altered immigrant movements and the reciprocal flow of trade goods and agricultural exports. This northern routeway system effectively integrated Upper Midwest lake ports with the eastern seaboard and Europe. The bridging canals in the Lower Midwest initiated the shift of the Mississippi-Ohio-Wabash-Illinois river towns' exchange ties to the mercantile hinterland of New York City.

A national trunk and bridge line transport system intertwined the eastern United States by mid-nineteenth century. The Old Northwest emerged as an expanding midwestern regional settlement and economic development sphere (Parker 1975). Walton argues that during the antebellum period, three commercial gateways integrated the Old Northwest with the seaboard national nodes and world system (1987, 230–34) (fig. 3.1). A northern commercial gateway embraced the Great Lakes–Erie Canal–Hudson system that connected Chicago with the terminus of New York. A northeastern or middle commercial gateway linked the National Road and Ohio system with Wheeling and Pittsburgh on the upper Ohio River to Philadelphia and Baltimore. The southern commercial gateway tied upstream entrepôts of St. Louis, Louisville, and Cincinnati on the Mississippi-Ohio system with New Orleans.

Growth of Regional Settlement Infrastructures

Frontier settlement networks expanded with the evolution of urban hierarchies (D. R. Meyer 1980), urban growth (Muller 1977), and transport network development (Taaffe and Gauthier 1973). A four-tier American urban system spread into midcontinent by 1850. Three-level, regional urban hierarchies comprising lower-level, subregional, and regional nodes connected with seaboard national nodes (Conzen 1975, 1977; D. R. Meyer 1980; Muller 1976, 1977). With rapid population increases and expansions in road-water networks, sustained settlement and economic growth emerged where intra- and interregional linkages improved interactions with regional and national nodes. Regional settlement frameworks improved with increased density and complexity of trunk, bridge, and feeder lines.

With inland movement of the transAppalachian frontier, interior unraveling points evolved as dynamic outposts of an American mercantile economy (Vance 1970, 80–128). Greater pioneer settlement growth occurred in attractive destination areas fringing gateway entrepôts with their high-profile visibility and accessibility. Initially, they served as primary collecting points for resources shipped back to original unraveling points on the eastern seaboard. D. R. Meyer argues that "the size of a node that can emerge on the basis of physical movement of commodities and passengers is related to the amount of stock a node

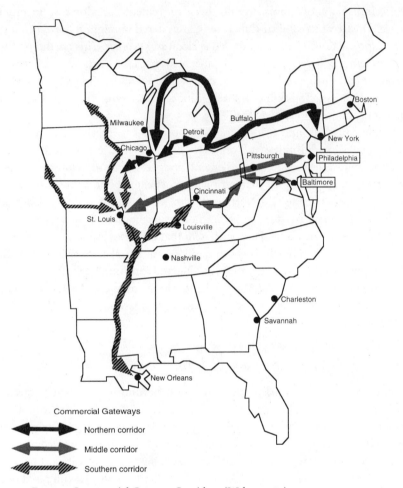

FIG. 3.1. Commercial Gateway Corridors (Walton 1987)

can aggregate for redistribution to other nodes and the degree of linkage the node can achieve" (1980, 127). With increasing population, demand for goods, and standard of living, regional entrepôts developed complex collection, distribution, and service functions. Midcontinent regional nodes formed river and lake alignments (Vance 1970, 97). They connected with national nodes that functioned as unraveling points for distribution and collection linking the interior, eastern seaboard, and Europe.

Fundamental mercantile centers were the predominant type of urban place in expanding regional settlement frontiers. In pioneer farming areas, they were small in population and simple in trading structure (Vance 1970, 83–86). Pivotal lower-level nodes provided essential mercantile, distributive, and county seat functions (fig. 3.2). Essential consumer travel of dispersed farmers and physical movement of commodities and passengers were primary processes that influenced their formation, size, and location (D. R. Meyer 1980, 127, 131). Lower-level nodes formed the basal building blocks of a frontier urban hierarchy and agricultural economy (Cronon 1991, 104). Elementary trading centers with greater accessibility within the expanding regional urban-transport networks increased their population size, connectivity, and hinterland area. They emerged as dynamic nodes for collecting and forwarding stock and distributing imported stock. Those that evolved as subregional nodes proffered higher-order mercantile, collecting, distributive, and service activities.

When the volume of stock of a frontier subregion achieved a level that encouraged entrepreneurs who controlled exchange to locate outside a regional node, the node chosen offered the best information access and physical movement of commodities and passengers. Entrepreneurs agglomerated in the next-highest urban node level, the subregional node, where population size and collection and distribution scale were considerably greater than in a lower-level node (D. R. Meyer 1980, 128–32). Subregional nodes were usually marketplace and courthouse centers in discrete, advantageous locations accessible to regional nodes in the urban-transport structure. Expansion of route networks in dynamic regional settlement areas augmented and altered connectivity to the subregional nodes with greater accessibility. Feeder and bridge roads linked subregional nodes to lower-level

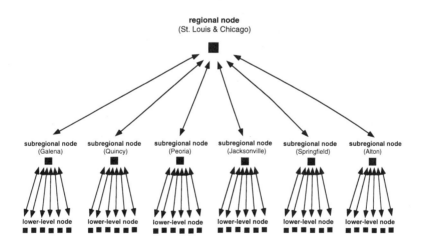

Note: End of the frontier three-tier regional urban hierarchy
was integrated into a four-tier American urban
system that included seaboard national nodes.

FIG. 3.2. Urban Hierarchy in Illinois, 1850 (D. R. Meyer 1980)

nodes within their tributary areas. Rapid population infilling and dispersion intensified reciprocal flows of commercial agricultural exports and manufactured goods in subregional nodes' expanding hinterlands. Three-tier frontier urban hierarchies occurred where effective overland-riverine transport networks enhanced mercantile flows. D. R. Meyer contends that a regional context for explaining frontier nodes' integration into an American city system is not adequate but requires a national context (1980). The shift from subsistence to marketplace space-economies in Illinois interrelated with an interdependent, expanding urban-transport system.

Two- and three-level regional urban hierarchies existed in Illinois by 1850. Two-tier urban hierarchies integrated subregional nodes and their hinterlands with lower-level nodes and their limited hinterlands. They existed in southern, east-central, and northwest Illinois. In a transitional stage of regional growth between subsistence and commercial agriculture, these regions possessed limited accessibility to regional marketplace centers. Extreme southern Illinois, with its persistent interior remoteness, developed only lower-level nodes and tiny, scattered communities. Such relatively isolated areas possessed weaker connections with each other, with interior subregional and regional nodes, and with distant Atlantic and Gulf seaboard national nodes. Greater accessibility and connectivity characterized emerging three-tier regional urban hierarchies in southwest, west-central, and northeast Illinois. Given higher levels of commercial agricultural and mercantile development, they unfolded as linchpin settlement areas essential for stable and sustained regional settlement and economic growth. Lower-level nodes, located at favorable water-land route junctures, aspired and competed for subregional nodal status. Expanding, maturing three-level urban hierarchies emerged in the Midwest where intraregional settlement networks connected to dynamic regional nodes, such as St. Louis, Chicago, Detroit, Indianapolis, and Cincinnati. Regional nodes functioned as mercantile gateways for developing regions. By 1850, three-tier regional urban networks integrated with interregional, national, and world economic systems (Agnew 1987; Conzen 1975, 1977; D. R. Meyer 1980, 1983, 1989; Vance 1970; Wallerstein 1989).

Muller proposes a model of selective frontier regional urban growth that included three developmental periods: pioneer periphery, specialized periphery, and transitional periphery (1977). "Pioneer periphery" marks the initial opening of the insular frontier to regional settlement (Muller 1977, 24–25). Relative isolation of nodes and hinterlands from external markets, low population densities, dependency on agricultural self-sufficiency, and minimal marketplace agriculture growth exemplified pioneering colonizations of unsettled lands. Penetration into unsettled frontier habitats and dependency upon natural movement corridors meant interregional communications were costly, irregular, and limited.

The second period of frontier regional urbanization growth represents a "specialized periphery" of economic development (Muller 1977, 25–26). Mainline movement corridors witnessed improvements in interregional and national integrations. Attractive settlement areas developed effective intraregional circulation webs that connected to interregional and national infrastructures. Advancements in transport linkages facilitated reductions in marketplace isolation, promoted competitive position of export products, increased nodality, and fostered population growth in urban places and their hinterlands. Access to external markets prompted growth and specialization of export crops and agricultural processing industries. Increasing mercantile activities, incipient manufacturing activities, and collecting, distributive, and service activities of regional nodes forged expansions in intraregional, national, and world interconnections.

Sequential growth of a frontier regional urban system concludes with the "transitional periphery" period, which coalesces with the integration of maximum road densities and diffusion of railroad networks (Muller 1977, 26–27). Interior peripheral areas were not dependent on regional nodes as markets but were now connected to more advantageous interregional, national, and international markets for their export commodities. The common availability of railroad service reinforced nodality and road networks.

In an expanding continental transport system, the American colonial period marked the initial transport growth phase of the emergence of "scattered ports" along the eastern seaboard (Taaffe and Gauthier 1973, 47). By the early 1800s, increasingly efficient water and land modes of transport in the Old Northwest entered the second phase of "penetration lines" in transport network development (47). As interregional trunk lines traversed transAppalachia, interior unraveling points increased their collecting and distributive specializations, control of exchanges, and market hinterlands. Penetrating trunk lines with spreading intraregional bridge and feeder lines formed effective connected networks. Bridge lines intensified competition between regional nodes for space-economy growth. Overlapping urban hinterlands emphasized the impact of available trunk and bridge lines on regional settlement and economic growth.

By 1850, the process of transport development entered the third phase of "interconnection" (Taaffe and Gauthier 1973, 47–48). Accelerated increases in the density of regional road networks occurred with feeder lines tapping expanding urban hinterlands. Trunk lines and intersecting bridge lines were imperative linkages in the integration of intra- and interregional road networks. The Wabash and Erie and Illinois and Michigan Canal corridors served as key bridge lines connecting navigable trunk systems. Improved efficiencies of the Great Lakes–Erie Canal and the Mississippi-Illinois-Ohio-Wabash River systems characterize the initial interconnection phase of midwestern transport network growth. Marketplace-biased immigrants did not migrate in a transport, urban, economic void. The frontier experience was compressed as regional space-economies increasingly tied to efficient trunk waterway corridors and expanding three-tier regional urban road networks. Complete interconnections within a spreading national transport system emerged with postbellum railroad dominance.

Evolution of Urban Road Networks in Illinois

Transport lines mark the structural framework through which movement of people, goods, and ideas flow (Taaffe and Gauthier 1973, 5–17). Urban places in a transport network proffer roadside services, taverns and inns, and marketplace functions for their hinterland and the traveling population. Nodal growth, stagnation, or decline closely link to changing accessibility. Relative accessibility of a market center includes its regional and national connections with other points and areas, its attractiveness as a settlement destination, and its location in the transport network. Pivotal point locations in transport structures comprise entry-and-exit points, crossroad points, line points, and termini points. Emerging frontier roads were interdependent of the points and areas they interconnected. Settlement, economic, and transport processes over time modify accessibility and perceived attractiveness of places and regions.

Illinois was gradually crisscrossed by a network of trails and roads linking southwest and southeast Illinois. Trunk lines traversed the state as immigrants opted for interior and cross-state destinations. Bridge lines integrated diverse regions, higher-level nodes, and trunk line overland and water routes. Feeder lines represented indispensable route ingredients for regional settlement and economic growth. They formed the web of spatial linkages that tied market centers to their immediate hinterlands. Within expanding three-tier regional urban hierarchies, lower-level nodes and isolated settlement clusters revealed marked reductions in the number of trails or roads that linked points or areas.

Urban points of attachment and attractive settlement districts in the developing regional settlement and economic structures metamorphosed from the late eighteenth to mid-nineteenth centuries in Illinois. Some subregional and lower-level nodes possessed, through their geographic location, greater centrality and ties with points and areas. Crossroads market centers experienced greater connectivity in a regional settlement context. County seat nodes evolved as crossroads market centers. Courthouse and market centers at the intersections of roads elaborated frontier social, economic, political, and transport structural linkages. Other early urban foci developed as wayside points along trails or roads.

Strategic junctures of navigable water channels and salient land routes were critical points of attachment. Maximum levels of accessibility and connectivity occurred where riverside and lakeside nodes emerged as transshipment points or break-in-bulk points in pivotal settlement areas. Extensive tributary areas spread downstream and especially upstream from riverside foci in movement-settlement corridors. Roads diverged from riverside and lakeside subregional and regional nodes to tap and mold inland mercantile tributary areas. Focal riverside nodes in the emerging regional settlement system of Illinois captured the interstice areas between riparian movement, settlement, and collecting corridors. As a consequence, road linkages from scattered areas converged on key mercantile-transshipment points. Continental interior market centers of varying scale and function required intra- and interregional road linkages in order to thrive and grow. Navigable channels, rivers, canals, and the Great Lakes were essential in the Old Northwest for interregional and international integrations prior to the railroad epoch.

Another of the essential foci in regional settlement evolution was the gateway node that linked interregional circulations. Located at critical junctures of trunk water and land links, gateways shifted in importance with fluctuating migration streams and economic-transport forces over time. Settlement timing, transport improvements, and regional economic growth influenced changing historical-geographic significance of gateways. Besides relative accessibility, other imperatives mark gateways (Taaffe and Gauthier 1973, 11–17). They operate as entry-and-exit or termini points and as break-in-bulk, transshipment, or break-in-freight-rate structure points in regional settlement growth. They also emerge in transitional zones owing to contrasting habitats, land uses, and stages of regional economic growth. Other transitional borders occur where nodes experience the divergence of routes in one direction and the convergence in the other. From gateway foci, roads fanned out into adjacent tributary areas or traversed the region to the next magnetic points or areas at the frontier's settlement edge.

Expanding overland routes and navigable waterways were interdependent in frontier Illinois (Boylan 1933; Taaffe and Gauthier 1973, 34–72). Expanding urban road networks were a sequential procession from the French colonial and territorial period to the frontier's closing. Circulation development included three stages: penetration, expansion, and consolidation. The penetration stage embraced crude trails and roads during the late French colonial, territorial, and early statehood periods. Slow population and economic growth etched a simple skeletal framework of trails and roads. The 1822 road map marks elemental route configurations in the early penetration stage in southern Illinois (Carey and Lea 1822). The 1828 road map unfolds the spread of routes into west-central Illinois in the late penetration stage (Knight 1828). The nexus of the road network shifted in the penetration stage from the colonial terminus of Kaskaskia to the entrepôt of St. Louis in the Mississippi Valley frontier.

The expansion stage of the road structure emerged with rapid population infilling in the 1830s and early 1840s. Regional settlement schemes expanded with the rapid increase in market centers and emergence of incipient commercial agriculture.

The 1839 road map underscores the initial intra- and interregional routes intersecting across Illinois in the early expansion stage (Young 1839). The National Road extended to Vandalia. The 1844 road map reveals significant changes in southern, central, and northern Illinois linkages in the late expansion stage (Morse and Breese 1844). Northern Illinois emerged with an expanding regional road structure that linked Galena and Chicago.

Prior to the railroad's dominance, well-integrated road infrastructures were engineered in Illinois (Taaffe and Gauthier 1973, 56–60). From a historical-geographical perspective, roads and navigable waterways were not mutually exclusive transport elements. As interdependent transport systems, wagon roads and steamboat channels doomed traditional frontier-dominated cultural and economic patterns. By the closing of the frontier, increasing marketplace agriculture expanded with the maximization of route densities. The consolidation stage connected rival accessible regional and subregional nodes. These interconnections marked the prime roads with the greatest traffic volume of goods and people and the most frequent common-carrier schedules of teamsters and stagecoaches (Taaffe and Gauthier 1973, 48–49). The 1850 road map corroborates a century spanning structural progression that culminates in the consolidation stage (Cowperthwait 1850). The emergence of rail networks in the 1850s fueled population and economic growth, competition of varied ranked nodes, and spread of commercial agriculture. Later generations attempted to perfect the underlying 1850 road alignments and structures (Boylan 1933, 22). (The five road maps are from the Illinois State Historical Library in Springfield.)

Lines on the maps marking roads were both real and imagined linkages available for immigrants who had caught Illinois fever. Land and water movement corridors developed as interrelated systems linking hierarchical nodes and successive, attractive destinations. Western promoters' approximations of important trunk and bridge roads spreading across the frontier landscape were not necessarily accurate on the maps during the frontier period. Feeder roads scratched into the pioneering habitat that tied lower-level nodes or radiated from larger nodes into their hinterlands were generally absent from early road maps. Public roads were generally routes joining lower-level nodes (Boylan 1933). Routes connecting county seat and market centers formed integrating intra- and interregional bridge lines crisscrossing the state. Roads designated as important public roads laid out at specific time periods in Boylan's 1933 seminal study, "Illinois Highways, 1700–1848," were not frequently demarcated on early road maps.

A number of factors explain missing roads. Distance between frontier Illinois and Philadelphia mapmakers created a problem of reliable information about new roads. From an eastern mapmaker's point of view, many bridge and most feeder routes were not necessary immigrant information in comparison with trunk routes. New routes were not overnight incisions into the wilderness habitat or encoded into immigrants' information feedback. Construction and maintenance of roads underscored at best a difficult, fragile transport process in remote settlement frontiers.

Penetration Stage

Frontier trails were initially superimposed over antiquarian trace-blazers: buffaloes, deer, and Amerindians. Interregional movements of Amerindians tied to principal rivers and lakes in the eastern United States. Friis argues that "the riverway was the natural pathway that complemented and often was part of their overland paths and trails. War paths, trading paths, and trails interlaced much of the continent" (1974, 8). Amerindians, explorers, fur traders, woodland frontiersmen, and a dispersing American society overlaid these waterway channels and their banks with a succession of transport modes and settlement patterns. The navigable Wabash-Ohio-Mississippi Rivers bordered Illinois on three sides. The Kaskaskia and Illinois Rivers traversed the state, northeast-southwest. The bisecting Illinois Valley was strategically located as a southwest-northeast bridge linkage between the Mississippi River and Great Lakes movement corridors. Early crisscrossing roads connected gateway foci, intervening navigable watershed areas with riverside nodes, and isolated interiors with peripheral locations. Frontier roads evolved as symbols of movement, communication, interaction, settlement, travel, and progress.

Road Structure in 1822

The early penetration stage perpetuated a simple skeletal road framework. Four years after statehood, the 1822 road map depicts the slow, colonizing settlement period that had extended over a century (fig. 3.3). Minimal settlement growth engendered few significant modifications to the earlier road network of the French colonial and Illinois territorial periods. During the French regime, an all-water route linked the French Canada colonial core of Quebec and Montreal on the St. Lawrence River by way of the Chicago portage and Illinois River with the remote Illinois Country. The Marquette and Jolliet waterway emerged as a favored linkage from Lake Michigan to the Mississippi River settlements. Kaskaskia (1703), Cahokia (1699), Prairie du Rocher (c. 1723), and Fort de Chartres (1720) were situated in the floodplain strip enclosed by the Mississippi River and its eastern bluff.

The American Bottom acquired "siren" destination status between 1778 and 1803. The Mississippi floodplain area contiguous to the French community of St. Louis in Spanish Territory marked the western verge of the new American republic (Boylan 1933, 15). French colonial attachment points were linked by paralleling roads in the Mississippi bottomlands and bluff fringe. Economic survival of the tiny agricultural villages was particularly dependent on the upriver Amerindian fur trade. Prior to Lewis and Clark, Kaskaskia and Cahokia were superseded in the

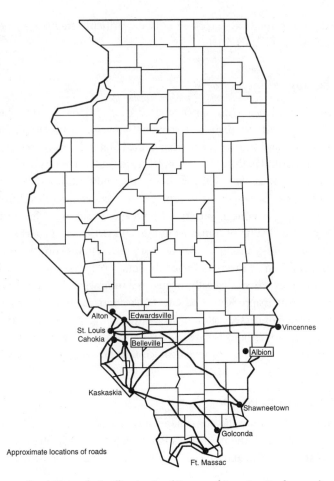

FIG. 3.3. Road Networks in Illinois, 1822 (Carey and Lea 1822; Boylan 1933)

upstream fur trade by the commercial hegemony of St. Louis. Kaskaskia was situated at the southern apex of the American Bottom near the juncture of the Kaskaskia and Mississippi Rivers. The mercantile outpost of Kaskaskia evolved at a strategic crossroads point where trunk lines intersected the Mississippi River and overland conduits (Boylan 1933; Corliss 1937; Friis 1974; Lewis 1933; Moore 1902; Ramey 1949; Tevebaugh 1952; Walsh 1947).

Early trunk lines integrating distant French colonial points of attachment terminated at Kaskaskia: the Fort Detroit–Kaskaskia Trace and the Vincennes-Kaskaskia Trail. Kaskaskia developed as the commercial, political center for Illinois Country midway between Quebec in French Canada and New Orleans in French Louisiana. American settlers arriving after the formation of the republic selected attractive destinations in the eighty-mile-long American Bottom floodplains and bordering uplands. It also served as the county seat of Randolph County when it was separated from St. Clair County in 1795. In 1809, Kaskaskia originated as the territorial capital and in 1818 as the first state capital. After the 1844 flood, the county seat of Randolph County was shifted to Chester, high on the Mississippi bluffs (Buck 1967, 82).

In the early pioneering period, the frontier metropolis of Kaskaskia emerged as the nexus through which frontiersmen with "Illinois fever" dispersed (fig. 3.3). The northern apex of the American Bottom and bordering upland rim was the preferred destination adjacent to St. Louis. A number of trunk lines converged on Kaskaskia from distant points (Boylan 1933; Moore 1902; Walsh 1947). Wilderness Road extensions arriving from central Kentucky entered Illinois at the gateways of Shawneetown and Vincennes. The Shawneetown-Kaskaskia Road was more important for immigrants arriving by flatboats on the Ohio River and disembarking overland at Shawneetown. The Vincennes-Kaskaskia Road was of greater importance for those traveling the overland route from the Falls of the Ohio River.

The Nashville-Saline Trail bifurcated at Princeton, Kentucky, and crossed the Ohio River into southern Illinois at Ford's Ferry (Cave in Rock) in Hardin County and Lusk's Ferry (Golconda) in Pope County. A trail from Ford's Ferry connected with the Shawneetown-Kaskaskia Road. Lusk's Ferry overshadowed Ford's Ferry because it had more direct access to southwest Illinois. Golconda emerged as an important point of entry, given the Golconda-Kaskaskia Road. An old French military route rarely utilized was the Fort Massac–Kaskaskia Trace. By the time George Rogers Clark invaded French Illinois in 1778 to capture Kaskaskia, Fort Massac on the Ohio River—now Metropolis in Massac County—had been abandoned. The trace proved difficult for Clark's men to follow, given its poor trail markings and infrequent use. Yet it suited a military tactician who decided to attack the village of Kaskaskia from an inland position rather than from the expected upstream Mississippi River approach (Boylan 1933, 8–10).

The persistent commercial-political connections of Kaskaskia shaped the inland divergence of rudimentary routes (fig. 3.3). During the late eighteenth and early nineteenth centuries, Kaskaskia tapped settlement clusters in its upland hinterland. Routes radiating from the pivotal focus in southwest Illinois included Kaskaskia-Cahokia; Kaskaskia–Belleville–French Village; Kaskaskia-Belleville; Kaskaskia-Belleville, west of the Kaskaskia River; Kaskaskia-Covington; and Kaskaskia-Chester-Murphysboro (Boylan 1933; Moore 1902; Walsh 1947). The Kaskaskia-Cahokia Road in the American Bottom conformed to the Mississippi bluffs by way of Prairie du Rocher and Harrisonville. It probably marks the oldest land highway in Illinois (Boylan 1933, 10). In 1790, Cahokia was established as the county seat of the first Illinois county, St. Clair. Given the more rapid growth of the upland settlements, frequent flooding problems, concern for safety, and convenience of accessibility to courthouse functions, the county seat of St. Clair County transferred inland eight miles to Belleville in 1814 (Boylan 1933, 15).

By early statehood, three bridge routes connected Kaskaskia and Belleville with rapidly growing upland settlements: Turkey Hill, Ridge Prairie, Looking Glass Prairie, Twelve Mile Prairie, and High Prairie. The Kaskaskia–Belleville–French Village Road was the eastward route via the upland settlements of Florence, Walsh, Preston, and Baldwin in Randolph County. The Kaskaskia River was crossed at New Athens and continued northward to Freeburg, Turkey Hill, and Belleville in St. Clair County. A northwest branching route extended to French Village, situated at the entrance to a bluff valley. The initial segment of the Kaskaskia-Belleville Road coincided with the Kaskaskia-Cahokia Road. Before reaching Prairie du Rocher, the route branched inland through a bluff valley and then northward by way of the upland settlements of Ruma and Red Bud in Randolph County, Hecker in Monroe County, and Georgetown (Smithton) and Belleville in St. Clair County. The Kaskaskia-Belleville Road west of the Kaskaskia River also paralleled the Kaskaskia-Cahokia Road to the Mississippi bluffs. From there, the route coincided with the Kaskaskia bluffs. Near Horse Creek, northwest of Evansville on the Kaskaskia River, the trail thrust northward to Horse Prairie east of Red Bud, then to Belleville (Boylan 1933, 15–16; Moore 1902).

Cahokia, the northern commercial outpost of the French colonial district in the American Bottom, rivaled the mercantile-political center of Kaskaskia. During the late eighteenth century, both Kaskaskia and Cahokia were depopulated as French settlers removed westward across the Mississippi River to St. Genevieve and St. Louis after the French and Indian War. By 1800, because of its proximity and ties with St. Louis, Cahokia succeeded Kaskaskia as the largest French population center in Illinois. Initially, Cahokia benefited from the nearby emerging American settlements in the adjacent floodplain and rapidly growing eastern uplands. Two high-profile upland settlements evolved by statehood, Goshen near Edwardsville and Turkey Hill near Belleville. New Design near Waterloo, which had been the earliest significant American settlement, failed to keep pace with the population growth of its northern settlement rivals.

Kaskaskia remained second in population size to Cahokia in 1810. Buck argues that Kaskaskia experienced a new lease on life with its multiple political functions: county seat, territorial capital, and first state capital (1967, 80–83). Acquisition of a land office, a weekly newspaper, and greater marketplace functions caused the population of Kaskaskia to rise slightly above Cahokia by statehood in 1818. This reversal of previous decadal declines was short-lived. The removal of the capital and newspaper to Vandalia in 1820 set into motion economic and settlement declines. Situated on the west bank of the middle Kaskaskia River, Vandalia lay in the path of the projected westward-penetrating National Road. In midstate, the new capital was perceived as being centrally located to emerging settlement patterns. Frontiersmen concentrated in the American Bottom and bordering upland areas adjacent to St. Louis. Yet immigrants employing the overland trunk lines dispersing from

Shawneetown, Golconda, and Vincennes witnessed the alteration of the terminus focus from Kaskaskia to the entrepôt of St. Louis.

During the incipient frontier period, Kaskaskia was located at the core of developing settlements. Trails consequently converged on this key urban location (fig. 3.3). By statehood, the settlement structure had advanced a two-prong, northward settlement penetration astride the Wabash-Mississippi Rivers. Proximity to the commercial center of St. Louis, a midcontinental location, and navigability of the Mississippi trunk channel molded dynamic settlement destinations. The northern apex of the bordering Mississippi Valley and uplands, collectively known as the American Bottom, emerged as the new core of Illinois' settlement structure. Geographical settlement positioning of Kaskaskia reversed through its locational transformation from core to periphery status. Alluring settlements, such as Goshen and Turkey Hill, functioned as springboards for the northward settlement thrusts in the 1820s. Settlers preferred established settlement destinations that perpetuated a St. Louis marketplace connection. New, attractive destinations formed in the Mississippi-Illinois corridors in the Military Tract and Sangamon Country.

During the early penetration stage, two additional trunk routes converged in southwest Illinois (Boylan 1933; Corliss 1937; Ramey 1949; Tevebaugh 1952; Walsh 1947). The Vincennes–St. Louis Road spread westward through present-day Lawrenceville, Salem, Carlyle, and Cahokia. It branched from the Vincennes-Kaskaskia Road in the vicinity of Salem in Marion County. Most early roads were not thoroughfares for wagons. Corliss suggests that the Vincennes–St. Louis Road was the closest route to a highway in frontier Illinois (1937, 10). The Shawneetown–St. Louis Road bypassed Kaskaskia and thrust northwest towards Carlyle on the Kaskaskia River in Clinton County, where it intersected with the Vincennes–St. Louis Road. At Carlyle, a northwest branch road linked with Edwardsville, adjacent Goshen, and Alton. The road was known as the Shawneetown-Goshen Road. A rudimentary trail extended northward from Shawneetown to Vincennes in the Wabash Valley corridor, which connected intervening settlement points of Carmi, Albion, and Mt. Carmel.

Information circulation via early frontier road networks were cultural, social, and economic imperatives. Mail routes generally coincided with trunk and bridge routes, but private routes existed prior to the development of a discrete road structure in a remote frontier (Tevebaugh 1952). Tevebaugh distinguishes between a mail route, a line over which mail was transported under contract with the United States General Post Office, and a post road, a route designated by Congress over which public mail could be carried (vi). Frontier mail service in Illinois Country originated in 1800 with monthly service on a private route from Louisville to Vincennes and Kaskaskia in Indiana Territory. By 1830, Illinois frontier mail ceased its horseback characteristics and adopted stagecoaches as carriers (v).

By 1805, five post roads were information conduits in Illinois Country: Vincennes-Kaskaskia; Vincennes–Cahokia–St. Louis; Kaskaskia-Cahokia; Smithland, Kentucky–Ft. Massac–Cape Girardeau; and Cahokia–St. Louis (Tevebaugh 1952, 27–36). These mail routes were not permanently fixed, as settlement patterns and nodes changed. Maintaining mail service was difficult during the territorial period as a consequence of the War of 1812 and continued Amerindian problems. By statehood in 1818, the primary mail routes in slowly growing Illinois included Shawneetown–Saline–Kaskaskia–St. Genevieve; Kaskaskia–Cahokia–St. Louis; Smithland, Kentucky–Ft. Massac–Cape Girardeau; Kaskaskia-Vienna; Cahokia–Edwardsville–Turkey Hill–Cahokia; and Vincennes-Palmyra-Carmi-Shawneetown (37–56). Postal routes binding Cahokia with the Goshen and Turkey Hill upland settlements and Kaskaskia with the Shawnee Hills county seat of Vienna in Johnson County increased the pace of inland settlement expansions. The early mail delivery system was limited to bimonthly service for interior areas or new routes; rarely were there weekly contacts, with the exception of main routes (67).

The expansion of road and mail routes during the early penetration stage diverged from Vincennes, Shawneetown, Kaskaskia, and St. Louis into their wilderness peripheries (Tevebaugh 1952, 57–82). New post roads attached the American Bottom with inland settlements and the new capital at Vandalia. Major post road expansions coalesced with the congressional directive "that mail service should be arranged from the nearest post office on any post road to any county seat already established or to be established in the future" (57). By the early 1820s, a network of mail routes crisscrossed Illinois south of a line from Vincennes to Alton. Settlements north of that line without a post office were quickly integrated into the mail delivery system during the late penetration stage (83–105).

Post offices were integral ingredients in evolving regional settlement systems. Accessible lower-level nodes at crossroads locations dispensed fundamental market center and generally county seat activities. Where land and water routes intersected on the margins of Illinois, riverside urban-postal centers provided transshipment activities. By 1823, small gateway foci included Mt. Carmel in Wabash County, Shawneetown in Gallatin County, Elizabethtown in Hardin County, Golconda in Pope County, Ft. Massac (Metropolis) in Massac County, Kaskaskia in Randolph County, Cahokia in St. Clair County, and Alton in Madison County (Tevebaugh 1952, 82). A few small, inland postal centers were aligned on routes: Vienna in Johnson County, Frankfort in Franklin County, and Equality in Gallatin County. Crossroads locations improved interior frontier connectivity to intraregional linkages. Market and courthouse centers with postal hub advantages linked within the road-mail structure of the early 1820s. Albion in Edwards County, Carmi in White County, Mt. Vernon in Jefferson County, Carlyle in Clinton County, Vandalia in Fayette County, Belleville in St. Clair County, and Edwardsville in Madison County were crossroads lower-level nodes (fig. 3.3). By

1823, most communities in the slowly developing urban road network received mail delivery at least biweekly by horseback (80).

Tiny urban nodes, attractive settlement clusters, and primitive roads were essential components of road-mail networks during the early penetration stage. Frontier place images supported the fragileness, remoteness, and endurance of the pioneering experience. Sketches of early linkages reveal their haziness, uncertainties, and crudeness:

> There are two roads leading through the Ohio to Kaskaskia. The first leaves the Ohio at Robin's [Ford's] ferry, 17 miles below the Saline; distance to Kaskaskia, 135 miles. The other leaves the river at Lusk's ferry, 15 miles above the mouth of Cumberland. This is the shortest route by 15 or 20 miles. A post route passes from Vincennes to Kaskaskia, about 150 miles long. . . . There is a tolerable road between the mouth of Au Vase [Big Muddy] and Wood river, passing through Kaskaskia, Prairie du Rochers, St. Philippe, and Cahokia. Most of the settlements are connected by practicable roads, at least for packers and travellers on horseback. (Brown 1817, 28)

Frontier outposts offered minimal urban amenities and creature comforts. Key riverside gateways were situated on opposite verges of Illinois Country. Vincennes and St. Louis played important roles in the early settlement and economic growth of their immediate hinterlands and the Wabash-Mississippi movement-settlement corridors (fig. 3.3).

> Vincennes—The seat of justice for Knox county, stands on the east bank of the Wabash, one hundred miles from its junction with the Ohio. . . . It contains about one hundred houses, most of which are small and scattering; some have a neat and handsome aspect, while others are built in an uncouth manner, having a frame skeleton filled up with mud and stick walls. . . . The best buildings are a brick tavern, jail, and academy. . . . The plan of the town is handsomely designed; the streets are wide and cross each other at right angles. Almost every house has a garden in its rear, with high, substantial picket fences to prevent the thefts of the Indians. . . . The United States has a land office for the disposal of the public lands; and formerly kept a small garrison, in a little stockage near the bank of the river, for the protection of the inhabitants. (Brown 1817, 65–68)

The linchpin river town of the middle Mississippi Valley was an external force in the early settlement and economic advancements in western Illinois:

> St. Louis, the largest town of the territory, and at present the seat of government, stands on a high bank, fifteen miles below the entrance of the Missouri. The buildings are scattered along three parallel streets, extending upwards of two miles along the river, and each rising above the other, which gives to the town a neat and romantic appearance. Most of the houses are built of stone, and whitewashed on the outside. Almost every house has an extensive garden or park, around which high stone walls are built. Some of the buildings are very large and costly, and surrounded with

galleries. The population exceeds 3000 souls. It has a bank, printing-office, post-office, and Roman chapel. It already enjoys a handsome trade, and from its local advantages, promises to become a rich and populous city. The country, around and west of St. Louis, is for fifteen miles, one extended prairie, of a very luxuriant soil and in a high state of cultivation. There is a ferry from this town to the Illinois side of the Mississippi: from hence passes the main road to Kaskaskia. (Brown 1817, 204)

Other trunk line gateways were diminutive.

Shawneetown, above the mouth of the Saline, containing 30 or 40 log buildings; the inhabitants live by the profits of the salt trade. The growth of the town has been greatly retarded in consequence of the United States having reserved to themselves the property of the site of this place, the salt licks, as well as the intermediate tract between this and Saline river, 9 miles distant. It is a place of great resort for boats, and in time will no doubt become a place of consequence, and the lands in its vicinity are of a good quality. (Brown 1817, 27–28)

Kaskaskia—Situated on the right shore of the river of the same name, eleven miles from its mouth, and six from the Mississippi, in a direct line. It is at present the seat of the territorial government and chief town of Randolph county—contains 160 houses, scattered over an extensive plain; some of them are of stone. Almost every house has a spacious picketed garden it its rear. . . . The inhabitants are more than half French; they raise large stocks of horned cattle, horses, swine, poultry, etc. There is a post office, a land office for the sale of the public lands, and a printing office, from which is issued a weekly newspaper entitled the "Illinois Herald." This place was settled upwards of 100 years ago, by the French of Lower Canada. The surrounding lands are in a good state of cultivation. (Brown 1817, 27)

Prior to territorial status, Kaskaskia failed to compete commercially with its rival upstream gateway. By the Louisiana Purchase in 1803, Kaskaskia witnessed the dynamic American settlement core shifting to the northern margins of the American Bottom contiguous to the entrepôt of St. Louis. In the decade and a half prior to statehood, population growth aligned with a string of connected upland settlement clusters: New Design, Turkey Hill, and Goshen. The steamboat era's inception in 1811 marked the transport-economic momentum for the expansion of transshipment linkages with the southern commercial gateway and growth of mercantile-related activities at St. Louis. These changes punctuated its immediate western Illinois hinterland with a scattering of new settlements.

As colonization settlement points, Turkey Hill and Goshen had excellent accessibility to the St. Louis marketplace ferry (fig. 3.3). Two years before statehood, a key road connected Belleville and its surrounding upland settlements through French Village with St. Louis (Boylan 1933, 15–16). In 1819, a turnpike road, one hundred feet wide, was authorized and built from the Mississippi ferry at Illinoistown across the American Bottom to Six Mile Prairie adjacent to the bluffs, near present-day Collinsville (29). The population growth of Goshen was spurred because of access to rival river towns St. Louis and Alton. Expanding local, regional, national, and world economic ties of St. Louis emerged as fundamental migration pull factors. Turkey Hill and Goshen, the high-profile American settlement bridgeheads, experienced increasing population infilling by 1820 that facilitated rudimentary commercial agricultural development. Transformations in southwest Illinois to marketplace agriculture and the mercantile hegemony of St. Louis were major forces shifting the terminus of the early road network from Kaskaskia.

The roads of frontier Illinois were merely trails coarsely etched across expansive stretches of desolate woodlands and prairies (Ramey 1949; Walsh 1947; Tevebaugh 1952). Early roads were virtually useless during the winter snows and spring rains. In the remainder of the year, the overland paths were still difficult to traverse because of poor markings and numerous obstacles to pioneers, mail couriers, horses, oxen, wagons, and stagecoaches. George Flower, co-founder with Morris Birkbeck of the English settlement in Edwards County, commented on early road conditions:

> There were no roads on land, no steam-boats on the waters. The road, so-called, . . . was made by one man on horseback following in the track of another, every rider making the way a little easier to find, until you came to some slush, or swampy place, where all trace was lost, and you got through as others had done, by guessing at the direction, often riding at hazard for miles until you stumbled on the track again. And of these blind traces there were but three or four in the southern half of the State. No roads were worked, no watercourses bridged. . . . No man could feel sure that he was within the limits of the State, but from knowing that he was west of the Wabash and east of the Mississippi. (1882, 120–21)

During the early penetration stage, overland routes were few and far between, slow, difficult, dangerous, ineffective, and costly. Getting lost on early trails was easy given their primitiveness as paths, infrequent use, and poor markings. Even seasoned travelers and traders were not immune to puzzlement and indecision as to the exact route through the Illinois wilderness. The tracks through the dark, dense forests between settlements were marked by one notch on trees for a narrow footpath, two notches for a bridle trail, and three for a wagon road (Buck 1967, 120). Routes across prairies required rude signs on poles embedded in the ground or simply following the ruts (Corliss 1937, 7). Birkbeck was terse in his censure of early Illinois roads: "Roads as yet are in a state of nature" (1818a, 14).

Road Structure in 1828

During late penetration stage, the road-riparian system thrust from its southwest Illinois platform and St. Louis hub northward into west-central Illinois astride the Mississippi-Illinois movement-settlement corridors. Routes tenuously penetrated westward from the Wabash Valley corridor across east-central Illinois. Ten years after statehood, the 1828 road map documents a denser interconnecting road network with new interior nodes and peripheral settlement areas in southern Illinois. Entry points on the state's eastern and southern margins suggest diffusion pathways' directional-biases and immigrants' destination-biases. A substantive increase in nodes, routes, and complexity of the road network occurred between the early penetration stage (fig. 3.3) and the late penetration stage (fig. 3.4).

The road blueprint was still skeletal. As population infilled and altered the settlement structure of southern Illinois, the route web expanded. Settlement spearheads were directed northward into central Illinois. Primitive roads penetrated to the emerging isolated urban communities and popular settlement clusters. Settlement penetrations were most rapid straddling the fringing and traversing

FIG. 3.4. Road Networks in Illinois, 1828 (Boylan 1933; Knight 1828)

navigable watercourses. Settlers initiated a concerted effort to implant the empty interior void. Nodes and potential agricultural areas that had access to roads and markets were highly favored by the late 1820s.

St. Louis persisted as the road network terminus and gateway for southwest Illinois. Trunk lines converged on the Mississippi ferry crossing: Vincennes–St. Louis, Shawneetown–St. Louis/Goshen, and Golconda–Kaskaskia–St. Louis. The routes from Vincennes and Shawneetown merged at Carlyle on the Kaskaskia River and proceeded westward. The route from Golconda connected with St. Louis by way of the old French road between Kaskaskia and Cahokia. The Kaskaskia-Cahokia Road typified a quintessential bridge route. Diverging feeder routes integrated St. Louis with the American Bottom and the upland settlements of Goshen and Turkey Hill: Illinoistown Ferry–Six Mile Prairie–Edwardsville Road and Illinoistown Ferry–French Village–Belleville Road.

Roads converged on Edwardsville in the attractive Goshen settlement area. Routes linked it with Shawneetown, St. Louis, Alton, Springfield, and Kaskaskia (fig. 3.4). The Shawneetown Road represented a pivotal trunk line. The other roads from the riverside nodes of St. Louis and Alton were feeder routes. The Springfield Road marked a bridge route thrust into the heart of Sangamon Country and a tenuous trunk line penetration to Peoria and Chicago. The Kaskaskia-Belleville Road developed as a northward bridge route between the trunk routes from the entry points on the Ohio-Wabash Rivers. This old northward-penetrating bluff road linked the upland settlements that stretched northward like beads on a settlement chain. It also connected with Edwardsville and Alton.

Belleville was surrounded by numerous settlement clusters, the oldest and largest one being Turkey Hill. It developed multiple route linkages with the American Bottom, Edwardsville, Kaskaskia, and Shawneetown. A bridge road linked the Edwardsville and Belleville settlement areas. Two bridge routes connected Belleville with St. Louis: Belleville–French Village–Illinoistown Ferry and Belleville-Cahokia-Illinoistown Ferry Roads. Three roads converged on Belleville from Kaskaskia: Kaskaskia-Cahokia Road with a branch from Harrisonville through Waterloo to Belleville; Kaskaskia-Belleville Road, which ran northward through Red Bud and Hecker; and Kaskaskia–Belleville–French Village Road, which bisected Turkey Hill. These early route ties of the late territorial period reflected both northward, stepwise settlement movements and an attempt by Kaskaskia to tap the commercial needs of upland settlements.

Road alignments suggest by the late penetration stage some important characteristics of the early Illinois frontier period. Although Kaskaskia lost its state capital status and was not a major settlement destination, it persisted as an important divergence hub. The convergence of roads on the four primary hubs of Kaskaskia, St. Louis, Edwardsville, and Belleville revealed the nodes with accessibility and centrality in the southern Illinois road network. Convergence zones in the road structure marked areas with the greatest route densities. The denser, skeletal circulation network in southwest Illinois delineated the road interstice areas that represented the past and present locations of alluring settlement enclaves. The trunk routes from the Wabash–Ohio River corridors leaped across interior woodlands and scattered small prairies. Finally, the insular capital of Vandalia integrated with the primary settlement concentrations and gateways on the bordering Wabash-Ohio-Mississippi Rivers.

The road maps of 1822 (fig. 3.3) and 1828 (fig. 3.4) hint at persistence and discrete changes in the expanding road framework. The gateway of Shawneetown increased in importance with the divergence of three trunk routes and a bridge route, while Golconda possessed two trunk routes. Trunk routes from both entry points terminated with Kaskaskia, St. Louis, Edwardsville, Belleville, and Vandalia. These vital frontier urban communities and their hinterlands persisted as major immigrant destinations. The interior capital emerged with the highest centrality levels when the legislature remedied its accessibility problem by approving roads diverging from Vandalia to Shawneetown, America, Golconda, Palestine, Alton, Illinoistown, and Fairfield in 1823 (Boylan 1933, 43). But the 1828 road map reveals that the crude roads were not incorporated by eastern mapmakers.

Critical to regional settlement growth in southern and central Illinois during the late penetration stage was the ingress inland of traversing trunk lines (Ramey 1949, 30; Tevebaugh 1952, 105; Walsh 1947). Two trunk routes had a strong northward directional-bias. Running through the interior spine of southern Illinois was a overland route that developed as an important movement-settlement corridor. Golconda functioned as the gateway for binding Frankfort in Franklin County, Mt. Vernon in Jefferson County, and Salem in Marion County with the state capital of Vandalia. These crossroads points emerged as courthouse, market, and post centers. This trunk route extended northwest toward Springfield, which evolved as a central road nexus in Sangamon Country. St. Louis also connected with Springfield via Edwardsville. The trunk route extended northward to Peoria, then northeast to Fort Dearborn. Fort Dearborn (Chicago) and Fort Clark (Peoria) ties associated with earlier fur trade and military linkages.

Three penetrating routes diverged westward from the Wabash Valley corridor in east-central Illinois (fig. 3.4). Danville, a courthouse center, was connected to Indianapolis. It served as a tiny gateway node for a difficult road that pierced the Grand Prairie to Peoria. Paris, a county seat, was connected to an important ferry crossing on the Wabash River at Terre Haute. Two roads penetrated westward from this tiny point of entry. A southwest route connected Paris, Shelbyville, and Hillsboro. A northwest route integrated Paris and Springfield, where the route bifurcated westward into the Military Tract across the Illinois Valley to Rushville and Quincy on the Mississippi River or westward to Jacksonville.

Vandalia, the new state capital in 1820, was molded by the Illinois General Assembly to be the "epicenter" of state politics and the internal road network. Legislators anticipated that its hinterland would evolve as a magnetic settlement district, since a government land office had been located there in 1821. Located in Fayette County, numerous routes radiated from the state-county political center (Boylan 1933; Ramey 1949; Tevebaugh 1952, 83–105). It had the locational advantage of the westward-extending National Road. Midstate location was viewed as a plus factor in its evolution as a circulation hub. Its hinterland also represented a transitional settlement area between southern and central Illinois.

Shaping the centrality of remote, frontier Vandalia was a perceptually motivated attempt to contrive and maintain strong ties with the state's social, cultural, economic, and political "southern roots" (Boylan 1933, 18, 43). Social networks were expected to produce persistent interior population infillings in southern Illinois. Instead, Upland Southerners bypassed the southern interior. A northwest population surge spread into west-central Illinois. Vandalia never emerged as a core of a large, attractive destination area. By the early 1830s, Vandalia was peripheral to the mainstream settlement areas bisected by the Illinois Valley corridor: Sangamon Country and the Military Tract. The argument arose for a more centrally located capital to the extraordinary settlement growth areas evolving in west-central and northeast Illinois.

Vandalia, the capital of the state, and the seat of justice of Fayette county, laid out in 1818, by commissioners appointed for that purpose, under the authority of the state. It is situated on the west bank of the Kaskaskia river. . . . The site is high and undulating, entirely above the inundations of the river. The streets cross each other at right angles, and are 80 feet in width. The public square is a high and commanding situation, and is already ornamented with a temporary state house, and a brick bank. There are also in the town, several stores, a printing office, from which is issued a weekly paper, entitled the "Illinois Intelligencer," about 150 dwelling houses, and 700 inhabitants, among which are professional men, and mechanics of every description. . . . The advantages of Vandalia are by no means few or inconsiderable. Many intelligent men are still, however, of opinion that a more eligible situation might have been selected. . . . [T]he fertility of the surrounding country, must also contribute much to its improvement. Here must of course be a considerable market, to which the farmers of the vicinity will send their produce. . . . Vandalia is . . . 70 miles northeast of St. Louis, and on the mail route from Vincennes to that place. (Beck 1823, 161–63)

Springfield, a post town, and the seat of justice of Sangamo county, laid out in 1821. It is situated on Spring creek a branch of the Sangamo river. . . . Although this place is as yet in its infancy, the circumstance of its being the centre of a fertile and thickly-settled district of country, must soon render it of considerable importance. Springfield . . . 96 miles northeast of St. Louis, and 65 northwest of Vandalia. (Beck 1823, 157)

By the late penetration stage, the future capital of Springfield emerged as a cross-roads node and double the population size of Vandalia (fig. 3.4). The centrality of Vandalia as a movement hub of people and mail was an illusionary situation. Settlers passed through the surrounding area to more advantageous destinations. Its hinterland languished in becoming thickly settled. Its midstate, transitional location faded as an advantage with its Sangamon Country rival.

The network of mail routes circulating information in the late 1820s closely paralleled the road structure of evolving central Illinois and established southern Illinois (Ramey 1949, 28–30; Tevebaugh 1952, 83–105; Walsh 1947). The information delivery system was concentrated south of the projected National Road route and in west-central Illinois. Bordering riverside gateways integrated with the expanding regional and national flow of mail. These important postal nodes persisted as both points of entry and exit on the state's east side, Vincennes and Shawneetown, and west side, Kaskaskia and St. Louis. Other key crossroads market, courthouse, and postal centers on the verge of Illinois were Carmi in White County, Belleville in St. Clair County, Edwardsville in Madison County, and Paris in Edgar County. In the interior, important postal hubs formed at Vandalia and Springfield. Other inland crossroads mail delivery foci were Carlyle in Clinton County and Jacksonville in Morgan County. Peoria, far to the north, emerged as a postal hub because of its important intervening tie with Galena in extreme northwest Illinois and the rapidly settling Illinois Valley corridor midsection (Tevebaugh 1952, 105).

Jakle observed that each transport mode offered its characteristic views and orientated the traveler in different ways to the passing scene (1977, 22–27). As a form of movement, walking placed travelers closest to their immediate environment. Perhaps it indicated the pedestrian was simply too poor to travel by any other means. Horseback riding also placed travelers closer to their surroundings and permitted riders to cover more miles in a day. Wagons offered mobile families more trail comfort and opportunity to move a larger proportion of their possessions. Yet family and teamster wagons were limited to improved roads, which were still quite primordial with mere tracks; obstructions of brush, tree trunks, and fallen trees; no bridges; difficult fords; deep mud ruts; and swampy ground. Stagecoaches were not immediately available in insular frontier Illinois. Trunk routes had to improve considerably to permit the operation of coaches in the forested wilds, let alone provide scheduled service point-to-point. Roadside taverns, inns, and private homes offered minimal creature comforts for weary travelers from arduous westward traveling (38–41). The first stagecoach line operated on the Vincennes–St. Louis Road in 1820, linking Louisville at the Falls of the Ohio with the "Gateway to the West" (Corliss 1937, 10). By the late penetration stage, St. Louis emerged as the nodal focus of the early Illinois frontier period.

Expansion Stage

The frontier regional road networks of Illinois were transformed during the rapidly changing 1830s and early 1840s. Bridge and trunk routes crisscrossed the state. Varied regional settlement timing, population growth, and economic growth forged sharp contrasts in the expanding road structures. The expansion stage interconnected attractive settlement areas across the breadth of southern, central, and northern Illinois. The density of feeder routes substantially increased in the intraregional route webs. Earlier-settled southern Illinois reflected an established, denser road framework as population infilling and replication of market and courthouse centers continued. Central Illinois embraced a rapid dispersion of routes that formed a base network. Attractive destinations in west-central Illinois delineated a rapidly expanding route design. The lagging settlement of northern Illinois witnessed a quickening population pace. Its skeletal route structure was anchored to population centers at its extreme edges. By the expansion stage's end, a web of routes tied emerging courthouse and market centers of the northern tier counties with Chicago, Galena, and midstate.

Midstate centrality integrated south-north and east-west bridging road structures. Settlement increased after the Black Hawk War of 1832. The early expansion stage spawned a substantial building program of unimproved roads in 1833 (Boylan 1933, 45–47). The surge in "Illinois fever" between 1835 and 1839 generated a far greater road-building spree statewide. Citizens perceived rapid population and economic growth as justification for engineering a phenomenal road expansion. The General Assembly responded with an internal transportation improvements program. Boylan attests to a bimodal peak in roads laid out and declared public roads in 1837 and 1839 that centered in the rapid growth settlement areas (47–53). A further engraving of public roads occurred in 1841 and 1843 (54–55). The late expansion stage unfolded a mesh of routes that joined the state together.

Road Structure in 1839

The early expansion stage 1839 road map (fig. 3.5) marked a dramatic shift in the areal extent and route density from the late penetration stage 1828 road map (fig. 3.4). Vincennes, Shawneetown, and Golconda persisted as important gateways in southern Illinois. On the eastern verge, numerous small entry points ebbed and flowed with the rhythm of new settlers. In the Wabash Valley corridor, points of entry were aligned on a south-north axis. Some were riverside nodes with access to both steamboats and flatboats on the Wabash River, such as Mt. Carmel, Hutsonville, and York. Others were inland foci that paralleled with riverside exit points and ferries on the Wabash River in Indiana: Lawrenceville with Vincennes, Marshall and Paris with Terre Haute, and Danville with Covington.

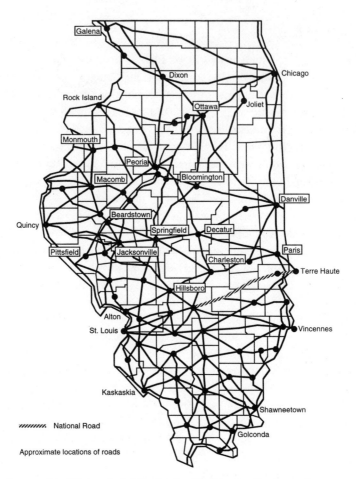

Fig. 3.5. Road Networks in Illinois, 1839 (Boylan 1933; Young 1839)

Terre Haute was a pivotal dispersion hub, since the Wabash River no longer formed a common political boundary. The riverside market and county seat center was a transshipment point at the juncture of the Wabash River (tributary steamboat conduit), the Wabash and Erie Canal, and the National Road (overland trunk line). Lawrenceville in Lawrence County and Danville in Vermilion County were inland entry points. Danville emerged with important diverging bridge routes because of its relative location. Its routes connected with emerging rival nodes in west-central Illinois and Chicago in northeast Illinois.

An important north-south trunk route traversed the Grand Prairie, connecting Chicago with the Wabash Valley corridor. The route evolved from the Old Vincennes Trace, or Hubbard's Trail. In 1823, Gordon S. Hubbard, an American Fur Company agent, carved a pack trail from Fort Dearborn to a trading post (present site of Danville) on the Big Vermilion River. Hubbard extended the route to Vincennes (Corliss 1937, 12). By the early expansion stage, the trunk route formed a permanent state road between Chicago and Vincennes through Danville, Paris, York, and Palestine (Boylan 1933, 20). Paralleling the Wabash River, an old bridge route linked Vincennes with Shawneetown. State Highway 1 parallels this north-south artery through the prairies and forest lands in the eastern verge of Illinois.

On the western margins, Kaskaskia continued as a gateway, even though it remained isolated from the booming northern settlement areas (fig. 3.5). Upstream on the Mississippi River, the riverside nodes of Alton and St. Louis competed as disembarkation points for southwest and west-central Illinois. Trunk line branches from Vincennes, Shawneetown, and Golconda converged on Alton in southwest Illinois. Alton integrated into the southern Illinois road structure that focused on the attractive destinations surrounding Belleville and Edwardsville. A dense route web formed in southwest Illinois. Bridge routes diverged to the pivotal nodes in west-central Illinois, thus linking Alton with Chicago and Galena by way of Jacksonville, Springfield, and Peoria. Alton had the advantage of upstream steamboat connections to the head of navigation on the Illinois River, Peru. "Bluff City" connected with the intermediary river towns, particularly the nexus of the Illinois Valley corridor and rival of Quincy in the Military Tract, Peoria.

Alton contested with the "Gateway of the West" in the upstream steamboat traffic on the Mississippi-Illinois Rivers that focused on Quincy, Galena, Beardstown, and Peoria. Gateway Quincy had numerous radiating routes into the Military Tract. Both Quincy and Alton served as exit points for settlers with transMississippi "state fevers" of Missouri and Iowa. The boomtown of Galena functioned as the gateway for the isolated lead mining region in northwest Illinois and southwest Wisconsin. Roads radiating from Galena into its hinterland furnished farmers an accessible market for agricultural products for immigrants caught up in "lead fever," mercantile opportunities, and artisan activities. Besides fertile soils, the western verge had the advantage of contiguous trunk steamboat arteries. Diverging roads from southern, eastern, and western riverside nodes contributed to the expansion of regional road networks.

A number of penetrating bridge routes intersected in the interior of central Illinois (fig. 3.5). The routeways acted as interregional trunk routes for immigrants and teamsters' wagons, individual horseback riders, drovers, and stagecoaches. In Sangamon Country, rivals Jacksonville and Springfield fused a framework of crisscrossing bridge routes. These market and courthouse centers formed higher connectivity levels. Pivotal bridge routes thrust northward to Peoria, Galena, and Chicago, westward to Quincy, eastward to Danville and Terre Haute, and southward to Alton and St. Louis. Jacksonville, the "Athens of the West," established by Yankees in Morgan County, effectively struggled commercially and culturally with the new state capital of Springfield in Sangamon County (Doyle 1978). Ottawa in the upper Illinois Valley evolved as a crossroads riverside node linking northern and central Illinois. The Bloomington connection was known as the Old Chicago Trail and to Chicagoans as Archer Road (Corliss 1937, 14).

A historic fur trade and military trail traversed western Illinois, connecting Fort Clark (Peoria) on the Illinois River with Prairie du Chien on the Mississippi River in southwest Wisconsin. Oliver Kellogg in 1825 established a south-north bridge route between Peoria and Galena in the Lead Country. Since Peoria's route linkages included Danville, Alton, and St. Louis by way of Jacksonville and Springfield, the Kellogg Trail expanded as a thrusting trunk route to Galena. Four years later, a mail route utilized the route and was followed by scheduled stagecoach service (Tevebaugh 1952, 105). A state road was laid out between Peoria and Galena in 1833 (Boylan 1933, 46). By the early expansion, stage wagons and immigrants ferried the Rock River at Dixon. The "Eldorado lead city" rivaled Chicago as a commercial, distributive, and wholesale center. In the early frontier period, Galena was larger in population than lakeside Chicago (Burchard 1925; Corliss 1937; Lee 1917; Rennick 1935).

A westward-penetrating trunk line slowly spread across the Old Northwest. Originating in 1811 from Cumberland, Maryland, the National Road never traversed the Prairie State as it terminated at Vandalia, the second capital. The movement corridor traversed midstate and opened for settlers, travelers, teamsters, drovers, stagecoaches, and postal riders during the summer of 1839 (Hardin 1963, 1967). Financial problems at the federal and state level, the building of the Illinois and Michigan Canal, the coming of a railroad network, and continued Missouri and Illinois debate over the exit point from Illinois of the trunk route at St. Louis or Alton doomed its western terminus at Vandalia (Hardin 1963). Roads extended westward to the rival Mississippi riverside nodes. The earliest route was the public road laid out in 1823 from the capital of Vandalia to Alton (Boylan 1933, 43). With the emergence of the national highway system in the early twentieth century, U.S. Highway 40 paralleled the National Road. Later, Interstate 70 aligned with the continental route in the Lower Middle West.

In early expansion stage, most of the new, unimproved roads were feeder lines that ensured crossroads lower-level nodes their fundamental imperatives of market and county seat activities. Feeder routes that interconnected courthouse trade centers fused as intraregional bridge routes. Because of their relative location and centrality, small juncture foci developed connectivity levels of at least four routes across much of southern and central Illinois (fig. 3.5). These tiny urban places, their hinterlands, and intersecting routes marked the essential nodes and strands of the evolving regional urban road networks. Earlier-settled southern Illinois, with its completed array of counties, possessed the greater number of this type of lower-level node than central and northern Illinois. The southern Illinois circulation network during the early expansion stage included the peripheral entrepôt of St. Louis and rival Alton.

The urban road structure of rapidly settling central Illinois embraced a different nodality. Slower-settling east-central Illinois possessed fewer crossroads lower-level nodes while integrating with bordering Terre Haute and the new state capital of Springfield. West-central Illinois was bisected by the Illinois Valley corridor. Sangamon Country with Springfield and Jacksonville and the Military Tract with Peoria and Quincy replicated dynamic, competitive nodes. East of the river, Sangamon Country was the earlier siren destination and included a greater number of crossroads lower-level nodes. The Military Tract between the Mississippi-Illinois Rivers witnessed a significant settlement increase after 1835. But fewer crossroads lower-level nodes formed in the early expansion stage.

Beardstown in Cass County, at the juncture of intersecting roads and a navigable tributary, emerged as a distinctive category of frontier lower-level nodes—the riverside, crossroads courthouse focus. It developed a greater variety of commercial, manufacturing, processing, distributive, and service functions than other small crossroads centers. Its relative location in the Illinois Valley corridor permitted the river town to configure a larger agricultural export hinterland that served marketplace-oriented farmers both in Sangamon Country and the Military Tract. It emerged as the epicenter of riverside activities in the lower Illinois River Valley. Peoria, the linchpin of the Illinois Valley, was the primary riverside competitor.

Settlement processes in interior northern Illinois spread slowly. Its 1830s overland circulation network persisted in the structural alignment of the penetration stage. Dynamic urban outposts emerged on opposite sides of this frontier region. Chicago and Galena were in the midst of economic booms. In the intervening emptiness, fewer crossroads lower-level nodes developed. Diverging bridge routes integrated lakeport Chicago with northeast, northwest, and west-central Illinois, northwest Indiana, and Wabash Country. Two alternative routes tied Chicago to Galena by way of Rock River ferries at Rockford and Dixon. The northern route became the preferred Chicago-Galena Road, or Stagecoach Trail. In the early expansion stage, the process of streamlining bridge routes established interregional trunk routes.

Road Structure in 1844

Economic hard times at the national and regional levels during the late 1830s and early 1840s reduced migration flows to Illinois. Yet more public roads were laid out statewide during this difficult period than amid the boom times (Boylan 1933, 44–55). A circulation structure of routes, nodes, and hinterlands symbolized the physical elements of the regional settlement process. Regional transformation of frontier living from self-sufficiency-biases to marketplace-biases required the spread of an intricate web of roads. The increasing expansion and integration of intra- and interregional bridge routes improved circulation within and between the regional urban road networks. The 1844 Illinois road map reveals an enhanced structure in the late expansion stage (fig. 3.6).

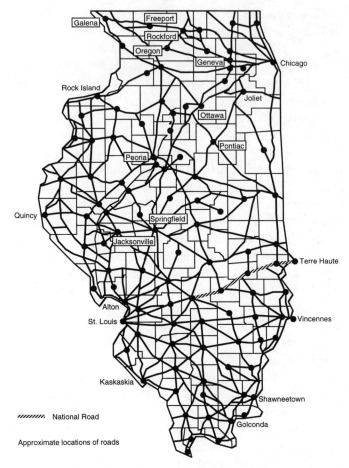

Galena Freeport
Rockford
Oregon
Geneva Chicago
Rock Island
Joliet
Ottawa
Pontiac
Peoria
Quincy
Springfield
Jacksonville
Terre Haute
Alton
St. Louis Vincennes
Kaskaskia
Shawneetown
National Road Golconda
Approximate locations of roads

FIG. 3.6. Road Networks in Illinois, 1844 (Boylan 1933; Morse and Breese 1844)

Increasing density of feeder roads in the internal route structures occurred in southern and west-central Illinois. More sparsely settled east-central and northern Illinois displayed road networks that perpetuated the early expansion stage where new bridge lines predominated. Numerous types of diminutive urban places existed during the frontier period. The smallest nodes were settlement clusters positioned in the interstice of the route networks with only a crude trail connecting it with a road or urban center. The next type of urban center, with a connectivity level of two, was an on-line point that engraved a small, elongated hinterland astride the road. Other foci had connectivity levels of three, thus improving their centrality and tributary size. But the critical basal blocks of the frontier regional urban road networks were market and courthouse centers that developed connectivity levels of at least four. Increases in population and economic and hinterland growth were sustainable in settlement areas with intersecting routes. Crossroads lower-level nodes and their hinterlands emerged as attractive destinations.

From the early expansion stage (fig. 3.5) to the late expansion stage (fig. 3.6), the complex web of crossroads lower-level nodes substantially increased. The majority of the newly emerging foci at road junctures were county seats. The internal regional urban road frameworks hint at hidden agendas related to settlement timing and accessibility differences between east-central and west-central Illinois. Slower settlement infillings in prairie-dominated east-central Illinois formed fewer additional crossroads lower-level nodes. West-central Illinois continued in the late expansion stage to display marked differences in its urban-transport structure. Sangamon Country possessed a greater number of crossroads foci than the Military Tract. Southern Illinois, with its older settlement and political structures, embraced an integrated route network linking courthouse and market centers.

Northern Illinois rapidly expanded its number of crossroads lower-level nodes. Foci were not evenly scattered across the breadth of northern Illinois. Instead, crossroads centers were concentrated in attractive movement-settlement corridors: the Rock and Fox River Valleys and the Illinois and Michigan Canal construction zone. Rapid growth of small urban places unfolded with on-line foci about every ten miles on the diverging Chicago roads, the Fox River Valley Road, and the roads paralleling the Illinois and Michigan Canal. Replication was most pronounced on the northwest-radiating roads within the expanding Chicago tributary. Chicago and Galena linked through Elgin, Geneva, Belvidere, Rockford, and Freeport. By late expansion stage, paralleling roads arrayed in the Illinois Valley corridor between Chicago and Alton.

Additional bridge routes in northern and east-central Illinois formed an expanded route web (fig. 3.6). The number of on-line and crossroads lower-level nodes significantly increased. A number of key bridge lines were engineered across the vast grasslands. Southern diverging routes from Chicago traversed the extensive Grand Prairie in east-central Illinois and linked with the Wabash Valley corridor and Sangamon Country. Wayside and juncture foci were few and far between for the weary travelers and immigrants. The early and late expansion stages were characterized by the reduction in the isolation of the expansive midstate prairies. A denser network of bridge routes interconnected points of entry on the eastern fringe of Illinois with the expanding urban networks in west-central and southwest Illinois. Elemental roads across the large-scale prairies tied the Wabash Valley corridor settlements with the vigorous old and new growth centers on opposite sides of sparsely settled northern Illinois.

The old lead mining center of Galena in northwest Illinois was commercially integrated in a tenuous fashion with distant Chicago. Its primary mercantile ties and lead exporting market connected southward with St. Louis. Although the distance was greater than to Chicago, the trunk route formed an efficient steamboat channel to the remote upper Mississippi Valley. Galena in Jo Daviess County functioned as a courthouse, market, and extractive resource center. It witnessed a slowly expanding hinterland, given its overland isolation. The lakeside market and courthouse center of Chicago in Cook County expanded its commercial hinterland via diverging roads during the early 1840s. Yet periodic road problems made it difficult for farmers to move agricultural products, which "discouraged a wider trade and limited the city's growth" (Cronon 1991, 57). A dense road web was best developed in southern and west-central Illinois. The mercantile hegemony of St. Louis in southwest and west-central Illinois was incontestable. Congruity of regional road networks and improved steamboat activities on the Mississippi-Illinois Rivers were commercially integrated (Mahoney 1990). Early Chicago road linkages were not an adequate transport-economic response to the waterway supremacy of St. Louis. By the late expansion stage, there were a far greater number of settlement destinations available statewide at the convergence of routes. Crisscrossing bridge routes formed trunk routes that connected old riverside St. Louis and upstart lakeside Chicago.

Consolidation Stage

Focal riverside and lakeside gateway nodes emerged as entrepôts in the expanding regional urban-transport systems of the Middle West. Regional road networks spread a warp and woof "of numerous threads, woven in and out, up and down," athwart Illinois (Boylan 1933, 22). Maximized route densities characterized the consolidation stage 1850 road map (fig. 3.7). Scheduled stagecoach service of six to seven trips per week was common between the regional nodes of Chicago and St. Louis and subregional nodes of Galena, Quincy, Peoria, Jacksonville, Springfield, Alton, and Terre Haute. Three stagecoach trips per week were readily available on routes concentrated in northern, west-central, and southwest Illinois (Conzen 1975, 366). Improved trunk and bridge road linkages fostered increased utilization by wagon teamsters of the connecting route web. Replicated tiny, on-line nodes provided wayside services for travelers and market centers for local farmers. Crossroads lower-level nodes benefited commercially by the increased movement activities.

In the consolidation stage, the road network of northern Illinois lagged behind other state sections, except for the Grand Prairie in east-central Illinois. The diverging web of northeast Illinois appears similar to the earlier road pattern in southwest Illinois. The mechanisms of road structure evolution were different. Interregional and national mainline roads converged on and terminated at St. Louis with its midcontinental steamboat hegemony. A progression of bridge and feeder

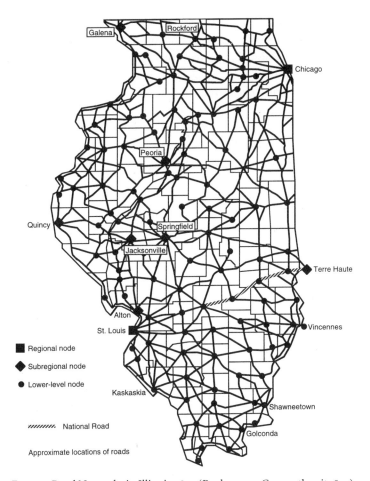

Galena

Rockford

Chicago

Peoria

Quincy

Springfield

Jacksonville

Terre Haute

Alton

St. Louis

Vincennes

■ Regional node

◆ Subregional node

● Lower-level node

Kaskaskia

Shawneetown

//////// National Road

Golconda

Approximate locations of roads

FIG. 3.7. Road Networks in Illinois, 1850 (Boylan 1933; Cowperthwait 1850)

roads entwined in southwest Illinois, which fringed the regional node. Farmers and merchants in its extensive western Illinois hinterland accessed its mercantile, collecting, distributive, service, and manufacturing activities. By contrast, Chicago, at the southern tip of Lake Michigan, developed as the western terminus of the northern movement corridor. It was instrumental in building diverging roads to tap mercantile and commercial agriculture growth in its spreading hinterland.

Fewer feeder and bridge routes formed by the closing of the frontier in southern Illinois and Sangamon Country in west-central Illinois. Regional settlement longevity had fixed well-established urban road structures (Boylan 1933, 55–57). A substantial decline in the formation rate of crossroads lower-level nodes marked the emergence of the consolidation stage. With the county political system virtually in place by 1850, fewer crossroads commercial centers emerged as county seats.

Southern Illinois achieved saturation level with crossroads marketplace foci. Central Illinois passed southern Illinois with juncture market centers. Many additional ones were situated in prairie-dominated east-central Illinois and in prairies of the northern Military Tract that were slowly infilling with settlements.

The flood of immigrants dispersing across northern Illinois in the 1840s spawned the formation of numerous crossroads lower-level nodes. Northeast Illinois was increasingly interwoven into the mercantile dominance of the lakefront entrepôt while it added the largest number of crossroads foci. Fewer small urban centers at road junctures evolved in distant, slower-settling northwest Illinois. A major urban transformation emerged at the juncture of the Rock River and the trunk line employed by wagons, stagecoaches, and immigrants traversing northern Illinois. Rockford evolved as a dynamic crossroads market and courthouse center in Winnebago County. It was situated midway on the Chicago-Galena Road at the strategic Rock River ferry crossing and at a nexus location of a paralleling road in the valley. Pooley argues that Rockford emerged as the metropolis of the northern prairies because it experienced the most rapid and steady growth of any of the towns in the "siren" Rock River Country (1968, 435).

The consolidation stage initiated a period of fewer dramatic road changes and maximization of the intraregional road densities (fig. 3.7). Longer-settled southern Illinois and west-central Illinois witnessed few alterations to their regional road structures. A mesh of feeder and bridge routes furnished farmers with improved—but still difficult—accessibility to marketplace centers within their regional urban hierarchies. In east-central Illinois, additional bridge roads for improved interregional connections were inscribed across the extensive wet and dry grasslands known as the Grand Prairie. Improved John Deere plows, drainage tiles, and rail lines were needed for opening up the interiors of the larger prairies. This later settlement and economic development promoted the demand for renewed building of feeder roads to the rail points. In remote northwest Illinois, a similar road pattern evolved as a few additional bridge roads traversed the larger prairies and undulating topography.

In northeast Illinois, gateway Chicago expanded its mercantile influence and immediate hinterland. As the lakeside terminus of the Illinois and Michigan Canal, it tapped developing commercial agricultural districts of the upper and middle Illinois Valley. Chicago thrust its radiating intra- and interregional road tentacles westward across northern Illinois, southwest into west-central Illinois, and southward into east-central Illinois. Cronon maintains that farmers increasingly chose Chicago as their market destination "because they received more cash for their crops there, and because they could buy more and better supplies at lower prices" (1991, 60). Yet Chicago boosters seldom emphasized natural transportation advantages, since its hinterland's westward extension was minimal, definitely not to the Rocky Mountains (37).

The steamboat had been the driving mechanism for the successful marketplace agricultural focus of farmers in the Illinois Valley corridor. The improved road structure of west-central Illinois in the agricultural borderlands paralleling the riparian channels of the Mississippi-Illinois Rivers ensured farmers greater accessibility to riverside nodes, such as Peoria, Quincy, and Beardstown, and the downstream mercantile linchpin of St. Louis. Lakefront Chicago had a difficult time competing with its riverfront adversary of St. Louis in the late 1830s and 1840s. Since the railroad was liberated from geography, the emergence of artificial railroad corridors nurtured a new capitalistic logic to midwestern and Far West economic development (Cronon 1991, 63, 74, 81).

The expansion of Chicago's radiating rail lines and its evolution as a hub of regional and national rail networks in the 1850s and postbellum period metamorphosed the commercial ties of farmers and merchants across the state. Engineered road structures in the regional settlement landscapes were virtually unaltered by the closing of the Illinois frontier. Regional and subregional nodes emerged as the dominant regional settlement road ligaments of converging and diverging movements. Railroads sought out these population centers in order to tap their mercantile markets and their potentially rich agricultural hinterlands. Population and economic growth of competing nodes and their tributary areas quickened. Smaller lower-level nodes in the road interstice areas, on-line, or at crossroads locations were abandoned or died a slow death if circumvented by the railroad. With the arrival of intersecting rail lines, many established crossroads market and courthouse centers experienced heightened prosperity in the late nineteenth century. Because of their deep-rooted feeder road structure, they effectively struggled with the replicated railroad towns.

Expanding regional urban road networks engendered a procession of settlement patterns, linkages, nodes, and hierarchies across colonial, territorial, and early statehood periods of frontier Illinois. The road structures established by 1850 delineate the strategic patterns that later generations attempted to perfect (Boylan 1933, 22). The stages of urban road network evolution parallel the pioneer periphery, specialized periphery, and transitional periphery periods of Muller's model of selective frontier regional urban growth (1977). The penetration stage corresponds to the pioneer periphery period (figs. 3.3, 3.4). Route density reflected remoteness from markets, sparse population, and agricultural self-sufficiency as the settlers colonized new settlement frontiers (24–25). Trunk roads dispersed across Illinois Country to the unraveling point of St. Louis. It was centrally situated in the Mississippi Valley at the western verge of an expanding continental America.

The expansion stage integrates with the specialized periphery period of regional urbanization (Muller 1977, 25–26). Increases in trunk, bridge, and feeder lines disclose the spread of salient intra- and interregional connections as nodal and route densities rapidly expanded (figs. 3.5, 3.6). Complexity and density of the

regional urban road networks contributed to the transformation of the agricultural economy from subsistence to a marketplace-bias. Farmers' crop and livestock export products were integrated to local, regional, interregional, national,
and world markets. Entrepôts served as the ingress and egress foci for developing
mercantile, service, collecting, distributive, and manufacturing activities.

The consolidation stage associates with the transitional periphery period in the
sequential growth of regional urban systems (Muller 1977, 26–27). Maximum regularity, density, and complexity in the intra- and interregional urban road networks coalesced by the closing Illinois frontier (fig. 3.7). Three-tier regional urban
hierarchies of regional, subregional, and lower-level nodes in southwest, west-
central, and northeast Illinois effectively integrated with an evolving four-tier

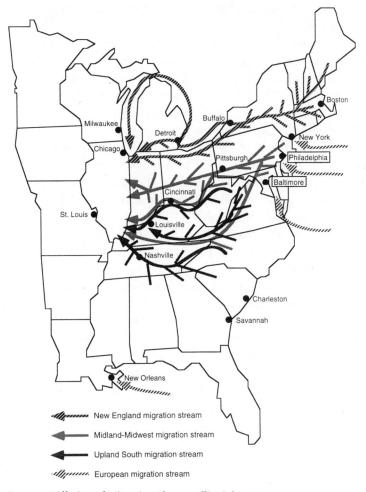

FIG. 3.8. Diffusion of Migration Flows to Illinois by 1850

American system of cities. Emerging interregional and national space-economies interconnected midcontinental Illinois with seaboard national nodes and the world economic system. National movement corridors, regional road networks, and available navigable watercourses were interdependent. Dispersing from hearth areas, secondary areas, and regional way stations in the expanding American culture region system, diverse migration flows converged on midcontinental Illinois (fig. 3.8).

Mahoney argues that as the St. Louis–dominated steamboat system improved, "the roads were drawn toward the rivers, becoming 'tributaries' on land by which interior residents reached the nearest navigable river" (1990, 128). Illinois' urban-transportation networks were enhanced further with the rapid spread of rail infrastructures in the ante- and postbellum periods. Roads had been engineered, overlaid, and integrated for over a century in frontier Illinois. Urban road networks were fundamental building blocks to regional settlement growth. Nodes, roads, and navigable waterways were not mutually exclusive. The urban road structures and navigable riverine corridors formed attractive settlement destinations.

4

Riparian Corridors of Internal Development

No state or territory in North America can boast of superior facilities of internal navigation. Nearly 1000 miles, or in other words, two-thirds of its frontier is washed by the Wabash, Ohio, and Mississippi. The placid Illinois traverses this territory in a southwestern direction, nearly 400 miles.
—Brown 1817

R oads, waterways, and canals served as transport-settlement growth corridors. Accessibility to and remoteness from navigable waterways molded urban mercantile hinterlands. The Ohio-Mississippi-Missouri Rivers, the Great Lakes–Erie Canal, backcountry tributaries, and bridging canals impressed well-defined diffusion paths. Fixed routeways directed settlers to attractive destination areas. Water arteries played a primary role in diffusing population, shaping settlements, collecting and transporting goods, and stimulating economic activities. The agricultural frontier transformed from self-sufficiency to a commercial-bias that reached beyond local and regional to national and world markets. Keelboats, flatboats, and steamboats ensured farmers participation in marketplace exchanges. Steamboats penetrated upriver backcountries. Distinctive riparian movement-settlement corridors were molded in midcontinental Illinois.

Impact of Western Rivers

Western promoters underscored the salient impact of waterways on future settlement and economic expansions in transAppalachia. The Ohio-Mississippi-Missouri River systems' mercantile role during the pioneer period forged startling differences in population and commercial modifications between riverine corridors versus inaccessible interiors and river towns versus landlocked towns (Haites, Mak, and Walton 1975; Hunter 1949; Mahoney 1990). The fundamental benefits of transplanting to riverine movement-settlement corridors were recognized by pioneer farmers inter-

80

ested in accessibility to marketplaces. Subtle, requisite rewards that were garnered from producing surplus agricultural products for a space-economy were instrumental in immigrants' destination selections.

Flatboating Significance

Samuel Brown stressed the vital importance of available waterways for flatboats and steamboats (1817, 17–18). Passage across Illinois Country was practical on the southwest-flowing Illinois River, a key navigable tributary of the Mississippi River. "Unlike the other great rivers of the western country, its current is mild and unbroken by rapids, meandering at leisure through one of the finest countries in the world" (18). The lower courses of numerous lesser tributaries of the Wabash (Little Wabash, Embarras, and Vermilion), Ohio (Saline), Mississippi (Big Muddy, Kaskaskia, and Rock), and Illinois (Sangamon and Spoon) Rivers were utilized by flatboats (fig. 4.1). Many larger creeks were useful for flats, but not always in regular yearly or seasonal cycles. During high spring runoff, farmers pursued the advantages of flatboat trading while recognizing the lesser watercourses' hazards, the long downstream journey to New Orleans, and the tedious overland return trip home.

The nature of flatboating contributed to the attractiveness of many rivers and larger creeks in Illinois as movement-settlement corridors during the early frontier period. Pioneering family units or groups of families frequently employed flatboats in migrating to the New West on the internal westward highway: the Ohio River. Flatboats were perceived as "a mixture of log cabin, fort, floating barnyard and country grocery" (Buley 1950, 1:415). Petersen argues that the Ohio Valley was the hearth area for flatboat evolution into two distinctive types. Smaller flats were frequently known as "Kentucky boats" because of their destination in Kentucky or the lower Ohio Valley. Larger flatboats destined for the lower Mississippi Valley export trade were designated "New Orleans boats" (1937, 50–51).

Upon harvesting the fruits of the land, individual farmers or neighbor groups could easily "build a flatboat, load it with produce, and float it to market" (Haites and Mak 1970–71, 154). Basically a large, oblong box, flatboats floated downstream with the current to be broken up at the voyage terminus and sold for lumber. Flatboats carried a variety of export products from the successive settlement frontiers of transAppalachia: pork, bacon, beef, flour, wheat, corn, cornmeal, oats, apples, tobacco, lard, whiskey, hides, furs, lumber, livestock, flax, beeswax, lime, and poultry (Buley 1950, 1:530; Gates 1960, 175–77). Prior to 1850, flatboats cost between $40 to $140 to construct and transported between twenty-five to a hundred tons of cargo (Cronon 1991, 103; Schieber 1969, 279).

Flatboats on the western rivers were crucial to farmers' economic well-being, initial agricultural marketplace activities, St. Louis market orientation, and southern commercial exposure. Flatboating heightened the early attractiveness of the lower Illinois Valley as a settlement-economic ribbon that in time would traverse the state.

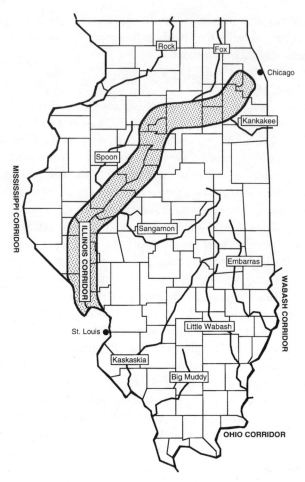

FIG. 4.1. Waterway Channels of Illinois

Persistence of the flatboat trade was enhanced because flats could negotiate upstream areas of the Illinois River that early steamboats could not penetrate. Flats also could navigate during periods of low water. Another important advantage was their capability of floating downstream during high water in the spring on the backcountry tributaries, such as the Little Wabash, Embarras, Vermilion, Big Muddy, Kaskaskia, Spoon, and Sangamon. Endurance of flats was influenced by urban market opportunities on the navigable river systems (Hunter 1949, 57; Schieber 1969, 287).

Walton notes that "flatboating reaped a bountiful, if indirect, harvest from the new steamboat technology, from improvements in steamboating and from river improvements" (1987, 236). Steamboats reduced flatboat labor costs by shortening return passage times and diminishing upriver impediments. It rewarded repeat trips and encouraged such innovations as larger flats and economizing of labor crews. Because of endurance, simplicity, and versatility, flats sustained an economic vitality on trunk arteries' lesser tributaries in insular frontiers. Walton argues that dependable steamboats and flatboats were essential "to improving market linkages between the continental interior and the seaboard and abroad" (229).

Rhythm of the Rivers

The evolving commercial life of the riparian settlement frontiers mirrored a distinctive seasonal rhythm (Hunter 1933–34, 6–23). Seasonal agricultural and trade behavior tied with intense activity in the spring and fall with slack time in the summer and winter. Out of necessity, trading seasons synchronized with the frenzied seasonal cadence of spring planting and autumn harvesting. Flatboat trading was conditioned by the geographical constraints of an environmental hydrology system. Because rivers formed the fluid backbone of the transport network, trading was economically feasible for surplus exports only during peak water volume periods and unhindered navigation of the rivers in the spring and fall.

Given the seasonal rhythm of the environment and rivers, Hunter contends that transport rates and market prices at terminal nodes "varied inversely with the height of the rivers" (1933–34, 8–9). Low water rates on steamboats were prohibitive for the majority of the agricultural exports, manufactures, raw materials, imported or domestic goods, or even passengers on an extensive portion of the Mississippi system. Movement seasons were not a smooth continuum, given the size of the drainage basin and meteorological conditions that varied by months, seasons, years, and weather cycles. Irregularities of nature, delays, and failures of the inland steamboat system often incapacitated life-styles, commerce, and manufacturing. Because of routine and destructive suspensions of trade channels, financial and psychological impacts on farmers' hopes and dreams for that season or year were disheartening.

Spring rise emerged as the critical trading season. It was a more reliable and longer passable period for steamboats because of the combination of melting snow and ice and spring rainstorms (Hunter 1933–34, 7–8). Secondary tributaries of the Ohio-Mississippi networks were navigable by any transport mode only for abbreviated time periods, if at all in some years. The persistence of flatboats on the lesser inland tributaries were fundamental to migration, settlement, and economic growth in midcontinent. Remote settlements possessed difficult logistical problems for exporting agricultural surpluses. Settlers prized smaller navigable waterways for flatboats as favorable settlement habitats.

Wabash Valley Corridor

Western river highways served farmers well in shipping their exports, since flats were so common on Ohio-Mississippi tributaries (Buley 1950, 1:410–11). Settlers in the Wabash Valley corridor shipped their surplus agricultural products primarily to the commercial gateway of New Orleans (fig. 4.1). Local buyers, merchants, and farmers situated peripheral to the navigable channels shipped the great bulk of the Old Northwest exports during the pioneer period by flatboat. Flats were as profitable as steamboats because of their competitive edge in downstream shipping costs. Most young men in agricultural areas peripheral to trade channels completed at least one trip to New Orleans, either to convey the family's farm surplus to market or as hired hands (Schieber 1969, 281). With improved steamboats and a decline in upriver passenger charges, flatboating operations were stimulated, since river men no longer had to trek back across country to their point of origin (Schieber 1969, 287; Taylor 1951, 64).

Flats on the Wabash River and its tributaries remained a steamboat rival for shipping farm exports until the mid-1840s (Clark 1966, 24–25; Haites and Mak 1970–71). Wabash Valley flatboats were a competitor of the Wabash and Erie Canal. As many as 1,200 to 1,500 flats descended the Wabash-Ohio-Mississippi Rivers to the Crescent City in one year (Benton 1903, 104). In 1828, the Wabash River alone had that many flatboats bound for southern markets. The flat export trade witnessed an annual increase estimated at 33 percent between 1820 and 1828 (Cammack 1954, 38). Abnormal dry seasons considerably reduced navigability of trunk line waterways, especially the secondary tributaries, owing to increased obstructions and lower draught for steamboats and even flatboats. The Wabash Valley corridor as an attractive settlement destination in Illinois and Indiana exemplifies the impact of the productivity and endurance of flats alongside the gradual increasing utilization of steamboats (Walton 1987).

After the Cumberland, the Wabash River for many years was the next key Ohio River tributary for steamboat traffic. Although steamboating on the Wabash River originated by 1818, it persisted as an insignificant mover of agricultural goods until the early 1830s. The retarded upstream expansion related to a few difficult rapids and other navigational impediments (Hunter 1949, 37–39). Lafayette, almost 370 miles from the mouth of the Wabash, marked the navigation head. Downstream, the principal river towns were Terre Haute and Vincennes. Steamboats plying the Wabash River in 1837 averaged about eighty-five tons, almost half the size of those on the Ohio-Mississippi Rivers. Lagging upstream settlement, greater navigational hazards, a need for a draft reduction, and greater trunk line trading profitability retarded steamboating on the lesser conduits (Haites, Mak, and Walton 1975, 49–52).

Mississippi Valley Corridor

The crucial linkages between availability of cheap water transportation, population growth, commercial enterprises, and economic growth were deeply rooted in flatboats and the inaugural era of steamboats on the rivers (Walton 1987, 226). By 1830, the largest proportion of population residing in Illinois congregated in the Mississippi-Illinois corridors (fig. 4.1). North argues that "the dramatic techno- logical change in inland transportation was not the advent of the railroad, but rather the development of the steamship on inland waters" (1974, 107). Improve- ments in steamboats increased land sales and agricultural production after 1825 in the upstream and downstream hinterland of St. Louis.

Later modifications and declines in freight and passenger rates increased the productivity and competitive edge of steamboats over other river transport modes. North concludes that "the consequent fall in rates for upstream river transportation after 1816 directly reflects the use of steamboats on the Mississippi River and its tributaries" (1974, 107). Vital settlement changes paralleled the con- version from subsistence to commercial agriculture astride the Mississippi-Illinois Rivers in western Illinois after 1830 (Haites and Mak 1970–71, 1971; Haites, Mak, and Walton 1975; Hunter 1933–34, 1949; Mahoney 1990; Walton 1987). Upstream, Mississippi steamboats gradually evolved because of the obstacles of the Des Moines or Keokuk (Lower Rapids) and Rock Island (Upper Rapids) Rapids, nar- rower channels, minimum depth, and later settlement of the Upper Middle West (Hunter 1949, 43–44; Mahoney 1990, 79–80).

Steamboats were the driving impetus for early settlement and economic devel- opments in the upper Mississippi Valley. Three commercial corridor segments emerged, each different in the nature of their traffic (Petersen 1937, 335–36). The first section stretched for about 200 miles from St. Louis to the physical barrier of the Lower Rapids. The second segment extended about 225 miles between the Lower Rapids and the lead mining district of Galena. The longest segment reached for about 275 miles between the lead fields and the Falls of St. Anthony at St. Paul, Minnesota. By the late 1840s, the lower river segment, which included the riverside nodes of Hannibal in Missouri, Quincy in Illinois, and Keokuk in Iowa, were linked by daily, short line steamboat service with St. Louis.

Not until after 1840 did steamboats increase significantly in the upper segment above Galena; it was not until the 1850s for its tributaries, Des Moines–Wisconsin– Minnesota. The small steamboats that operated irregularly were linked to the pre- requisites of the fur trade and the federal government at Fort Snelling and St. Paul. Freight traffic embraced troops and supplies for military posts, Amerindian annu- ities for distribution, and merchandise and furs for the operators of the fur trade (Haites, Mak, and Walton 1975, 49–50; Hunter 1949, 45; Petersen 1937, 190–203). Petersen argues that the military and Amerindian frontiers' commercial activities during the antebellum period were geographically basic processes in vitalizing steamboating beyond the settlers' frontier on the upper Mississippi (203).

The mining rush, shipment of supplies, and lead exports downstream sup- ported steamboat traffic in the second upper Mississippi segment from 1823 to

1848 (Hunter 1949, 43–45; Mahoney 1990, 162–63, 182–85, 198–202; Petersen 1937, 204–26). Lead mining focused in northeast Iowa, southwest Wisconsin, and northwest Illinois. The pivotal lead mining activities occurred in the Fever River settlements of Jo Daviess County, Illinois. Lead freight from this tri-state mineral region were initially transported downstream on flatboats to St. Louis, beginning in 1816. Only six steamboats operated between St. Louis and Galena by 1822 (Hunter 1949, 43–45). The value of lead was the salient factor in stimulating the growth of Galena, St. Louis, and settlements in western Illinois abutting the Mississippi River in the 1840s. At the "Gateway of the West" in 1848, the fur trade was valued at $300,000 and the Santa Fe Trail trade at $500,000. A year earlier, the value of lead was $1,654,077.60 (Petersen 1937, 209).

Petersen divides the lead mining history into three stages: initial growth, 1823–29; decline and hard times, 1829–35; and extraordinary growth, 1835–48 (1937, 207). Galena emerged as the entrepôt of the mining region in northwest Illinois and southwest Wisconsin (Mahoney 1990, 162, 182; Petersen 1937, 214). It was situated on the Fever River, a small tributary of the Mississippi River some four hundred miles from St. Louis and three hundred miles from Fort Snelling. Steamboat traffic fluctuated with population growth, lead production, market conditions, and navigational obstacles. Arrivals and departures of steamboats peaked after the winter ice breakup and during the spring crest of this narrow, secondary channel. By 1828, arrivals numbered 99 at Galena, 153 in 1835, and 350 in 1837 and annually averaged 300 in the 1840s (Schockel 1916, 215; Hunter 1949, 45). Steamboat size ranged between 92 and 200 tons, averaging 129. Steamboat supremacy prevailed on the Fever or Galena River between 1835 and 1855. The arrival of the railroad in 1855 heralded the demise of the steamboat trade (Schockel 1916, 214).

Mining supplies, manufactured goods, and foodstuffs destined for the Lead Country required a two-month transshipment from eastern seaboard cities, the Gulf of Mexico, and the "Father of Waters." Refined food products from New Orleans moved directly upstream. Galena's dominance of the lead trade is substantiated from its pounds of lead shipped to St. Louis: in 1839, 26,250,000 pounds; in 1841, 32,438,000 pounds; in 1843, 39,148,270 pounds; in 1845, 54,494,860 pounds; in 1847, 54,085,920 pounds; and in 1849, 44,035,380 pounds (Mahoney 1990, 183; Schockel 1916, 216). Agriculture emerged early as a supplier of crops and livestock products for the mining district. By 1840, the 876 farmers substantially outnumbered the 617 miners in Jo Daviess County. Traditional frontier agricultural productions—corn, oats, wheat, hay, potatoes, and livestock—were the mainstay along with dairying (Schockel 1916, 208). With its mercantile, agricultural processing, manufacturing, and distributive activities, Galena developed a hegemony over northwest Illinois and the upper Mississippi Valley between 1840 and 1855. Steamboat traffic operated daily between Galena, St. Louis, and St. Paul (216).

The key Illinois river town in the lower segment between Galena and St. Louis–Alton was Quincy (Pooley 1968, 405). In 1825, the town was designated the county seat of Adams County, both named for the recently inaugurated president (Brown 1982, 246). With the opening of the land office in 1831 and the land speculation boom of the mid-1830s, Quincy's population expanded from 600 in 1834 to 1,500 four years later to 2,319 in 1840 and 6,902 in 1850 (Brown 1982, 246; Carlson 1951, 66). Pooley noted that 300 steamboats arrived or left during the Panic of 1837 (1968, 405). By 1841, 1,000 to 1,200 vessels arrived to pick up and unload freight and passengers (Carlson 1951, 89). Quincy emerged as the largest town, an important agricultural processing center, and leading mercantile center in the Military Tract, easily outstripping Peoria's population on the Illinois River during the pioneer period. The adjacent hinterland of Quincy rapidly transformed by the mid-1830s and 1840s into a marketplace economy as farmers acknowledged its importance as a transshipment point for downstream agricultural exports.

Typical incipient manufacturing industries of a dynamic riverside gateway evolved during the antebellum period in Quincy. Early industrial development comprised cooperage, woodworking, pork packing, flour milling, and leather working industries and stove, foundry, plow, wagon, carriage, distillery, and furniture makers (Wilkey 1939). Two not-so-typical pioneer industries were stove-making and large-scale distilling. Manufactured products were important to the swiftly expanding local and hinterland markets. The downriver export trade of processed agricultural and manufactured goods tied to St. Louis, New Orleans, and eastern seaboard markets (Clark 1966, 148). Usually when river ice was no longer a problem in March, large pork shipments from the winter processing season were the chief downstream steamboat cargo (Wilkey 1939, 480). In most years, during high spring flow in April, water depth permitted the larger downstream New Orleans vessels to reach as far as Quincy. The remainder of the year, the smaller upper Mississippi steamboats that operated above St. Louis predominated.

Agricultural, manufacturing, and mercantile activities increased in diversity, scale, and value. The river entrepôt of Quincy emerged in a linchpin exchange position in the upper Mississippi Valley as its hinterland extended upstream and downstream. Quincy represented a pivotal, smaller urban spearhead in the upper Mississippi Valley and western settlement verge of Illinois (Brown 1982; Wilkey 1939). The rapid immigrant influx of Yankees, Irish, and Germans stimulated the economic growth of Quincy (Brown 1982, 246–48). Of the steamboat arrivals in St. Louis, 22 to 28 percent originated from the upper Mississippi, primarily from the Illinois side, between 1847 and 1850 (Barrows 1910, 92). By 1850, daily steamboats linked St. Louis and Quincy, the second-largest city of Illinois behind the swiftly growing lakeport of Chicago (Pooley 1968, 414–15). The regional railroad network that tied Quincy to Chicago greatly increased its meat-packing export and manufacturing activities (Walsh 1978, 1982).

The economic vitality of "Gem City" was spurred during the Civil War. Military demands for steamboats, government orders for manufactured products, and wartime food needs ensured farmers good times (Brown 1982, 252). Quincy's population doubled to 24,052, so that by 1870 it once again passed Peoria as the second-largest city in Illinois. Brown argues that as competition between river and rail accelerated after the Civil War, Quincy was "no longer the last point on the line, the city on the edge of the Mississippi. It was becoming merely a point in the middle of the United States instead of the central national crossroads that its residents had envisioned" (255–56). Its population growth moderated and failed to keep pace with Peoria, Rockford, Springfield, and Joliet in the late 1800s. Economic expansion of Quincy stagnated as railroad networks brought about the demise of river commerce, shifted grain trade patterns, and created new destinations for foreigners in urban-industrial America.

Downstream on the Mississippi River, Alton experienced similar population and economic expansion patterns with the ascendancy of river commerce (fig. 4.1). Founded in 1817 in Madison County, it persisted as a significant river town on the Illinois side near the juncture of the Missouri-Mississippi-Illinois Rivers. It competed actively with its Missouri rival. St. Louis had the historical timing of involvement with the steamboat trade from its inception and its upstream fur and lead trade hegemony (Mahoney 1990, 213–14). Between St. Louis and Alton, a rock ledge appeared during low water that often hindered upstream steamboat travel. Alton was located about eight miles upstream from the confluence of the Missouri-Mississippi Rivers. St. Louis had the advantage of the increasing volume, depth, and width of the Mississippi River.

The regional commercial rivalry of St. Louis and Alton was won by 1840. Its extraordinary transshipment point location, its transferring of wholesaling purchases from Philadelphia to New York, and its dominance of the lead trade enhanced the mercantile control of St. Louis (Mahoney 1990, 214, 244–46). All freight and passengers were unloaded from the palatial lower-river steamboats to the smaller upper-river vessels. Upstream travel necessitated a reduction in the steamboats' tonnage, length, draft, and navigation season. Reduced width and depth, irregularity in seasonal water flow, increased ice problems in the northern regions, and natural obstacles of rapids, sand and gravel bars, and sawyers upstream assured the mercantile leadership of St. Louis over the upper Mississippi Valley. The entrepôt embraced a pivotal location where upper-river commerce terminated and lower-river trade commenced (Belcher 1947, 29). St. Louis was the "Gateway to the West" via the Missouri River and westward wagon trails. It also was the "Gateway to the Back Country of the North" astride the upper Mississippi River.

Alton operated in the mercantile shadow of St. Louis (Mahoney 1990, 244–46). Vigorous upstream commercial activity and the supplying of arriving immigrants who settled its contiguous hinterland and the lower Illinois Valley stimulated its population growth and economic competitiveness in the late 1820s and 1830s. Although the river town had an ideal vessel landing, Peck noted settlement problems related to "being surrounded on the west and north with abrupt hills and bluffs" (1831, 295). He also recognized that St. Louis was "a place admirably located, and of great business. It now draws a considerable portion of the trade of Illinois, and will be a powerful rival to compete with. These difficulties leave the future prospects of the rise of a great commercial city shortly at this point, a little problematical at the present" (295–96). Manufactured goods arrived at Alton through St. Louis from the Ohio Valley and eastern seaboard by 1830. Coopers supplied the local and St. Louis market with various-sized casks and barrels, and cabinet makers provided furniture (296).

The driving economic forces that transformed Alton's cityscape in the 1830s were the impact of upstream steamboat commerce and evolving marketplace agriculture in its upland hinterland of Goshen. Concerning its upriver mercantilism and expanding inland hinterland, Peck remarked: "Seven or eight steamboats are owned here in whole or in part, and arrivals and departures occur every day and at all times in the day during the season. Alton now commands a large proportion of the trade of the upper Mississippi and Illinois rivers, and of the interior country for one hundred miles" (1837, 149). Mahoney notes that upstream Peoria, Pekin, and Galena were linked to Alton's wharf for goods (1990, 215). It emerged as a smaller urban spearhead of commercial, distributive, and agricultural processing and manufacturing activities in western Illinois. Walsh notes the rise in the mid-1840s of Alton, Quincy, Beardstown, Pekin, and Peoria as important pork-packing centers on the Mississippi-Illinois riparian systems (1978, 1982).

Farmers upstream from the mercantile entrepôt of the middle Mississippi Valley had the advantage of multiple destinations for shipping their agricultural surplus products: St. Louis, New Orleans, urban markets in between, and plantations. By 1830, St. Louis emerged as the crossroads mercantile urban spearhead of mid-continent (Belcher 1947, 11–54; Wade 1958, 1959). The steamboat and flatboat trade did not move through St. Louis but flowed from the gateway to points south and the commercial terminus of New Orleans (Cronon 1991, 106–7; McDermott 1965, 15). With improved steamboats, commercial traffic flowed from St. Louis upstream on the Mississippi-Illinois-Missouri-Ohio Rivers. Early on, the linchpin commercial center developed a collecting, distributive, wholesale, service, and manufacturing hegemony. St. Louis reflected the many facets of its upstream and downstream riparian economic linkages. The centrality and accessibility of the St. Louis break-in-bulk point amplified its terminal, riverside activities. The English traveler William Oliver observed: "There is here a daily and extensive market for all country produce, which drains a large portion of the surrounding district, within a distance of sixty or seventy miles. Large quantities of pork, fowls, eggs, butter, game, fruit, etc. are disposed of for ready case. The city, of course, requires a considerable supply, but the numerous and crowded steamers are doubtless the cause of such a constant and large demand. . . . Large steamers are very frequently arriving and departing, and there is a constant bustle of lading and dislading at the levee" (1843, 88–89).

With a similar geographical commercial situation with respect to the upriver Ohio Country, Louisville at the Falls of the Ohio River competed with its commercial rival, Cincinnati. Greater channel width and minimum water depth downstream from Louisville and St. Louis permitted larger New Orleans steamboats to operate on the lower Ohio and Mississippi Rivers. Upriver tributaries of the Mississippi-Ohio systems required smaller steamboats. During the steamboat climax in the decade and a half prior to 1850, the average size of trunk route steamboats was 310 tons (Haites, Mak, and Walton 1975). Because of increased channel hindrances and reduced commercial traffic, smaller steamboat packets employed on the upstream and tributary routes from St. Louis and Louisville were about half the size.

Illinois Valley Corridor

Among the upper Mississippi tributaries after the Missouri, the Illinois was next in prominence in steamboat traffic development (Hunter 1949, 46). Traversing from northeast to southwest, the Illinois Valley corridor linked northeast, west-central, and southwest Illinois (fig. 4.1). With its headwater tributaries in proximity to Lake Michigan, its mouth above Alton on the Mississippi, and a number of sizable tributaries, the water channel was perceived to possess incredible potential settlement and economic growth. Being a potent movement-settlement corridor, the Illinois Valley experienced a procession of colonizations: Amerindian settlements, French explorers and fur traders, backwoods frontiersmen from the Upland South in the lower valley, and Yankees and foreigners in the upper valley. Valley topography and drainage between its headwaters and Lake Michigan marked a key continental divide portage in the interior for Amerindians, French, and Americans (Conzen 1988, 3–25).

Upper Illinois Valley

The upper valley corridor between the navigation head at Peru and Lake Michigan was recognized a century and a half earlier by the French as a natural canal route linking the Mississippi and Great Lakes basins. Early western boosters argued the commercial significance of a canal in the territory of Illinois: "A trifling expence, comparatively to the importance of the undertaking, will unite the Illinois to the Chicago in all seasons of the year. Then the lead of Missouri, and the cotton of Tennessee will find their way to Detroit and Buffalo" (Brown 1817, 34). A few years later, another canal proponent strongly supported the linkage as a key element in the state's internal improvements: "A mere glance at the map of Illinois will be sufficient to convince a person of the least observation, that the union of Lake Michigan with the Illinois river, by means of a canal, is not only practicable, but of easy accomplishment" (Beck 1823, 19).

Later, Peck argued that canal construction activities through 1836 were a migration enticement to northerners and foreigners (1837, 52–59). Its settlement and agricultural impact on northeast Illinois, bordering canal lands, and Illinois Valley corridor spelled prosperity. "The project of this canal is a vast enterprise for so young a state, but truly national in its character, and will constitute one of the main arteries in eastern and western communication. The work is going forward, and from five to eight years is the period estimated for its completion. Already commerce, in no small extent, is passing along that line. Merchants from St. Louis, from along the Illinois river, from Galena and the Wisconsin territory, and especially from the Wabash river as far south as Terre Haute, bring their goods that way" (57–58). The illusionary hype concerning the salient influence of the canal on settlement and directional shift in commerce was obviously overblown, but only ten years ahead of reality (Coard 1941; Putnam 1918).

In 1827, the federal government granted Illinois odd-numbered 640-acre sections within five miles of the intended canal route. Land sales were to finance the construction (Conzen 1988, 7–8). Ground was finally broken on July 4, 1836, but cash flow problems suspended canal building in 1841. The termini canal towns were to be Chicago and Ottawa astride the almost hundred-mile-long Illinois and Michigan Canal. By completion in 1848, the canal was extended beyond the rapids and shoals of the Illinois just upstream from Peru (Putnam 1918). Conzen contends that no single locality more directly interconnects the Mississippi and Great Lakes basins in the Middle West (1988, 3). The canal corridor emerged as a pivotal locality in the growth of diverse agricultural, manufacturing, and mineral resource activities.

Prior to the impetus of the canal, the Illinois River's backcountry was settled slowly because of the difficulty of regional and national economic integrations. Steamboats were infrequent to the head of navigation at Peru in La Salle County. In the twelve months following July 1, 1841, Peru was the point of origin for 143 of the 432 steamboat arrivals at Peoria. A daily packet operated between Peoria and Peru during navigational season. By 1840, ten vessels operated only on the Illinois River (Hunter 1949, 46). Like other lesser channels of the Mississippi system, steamboats were considerably smaller in size than those utilized in the New Orleans trade, averaging 75 to 150 tons. Each riverside point of attachment originating in the 1830s and 1840s inaugurated a gateway between an agricultural hinterland and expanding world economic system. Its significance was gauged by the geographical extent, population, and agricultural productivity of its hinterland (Barrows 1910, 87–88).

Lower Illinois Valley

On the lower Illinois River, the inception of downstream flatboats to St. Louis and New Orleans occurred by statehood (fig. 4.1). Conger writes of a family from Lewistown, the county seat of Fulton County, that actively employed keelboats: "The Phelpses had a keelboat built for their own trade to St. Louis which was run by Norman Scovill as its captain. I was present at one time when they were loading this boat at Thompson's Lake. The cargo consisted of barrels of pork and honey, packages of deerskins, and furs, barrels of dried venison, ham, beeswax and tallow, sack of pecans, hickory nuts, ginseng and feathers, and dry hides. In an ordinary stage of water it took about four days to run a keelboat to St. Louis, by poles, oars and sails, and from twenty to twenty-five days to return" (1932, 148). Prior to 1830, the nearest cash market for the riparian movement-settlement corridors of the upper Mississippi and the lower Illinois Rivers in western Illinois was the mercantile, collection, and distribution entrepôt of St. Louis.

The transformation from subsistence to commercial agriculture was slow in west-central Illinois preceding regular upstream steamboat traffic. Ambitious pioneer farmers learned from experience that to engage in marketplace agriculture, their distance from flatboat and steamboat riverside landings could be no more than ten to twenty miles (Carlson 1951, 86–88). Beyond this distance, wagon travel was practically prohibitive, owing to transport costs, and too time consuming for hauling grain and other bulky exports. Farmers were tied to local markets rather than distant markets. The well-drained, fertile mesopotamia peninsula between the Mississippi-Illinois Rivers in the Military Tract and western Sangamon Country contiguous to the lower Illinois Valley were favorably situated to waterborne mercantile operations.

Resourceful farmers emerged as their own merchant-traders. Ford describes the hardships of exchange:

> A farmer would produce or get together a quantity of corn, flour, bacon, and such articles. He would build a flat-bottomed boat on the shore of some river or large creek, load his wares into it, and, awaiting the rise of water . . . would float down to New Orleans. The voyage was long, tedious, and expensive. When he arrived there, he found himself in a strange city, filled with sharpers ready to take advantage of his necessities. Everybody combined against him to profit by his ignorance of business, want of friends or commercial connexions; and nine times out of ten he returned a broken merchant. His journey home was performed on foot, through three or four nations of Indians inhabiting the western parts of Mississippi, Tennessee, and Kentucky. He returned to a desolate farm, which had been neglected whilst he was gone. One crop was lost by absence, and another by taking it to market. (1854, 98–99)

During the 1830s and 1840s, improving road structures integrated lower-level nodes and their tributary areas to the economic spheres of riverside Quincy and

Peoria in the Military Tract. Road network improvements transformed the agricultural landscape from self-sufficiency to marketplace pursuits. Yet without increasing numbers and regularity of steamboats, the expansion of commercial agriculture would have remained retarded. Relative location and rivalry of the river towns on opposite sides of the Military Tract spawned attractive destinations in their respective hinterlands. Substantial population growth forged economic growth. Traditional agricultural processing industries of western river towns during the frontier period emerged by the late 1830s. During the 1840s, the two growth poles in the Military Tract witnessed greater manufacturing diversification and expansion of interregional and national markets than their rival subregional nodes in the Sangamon Country, Jacksonville and Springfield. Curtis stresses that the triangular Military Tract's five hundred miles of bordering navigable channels left "no part of the tract more than 45 miles, and the greater part not exceeding 20 miles from steamboat navigation" (1852, 225).

Inland Jacksonville and Springfield in Sangamon Country lacked the benefits of direct steamboat accessibility to St. Louis and New Orleans. Their ties with steamboat mercantilism depended on road ties with Meredosia, Beardstown, Havana, and Pekin on the Illinois River. Pooley argues that these riverside foci were prototypal steamboat towns with their flour mills, saw mills, and pork-packing industry connected to their countryside (1968, 379). Small river towns were the entry-and-exit points of interaction between backcountry and space-economies. These steamboat centers gained advantages from their intermediate locations between Peoria and St. Louis. Commercial expansions corresponded with increasing agricultural exports and growing demands of their hinterland's population.

Upstream steamboat ingress was delayed on the Illinois River by more than a decade, as it universally was on Mississippi-Ohio tributaries. Steamboat travel originated in 1828 and grew slowly, with only three steamboats actively engaged in the carrying trade by 1833 (Hunter 1949, 46). Principal river towns in ascending order from the mouth were Beardstown (90 miles), Peoria (165 miles), and Peru (225 miles) (46). Founded in 1829, Beardstown emerged as the head of navigation for the larger New Orleans steamboats during high spring water (Mitchell 1837, 115). Almost daily service with St. Louis existed in 1831 (Barrows 1910, 85). In 1836, steamboat arrivals at Beardstown numbered about 225.

Although a small frontier river town, Beardstown marked a major exporting center for agricultural products from the Military Tract and Sangamon Country, particularly pork. In the 1840s and early 1850s, it was the "Porkopolis" of Illinois. It slaughtered a substantially greater number of hogs than its pork-packing rivals of Quincy and Oquawka on the Mississippi River and Meredosia, Canton, Pekin, and Peoria on the Illinois River (Carlson 1951, 125). Over 45,000 hogs were killed in the 1848–49 winter packing season at Beardstown. This production output exceeded Chicago's less-than-30,000 hogs annually prior to 1850. Still, Beardstown's packing production was small in comparison with the 124,000 hogs packed in St. Louis and minuscule when compared with the "Porkopolis" of the Ohio Valley, Cincinnati's 498,000 hogs. Lakeside Chicago in the early 1860s challenged its riverside rivals of Cincinnati and St. Louis as the key middle western pork packer (125). The railroad's ascendancy expanded the flow of dressed and live hogs to Chicago, which became the regional "Porkopolis" (Walsh 1978, 14; 1982, 51). Eventually it achieved the status of "Hog Butcher to the World" as it surpassed a million hogs butchered annually.

Agricultural processing industries were fundamental to midwestern economic growth. Pork packing was an elemental frontier industry in the transition from subsistence-bias to marketplace-bias. Hudson argues that merchant-wholesalers introduced the meat-packing business in the Wabash, Illinois, and Mississippi Valleys adjacent to the evolving corn-livestock agriculture areas (1994, 103). The export potentials of pork created economies of scale that produced centralization in both large and small riverside commercial entrepôts (Walsh 1978, 1982). As agricultural exports were diverted from steamboats to rail lines, river nodes declined in relative importance as rail termini emerged more dominant as processing centers in the postbellum period. Pork-packing hegemony on the Mississippi and Illinois Rivers was a response to abundant resources and the essential role of steamboats. Local hog productions and processings were tied with interregional southern plantation markets bordering the lower Mississippi Valley.

Beardstown exemplified a quintessential lower-level riverside node of the frontier period. In the late 1830s, it embraced typical agricultural-oriented frontier industries. An ambitious booster of "porkopolis" status remarked that there were "two tanneries, two forwarding houses, two steam flouring mills, one distillery, one brewery, and three pork establishments. . . . The exports are considerable, and consist of corn, pork, hides, and whiskey. Flour was exported a few years ago; but is now as high here as at New Orleans, all that can be made being required for home consumption. The chief article of export is pork, of which, in the winter of 1835–6, 12,000 head were put up; in the succeeding winter (the last), 15,000" (Mitchell 1837, 115–16). Post–Civil War Beardstown failed to compete with its west-central Illinois pork-packing rivals of Quincy and Peoria with their better rail connections.

The pivotal riverside node of the Illinois Valley corridor originated as the only successful settlement in the Military Tract prior to 1820, dating from 1819 (Pooley 1968, 398). Pioneers arrived from the Shoal Creek settlements in Clinton County, forty miles east of the Goshen and Turkey Hill settlements near St. Louis (Barrows 1910, 85). As an old settlement, Peoria sequentially transformed over a century and a half from an Amerindian village to a French one to American fur trading and military posts and finally to a river town. Beck commented: "No improvement has as yet been made, but from its local advantages, and the fertility of the surrounding country, there is no doubt but it will become a place of the first consequence" (1823, 147). Two years later, it was designated the county seat of the new county of Peoria. Settlement and economic growth were initially minuscule prior to significant increases in upstream steamboat travel. In December of 1829, the first steamboat, *Liberty,* reached Peoria (Drown 1851, 107). Peck remarked that in the summer of 1833, it was a tiny village of twenty-five families that doubled owing to emigration in a few weeks (1837, 270). Its population grew to about 1,500 by 1837, almost 1,600 in 1844, around 4,000 in 1847, and 5,890 in 1850 (Mitchell 1837, 138; Peck 1837, 270; Pooley 1968, 413). Carlson concluded that the phenomenal population growth of Peoria and its hinterland in the late 1840s directly tied to the building and opening of the Illinois and Michigan Canal (1951, 97). Its mercantile hegemony of the Illinois Valley corridor was shaped in the steamboat era. But it was further enhanced with the fruition of the canal as the corridor's export trade diverted from St. Louis and southward to New Orleans to Chicago and eastward to New York. The magnitude of the population, commercial, agricultural processing, and manufacturing growth forged Peoria as the key Military Tract city, supplanting Quincy.

The number of steamboats operating and arriving at Peoria substantiate the slow growth and then rapid takeoff of steamboating in the Illinois Valley. By 1833, three different steamboats, the *Exchange, Utility,* and *Peoria,* were making trips to Peoria. There were 7 in 1834, 44 in 1840, 60 in 1841, and 150 by 1844 (Drown 1851, 107). In the twelve months following July 1, 1841, Peoria witnessed 432 steamboat arrivals, 694 in 1845, 866 in 1847, 1,166 in 1848, and 1,286 in 1850 (Barrows 1910, 91; Hunter 1949, 46). Peoria expanded its riparian tributary area after the completion of the Illinois and Michigan Canal in 1848. Manufactured goods from the East and lumber from the North were brought to Chicago. Canal boats and steamboats dispersed them to Peoria and St. Louis.

The canal's influences on migration, settlement, and economic expansion were short-lived in contrast to the steamboat's impact on the Illinois Valley corridor (Coard 1941; Conzen 1988; Belcher 1947; Putnam 1918). Given expanding railroad networks in the ante- and postbellum periods, Peoria's connectivity with Chicago, St. Louis, other midwestern railroad hubs, and seaboard national nodes intensified as its commercial dominance expanded. Peoria in the middle Illinois Valley witnessed competitive struggles between river, canal and lake, and railroad transport modes during the 1850s. Steamboats did not experience an immediate demise because of the extending rail lines that captured the Mississippi-Illinois settlement corridors and interstice trade (Belcher 1947). East-west rail lines and radiating trunk and bridge railroads from Chicago enhanced Peoria's population and economic growth during the 1850s. It continued to vigorously interact with the two economic antagonists, St. Louis and Chicago. Trade volume in the middle Illinois Valley corridor shifted northeast to the lakeside node. By 1860, Chicago had emerged as the midcontinent railroad nexus. The pivotal rail focus embraced eleven trunk rail lines with twenty branch and extension lines, totaling almost five thousand miles (Belcher 1947, 71; Paxson 1911). Yet for Peoria and Quincy, improved steamboat traffic ties with St. Louis originated the dramatic settlement and economic growth of the riverside nodes and their tributary area.

Peoria emerged as the linchpin commercial, wholesaling, distributive, and manufacturing center of the Illinois Valley corridor. Barrows suggests that the following factors shaped its preeminence: (1) it was centrally located between the mouth and headwaters of the Illinois River; (2) the riverside node was literally midway between arch rivals St. Louis and Chicago; (3) its centrality and accessibility within the navigable portion of the waterway fostered control of upstream and downstream steamboat commercial exchanges; (4) early radiating roads were built that extended its mercantile sphere within the county and contiguous counties; (5) it established the first ferry to traverse the river and profited from the crossing trade; and (6) it particularly benefited from immigrants, business travelers, and drovers crossing the first bridge in 1849 (1910, 88–90).

Because of its centrality in the corridor, its expanding mercantile activity, and its river-crossing facilities, Peoria emerged as an overland transport nexus by the late 1830s (fig. 3.5). Major roads connected with rival nodes in west-central Illinois and rival entrepôts. Other small river towns in the corridor's midsection revealed an absence of converging roads. Peoria was at the crossroads of overland and waterway linkages that intensified its mercantile, collecting, and distributive growth and circulation integration via mail and stage routes. It evolved as an important break-in-bulk point. Larger steamboats from St. Louis terminated their upstream journey at Peoria because of slower settlement and economic growth and obstacles of low water and sandbars toward the navigation head at Peru. Smaller packets operated from this transshipment center toward the sparsely populated upriver backcountry.

Prior to 1850, steamboats were the driving mechanism of Peoria's population and economic growth. For a short period, the Illinois Valley corridor's economic ties were altered by the opening of the Illinois and Michigan Canal in 1848. New markets and reductions in distance-decay linkages with Chicago, the Great Lakes–Erie Canal, and New York modified economic life of the middle valley as the population shifted their interrelationships from west and south to the east. Barrows notes a number of canal-related factors that reversed mercantile exchange links: shipping grain in sacks on steamboats was more costly than in bulk on canal boats, and lakeside Chicago had better receiving, storage, and forwarding facilities for grain than riverside St. Louis and charged lower storage and commission fees (1910, 98).

Shipping costs from the valley's midsection to the eastern seaboard were less by way of the northern rather than the southern commercial gateway. Great Lakes' shipping charges for bulk cargo by the mid-1850s were approximately half the western river rates. Chicago's competitive freight charge advantages over St. Louis were a powerful factor to be weighed by farmers in the settlement corridor. In most years, prices of farm products were greater and costs for merchandise goods less in the lakeside node than in the riverside node. Prior to transshipment of grain from New Orleans during the summer to the eastern seaboard, there remained the problem of grain heating and humidity damage in the warehouses. Water passage of grain through the Gulf of Mexico in the cargo holds of ocean vessels always persisted as a hindrance to the southern gateway. Besides, the circuitous southern trade route required more time to reach its American and European destination ports. Finally, New Orleans as a national node could not compete with the commercial, manufacturing, and relative location advantages of New York as a transshipment focus at the Hudson River mouth connected to continental Europe.

Chicago at the terminus of the lakeside canal connection emerged as the commercial gateway of the Illinois Valley corridor in the 1850s. Its population and economic boom were further spurred by the building of radiating rail linkages into the Illinois Valley corridor and to Peoria. The rails linked Chicago to the extensive interstream prairies of east-central, west-central, and northern Illinois. By the late 1850s, both the steamboat and the canal water trade lost their economic control over the Illinois Valley corridor commerce to the railroad. Water traffic could not rival the "iron horse's" economic advantages: all-season trade, freight costs, capacity, reliability, network density, and swiftness of movement of goods and passengers (Barrows 1910, 99–104). By the Civil War, the rapid expansion of manufacturing and railroad connections spurred Peoria's phenomenal population growth, prosperity, and economic hegemony over west-central Illinois. It had been the "Queen City" of the steamboat era in the corridor.

Steamboats integrated a duplicity of settlement and economic growth patterns in western Illinois. The hegemony of rivers formed the backbone of the interior's antebellum transportation system (Hunter 1933–34, 23). Hunter argues that "the growth of the West and the rise of steamboat transportation were inseparable; they were geared together and each was dependent upon the other. The record of the steamboat's development reflected the horizontal extension of territorial settlement and the upward climb from a plane of relative self-sufficiency to one of economic interdependence" (1949, 32). Illinois' midcontinental location, bordering navigable waterways, and traversing complementary tributaries influenced successive "siren" settlement areas. Hunter underscores that "the railroad was of course to prove the solution for the problems of river transportation, a solution early perceived and increasingly advocated" (1933–34, 21). Yet steamboats were the salient factor that unlocked the Old Northwest (Walton 1987, 238). Railroad lines ultimately superimposed navigable trunk and tributary riparian arteries.

Self-Sufficiency to Marketplace Agriculture

The heart of the Corn Belt evolved in central Illinois by mid-nineteenth century. Hudson argues that two forces shaped the midwestern Corn Belt as a distinctive region (1994, 88–109). First, the initial Corn Belt was a cultural region created by transplanting migrants who followed discrete migration flows. They originated in five transAppalachian islands of good agricultural land: the Nashville Basin of Tennessee, the Bluegrass of Kentucky, the Pennyroyal Plateau astride and north of the Kentucky-Tennessee border, and the Scioto and Miami River Valleys of Ohio. Their Upland South cultural heritage was rooted in an area of the Piedmont and Great Valley stretching from Pennsylvania through Virginia to the Carolinas. These immigrants of English, Scotch-Irish, and German heritage who settled the five islands concentrated on increasing the quantity and quality of production. The foundation of this emerging Corn Belt agriculture was a bias toward fattening hogs and beef cattle on corn.

Second, the first Corn Belt was associated with the riparian commerce of the Mississippi-Ohio River system and their major tributaries of the Illinois and Wabash Valleys. The Corn Belt's area in Illinois included Sangamon Country and the Military Tract astride the Illinois River, southwestern Illinois contiguous to St. Louis, the Grand Prairie, and the Wabash River counties north of Palestine in Crawford County (Hudson 1994, 1–14). This Corn Belt was established across central Illinois before Chicago became a primary factor in the regional economy. The city was peripheral, geographically as well as functionally, prior to its hinterland rail linkages. The commercial orientation of the first Corn Belt was southward downstream on the Mississippi River system through St. Louis. The commercial axis rotated northward with the appearance of a rail network in the Mississippi Valley, and Chicago became the focal point.

By 1850, the shift from self-sufficiency to marketplace agriculture created more complex agricultural patterns or farming types than simply the advent of the first Corn Belt across the state's midsection. A corn-livestock farming region bordered the Mississippi-Illinois steamboat corridors in western Illinois (fig. 4.2). It embraced greater agricultural diversification and specialization and ranked above average for the state in most farming enterprises, such as corn, cattle, swine, and wheat production, percentage of improved land, and value of farms (Mahoney 1990; Meyer 1979; Nelson 1930). Tributary areas of corn-hog-type marketplace agriculture surrounded the Mississippi-Illinois riverside packing centers for a fifty-mile radius or more (Anderson 1929, 89–91; Bogue 1968; Carlson 1951, 124–27; Mahoney 1990, 158; Meyer 1979; Nelson 1930; Walsh 1978, 1982). According to Hudson, the antecedents of a prototype Corn Belt farming system evolved in this swine-cattle feeding region by the end of the frontier period (1994). Sangamon Country in west-central Illinois and southwest Illinois

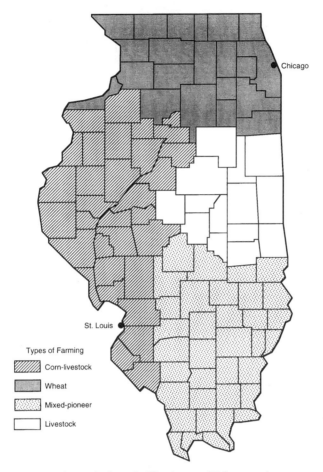

FIG. 4.2. Frontier Agriculture in Illinois, 1849 (Nelson 1930)

contiguous to the riverside nodes of Alton and St. Louis epitomized the distinctive corn-livestock marketplace-bias (Bogue 1968; Carlson 1951, 122–35; Mahoney 1990, 135–39, 165–66, 179–82; Meyer 1979).

Farmers' market choices by the late 1840s differed for those with accessibility to both or one of the waterborne commercial corridors: Mississippi-Illinois Rivers linked to St. Louis and New Orleans, and the Illinois River and the Illinois and Michigan Canal linked to Chicago and New York. The southern gateway's commercial hegemony unraveled as marketplace agricultural exports diverted toward the expanding northern gateway's mercantile hegemony. The linchpin, seaboard national node of New York tapped the northeast manufacturing base and strengthened its economic bonds with the interior as industrial goods flowed westward on the Great Lakes–Erie Canal system. Subsequent railroad expansions intensified and spread the corn-livestock farming system throughout west-central and southwest Illinois, the state, and the Middle West. During the postbellum era, the heartland's commercial agricultural and industrial activities strengthened and expanded in an interrelated national and world space-economy. Subregional and lower-level nodes in Illinois improved their interconnections in a maturing American urban-manufacturing system (Conzen 1977; D. R. Meyer 1980, 1983, 1989). Conzen argues that rail lines tended to reinforce established channels of commercial linkages (1975, 382).

While interurban relationships matured with the railroad, financial congruities of midwestern regional and subregional nodes were fundamental to integrating space-economies' mercantile, manufacturing, distributive, service, and transport sectors (Conzen 1977). D. R. Meyer argues that greater manufacturing specialization and rising levels of interaction for cities like Quincy, Peoria, and Alton meant their increased economic ties were with interregional and national market industries (1983). By contrast, their late-frontier emphasis fixed on local and regional manufactures. Powerful economic linkages in the late nineteenth century rapidly integrated maturing urban, manufacturing, and transport networks of west-central, southwest, and northern Illinois and the Middle West within national and world systems.

Earlier rapid settlement and economic changes promoted by improved steamboat connections in the Mississippi-Illinois riverine corridors in western Illinois were a classic example of the shift from agricultural self-sufficiency to a marketplace-bias. Deep-seated frontier self-sufficiency competed with a farmer's desire to produce salable crop-livestock surpluses for commercial exchange (Henlein 1959, 3). Between the 1830s and 1850s, midwestern agriculture witnessed vigorous expansions and reorganizations (Bidwell and Falconer 1925; Clark 1966; Danhof 1969; Earle 1987). Intensifying spatial interactions in the urban hierarchy of northeast America influenced the emerging complexity of farming types and agricultural patterns (Conzen 1977; Earle 1987). Hart maintains that early midwestern settlers coalesced, over time, an economically successful and ecologically sound farming system that supported an efficient infrastructure (1972, 265). Fast-growing entrepôts like St. Louis and Chicago quickly organized their surrounding countrysides' crop staple exportings and wide-ranging social-economic imperatives (Conzen 1975, 1977). By 1850, west-central Illinois was linked with mercantile antipodes in the Illinois Valley corridor.

Illinois revealed discrete regional agricultural economies and farming systems by 1850 (Mahoney 1990; Meyer 1979; Nelson 1930). Earlier-settled southern Illinois perpetuated a variety of farming enterprises while it concentrated on none (fig. 4.2). Within the mixed-pioneer farming area, swine and probably whiskey furnished the essential profit-motivation for the conversion of corn in a traditional pioneer self-sufficiency economy. The Ohio-Wabash-Mississippi-Illinois riverine corridors with access to steamboats developed more diversified and commercial farming types than in the remote, inland interiors (Mahoney 1990, 145–205; Nelson 1930, 91–95). Postbellum, the advent of regional rail networks spawned changes in marketplace specializations and farming types in southern Illinois. Sparsely settled east-central Illinois initially forged a livestock farming enterprise that reflected open-range ranching on the Grand Prairie and corn-cattle feeding in the western sections, such as McLean County (Hudson 1994). The graziers predominated where less than 20 percent of the land was in farms (Nelson 1930, 89–90).

Northern Illinois evolved a mono-staple crop export. Specialized wheat farmers produced nearly 50 percent of the wheat crop in the state in 1849 (Meyer 1979; Nelson 1930, 60). Grain farming spread from Lake Michigan to the Mississippi River as a middle western bread basket fed eastern seaboard and continental European populations (Mahoney 1990, 151–162, 187–95). A wheat-biased commercial agriculture developed for a number of reasons. Grains required relatively less labor and capital for production, processing, and distribution. Transportation facilities in northern Illinois that linked with the Great Lakes–Erie Canal improved significantly during the 1840s. Wheat farmers were accessible to national and world markets (Clark 1966, 84–91; Nelson 1930, 78–79). The Illinois and Michigan Canal furnished a new impetus for grain exports from the lakeside port. Chicago's hegemony over the lake grain trade emerged with its growth as a rail hub that linked heartland and eastern seaboard (Paxson 1911).

Agricultural patterns and farming types spread and changed with successive Illinois settlement frontiers (Meyer 1979). Earle contends that the emergence of railroad networks connected to seaboard national nodes, and competing regional nodes impacted the specialized staple regions emerging in the continental interior (1987). Radical restructuring of Illinois' regional agricultural specializations and farming types occurred during the late ante- and postbellum periods. Aberrations and displacements of frontier agricultural complexes must be understood beyond the traditional Turnerian interpretations (Turner 1920). Agricultural changes from self-sufficiency to marketplace-biases were shaped by the evolution of a "Thünen World City," a huge urban-industrial complex stretching from Boston to Baltimore in northeast America. New York emerged as the dominant "city" (Peet 1969, 1970–71). Peet proposes that this economic core was surrounded by a series of concentric agricultural zones best fitted to distance (1969). A logical, sequenced system of forces were fundamental to economic structure. Two major inputs were increasing central market demands and rapidly changing transport costs. As food and raw material demands increased in the "World City," agricultural zones were pushed outward into vacant interior areas. The frontier persisted as the outer verge of a dynamic world-economic system.

Vance's mercantile model stresses that the growth of local and regional settlement and commercial agricultural systems were driven by dynamic mercantile activities (1970). Wallerstein's capitalist economic expansion model argues that in an expanding continental America, essential zones of settler decolonization were incorporated into a spreading world-economy (1974, 1980, 1989). Mercantile entrepôts St. Louis and Chicago and subregional nodes in Illinois connected within the supply zone surrounding the dominant capitalist, mercantile "World City" in the northeast United States, New York. Regional and subregional nodes possessed their own micro-agricultural zones (Peet 1969; Vance 1970; Wallerstein 1974, 1980, 1989). Recently, Agnew's interdependent world-economy model suggests that America's geographical growth, economic expansions, and political developments were woven in world-economy relationships (1987). The eastern United States and Illinois experienced varied world-economy interactions and impacts over time. Expansions of settlement and agricultural infrastructures illustrate societies' inherent objective to sort out the land locally, regionally, nationally, and globally.

The Thünen (Peet 1969, 1970–71), mercantile (Vance 1970), capitalist economic expansion (Wallerstein 1974, 1980, 1989), and interdependent world-economy (Agnew 1987) models enhance interpretations of expanding frontier regional agriculture systems. Two Illinois examples follow. The open-range ranching zone retreated from the Grand Prairie in east-central Illinois because of expanding railroad networks, increasing infrastructure complexities, and developing agricultural and manufacturing technologies diffusing from "World City" and entrepôts, especially Chicago. Rather than open-range ranching, a corn-livestock feeding region or Corn Belt emerged that was short-lived as cash-grain farming evolved as the dominant farming system. Farming types and agricultural patterns change slowly. By 1870, the wheat country in northern Illinois changed from grain to corn-livestock farming. Chicago's rise as the dominant midwestern meat-packing center were key factors impacting agricultural changes and raising living standards. In northeast Illinois, new specializations emerged, dairying and truck farming.

Today, central Illinois embraces quintessential midwestern agricultural landscapes. Cash-grain farming in east-central Illinois and crop-livestock farming in west-central Illinois characterize rural agrarian life. Corn Belt agriculture emerged in central Illinois by 1850. Hudson (1994, 6–9) and Mitchell (1978, 83–85) argue that the practice of fattening cattle and hogs on corn in open feedlots during the winter, which occurred by 1840 in the Nashville Basin of Tennessee, the Bluegrass of Kentucky, and southwest Ohio, originated in western Virginia, the South Branch of the Potomac River. By 1850, the evolution of a marketplace-biased steer-hog-corn complex, or Corn Belt farming, was transplanted by immigrants from these settlement islands across central Indiana and central Illinois. By the late nineteenth century, distinctive zones of marketplace agriculture characterized the upper and lower versus eastern and western Middle West (Bidwell and

Falconer 1925; Danhof 1969; Gates 1960; North 1961; Peet 1969, 1970–71; Throne 1949).

Rivers functioned as integrators rather than as segregators of movement-settlement activities. Mainline waterways were supported by expanding regional road networks (Mahoney 1990, 128–29). The riverine settlement-economic interfaces were reinforced with the dispersion of railroad networks from regional hubs in the 1850s. Cronon maintains that as the railroad lowered land transportation costs, it permitted the "farmers to sell more grain and heightened their expectations about the scale of their own production" (1991, 109). Post–Civil War interstice voids between navigable channels and railroad trunk lines were rapidly transformed and integrated into national and world economic systems.

5

Emerging Regional Settlement Patterns

> The Illinois has proportionably a less number of islands
> than any of the western rivers, and is seldom obstructed by
> bars. In many places the banks are elevated, and present the
> most beautiful town sites, being surrounded on all sides by the
> most fertile lands.
> —Beck 1823

Pioneers converged on attractive settlement areas as national and regional transport networks slowly expanded. "Westward fever" was powerful and complex: "The advantages of the western country consist in the great fertility of the soil, the profusion of all the products of nature, whether of the animal, vegetable, or mineral kingdom, the cheapness of lands, and the newness of the country, which affords room and opportunity for enterprise. These, together with its commercial advantages, the total exemption from all taxes and political burthens, and the comparatively small portion of labour requisite to procure the necessaries of life, certainly render this a desirable home" (Hall 1828, 317). In a January 1817 letter written from Springfield, Ohio, to his brother who remained a farmer and blacksmith in Richmond, Vermont, Gershom Flagg observed: "The whole movement seems to be to the Westward and when they get there they go on beyond the Westward" (Buck 1912, 145). While crossing the Old Northwest, Morris Birkbeck noted: "Old America seems to be breaking up, and moving westward" (1818b, 31).

In assessing the American national character almost a century and a half ago, Tocqueville argued the "restlessness of character seems to me to be one of the distinctive traits of this people" (Mayer 1960, 182). Pierson stresses that Americans' restless temper shaped our character, attitudes, values, and look of the land (1954, 1962, 1964). He asserted that American history was linked to the "M-factor" of movement, migration, and mobility (Pierson 1962). During the nineteenth century, the westward drift of pioneers displaced and replaced America's natural habitats and Amerindian population. According to Zelinsky, "America is process"

(1973, 53). Spatially expressed, "[T]he American never arrives; he is always on his way" (58).

In the American settlement process, a vast difference existed between frontier dreams and realities (Billington 1958). "Gardens of the West" in the Old Northwest originated with Ohio. Writing to his mother in Richmond, Vermont, from St. Louis in February 1818, Flagg commented on emigrants' contraction of "state fevers": "For altho' you say the Ohio feever is abated in Vermont—the Missouri & Illinois feever Rages greatly in Ohio, Kentucky, & Tennessee and carries off thousands. When I got to Ohio my Ohio feever began to turn but I soon caught the Missouri feever which is very catchin and carried me off" (Buck 1912, 155). Flagg purchased a quarter-section of land six miles north of Edwardsville in Madison County, Illinois, in the spring of 1818, which he farmed until his death in 1857 (140). Four of his brothers followed him to Madison County. With each decade, "state fevers" were altered and shifted westward. Upland Southerners, New Englanders, Midlanders, Midwesterners, and foreigners were sequentially lured deeper into continental America. Indeed, mobile pioneers caught the western fervor long before Horace Greeley urged the obvious.

Improving regional transportation networks integrated with the evolving American culture region and urban-transport systems. Effective circulation linkages shaped enduring immigrant clusters as the Great Migration spread across the Northwest Territory. Mainstream roads and waterways emerged as integral connections within diffusion networks in the eastern United States. Agricultural settlements and urban spearheads thrust deeper into the interior each decade. Interstream areas lagged behind the population and economic growth of the navigable riverine corridors. Settlement assemblages unfolded sequential, segmented settlement patterns between the 1780s and 1850 in Illinois. Initially simplistic, insular and riparian settlements formed at the frontier's cutting edge. Rapid, successive settlement patterns in the 1820s, 1830s, and 1840s altered the spatial alignment of regional frontiers into complex, integrated settlement structures. Pivotal settlement areas with their cores and peripheries were elemental immigrant destinations. Interrelationships among developing local, regional, national, and even international networks were critical to economic growth, increasing population densities, the durability of migration clusters, and lateral settlement spatial expansions. I argue that midcontinental Illinois metamorphosed as an archetype of midwestern immigrant cultural mixing.

Dissecting Frontier Settlement Spatial Ordering

Fertile soils, featureless plains, gentle hills, bordering and traversing rivers, extensive prairies, and forested riverine corridors influenced settlement and migration patterns in Illinois. Frontier settlement patterns witnessed slow transformations, then rapid spread, multiplicity, and fluidity of subsequent spatial orderings. Brown lauded Illinois Territory in a brief, Edenic description of its future growth:

> The territorial population being at this moment 20,000 souls, and the ratio of increase 30 per cent per annum, it will require ten years to give Illinois the necessary qualification for being admitted into the Union. . . . Nature has been peculiarly bountiful to Illinois, for not only has she blessed this favored region with a temperate climate, and highly productive soil, but has prepared convenient channels of communication, for the transportation of products to market, and to facilitate settlement and internal intercourse. The Illinois, which hitherto has been little navigated, except by the North-West Company's boats, must in a few years become the theatre of an active commerce. American enterprize will force its way thither. (1817, 17–35)

Illinois emerged as the twenty-first state in the Union on December 3, 1818. The Ordinance of 1787 required a population of 60,000 for statehood. The Illinois Territory petition to Congress for admission guaranteed 40,000 persons. The Illinois census recorded 34,620 individuals between April 1 and June 1, 1818. The supplemental census revealed an official count of 40,258 when the constitutional convention assembled in Kaskaskia on August 3, 1818 (Alvord 1920, 461–62). The supplementary schedule was padded (Buck 1967, 61). Buck concluded that the number of inhabitants was probably 40,000 by the end of 1818 (97). At the time, the future Land of Lincoln possessed the smallest population of any state ever admitted into the Union (Howard 1972, 98).

Settlement Diffusion Processes

Hudson proposes that diffusion processes influencing settlement structure change over time within expanding frontiers (1969). His rural settlement model embraces three sequencing stages. Each stage comprises a spatial diffusion process with distinctive properties that shapes regional settlement differentiation. Settlement patterns of colonizing backwoods frontiersmen and yeoman farmers were linked to their desire for similar or improved environmental niches in comparison with their place of origin. Diffusion processes structured sequential settlement expansions within the matrices of "Illinois fever" place images and evolving regional urban-transport infrastructures.

The *stage of colonization* marks "the dispersal of settlement into new territory, or a new environment, or into an unoccupied portion of the old environment" (Hudson 1969, 366–69). Low population densities with both dispersed and clustered settlements prevail as an intrusive society searches out new areas (fig. 5.1). The following factors affect immigrants in the colonization process: absence of viable overland transport networks, bare subsistence nature of economy, minimal accessibility to regional trade and communication processes, tentative population growth, limited economic infrastructure, and inadequate geographic knowledge

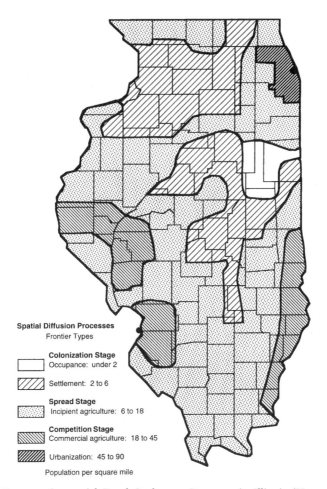

Spatial Diffusion Processes
Frontier Types

Colonization Stage
Occupance: under 2

Settlement: 2 to 6

Spread Stage
Incipient agriculture: 6 to 18

Competition Stage
Commercial agriculture: 18 to 45

Urbanization: 45 to 90

Population per square mile

FIG. 5.1. Sequential Rural Settlement Processes in Illinois (Hart 1974; Hudson 1969; Paullin 1932)

of destinations. The colonization process focuses on the settlement verge (Lewis 1984, 23). Simplistic spatial orderings mark settlement patterns of remote frontiers.

By the 1820s and 1830s, the *stage of spread* dominated the Illinois settlement frontier (Hudson 1969, 369–70). The spatial diffusion process of spread differentiates "increasing population density, creation of settlement clusters and eventual pressure on the environment, both physical and social" (367). Territorial size of immigrant clusters and lateral settlement expansions are functions of colonizing or related culture groups' population size. Upon closer scrutiny, vacant lands in earlier settled areas are colonized (Lewis 1984, 22). The expanding spread stage in Illinois directed settlers to earlier promoted, verge settlement areas: the American

Bottom, the Military Tract, and Sangamon Country. A gradual transformation from subsistence to a commercial-oriented economy evolved with readjusting urban-transport webs interwoven into the regional settlement frontiers. Lewis argues that settlement composition emerges clustered, rather than dispersed, with rapid population infilling as economic organization becomes more complex (1984, 22–23). Lateral settlement expansion continues as immigrants permeate the interstices between population clusters. The processes of colonization and spread function in the same area and at the same time as a diffusion continuum (Hudson 1969, 370).

With a state population increase of almost 400,000 in the 1840s, the spatial organization of regional settlement expansions embarked on the *stage of competition* in Hudson's settlement model (1969, 370–71). The process of competition "tends to produce great regularity in the settlement pattern" (367). A struggle unfolds between regional settlement networks and settlement areas to hold their territory intact and to increase their hinterlands. Competition occurs when immigrant groups from different source areas rapidly increase their population density and expand their territory while penetrating a settlement region. Larger places expand their trading hinterlands as less advantageously positioned trade centers decline in local and regional economic importance (371). The competition process reorganizes regional frontier places and areas in order to stabilize the economic environment to permit maximum settlement density (Lewis 1984, 22). The process of competition spatially orders greater complexities and specialization in regional settlement patterns and organizational activities. Segmented, complex settlement structures exemplified the rapidly integrating closing frontier.

Sequential Settlement Patterns

Immigrant diffusion processes engendered sequential, segmented settlement structures. Illinois' emerging frontier types are explored for six time slices: 1800, 1810, 1820, 1830, 1840, and 1850. Dissection of changing population densities embraces Hart's notion that early regional settlement developments augment idiosyncratic, successive frontier settlement types (1974, 73–74). They ordinarily succeeded one another at regular intervals across much of the eastern United States. *Frontier of occupance* (less than two persons per square mile) represents a sparsely populated, unsettled territory of scattered backwoods pioneers. Culturally distinctive and highly successful colonizers, these woodland frontiersmen formed settlement spearheads in transAppalachia (Jordan and Kaups 1989, 1–7). *Frontier of settlement* (two to six persons per square mile) corresponds to a diversified frontier subsistence economy increasingly shaped by pioneer hunter-farmers. The frontiers of occupance and settlement represent the population distribution patterns formed during the process of colonization (Hudson 1969) (fig. 5.1).

Rapid frontier settlement growth triggers the *frontier of incipient agriculture* (six to eighteen persons per square mile). It reflects the duality of an insular regional economy comprising persistent pioneer hunting and self-sufficient farming with their limited market accessibility and outer reaches of yeoman farmers' commercial agricultural activities. The diffusion process of spread generates the transplanting and dispersal of predisposed farmers who inscribe an agricultural-oriented landscape and economic framework (Hudson 1969). *Frontier of commercial agriculture* (eighteen to forty-five persons per square mile) depicts a sorting of regional economic growth that emphasizes a decision-making process controlled by a marketplace-bias and crop-livestock specializations. The resultant intraregional settlement organization interacts with interregional, national, and international linkages.

Frontier of urbanization (forty-five or more persons per square mile) coincides with the minimal population density necessary for urban places to grow beyond simple agricultural processing, market, and courthouse functions. Greater entrepôt and hinterland population size meant that incipient higher-threshold manufacturing, commercial, service, and distributive activities emerge. Regional, subregional, and lower-level nodes integrate in expanding national urban-transport infrastructures. The competition stage of settlement diffusion concurs with greater rewards available in the frontiers of commercial agriculture and urbanization (Hudson 1969) (fig. 5.1). Geographical analysis of six decadal slices of changing settlement structures documents salient immigrant destinations.

Evolving Settlement Patterns

Mobile pioneers faced the predicament of physical and psychological separation as they moved from seaboard core and peripheral areas into the remote interior. The frontier types arrayed from 1800 to 1850 across Illinois underscore spatial ordering that lessened immigrants' fear of "terrae incognitae." Interdependent settlement arrays were influenced by migration fundamentals that motivated immigrants to attractive destinations. The continuity of settlement structures record the persistence of collective immigrant sentiments and intentions. The imperative benefits of settlement, economic, urban, and transport structures were expected by the influx of success-driven immigrants. Rapid population growth in the 1820s, 1830s, and 1840s triggered increasing changes in settlement patterns.

Illinois French Settlement Corridor

At the beginning of the eighteenth century, Illinois Country, or Upper Louisiana, unfolded as a settlement colony of Lower Canada. This religious-commercial enterprise developed in tandem with Lower Louisiana (Meinig 1986, 201). In this north-south French colonization corridor, Cahokia (1699), Prairie du Rocher (c. 1723), and

Kaskaskia (1703) were situated. Fifteen miles upstream from Kaskaskia, near Prairie du Rocher, Fort de Chartres was established in 1720 as the seat of military and civil authority (Alvord 1920, 153). Destroyed by a Mississippi flood seven years after being constructed, the rebuilt limestone fort symbolized the French continental strategy of passive defense. This imperial military outpost never fired a cannon to protect its politically strategic midcontinental location (Howard 1972, 39).

The French villages in the movement-settlement corridor focused on upstream Mississippi fur trading, agricultural production from the narrow farming strips or long lots, and Christianizing and civilizing Amerindians at the missions. The settlement district emerged as a pivotal, petite French colonization enclave. Kaskaskia, the mercantile hub, and Fort de Chartres, the political nexus, were the salient Illinois Country links. These intermediary foci between Montreal, over a thousand miles to the northeast, and New Orleans, almost a thousand miles to the south, were historically and geographically significant in the French grand continental scheme (Meinig 1986, 201–2). Victor Collot, a French traveler in the Mississippi Valley after the American Revolution, visited the settlement ribbon in the American Bottom in 1796. He described the area as "superior to any description which has been made, for local beauty, fertility, climate, and the means of every kind which nature has lavished upon it for the facility of commerce. This country is a delightful valley, where winds one of the most majestic rivers on the globe" (Collot 1908, 286).

Wade argues that "towns were the spearheads of the American frontier" (1958, 1959). Pierre Laclede from New Orleans originated St. Louis in 1764 near the confluence of the Missouri-Illinois-Mississippi Rivers for the purpose of monopolizing the upstream Amerindian fur trade (Adler 1991; McDermott 1965, 1969; Wade 1959, 3–7). St. Louis and its vast hinterland were centrally located in midcontinent. It was situated at the northeast border of Spanish Territory and extreme western verge of the American frontier. The French outpost's commercial monopoly served as a pull factor for American pioneers who settled the American Bottom (Alvord 1920, 262). When Americans arrived to possess the frontier urban outpost after the Louisiana Purchase in 1803, its population had barely attained one thousand people (Wade 1959, 7).

Political disorders and restraints after the French and Indian War in 1763 and the Revolutionary War prompted a French exodus from east of the Mississippi River. Enterprising large landholders, officers of the garrison, rich merchants, and habitants from Illinois Country transferred across the river to the Spanish borderlands of Missouri (Alvord 1920; Buck 1967). The French egress continued after 1790, when disputes arose with American settlers over French land claims based on original occupation or royal grants. French settlers often claimed extensive tracts of land with vague boundaries. Another push factor coincided with the passage of the Ordinance of 1787 that prohibited slavery in the Northwest Territory.

Aspiring French habitants were frequent slave owners (Busch 1922, 99; Pooley 1968, 317). After the Revolutionary War, the Edenic American Bottom emerged as a deep-seated place image in frontiersmen's Mississippi Valley mental maps. The American Bottom was perceptually separated from Spanish possessions west of the river (Pooley 1968, 315). The ancient Cahokia Mounds and French colonial settlements in the American Bottom were pivotal antecedent settlements within continental strategies.

Distribution of Settlement: 1800

In the 1800 census, Illinois Country was a part of Indiana Territory. The frontier of occupance (less than two persons per square mile) predominated in the American wilderness (fig. 5.2). The Illinois population of 2,458 was comparable to the maximum French numbers half a century earlier (Alvord 1920, 407–8). Americans counterbalanced the four-decade withdrawal of French across the Mississippi River. St. Louis and St. Genevieve and their hinterlands in New Spain were principal destinations. The American Bottom possessed 93 percent of the 1,498 French settlers in Illinois Country. They clustered in three villages—Cahokia with a population of 719, Kaskaskia with 467, and Prairie du Rocher with 212—and at Peoria, on the Illinois River, with about 100. French settlers were not homogeneous in their cultural traits and population origins. Reynolds discerned subtle differences: "Kaskaskia and Prairie du Rocher were mostly colonized from Mobile and New Orleans, and Cahokia from Canada. The language possessed a shade of difference, as well as their habits. In the first-named village, the inhabitants partook of the sunny South, more than those who settled in Cahokia from Canada. A shade more of relaxation, gaiety, hilarity, and dancing, prevailed in Kaskaskia and Prairie du Rocher than in Cahokia. It may be, the immigrants from France to the north and south of the continent of North America, may have been from different provinces of the mother-country" (1879, 37).

The frontier of settlement (two to six persons per square mile) in southwest Illinois was initially shaped by colonial French settlers. Woodland frontiersmen slowly colonized the century-old settlement enclave in the American Bottom. Possessing a powerful place image in the distant Mississippi Valley, its legibility and imageability were enhanced by the earlier French colonial occupation and firsthand reports of explorers, Clark's veterans, and fur traders. It was perceived as a frontier environment of extreme fertility and was recognized for its midcontinental centrality. Market ties with St. Louis and New Orleans consolidated the essential place image qualities of this inaugural American settlement in Illinois Country. The 1800 census counted 960 colonizing Americans among the woodland Amerindians.

At the southern verge, the military outpost of Fort Massac on the Ohio River, near modern-day Metropolis, had 90 inhabitants (Alvord 1920, 407–8). Americans' settlement predilections, 91 percent of the total, focused on the century-old

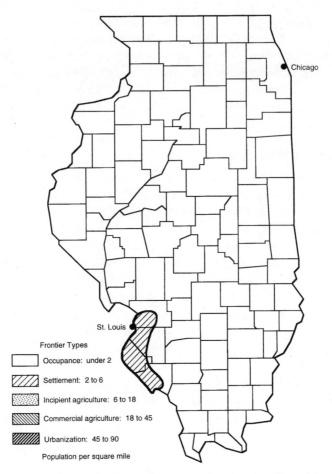

FIG. 5.2. Settlement Patterns in Illinois, 1800 (Hart 1974; Paullin 1932)

French settlement corridor of the American Bottom. Almost two-thirds of the pioneers settled in tiny, dispersed settlements comprising nuclear families or small,
socially cohesive kinship settlements in the bottomlands of Monroe County
(Alvord 1920, 407; Reynolds 1879, 19). Farmstead dispersals arrayed as loose settlement clusters numbering 250 settlers astride Fountain (Eagle) Creek, which
flowed southwest across the bottomlands before entering the Mississippi River.
Dispersed and clustered settlements were situated eight to fifteen miles inland
from the Mississippi River (Alvord 1920, 407; Reynolds 1879, 19). Almost one-third
of the frontiersmen formed an eastern settlement periphery astride the bluffs.
They were concentrated in the early upland clustered settlements stretching
south-north from New Design to Bellefontaine. James Lemen, a Scotch-Irish

Virginian and pathfinder of New Design, attracted pioneers of Scotch-Irish and Irish ancestry in the late nineteenth century to the American Bottom (Boggess 1968, 91–92; *Combined History of Randolph, Monroe and Perry Counties, Illinois* 1883, 330). Midland–Upland South woodland frontiersmen were extremely resourceful colonizers (Jordan and Kaups 1989, 1–7). The physical and human frontier conditions "often forced the backwoods' people into singular and different employments and conditions of life. Sometimes they were compelled to act as mechanics, to make their ploughs, harness, and other farming implements. Also, to tan their leather. At times they were forced to hunt game to sustain their families" (Reynolds 1879, 40).

Two nucleated settlements were colonized north and south of New Design. Turkey Hill was founded in 1798 east and southeast of contemporary Belleville. The Turkey Hill pathfinder was William Scott, born in Botetourt County, Virginia. He arrived from Kentucky with his extended family in late fall, passing through Fort Massac to New Design by wagon. After Christmas, he established his diminutive kinship settlement at Turkey Hill in advance of the frontier's edge (*History of St. Clair County, Illinois* 1881, 48–49). Pioneers primarily from Kentucky originated the Horse Prairie settlement about 1800, east of present-day Red Bud in Randolph County. These incipient, loosely clustered settlements reflect the significance of favorable micro-scale destinations etched within the macro-scale American Bottom.

American colonizers migrated within socially cohesive kinship networks. Ostergren stresses that "migration in family units underscores the seriousness and the permanence" of the relocation diffusion process in a frontier setting (1982, 318). As intrinsic as behavioral, cultural, and psychological attributes, sense of place and geographical propinquity played important roles in settlement selections. Pioneers dispersing within chain migration linkages underscored community cooperation, bonds, and durability to survive frontier hardships. Advantages of social proximity in a community embodied intensified communication, convenience, and neighborly help (McQuillan 1978, 141). American Bottom pioneers had selected a frontier verge where physical separation and psychological isolation encouraged clustering for social and economic well-being as well as for physical protection for mutual survival.

Distribution of Settlement: 1810

Formed in 1809, Illinois Territory included Illinois, Wisconsin, the western Upper Peninsula of Michigan, and northeast Minnesota. Of the 12,282 inhabitants in 1810, the vast majority were in southwest Illinois. The Amerindians dominated the frontier of occupance wilderness in Illinois Country (fig. 5.3). The initial American colonization scheme shaped by slowly probing colonizers did not exhibit stagnation. Instead, the emerging patterns of the frontier of settlement embraced spatial convergence in the southern half of the American Bottom, contiguous to gateway St. Louis. For over two decades, a gradual ingress of woodland frontiersmen transplanted a preadaptive Midland–Upland South settlement veneer over a declining French settlement landscape. Colonizing pioneers fixed an elongated frontier of settlement in the Mississippi floodplain that spilled over onto the limestone bluffs.

The Mississippi River bisected the old French colonial settlement corridor. French egress from the east side of the river, commercial hegemony of St. Louis, trade linkages of St. Louis with New Orleans, and old lead mining settlements in the eastern Ozarks meant the Missouri side developed a more expansive frontier

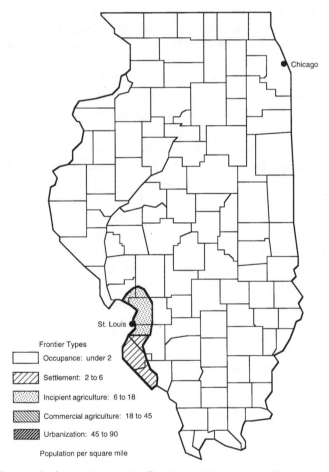

FIG. 5.3. Settlement Patterns in Illinois, 1810 (Hart 1974; Paullin 1932)

of settlement. An elongated south-north settlement ribbon extended between the confluences of the Ohio and Missouri Rivers with the Mississippi River. It was anchored at opposite ends by St. Genevieve and St. Louis. Both mirrored their older French village counterparts of Kaskaskia and Cahokia, across the channel from whence emigrated their population. Kaskaskia French farmers originated a permanent village and lead port at St. Genevieve in the early 1730s. Porterfield suggests that the village displayed minimal organization (1969); but the quintessential long, narrow agricultural plots with each family's home astride the river revealed an inherent planning for easy access to both their fields and mode of transport. Le Grand Champ, or the Big Field, was a flood-prone area prompting the relocation of St. Genevieve to the present village site about two miles from the old village as early as 1778.

The entrepôt metropolis of the Mississippi Valley grew slowly prior to 1810 (Adler 1991, 15–16, 22–23; Wade 1959, 59–64). The mercantile hegemony of St. Louis was tied to furs and lead, which depended less on population size than on its advantageous, accessible midcontinental location. Wade notes: "The town was the child of a fur company, and that business remained for three-quarters of a century its most important interest. Not only was this trade the core of St. Louis's economy, but the river metropolis was the commercial heart of America's fur empire" (1959, 60). As its Mississippi River hinterland grew in population, the river town emerged as a growing local and regional market center. Among the early western urban spearheads, the hinterland of St. Louis persisted with an Amerindian problem that diluted the flow of American pioneers and lessened its economic expansion.

By 1810, settlement aggregations concentrated in the northern apex of the American Bottom. Infilling in this core settlement area substantially increased the population density and caused lateral spread beyond the Mississippi bluff valleys into the bordering upland tracts of Goshen and Turkey Hill. The process of spread inscribed a frontier of incipient agriculture (six to eighteen persons per square mile) upon these peripheral upland settlements that experienced sequential settlement patterns (figs. 5.2, 5.3). Turkey Hill (1798) and Goshen (1800) were among the oldest American settlements in southwest Illinois. Goshen, the larger of the two inland settlements, was primarily west and southwest of Edwardsville.

Small kinship communities were colonized complementary to the Goshen and Turkey Hill settlements. Ridge Prairie, between Goshen and Turkey Hill, was initially comprised of kinship units from the ridges and valleys of Virginia who outmigrated from Kentucky to the American Bottom. Originating in 1802, some Ridge Prairie settlers had relocated northward from the older New Design settlement (*History of St. Clair County, Illinois* 1881, 50–51). Silver Creek, a tributary of the Kaskaskia River in eastern St. Clair County, was settled in 1804. High Prairie, south of Belleville between Turkey Hill and New Design, was slowly settled around 1805. Ten miles east of the Kaskaskia River, along Plum Creek in Randolph County, fifteen families from South Carolina established a small colonizing community (Reynolds 1879, 44–48, 61–64). The population growth of the older New Design settlement failed to keep pace with the northern upland settlements of Goshen and Turkey Hill, with their greater accessibility to St. Louis.

Morse wrote in 1810 that only three towns of any consequence existed in Illinois Territory: Kaskaskia (622 persons), Cahokia (711 persons), and Goshen (1,725 persons) (1812, 453). His population numbers were for the entire settlement island. Pioneers perceived the Goshen settlement with a vivid biblical place imagery as they sought harmony, safety, and order in a wilderness. They foresaw an analogous episode with their Hebrew brothers in the relative location of their fertile upland tracts and the Mississippi floodplains in the American Bottom. Goshen in Old Testament history was a northeast Nile delta settlement that Abraham's descendants inhabited with their sheep, goats, and camels until the exodus from Egypt under the leadership of Moses. Peck perceived Illinois Country as the "Canaan" of America, a quintessential promised land, deep in the interior, flowing with milk and honey even as Canaan did for the Hebrews after forty years in the Sinai wilderness (1837, 328).

Successive frontier settlement patterns forged by the processes of colonization and spread intensified the ripple effect into the eastern-bordering forested uplands with their small prairie niches. Goshen and Turkey Hill formed pulsating, bipolar settlement clusters. Backwoods frontiersmen infilled the old French settlement remnant in the American Bottom, creating an American-French settlement veneer. By 1810, the settlement topography evolved into the pivotal elements of the initial "siren" destination in Illinois. Pioneers perpetuated the settlement district as the American Bottom.

Distribution of Settlement: 1820

Illinois emerged as a state in 1818. Continental expansion by the French created a point of attachment at the confluence of the Kaskaskia and Mississippi Rivers in 1703. For over a century, Kaskaskia persisted as the commercial, cultural, and political linchpin of Illinois Country. During the territorial period, the village witnessed considerable population decline and economic stagnation, yet it emerged as the first state capital. The French population dwindled by statehood to 1,500 (Buck 1967, 93). Ford wrote, "In the year 1818, the settled part of the State extended a little north of Edwardsville and Alton; south, along the Mississippi to the mouth of the Ohio; east, in the direction of Carlyle to the Wabash; and down the Wabash and the Ohio, to the mouth of the last-named river. But there was yet a very large unsettled wilderness tract of country, within these boundaries, lying between the Kaskaskia river and the Wabash; and between the Kaskaskia and the Ohio, of three days' journey across it" (1854, 38).

Flower stresses the human isolation that reigned supreme as a hardy back-woods society colonized a new insular frontier in southern Illinois around the time of statehood: "Let us glance at the situation of these settlers, a thousand miles inland. . . . A forest from the Atlantic shore behind them, but thinly settled with small villages, far apart from each other. To the west, one vast uninhabited wilderness of prairie, interspersed with timber, extending two thousand miles to the Pacific Ocean. Excepting St. Louis, on the Mississippi, then a small place, and Kaskaskia, yet smaller, there were no inhabitants west of us. About the same time, one or two small American settlements were forming a few miles east of the Mississippi, as we were planting ourselves a few miles west of the Wabash" (1882, 120).

The 1820 population distribution map resembles Ford's description of settle-ment patterns for the 55,211 pioneers dispersed across Illinois' southern margins (1854, 38) (fig. 5.4). The process of colonization predominated as the frontier of occupance extended from the interior of southern Illinois northward across the Amerindian lands to northern Illinois. A small frontier of occupance persisted in the flood-prone Ohio-Mississippi confluence area and the rugged outcropping of the southern Illinois Ozarks, the Shawnee Hills. The frontier of settlement formed a horseshoe pattern across southern Illinois. Woodland frontiersmen settled in proximity to early trails extending from gateway Shawneetown and ferry crossings on the Ohio River to Kaskaskia, St. Louis, and Goshen. Government land office hinterlands at Shawneetown, Kaskaskia, and Edwardsville were also favorite desti-nations. Valley corridors of the Wabash, Ohio, Big Muddy, Kaskaskia, Mississippi, and Illinois were also preferred settlement choices.

The spread process infilled and laterally expanded the two "siren" riparian movement-settlement corridors situated on opposite sides of southern Illinois. The lower Wabash Valley settlements extending northward from Shawneetown focused on Vincennes. For over half a century, the American Bottom persisted as a premier settlement destination contiguous to the middle Mississippi Valley gate-way. Historical timing, relative location, and accessibility to variant mercantile markets from the entrepôt of St. Louis, lower Mississippi Valley plantations, and New Orleans marked these settlement ribbons for continued population growth. Each riverine settlement core merged into the frontier of incipient agriculture. Immigrants' destinations fused with their desire and need for accessibility to local, regional, national, and even global markets. In the early formation of frontier space-economies, pioneer hunter-farmers and yeoman farmers recognized that trade was impossible without effective water linkages.

The American Bottom in southwest Illinois, contiguous to the spearhead en-trepôt of St. Louis, had a salient locational advantage over the lower Wabash Valley settlement enclave in southeast Illinois. In the Northwest Territory, the key to frontier settlement and economic expansion was river transportation.

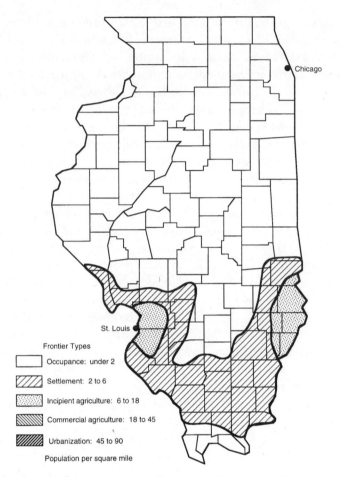

Frontier Types

- Occupance: under 2
- Settlement: 2 to 6
- Incipient agriculture: 6 to 18
- Commercial agriculture: 18 to 45
- Urbanization: 45 to 90

Population per square mile

Fig. 5.4. Settlement Patterns in Illinois, 1820 (Hart 1974; Paullin 1932)

St. Louis experienced the gradual impact of regional mercantile growth with the innovation of steam on inland waterway navigation after 1811, especially its upstream influence on freight and passengers (Wade 1959, 39–40). The gateway's potential was hyperbolized in 1811: "St. Louis will become the Memphis of the American Nile" (Wade 1959, 64). By 1820, arriving entrepreneurs and rapid commercial growth "began to redefine the character of St. Louis from a frontier outpost to a commercial center" (Adler 1991, 17). Its hinterland was transforming from self-sufficiency to a marketplace economy. Settlers acknowledged the mercantile hegemony of the entrepôt with its converging roads as the market for their agricultural surpluses and source of goods.

Distribution of Settlement: 1830

Laggard penetration of the National Road, the plodding pace of surveying the public domain, and slow development of regional road networks contributed to a moderate population increase of slightly over 100,000 during the 1820s in Illinois. Slightly over 80 percent of this population growth inundated the state during the last five years of the decade (Boggess 1968, 188). The distribution of 157,445 settlers in 1830 reveals persistence, succession, and lateral expansion of earlier frontier settlement areas (figs. 5.2–5.5). Substantial infilling of a backwoods pioneer culture occurred as Upland Southerners impressed accretion settlement spearheads in a northward-thrusting population front.

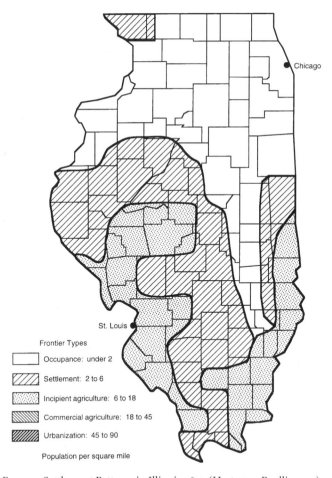

FIG. 5.5. Settlement Patterns in Illinois, 1830 (Hart 1974; Paullin 1932)

An intrusive society diffused at a snail's pace across the settlement frontiers of northern and central Illinois. The frontier of occupance persisted in northern and east-central Illinois, with a permanent Chicago still a dream (fig. 5.5). Yet a speculative land boom associated with the canal soon followed as Chicago was perceived "not as it was but as it could be: a metropolis of continental significance" (Cronon 1991, 31–41). A narrow band of the frontier of occupance persisted deep into southeast Illinois. Owing to inland physical isolation and slowly improving roads, the frontier of settlement survived in the interstice between the Wabash-Ohio-Mississippi Rivers in southern Illinois. The southern margins of the Military Tract between the Mississippi-Illinois corridors were initially colonized as two riverine settlement prongs. Given the availability of navigable waterways, the northward thrust and areal spread of the frontier of settlement was greater in west-central than in east-central Illinois. In east-central Illinois, the frontier of settlement coincided with the Wabash River and its tributaries, the Little Wabash and Embarras. The lead mining region of Galena in northwest Illinois emerged as an anomalous settlement cluster.

By 1830, distinctive settlement prongs formed on opposite sides of Illinois. Watercourses attracted probing pioneers as channels to new destinations and as settlement corridors. Increasing population infilling caused lateral spillover into peripheral areas and relocation to new destinations. The process of spread operating during the 1820s expanded the frontier of incipient agriculture as antipodal, south-north riverine movement-settlement corridors. Each settlement corridor experienced a succession of frontier settlement patterns (figs. 5.4, 5.5). The process of spread did not create a continuous settlement surface of six to eighteen persons per square mile (one to three pioneering families per 640 acres). Numerous small, empty, hollow frontiers and sparsely populated areas separated the magnetic destinations within these elongated riparian settlement areas.

Focal settlement clusters formed in intervening confluence areas when a sizable tributary merged with a navigable waterway. Within each settlement corridor, the early-arriving Upland Southerners were particularly attracted to the tributary valleys and bordering bluffs rather than the flood-prone lowlands. The Wabash-Mississippi-Illinois Rivers and their tributaries witnessed a number of these proto-typical settlement types essential to the diffusion process of spread. Rapid infilling and lateral areal expansion were constantly modified as pioneers reassessed their cognitive maps upon dispersing into new remote frontiers. The regularity of confluence settlement islands evolving in lowlands and adjacent interstream divides represents the natural advantages of site and situation inherent in certain environmental niches.

Settlement foci at the confluence of waterways served as significant points of entry, transshipment points, and trade points during the frontier's evolution. Points of pause in the migration process were comprehended by pioneers as important steps in the frontier settlement process. Typical migration decision-making pauses occurred at frontier settlement junctures: confluence of rivers, transshipment points (changing transport mode), and road intersections. Prior to the evolution of an effective regional road network and improved steam navigation on the inland rivers and Great Lakes, loose settlement enclaves in proximity to river junctures were pivotal settlement foci. These settlement clusters furnished the opportunity to replenish supplies and make repairs, to take a physical and emotional break from the monotony and rigors of travel, to visit socially with antecedent kinfolk and pioneer settlers, and to acquire geographical information concerning route choices and alternative destinations.

Archetype settlement clusters by 1830 evolved at ferry crossings with radiating roads (Lusk's Ferry, Golconda), gateway nodes with excellent connectivity (Shawneetown), stream confluences (Little Wabash–Wabash Rivers), and central crossroads locations (southern Franklin County) (figs. 3.3, 3.4, 4.1, 5.5). Confluence areas as colonizing settlements functioned as disembarkation points for further upstream movements. Household units migrating within social networks utilized such duplicated settlement stepping-stones as a means of reducing the hardships, physical separation, and emotional fears of relocating deeper into a remote frontier. Established settlement clusters were safety valves that furnished pioneers the opportunity to benefit from voices of experience who preceded them. Selection of final destinations in the upstream wilderness could be easily terminated, given alternatives on paralleling streams. Pioneers penetrating upstream on the Wabash River had two classic examples of paralleling tributaries in Illinois: the Little Wabash and Embarras Rivers. Settlement along both the master and the secondary streams produced a ripple effect of lateral settlement expansion into the interstice land tracts.

The Ohio-Wabash corridor fragmented into appealing settlement enclaves with intervening, unsettled tracts. The Shawneetown hinterland in southeast Illinois, bordering the Ohio River, possessed the greater width of the frontier of incipient agriculture. It was associated with the gateway node and land office center of Shawneetown with its nearby salt works. In addition, Shawneetown and Golconda (Lusk's Ferry) were points of entry for two major roads linking the Upland South with southern Illinois: the Wilderness Road and the Nashville-Saline Trail. Dispersed farmsteads and loosely clustered settlements formed astride and in the interstice between the northwest-radiating roads from Shawneetown and Golconda.

The frontier of incipient agriculture penetrated the interior of southern Illinois in Franklin County. The habitat bordering modern-day Franklin and Williamson Counties had two essential attributes that spawned the process of spread in an isolated inland location. The area marked an upland divide for a Saline River branch that flows into the Ohio River and Big Muddy River branches that empty into the

Mississippi River. The numerous upland divides between the forks of the Big Muddy were elemental environmental niches favored by woodland frontiersmen. A cross-roads area developed in this vicinity as the southern Illinois road network expanded. Roads extended northwest to the key early overland destinations: Kaskaskia and the St. Louis–Goshen area. This settlement island was also bisected by a southwest-northeast trending road that connected the clustered settlements in the Mississippi bluffs of Union County with the confluence area of the Little Wabash–Wabash Rivers. In time, an overland route thrust northward to Vandalia and northwest to Sangamon County. Intersecting roads produced a level of connectivity and centrality that other inland areas of southern Illinois never replicated.

The Wabash Valley corridor fragmented into discrete settlement enclaves (fig. 5.5). The initial settlement island north of Shawneetown in the corridor evolved in the lower Little Wabash Valley. Remnants of the old English colony of Birkbeck and Flower in Edwards County persisted at the northern apex of the settlement district. Settlement clusters developed along the Shawneetown-Carmi-Albion Road, but the greatest areal breadth evolved in the intervening area between the lower Little Wabash and lower Wabash Rivers. This mesopotamian settlement ribbon averaged about ten to fifteen miles in width.

Another ribbon settlement island extended upstream between the Embarras and Wabash Rivers. These north-south, paralleling rivers marked quintessential smaller settlement corridors. The core of the settlement district, the frontier of incipient agriculture, extended northward about a hundred miles from Lawrence County to southeast Vermilion County in eastern Illinois. Segmented settlement clusters formed adjacent to three gateways on the Wabash River in bordering Indiana: Vincennes, Terre Haute, and Covington. These points of attachment connected to the expanding southeast-northwest trending road network in the Hoosier State. Each riverside node with its settlement hinterland interconnected via the Wabash River. The tributary areas stretched greater distances upstream and downstream from the respective gateways than their lateral spread toward the Embarras River.

The settlement cluster contiguous with Vincennes, the old French colonial settlement and trading outpost, developed in the stream divide of the Embarras-Wabash Rivers in Lawrence and Crawford Counties (figs. 3.4, 5.5). French colonists had imprinted a long lot settlement form in Illinois Country across from Vincennes, even as the Kaskaskia habitants colonized St. Genevieve across the Mississippi River in Missouri. The Wabash waterway had been one of the natural pathways linking Lower Canada and Illinois Country. An important branch of the Wilderness Road from the Falls of the Ohio River connected with Vincennes. The Vincennes–St. Louis Trace bifurcated with a branch to Kaskaskia and the main trail to Cahokia and St. Louis. The Vincennes ferry was operating by the turn of the eighteenth century. Being situated on a trunk line that linked Louisville and St. Louis, this key ferry was stationed on the Illinois side.

The next riverine settlement cluster embraced the eastern half of Clark and Edgar Counties, bordering Terre Haute. Its accessibility improved with steamboating on the Wabash River and the arrival of the National Road in the late 1820s (Cammack 1954). Its Illinois hinterland expanded in the early 1830s with the westward penetration of two roads: the National Road through Clark County to Vandalia and a Terre Haute–Decatur–Springfield Road through Paris, county seat of Edgar County. As the gateway market center for this portion of east-central Illinois, Terre Haute had a rival about twenty miles downstream. A ferry originated in 1818 at Darwin, county seat of Clark County from 1823 to 1838. By the time of the National Road, the ferry at Terre Haute dominated immigrant and wagon traffic crossing of the Wabash River. Marshall on the National Road became the new county seat.

The last settlement enclave evolved in the confluence area of the Little Vermilion–Vermilion Rivers with the Wabash River. Southeast Vermilion County became attractive beginning in the mid-1820s with the production of salt at the salines near Danville. Originating in 1826, the Indiana entry-and-exit point was Covington at the big bend of the Wabash River. Flatboats, steamboats, a ferry, and road linkage with Indianapolis through Crawfordsville contributed to making Covington a market center for a hinterland of incipient agriculture. The accessibility of the Vermilion County tributary area to Covington improved slightly by the mid-1830s as the road from Indianapolis penetrated the empty prairies beyond Danville to link with Springfield in Sangamon Country. Even after the establishment of a federal land office at Danville in 1831, the pace of migration remained lethargic. The northern half of east-central Illinois as a yeoman farmers' domain was neglected and delayed until post-1850s. The area remained a hollow frontier, given the geography of the Grand Prairie (Winsor 1987). Resource evaluation engendered a cattlemen's domain, with large landholders, farm tenancy, and a marketplace farming economy in the late nineteenth century (Bogue 1959; Gates 1932, 1945, 1948; Poggi 1934). On the distant technology horizon in 1830 were heavy steel plows and drainage tiles for the extensive, featureless prairie peninsula (Bogue 1959).

The south-north settlement patterns in 1830 closely conformed to the paralleling streams. Sequential settlements dispersed inland from the Wabash River with each decade (figs. 5.3–5.5). The frontier of incipient agriculture evolved as a fifteen- to twenty-mile-wide settlement ribbon between the Wabash and North Fork of the Embarras Rivers. This meant that a farmer was within one or two days' travel of Wabash River transshipment points. The frontier of settlement extended between the North Fork of the Embarras and Embarras Rivers, about ten to fifteen miles wide. In Vermilion County, the southeast-flowing Wabash tributaries promoted a greater inland settlement penetration.

In western Illinois, the Mississippi-Illinois movement corridors witnessed a settlement momentum in the 1820s. For half a century, American settlements tenuously established a regular succession of settlement clusters northward on the navigable channels and inland along the tributaries. Owing to the environmental hazards of the floodplains, upstream valleys of the rivers and creeks that bisected the bluffs and adjoining interstream divides emerged as preferred early settlement sites. Tributaries of the two rivers navigable for flatboats were particularly prized for settlement. A south-north ordering of small settlement clusters juxtaposed in the upland divides of the Mississippi-Illinois tributaries.

These settlement intrusions spread laterally in western Illinois. In the southern portion of the Mississippi Valley corridor, the greater width of the frontier of incipient agriculture in Union County linked to an early channelized migration of German Americans from North Carolina (Meyer 1976c, 156). The dissected interstream divides separating the headwater creeks of the Cache River, an Ohio River tributary, and the creeks flowing into the Mississippi embraced an environmental setting similar to their origins in the Carolina piedmont. The next upstream settlements paralleled the Big Muddy River and its tributary creeks in Jackson County and St. Marys River in Randolph County.

A succession of settlement frontiers leapfrogged upstream through and laterally away from the Illinois Valley corridor (figs. 5.4–5.5). Woodland pioneers, with their preadaptive cultural strategies, intruded their diminutive settlements into a familiar habitat. From south to north on the east side of the Illinois River, colonization footholds were transplanted at Otter, Macoupin, Apple, Sandy, Mauvaise Terre, Indian, and Quiver Creeks and Mackinaw River. Fewer small arteries entered the west side: McKee Creek, La Moine River, Sugar Creek, and Spoon River. The process of spread infilled intervening areas between the minor tributaries. Inland settlement dispersal extended away from the channel a greater distance on the east side of the corridor, given the allure of Sangamon Country.

By 1830, the Mississippi-Illinois settlement corridors were segmented into several discrete place-specific destinations: the American Bottom, the lower and middle Kaskaskia Valley, the Goshen–Turkey Hill area, the lower Illinois Valley, and Sangamon Country. Sequential settlement patterns dispersed further inland during the 1820s astride the two major tributaries of the Mississippi-Illinois Rivers: Kaskaskia and Sangamon. These riverine settlement ribbons experienced the frontier of incipient agriculture. Lateral spread from the riparian settlement impress spawned population thrusts straddling smaller streams and expanding road networks. Two settlement clusters emerged as captivating immigrant destinations.

The Goshen–Turkey Hill area and northern part of the American Bottom endured as a principal destination for half a century. This dynamic settlement area possessed the following attributes: availability of large amounts of cheap, fertile land, "siren" place image, centrality, and access to markets. The settlement veneer superimposed the interstice and the roads converging on the adjoining mercantile entrepôt of St. Louis, its smaller rival of Alton, and the old French village of

Cahokia (figs. 3.4, 5.5). Frontier demographic fronts expanded astride the creeks in the northern colonization fringe of the Goshen–Turkey Hill area. The northward-expanding road network formed a skeletal settlement framework between riverside Alton and upland Edwardsville to Jacksonville and Springfield in Sangamon Country.

The Goshen–Turkey Hill settlements spread eastward toward Vandalia. The interior settlement clusters surrounding the state capital in the middle Kaskaskia Valley coalesced with the lower Kaskaskia Valley settlements in proximity to the old French village of Kaskaskia near the Mississippi-Kaskaskia Rivers juncture. Settlements thrust upstream on the major north-south, paralleling tributaries of the Kaskaskia River: Silver, Shoal, and Hurricane Creeks. In the 1820s, the frontier of incipient agriculture spread as much as twenty-five or more miles upstream on these creeks. During maximum spring runoff, flatboats could descend the almost hundred miles by way of the creeks to the Kaskaskia River and Mississippi River.

Edenic Sangamon Country rose to ascendancy as the leading immigrant destination in Illinois. Sangamon Country embraced more than the narrowly defined valley. Jacksonville and Springfield served as rival settlement-growth poles. Jacksonville, the county seat of Morgan County, was situated about twenty miles inland from the Illinois River. Springfield, the future capital and county seat of Sangamon County, was located about thirty miles east of Jacksonville in the middle Sangamon Valley. A rapid succession of frontier types, from occupance to incipient agriculture, mirrored the dynamics of colonization and spread processes as immigrants focused on Sangamon Country in the 1820s (figs. 5.4, 5.5). Southwestern Sangamon Country was traversed by northeast-southwest-flowing Illinois tributaries. Pioneers penetrated the riparian woodlands and broadened the frontier of incipient agriculture to about twenty-five miles wide in Jersey and Greene Counties in the lower Illinois Valley. Sangamon Country achieved its greatest width of almost seventy-five miles from the Illinois River astride the Sangamon River and its tributaries. Northern Sangamon Country was located within the federal land district of Springfield. Sangamon Valley, the southern periphery of Sangamon Country, and northern margins of the Goshen–Turkey Hill area marked a highly favored ecological niche, a woodland habitat. Small prairie peninsulas and larger prairies emerged deeper in the interior. This middle perceptual ground where Sangamon Country merged with the Goshen–Turkey Hill area lay within the federal land district of Edwardsville. West-central Illinois unfolded as a key migration destination area. By 1830, the primary watersheds of the Prairie State emerged as the pivotal areas of initial agricultural occupation (Cronon 1991, 103).

Distribution of Settlement: 1840

Segmented settlement patterns were arrayed from south-north and east-west by 1840 (fig. 5.6). The early 1830s served as a forerunner of divergent immigrant

inundations, extraordinary increases in land sales, and rapid growth of new, alluring destinations as additional government land offices were opened for a total of
ten by 1840. The seeds for inaugurating rapid changes in settlement patterns were
triggered by the influence of the northern commercial gateway (Walton 1987, 230).
The competition stage of settlement diffusion and marketplace agriculture
loomed on the horizon in midcontinental Illinois.

The structure of the population patterns in 1840 delineates the tenacity of the
colonization process. Its areal extent was greatly reduced and limited to east-
central and northern Illinois. Persistence of the colonization process over an extended period of time hints at the regional problems of limited accessibility and
inadequate agricultural technology. Although northern Illinois by the late 1830s

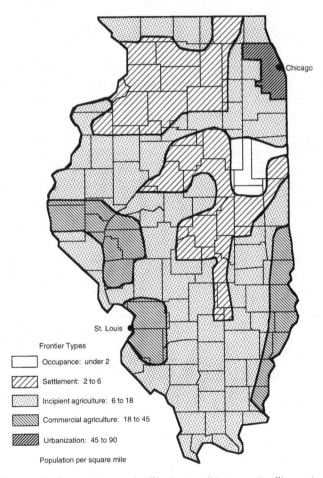

FIG. 5.6. Settlement Patterns in Illinois, 1840 (Hart 1974; Paullin 1932)

accumulated a spectacular influx of immigrants, rapid succession of settlement frontiers was limited to those areas accessible to markets. The frontier of occupance persisted in the Grand Prairie of east-central Illinois. Avoided in initial settlement appraisal, it survived into the 1840s as an archetypal hollow frontier. Grand Prairie's appeal as an immigrant destination lingered until after the Civil War.

The frontier of settlement bifurcated on either side of the Illinois River. The northern Illinois area conformed to the Rock River Valley, poorly accessible areas, and extensive prairies. The nearly empty east-central Illinois area coincided with the Grand Prairie's wide expanse and isolated interior tracts. Extensive wet and dry prairies dominated the Danville federal land district. The prairie peninsula extended into the eastern portion of the Springfield, northern part of the Palestine, northern sector of the Vandalia, and northeast segment of the Edwardsville federal land districts. The areal extent of the frontiers of occupance and settlement corresponded to the settlement endurance of the colonization phase.

The process of spread rapidly unfolded the frontier of incipient agriculture by 1840 (fig. 5.6). Immigrant farmers expected remote regional frontiers to offer the fruits of success and prosperity available from expanding commercial agriculture activities and requisite economic, transportation, and urban infrastructures. For the first time, the frontier of incipient agriculture areally dominated the state's breadth. Expanding road networks and riverine corridors of the Wabash-Ohio-Mississippi-Illinois Rivers engendered settlement structures with marketplace space-economies.

A rapid increase in population to almost half a million by 1840 launched the terminal phase of competition in Hudson's frontier settlement model (1969). Swiftly growing regional settlement clusters and urban centers evolved in a competitive struggle that typifies its essential characteristic (370–73). Population density structure pinpointed preferred, maturing, and new destinations in Illinois by the late 1830s. Motivated by economic well-being, large-scale infilling of immigrant farmers and urban dwellers characterized the salient settlement areas of the frontiers of commercial agriculture (eighteen to forty-five persons per square mile) and urbanization (forty-five or more persons per square mile). Lewis argues that the competition process marks increasing complex economic networks and technology changes (1984, 22).

The 1830s brought about significant transportation innovations that increased the effective movement of people, goods, bulk materials, and agricultural exports in the eastern United States. Improved steam navigation and boat technology on the Great Lakes system and navigable rivers, improvements in flatboats, and evolution of a bridging canal network in the Lower Middle West were important transport changes. Upgrading the National Road, improved wagon roads, and expansions in regional road networks in Illinois contributed to a substantial population increase of over 300,000 by 1840 (Meyer 1948; Taylor 1951; Vance 1990) (figs. 3.4, 3.5).

The premier frontier settlement nexuses developed marketplace agricultural-biases. Southern Illinois emerged by 1840 with two early commercial agricultural cores: southwest and southeast Illinois (fig. 5.6). The immediate Illinois hinterland of St. Louis included the American Bottom's northern part with Alton and the Goshen–Turkey Hill area. Southwest Illinois, with its converging roads, expanded the tributary area of St. Louis. The relative location of "River City" on the Mississippi trunkline fostered an extensive upstream mercantile hegemony. The accessible mercantile entrepôt had an effective ingress to the southern commercial terminus. Commercial agriculture developed early in the Wabash Valley corridor because of availability of steamboats and flatboats for transporting surpluses to New Orleans. Marketplace agriculture extended northward from Shawneetown to Terre Haute. Inland spread was restricted to paralleling Wabash tributaries that were accessible to flatboats.

Two commercial agricultural cores developed in west-central Illinois, separated by the Illinois River. Southwest Sangamon Country with Jacksonville was connected to the Alton-Goshen settlement area. Farmers at this time were market-biased toward St. Louis and a southern export trade. A narrow band of commercial agriculture formed across the southern part of the Military Tract between the Mississippi-Illinois Rivers. The Quincy settlement island interconnected with St. Louis and New Orleans. Both "siren" settlement districts witnessed modifications in their road networks and sequential settlement patterns.

Three attractive settlement areas formed in northern Illinois after the Black Hawk War of 1832 (fig. 5.6). Each settlement cluster grew in conjunction with a dynamic urban center: Galena, Rockford, and Chicago. These destinations were connected by the long haul over the Chicago-Galena Road. Galena Country encompassed a small frontier of incipient agriculture in Jo Daviess and Stephenson Counties that was tributary to the lead entrepôt in northwest Illinois. Rockford, situated at the Chicago-Galena Road ferry and an advantageous mill site on the Rock River, slowly evolved as the market center for the Rock River Country in north-central Illinois. By 1840, the county seat of Winnebago County served a small hinterland in the frontier of incipient agriculture with its tenuous east-west post road ties.

Northeast Illinois, with its lakeside gateway, evolved as the western terminus of the northern commercial gateway. Improved Great Lakes steam navigation enhanced Chicago's integration to the eastern terminus of New York. Accessibility of settlement clusters to local, regional, national, and international markets was enhanced with improved roads radiating from Chicago at Lake Michigan's southern tip (figs. 3.5, 3.6). Chicago tapped the frontier of incipient agriculture in its hinterland fringe and astride the future Illinois and Michigan Canal. Its population and economic growth were mercurial as the processes of colonization, spread, and competition rapidly reshaped settlement patterns. Settlement transformations in Cook County shifted from the frontier of occupance in 1830 (fig. 5.5) to the frontier of urbanization in 1840 (fig. 5.6). Its agricultural hinterland changed from subsistence to a marketplace space-economy.

Distribution of Settlement: 1850

During the frontier period, immigrants cleared patches in the forests and prairies, broke the soil, and planted town sites. The wilderness was transformed with an array of cultural artifacts: farmsteads, fields, river landings, roads, mills, and urban places. Prior to the mid-1830s, the fundamental processes of "setting up" settlement and economic impresses were their primary concerns. The preadaptive, backwoods cultural strategy of pioneers effectively dispersed their agricultural settlements and urban places at riverside, isolated, and crossroads locations. Dispersed and clustered settlements stressed choosing sites for initial dwellings, agricultural lands, and communities adjacent to rivers and their larger tributaries. Small, local agricultural market-biases dominated remote frontier settlements. Agricultural transformations from self-sufficiency to marketplace exposures meant navigable rivers evolved as primary movement-settlement corridors. By 1850, the greatest population densities persisted astride the navigable riparian corridors with the exception of Chicago's contiguous hinterland (Cronon 1991, 103).

Smaller streams furnished mill sites for the frontier's incipient agricultural processing and manufacturing activities linked to settlers' needs: grain and lumber. Early milling, crossroads, and county seat sites emerged as important entrepreneurial communities or "urban building blocks" with their tiny agricultural hinterlands. Lower-level nodes, especially courthouse centers, functioned as elemental mercantile, distributive, manufacturing, social, and political centers. Processing and distribution of local agricultural products and furnishing goods and services for local population consumption were cultural and economic imperatives. Expanding regional road networks connected county seats with larger places, which improved their accessibility and mercantile competitiveness.

Riverside, lakeside, and crossroads market centers located at road convergences were particularly favored immigrant destinations. Subregional nodes—Alton, Jacksonville, Springfield, Quincy, Peoria, Galena, and their tributary areas—witnessed agricultural, mercantile, service, distributive, and incipient manufacturing growth by 1850. Riverside foci in western Illinois particularly met the fundamental locational, transport, economic, and geographic imperatives. During the height of the steamboat's impact, upstream Mississippi-Illinois river towns within the mercantile hegemony of St. Louis experienced immigrant cultural mixing and diverse economic activities. Riverside commercial hinterlands interconnected with interregional, national, and world economic systems through New Orleans.

During the 1840s, the lakeside regional node of Chicago swiftly developed its own radial overland and water/canal movement-settlement corridors as a means of exerting a mercantile influence over northern Illinois and the Illinois Valley corridor. The hegemony of Chicago over settlement and regional growth in its expanding hinterland gained from its integration through New York with national and world market infrastructures (Agnew 1987; Wallerstein 1989). Immigrants disembarked from the gateway into the recently settled northern Illinois backcountry. Population, commercial agriculture, and mercantile expansions in Chicago's hinterland mushroomed with the growth of regional and national rail networks. The city connected with competitive midwestern regional nodes and seaboard national nodes.

After over half a century, settlement patterns in 1850 reveal that the frontier of occupance ceased to exist in the Illinois settlement landscape (fig. 5.7). The frontier of settlement persisted on either side of the Illinois Valley corridor at the self-sufficiency level. The largest settlement void survived across the horizontal expanse of east-central Illinois. The hollow frontier of the Grand Prairie required the railroad, steel plows, and drainage tiles after the Civil War. The frontier of incipient agriculture depicted the inaccessibility of interior places as farmers remained in subsistence agriculture, except for those located on the margins who overcame the barrier of distance. An extensive frontier of incipient agriculture extended northward from the Ohio River through the forested southern and mixed forest–prairie areas of east-central Illinois. Interior areas lagged in settlement and economic advancement until the Illinois Central Railroad traversed eastern Illinois in the 1850s. Two smaller areas of the frontier of incipient agriculture survived in northern and west-central Illinois. Isolation, settlement timing, minimal road development, limited accessibility to waterways, and extensive prairies perpetuated sparse settlements.

The frontier of commercial agriculture dispersed across almost half of Illinois by 1850. The process of competition inscribed both a linearity and increasing lateral spread in the progression of settlement and economic expansions. Linear settlement areas emerged astride the movement corridors of the navigable waterways and Chicago-Galena Road. In the frontier of commercial agriculture, farmers integrated their crop and livestock exports to potential local, regional, interregional, national, and international marketplace economic systems. Steamboats functioned as the principal transport means that shaped dynamic spatial growth and interactions. Regional settlement organization was spurred, aligned, and consolidated along mainline channels. Where steamboat regularity was reduced by shipping obstacles, such as on the Wabash, Big Muddy, Kaskaskia, and Sangamon Rivers, riparian movement-settlement corridors depended on the persistence of flatboating for marketplace economic exposure.

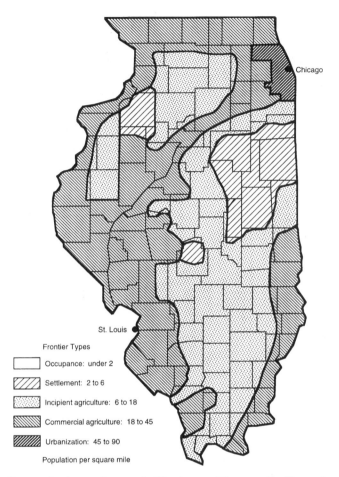

FIG. 5.7. Settlement Patterns in Illinois, 1850 (Hart 1974; Paullin 1932)

Expanding regional road networks reinforced intra- and interregional overland and navigable waterway interconnections (figs. 3.5–3.7). Regional, subregional, and lower-level nodes emerged as foci of road convergences and divergences that fused tributary areas. Key riverside and lakeside nodes rapidly expanded their commercial hegemony. A few interior nodes along major roads, astride rivers, and within attractive settlement districts evolved as important regional mercantile network components. In northern Illinois, Rockford, straddling the Chicago-Galena Road where it crosses the Rock River, was centrally situated in the captivating Rock River Country. As an evolving interior node, its settlement and economic expansions were not linked to a navigable steamboat channel.

The population distribution map of 1850 delineates the maximum integration of steamboats on the navigable trunk and tributary channels bordering and penetrating Illinois (fig. 5.7). Efficient use of waterways affected the growth of marketplace agriculture as it expanded upstream towards the heads of navigation and laterally inland. Smaller steamboats and downstream flatboats navigated the Wabash and upper Mississippi backcountry channels. The Ohio-Wabash corridor represented a narrow ribbon settlement that linked small river landings—Terre Haute, Vincennes, and Shawneetown—near the confluence of the two rivers. The upstream Mississippi River region of Illinois slowly developed a commercial agricultural focus given its settlement timing, transport hindrances, and location. Galena was situated on a tiny channel that experienced a short navigation season. As a lead exporter, its fortunes were tied to the mineral cycle, not to grain and livestock exports.

In western Illinois, attractive settlements paralleled the Mississippi-Illinois Rivers. The bifurcated, Y-shaped riparian movement-settlement corridors were steamboat-dependent. The gateway entrepôt of St. Louis forged an extensive mercantile hinterland upstream in the Mississippi-Illinois corridor. This settlement and economic growth channel integrated subregional riverside nodes (Alton, Quincy, Peoria, and Galena), lower-level riverside nodes (Beardstown, Havana, Pekin, and Peru), and inland subregional nodes (Jacksonville and Springfield) via efficient steamboat and regional road linkages. The greatest breadth and vitality of settlement and commercial agricultural expansions emerged where steamboats and converging road networks complemented each other in southwest and west-central Illinois.

The mercantile and commercial agricultural hinterlands of St. Louis were interdependent. Downstream from St. Louis, the smaller tributaries of the Big Muddy and Kaskaskia Rivers continued to depend on flatboats, thus producing an inland expansion of the frontier of commercial agriculture from the Mississippi River trunk line. Marketplace agriculture spread throughout the American Bottom and Goshen–Turkey Hill settlement areas in southwest Illinois. The road network converged on riverside rivals, the regional node of St. Louis and the subregional node of Alton. The upriver Mississippi segment from St. Louis to Quincy and the lower and middle sections of the Illinois River to just north of Peoria developed greater linear extension and width in commercial agriculture. The Military Tract, Sangamon Country, and the Illinois Valley corridor forged dynamic marketplace infrastructures. Commercial ties to interregional, national, and world markets were assured through St. Louis, the mercantile linchpin of the Mississippi Valley.

Two other movement-settlement corridors expanded in the 1840s (fig. 5.7). Linking the upper Illinois River from the head of steamboat navigation at Peru to the terminal node of the Illinois and Michigan Canal at Chicago in 1848 engendered major commercial shifts in the state. A narrow riparian, marketplace agricultural zone emerged contiguous to the canal in northeast Illinois. This marketplace-biased corridor bisected the frontiers of settlement and incipient agriculture that persisted in north-central and east-central Illinois. The canal permitted Chicago to intersperse effectively and expand its spatial interactions into west-central Illinois astride the Illinois Valley corridor.

The dynamic growth of the lakeside gateway of Chicago reflected its western terminus location in the northern movement corridor and its centrality in midcontinental America. Early growth stimuli were tied to large amounts of cheap, fertile lands and steam navigation on the northern lake-canal trunk line. Arriving immigrants were lured by potentially available commercial agricultural and urban activities. Chicago's diverging road network was essential for its population and economic expansions as it integrated northeast and distant northwest Illinois (Lee 1917; Quaife 1923; Ramey 1949). Population densities, commercial agriculture activities, and mercantile exchanges spread from Chicago to the Fox River Valley straddling the radiating roads (figs. 3.5–3.7, 5.5–5.7). The Chicago-Galena Road developed as a movement-settlement corridor across the northern tier counties. A wheat export staple area interconnected through Chicago via the northern commercial gateway to eastern seaboard and western European markets (Agnew 1987; Clark 1966; Meyer 1979, 11; Peet 1969, 1970–71).

In the 1840s, the rapid settlement growth of the Fox River counties with their many mill sites exceeded the population increases of the counties astride the Illinois and Michigan Canal. The immediate hinterland population of Chicago in Cook County grew significantly. The frontier of urbanization marked a leap beyond simple processing of agricultural products, commercial activities, and courthouse functions. The regional node straddled an emerging commercial agricultural West and penetrating, manufacturing Northeast. Chicago evolved as the mercantile, manufacturing, distributive, and collecting entrepôt for the expanding commercial agriculture of northern Illinois (Pooley 1968, 489–90). The fundamentals for a diverse incipient manufacturing base in Chicago were antecedent to the railroad (Pierce 1937). By 1850, northeast Illinois formed the "siren" settlement district in the state.

Rail lines in the 1850s superimposed and reinforced prototype transport modes and networks. The establishment of numerous trunk and bridge rail lines from the evolving railroad hub of Chicago quickly and effectively interconnected an expanded tributary area. The emerging rail network dynamically enlarged its mercantile hegemony northwestward, westward, southwestward, and southward across Illinois and into the neighboring states prior to the Civil War (Paxson 1911). The railroad served as the key factor in the settlement and economic development of isolated intervening areas between navigable waterways and particularly the extensive prairies of central and northern Illinois (Lee 1917).

Chicago's population grew rapidly with the opening of the Illinois and Michigan Canal: in 1840, the population was 4,470; in 1845, 12,088; and in 1850, 29,963.

Yet in 1850, St. Louis, mercantile entrepôt of the middle Mississippi Valley, was two and a half times larger in population, with 77,860, than its lakeside rival (Belcher 1947, 23–24). Chicago's numbers soared to 109,260 by 1860, but St. Louis persisted as the larger city with 160,773 people. By 1870, the rival national nodes were equivalent in size. The railroad, mercantile, manufacturing, and service center of Chicago leaped ahead in population by 1880 with 503,185 over St. Louis's 359,518. Chicago never looked back in the race for economic supremacy in the interior.

River City Versus Lake City

Commerce developed as the essential activity of St. Louis (Belcher 1947). Wade argues that the gateway evolved both as a "distribution center for Eastern goods on the Mississippi frontier and the dispatching point for Western produce to the outside world" (1959, 63–64). Its mercantile linkages operated at regional, continental, and global economies of scale. Trappers from the entrepôt accumulated furs in the Rocky Mountains as its traders bickered over prices in New Orleans, New York, and London. Lead mined in Wisconsin, Illinois, and Missouri was processed in proximity to the riverside node and marketed in Pittsburgh and Philadelphia. St. Louis served as the ingress focal point for trade goods and immigrants heading upstream on the Missouri-Mississippi-Illinois Rivers. It also emerged as the egress transshipment point for agricultural exports from its upstream tributary area and abutting Illinois hinterland for the downstream journey to New Orleans, the eastern seaboard, and Europe.

Louisville, Cincinnati, and St. Louis were riverside urban spearheads in the Ohio-Mississippi Valley settlement frontiers of the Lower Middle West (Adler 1991; Hunter 1949; Wade 1959). Mercantile activities related to the river trade dominated their economic growth. Louisville developed at the Falls of the Ohio and peripheral to the Bluegrass Region. This strategic transshipment location meant an early rapid growth and commercial dominance of the Ohio Valley corridor in the 1820s and 1830s, both upstream to Pittsburgh and downstream to New Orleans. Louisville's rival, Cincinnati, was vitally positioned midway between Pittsburgh and the mouth of the Ohio. Cincinnati had the geographical advantage of an extensive hinterland of fertile farm country in the three bordering states of Ohio, Kentucky, and Indiana. The rapid commercial growth of Cincinnati during the 1840s allowed it to succeed Louisville as the mercantile mart, transshipment point, and steamboating center on the Ohio River.

By the late 1830s and 1840s, St. Louis ascended to riverside mercantile linchpin in the continental interior (Adler 1991; Mahoney 1990). Centrality within the Mississippi drainage basin, access to radial tributary channels, and being midpoint of the trunk line artery and a break-in-bulk point shaped an extensive upstream trading hinterland for St. Louis. As the transshipment point for the upper Mississippi Valley steamboat traffic, it extended commercial linkages northward. The commercial control of an inland empire was short-lived for St. Louis, however, because of rapidly growing Chicago at the southern tip of Lake Michigan (Belcher 1947). St. Louis emerged in a commercial struggle with its rival by the late 1840s.

Ten years later, the "Gateway to the West" witnessed the increasing dissolution of its midcontinental trade dominance to its mercantile rival, lakeside Chicago (Adler 1991, 1; Cronon 1991, 295–309). Situated on the west bank of the Mississippi River, the regional node of St. Louis was fused to its waterborne, southern agricultural and western resource export traffic. It had a difficult time competing with the Illinois and Michigan Canal and Great Lakes–Erie Canal commercial linkages of Chicago (Adler 1991; Belcher 1947; Putnam 1918; Schnell 1977). Rail lines converged on Chicago from the East, diverged from the transshipment point, and traversed Illinois with trunk and bridge lines. The lake port possessed transport and commercial advantages that St. Louis would not experience until post–Civil War (Paxson 1911).

Schnell argued that in the economic rivalry between "River City" and "Lake City," St. Louis suffered from several locational disadvantages (1977). It was not favorably positioned for linking with westward-penetrating rail lines from New York, Boston, or Philadelphia. The expanding mercantile patterns of Chicago reinforced economic ties with eastern financial interests whose entrepreneurs readily furnished it speculative capital for railroad building. Since the eastern rail lines paralleled the northern commercial gateway, Chicago exploited its commercial and capital connections with the northeast seaboard, New York, and Boston. Yet the traditional trade ligaments of St. Louis persisted with the moneyless business links of the South and West. Recently, Adler concluded that sectionalism, financial crises, and particularly Yankee venture capital, economic power, and eastern cultural institutions redefined antebellum commercial developments in the urban West (1991, 175–77). With competitive capital flows and a mercantile edge over St. Louis, midwestern mercantile hegemony shifted three hundred miles northeastward to Chicago.

The loss of the Illinois Valley corridor's grain export trade was a limited setback for St. Louis's trading hinterland. Putnam concluded that in the 1850s, St. Louis expanded her mercantile interests through wholesaling (1918, 103–8). Wholesale grocers established new markets for sugar, coffee, and tobacco in the lower Mississippi Valley trade. St. Louis remained the distributive center for the rapidly emerging trans-Mississippi West via the accessible Missouri River. Still, eastern manufactured goods flowed more efficiently and cheaply through Chicago than New Orleans. A growing manufacturing and wholesale base; construction of radiating transcontinental rail lines westward to the Pacific rim and southwest to the Gulf of Mexico; converging rail lines on the riverside mercantile metropolis; the bridging of the Mississippi River with the Eads Bridge in 1874; and rapid population growth after the Civil War generated new economic stimuli for St. Louis's commercial hinterland expansion.

6

Upland South Immigrant Regions

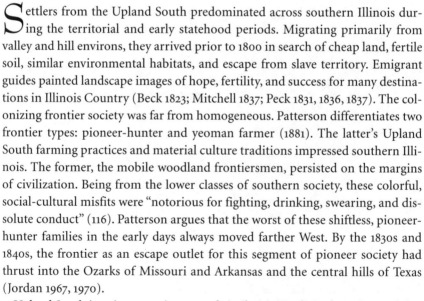

These bottoms, especially the American, are the best regions
in the United States for raising stock, particularly horses,
cattle, and swine. Seventy-five bushels of corn to the acre is an
ordinary crop.
—Peck 1836

Settlers from the Upland South predominated across southern Illinois during the territorial and early statehood periods. Migrating primarily from
valley and hill environs, they arrived prior to 1800 in search of cheap land, fertile
soil, similar environmental habitats, and escape from slave territory. Emigrant
guides painted landscape images of hope, fertility, and success for many destinations in Illinois Country (Beck 1823; Mitchell 1837; Peck 1831, 1836, 1837). The colonizing frontier society was far from homogeneous. Patterson differentiates two
frontier types: pioneer-hunter and yeoman farmer (1881). The latter's Upland
South farming practices and material culture traditions impressed southern Illinois. The former, the mobile woodland frontiersmen, persisted on the margins
of civilization. Being from the lower classes of southern society, these colorful,
social-cultural misfits were "notorious for fighting, drinking, swearing, and dis-
solute conduct" (116). Patterson argues that the worst of these shiftless, pioneer-
hunter families in the early days always moved farther West. By the 1830s and
1840s, the frontier as an escape outlet for this segment of pioneer society had
thrust into the Ozarks of Missouri and Arkansas and the central hills of Texas
(Jordan 1967, 1970).

Upland South immigrant regions reveal similarities in their clustering and dispersion patterns in Illinois by 1850. Structural patterns delineate the northern extent of southernness. Upland Southerners spread westward and northwestward
within a dynamic American diffusion network into the Lower Midwest (fig. 3.8).
I propose the emergence of a cultural core within the Upland South culture

region. As a key component of a new regional way station, it interconnected in the expanding four-tier urban-transport and culture region systems.

Families, relatives, and friends within the Upland South migration stream partic- ipated in a stepwise migration process. Originally, their descendants out-migrated from Pennsylvania, Virginia, and the Carolinas. They moved in transgenerational stages to Tennessee, Kentucky, Indiana, and Illinois. The neighborhood effect oper- ating within the social network of relatives and friends developed powerful chain migrations. Effective social networks interconnected origins and destinations that spawned stepwise movements between integrated, duplicated immigrant clusters. Channelized migration flows followed similar routes in the spreading Upland South culture region system.

Upland South migration clusters in Illinois interconnected with trans- Appalachian regional way stations in central Kentucky (Bluegrass Region), central Tennessee (Nashville Region), and southwest Ohio and southeast Indiana. Upland South secondary areas that had evolved in the late colonial period in western Vir- ginia and the North Carolina piedmont were also source regions in the diffusion system (Mitchell 1978, 74–78). Southern and central Illinois marked sequential stepping-stones in the circuitous spread of Upland Southerners. The Upland South settlement network dispersing northwestward achieved an increased level of mobility with improving road networks. Distinctive Upland South migration fields emerged in southern and central Illinois by 1850 (Meyer 1976b). Upland Southerners penetrated farther north of the National Road than scholars have recognized.

Making Maps of Immigrant Regions

County birthplace data or lifetime migration patterns of twenty-three native- born and ten foreign-born immigrant groups were obtained from the 1850 United States manuscript schedules. Adult males twenty years and older provide state and country of birth data. I examine the spatial sorting of thirty-three immigrant groups arrayed in Illinois' ninety-nine counties in 1850 (table 6.1). Standardized values (z-scores) depict immigrant patterns by scaling birthplace data with re- spect to their mean and standard deviation. This statistical method permits com- parative analysis of both larger and smaller immigrant groups' patterns at the county scale. Meinig provides a useful typology for delimiting the internal struc- ture of culture regions (1965). Zones of concentration emerge when a culture group disperses unhindered in its territorial expansion. Such a condition did not prevail when immigrant groups spread across midwestern plains in the early nineteenth century. Yet the conceptual framework of decreasing levels of immi- grant concentrations is applicable to analyzing the core-periphery structure of immigrant regions.

TABLE 6.1 Birthplaces of Adult Male Immigrants in Illinois, 1850

Birthplace	Number	Percentage	Cumulative Percentage
New York	23,054	11.7	11.7
Kentucky	20,066	10.2	21.9
Ohio	17,069	8.7	30.6
Germany	15,889	8.1	38.7
Illinois	14,319	7.3	46.0
Pennsylvania	13,451	6.8	52.8
Tennessee	12,079	6.1	58.9
Ireland	12,075	6.1	65.0
Virginia	11,602	5.9	70.9
England	7,911	4.0	74.9
North Carolina	6,740	3.4	78.3
Indiana	6,180	3.2	81.5
Vermont	5,000	2.6	84.1
Massachusetts	4,370	2.2	86.3
Connecticut	3,134	1.6	87.9
New Jersey	2,899	1.5	89.4
Maryland	2,891	1.5	90.9
Canada	2,436	1.3	92.2
South Carolina	2,223	1.1	93.3
Scotland	2,109	1.1	94.4
New Hampshire	2,074	1.1	95.5
France	1,442	.7	96.2
Missouri	1,333	.7	96.9
Maine	1,195	.6	97.5
Norway	823	.4	97.9
Delaware	650	.3	98.2
Georgia	646	.3	98.5
Switzerland	610	.3	98.8
Rhode Island	479	.2	99.0
Alabama	435	.2	99.2
Sweden	331	.2	99.4
Wales	256	.1	99.5
Michigan	220	.1	99.6
Other native-born	482	.2	99.8
Other foreign-born	423	.2	100.0
Total	196,896		

Source: Seventh Census Population Schedules, 1850

Distributional patterns divide into four levels of immigrant concentrations: core, domain, sphere, and avoidance. The immigrant concentration of *core* counties exceeds +1.50 standard deviation from the mean for that immigrant group. Core areas represent the concentration zone with the greatest density of occupancy by an immigrant group, that is, Ohioans or Germans. *Domain* concentrations associate usually with lateral spread of immigrants from core areas into contiguous counties. The slightly lesser dominance of an immigrant group represents a deviation range of +1.50 to +.75. Average or normal immigrant concentrations typify *sphere* counties and range between +.75 to −.25 deviation. Sphere concentrations delimit the zone of outer influence of an immigrant group. Peripheral in location, they reveal the dilution of material culture imprinting in the vernacular landscape by a dominant culture group. This investigation of diverse immigrant patterns comprises a fourth zone of concentration called *avoidance* areas. Immigrant groups did not disperse evenly in a state or large region. County z-scores ranging between −.25 to −2.00 standard deviation exemplify avoidance areas. The above four z-score intervals reveal the most representative distributional patterns.

Primary Upland South Population Sources

A dynamic Upland South backwoods culture rapidly colonized the eastern United States (Jordan and Kaups 1989; Mitchell 1978; Newton 1974; Mitchell and Newton 1988). The Northwest Territory, principally the Ohio Valley corridor, emerged as a primary destination for out-migrating Upland Southerners (Anderson 1943; Barnhart 1935a, 1935b, 1937a, 1937b, 1939, 1940, 1951; Turner 1897, 1906, 1920, 1935). Heightened "Illinois fever" altered the directional-bias of their movements northwestward (Barnhart 1939). Lifetime out-migration from southern states with extensive uplands comprised 388,059 Virginians, 283,077 North Carolinians, 257,643 Kentuckians, and 241,606 Tennesseans by 1850. Upland Southerners' destination states reveal migration processes that define massive population shifts into the interior (Lynch 1943; Owsley 1945).

Virginians emigrated to Ohio (22.1 percent), Kentucky (14.1 percent), Tennessee (12.0 percent), Indiana (10.8 percent), Missouri (10.5 percent), and Illinois (6.4 percent). The fusion of Tidewater and Midland material culture contributed to the creation of an Upland South cultural complex. Scholars differ on the precise hearth area whose geographic range stretches from southeast Pennsylvania through the Great Valley to the piedmont of the Carolinas (Newton 1974; Mitchell 1978). Recently, Jordan and Kaups argued for the fusion of Finnish and Indian woodland culture between 1640 and 1680 in the lower Delaware River Valley as the core area that molded Midland backwoods frontier culture (1989). In the late 1700s and early 1800s, Midlanders of Pennsylvanian origins provided the cultural imprint that configured a westward-penetrating domain area in the Lower Middle West.

The Shenandoah Valley of Virginia evolved as a staging area as the preadaptive forest culture complex diffused southwestward through the Great Valley and into the piedmont of the Carolinas. By the late 1700s and early 1800s, the Midland–Upland South cultural complex thrust northwestward through the Wilderness

Gap into transAppalachia (Jordan and Kaups 1989; Mitchell 1972, 1974, 1978; Mitchell and Newton 1988; Newton 1974). The tricultural nature of Virginians (Tidewater South, Midland, and Upland South) is supported by their destinations. Pioneer-hunters, yeoman farmers, and small plantation owners from Virginia migrated to Kentucky. The Bluegrass Region was attractive to yeoman farmers and small slave owners who shaped an agricultural settlement complex of steers, hogs, horses, flax, corn, and tobacco (Mitchell 1978). Kentucky was in number of settlers, politics, and culture a "daughter state" of Virginia (Barnhart 1941; Braderman 1939). Virginians crossed the Ohio River into Illinois (Eckenrode 1918).

North Carolinians out-migrated to Tennessee (25.4 percent), Georgia (13.3 percent), Indiana (11.7 percent), Alabama (10.1 percent), Mississippi (7.6 percent), Missouri (6.0 percent), Kentucky (5.0 percent), Illinois (4.9 percent), and Arkansas (3.1 percent). The state destinations of Virginians and North Carolinians reveal the dual character of their cultural-agricultural-environmental habitats. Stepwise migration patterns into adjacent states replicated "daughter states." First, Tennessee and then Kentucky became linked in the Upland South social networks spreading from piedmont North Carolina (Wooten 1953). Emigrants from the lowlands of North Carolina dispersed into Georgia tidewater areas. Indiana and Illinois attracted large numbers of Tar Heel Quakers. They moved to small, backwoods-pioneer clusters as individuals and groups within social-religious networks (Lindley 1912; Monaghan 1945; Rose 1986a).

Kentuckians' state destinations were principally Missouri (27.1 percent), Indiana (26.7 percent), Illinois (19.3 percent), Ohio (5.4 percent), Tennessee (4.9 percent), and Iowa (3.5 percent). In the early 1800s, Kentuckians emerged as an important population source or "mother state" for the Ohio Valley corridor states as they transplanted northwestward (Barnhart 1937a, 1937b, 1939, 1951; Chaddock 1908; Lang 1954; Lawlis 1947a, 1947b, 1947c; Rose 1985a, 1986c). Yeoman farmers from central Kentucky transferred across the Ohio River a mixed agricultural complex of corn, wheat, rye, hogs, and cattle. The mixed agricultural complex emerged fundamental to a marketplace agriculture in the Lower Middle West and an evolutionary root of Corn Belt commercial agriculture (Mitchell 1978; Power 1953a, 1953b).

Tennesseans' lifetime out-migration was directed to Missouri (18.6 percent), Arkansas (14.0 percent), Illinois (13.4 percent), Mississippi (11.4 percent), Kentucky (9.8 percent), Alabama (9.3 percent), Texas (7.3 percent), Indiana (5.3), and Georgia (3.4 percent). Their geographic mobility was principally a westward shift. As a proportion of the total population, Arkansas developed as a child of Tennessee, but Missouri and Illinois were more important destinations for yeoman farmers (Rogers 1968). A strong directional-bias of Upland Southerners transferring to southern Illinois was a natural outcome.

Primary Upland South Immigrant Patterns

Southern immigrants were the earliest native-born groups to settle the Prairie State. Upland Southerners dominated among the southern element, who comprised 35.3 percent of the native-born immigrants in Illinois by 1850 (table 6.2). Levels of immigrant cohesiveness varied with cultural backgrounds and potential destinations. Some southerners tended to concentrate within relatively few counties, whereas others dispersed into numerous counties. Kentuckians and Tennesseans epitomized an Upland South cultural heritage. These large migration streams were similarly distributed in core, domain, sphere, and avoidance concentration type counties (table 6.3). Immigrants from Virginia and North Carolina revealed both Lowland and Upland South cultural traditions. Upland traditions dominated, given the physical character of the source regions at the time. Virginians dispersed more widely across Illinois, given their greater proportions in avoidance areas. The immigrant patterns of Upland Southerners corroborate that settlement processes did not operate across smooth, uninterrupted immigrant surfaces. I posit that Kentuckians, the largest Upland South group, delineate the structural patterns that smaller groups typified and infilled. The spatial configurations of the four immigrant concentration types document the structural patterns and northward thrust of the primary Upland South groups.

Kentucky Immigrant Region

Kentuckians were the second largest immigrant group, 10.2 percent, but the largest Upland South immigrant group in Illinois by 1850 (tables 6.1, 6.2). Prior to the tremendous influx of New Yorkers in the late 1830s and 1840s, Kentuckians

Table 6.2 Birthplaces of Adult Male Upland Southerners in Illinois, 1850

Birthplace	Number	Percentage of Native-Born
Kentucky	20,066	13.15
Tennessee	12,079	7.92
Virginia	11,602	7.60
North Carolina	6,740	4.42
South Carolina	2,223	1.46
Georgia	646	.42
Alabama	435	.29
Mississippi	113	.07
Arkansas	42	.03
Total native-born	152,591	35.29

Source: Seventh Census Population Schedules, 1850

TABLE 6.3 Upland South Immigrants' Concentration Patterns in Illinois, 1850

Birthplace	Core Concentrations		Domain Concentrations		Sphere Concentrations		Avoidance Areas	
	No. Counties	% Migrants	No. Counties	% Migrants	No. Counties	% Migrants	No. Counties	% Migrants
Kentucky	9	30.2	10	20.4	30	32.6	50	16.8
Tennessee	10	32.7	11	22.7	24	30.2	54	14.4
Virginia	8	24.8	11	23.0	23	25.9	57	26.3
N. Carolina	6	21.0	13	26.1	28	35.6	52	17.3
S. Carolina	4	23.3	11	26.1	26	34.5	58	16.1

earlier had been the largest native-born immigrant group in the state. Initially, they settled extreme southern Illinois (Meyer 1976c). In the 1820s and especially after the Black Hawk War of 1832, they thrust north beyond the proposed National Road in overwhelming numbers. Kentuckians established a west-east settlement zone across the state's midsection (fig. 6.1). Bimodal migration clusters evolved on opposite sides of central Illinois with some 50 percent of all Kentuckians residing in these core and domain counties (table 6.3).

Two destinations comprised the largest Kentucky migration cluster in west-central Illinois. It included the southern portion of the Military Tract and Sangamon Country. This Kentuckian cluster formed a large, contiguous block of counties

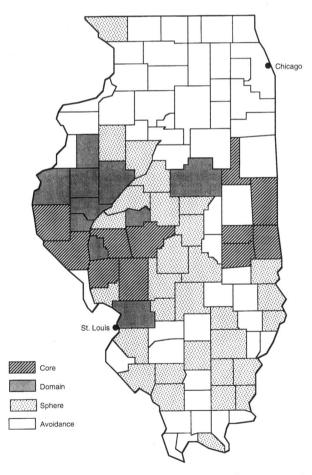

FIG. 6.1. Kentucky Immigrants in Illinois, 1850 (*Seventh Census Population Schedules, 1850*)

with a complete array of core, domain, and sphere counties straddling the lower Illinois River Valley. Immigrants read or heard attractive descriptions of the adjacent habitats in west-central Illinois. Between the Mississippi and Illinois Rivers, the Military Tract, with its dynamic, subregional nodes of Quincy in Adams County and Peoria in Peoria Country and their trade hinterlands, lured large numbers of Kentuckians (D. K. Meyer 1980).

Sangamon Country, east of the Illinois River, contained the dynamic, subregional nodes of Jacksonville in Morgan County and, some thirty miles eastward, Springfield in Sangamon County, the new capital. The intervening area and their individual trade areas had magnetic appeal for Kentuckians in the 1830s and 1840s (figs. 3.5, 3.6). Adjoining the southern portion of Sangamon Country was an earlier Upland South destination, the Goshen settlement. It evolved at the northern apex of the American Bottom. Goshen was situated in proximity to the subregional urban node of Alton on the Mississippi River in Madison County. A government land office operated in Edwardsville, some ten miles southeast of Alton. Both nodes existed in the hinterland of the entrepôt of St. Louis, some twenty miles southwest.

The six core counties in west-central Illinois straddling the Illinois Valley corridor had slightly over one-fifth of the adult male Kentuckians (fig. 6.1). Sangamon County had the largest number of Kentuckians in the state, some 1,100. Combining the core and domain counties reveals that the number of Kentuckians in the Military Tract (19.6 percent) and in Sangamon Country (21.2 percent) were similar in size. Their numbers corresponded to four out of ten Kentuckians in the state. Improved accessibility via the available water and land routes in the 1830s and 1840s was a primary factor contributing to the emergence of a large Kentuckian concentration that spilled over into contiguous counties in west-central Illinois.

In the early decades of settlement, a transient majority characterized community life. Faragher substantiates the significance of the stayer minority who comprised the "core of families that provided the continuity and cohesion necessary for communal life" (1986, 50–52). Small covenant communities bonded by relatives and friends served as powerful migration stimuli at the micro-scale destination level. Sugar Creek typifies geographical clustering of rural kinship pioneer neighborhoods in "siren" Sangamon Country (Faragher 1986). This commonplace frontier social community evolved in a timbered valley surrounded by prairie that lay immediately south of Springfield. Sugar Creek prior to 1840 was Upland South, with three-quarters of the heads of household out-migrating directly from Kentucky, Tennessee, and the upcountry of Virginia and the Carolinas (45). The remainder arrived from Ohio, Indiana, and Illinois but had been born in the South. During the Great Migration, many socially cohesive rural settlements emerged with the duplicity of backcountry frontier communities north of the Ohio River.

A much smaller Kentucky migration cluster emerged in east-central Illinois in the Wabash–Embarras–Little Wabash interstice river areas. The migration cluster does not exhibit the decreasing concentration types from a central core. The more recent settlement of this mixed timber and prairie country actually portrays the process of colonization and establishment of a discrete core. Initially, Upland Southerners favored timbered areas of the Shelbyville Moraine, tributary banks of the Wabash River, and edges of the large prairies where grasslands and trees interspersed. The spread process had not occurred to the degree where lateral expansion had created adjacent domain counties. The three core counties and the one domain county included some 10 percent of the state total of Kentuckians.

Land and water routes linked this Kentuckian cluster with central and western Kentucky. The peripheral subregional node of Terre Haute on the Wabash River served east-central Illinois. Upland Southerners dispersed via a slowly expanding regional road network that focused on the Kentuckian core cluster in east-central Illinois (figs. 3.3–3.7, 4.1, 6.1). Gateway Vincennes integrated with Louisville and Lexington. Kentuckians especially out-migrated from the Bluegrass Region. Immigrants from western Kentucky dispersed via available waterways and particularly the Nashville-Saline Trail, which linked with the spreading southern Illinois urban-transport network. Accessibility and connections varied over time and space as Kentuckians out-migrated to destinations in southern, west-central, and east-central Illinois.

A small, channelized migration flow of Kentuckians operated between the mid-1820s and the 1840s in east-central Illinois but with minimal lateral dispersal into adjacent counties. After 1850, the Kentuckian channelized migration flow failed to persist. In the 1850s and 1860s, east-central Illinois was overrun with Ohioans and Indianians as the Illinois Central Railroad contributed to the extensive settlement of the Grand Prairie (Meyer 1984). Kentucky immigrants did not develop a northern transitional boundary in east-central Illinois. Instead, a rather abrupt cultural divide formed to the north, owing to a social-perceptual-physical barrier caused by a large Yankee migration cluster; flat, extensive, poorly drained prairies; and inaccessibility of markets.

Figure 6.1 depicts the process of competition between the two primary Kentucky immigrant destinations. West-central Illinois, with its navigable waterways of the Mississippi and the Illinois and its emerging urban-transport structure, simply had far greater centrality and interconnectivity. It was more efficiently integrated within the evolving, westward-spreading national urban-transportation system and expanding Upland South culture region network. Galena territory, as an anomaly, pulled diverse immigrant groups to the lead mining frontier. The intervening territory between the two Kentucky migration cores infilled with an average concentration of Kentuckians (sphere counties), except for the three counties dominated with poorly drained prairies (avoidance counties).

A two-prong Kentuckian front aligned astride the integrating midstate land and water transport networks in the 1830s and 1840s. These migration thrusts penetrated the two core clusters in west-central and east-central Illinois. These Kentuckian circulation probes joined in McLean County in north-central Illinois. Improved steam navigation on the Wabash-Illinois-Mississippi Rivers increased the accessibility of northern areas. Infilling of the interstice between the rivers associated with expansions and improvements of the regional road networks. If Kentucky immigrant regions for 1850 were available for Missouri, Iowa, and Indiana (Rose 1985a, 1986c), a three-prong, northward migration front straddling the Mississippi-Illinois-Wabash Rivers would be documented. Kentuckians infiltrated farther north of the Shelbyville Moraine and National Road than suggested by scholars.

Far south of this northward migration spearhead, southern Illinois served as an intervening settlement area between central Illinois and central and western Kentucky population sources. Southern Illinois was traversed rather than substantially infilled by Kentuckians. Counties astride the primary water and land routes emerged as sphere counties with normal concentrations. This settlement process occurred because many southern Illinois counties over almost half a century witnessed a northward and westward stepwise migration of Kentuckians exploring new frontiers. Prior to 1850, west-central Illinois astride the Illinois Valley corridor became the mesmeric Kentuckian migration cluster.

Tennessee Immigrant Region

Tennesseans were the seventh largest adult male group, 6.1 percent, in Illinois by 1850 (table 6.1). Among Upland South immigrant groups, Tennesseans and Virginians were in a virtual tie (table 6.2). Tennesseans were similarly distributed as the Kentuckians among the four immigrant concentration types (table 6.3). The structural patterns of the Tennessee immigrant region was quite different from the Kentuckians (figs. 6.1, 6.2). An elongated Tennessee immigrant surface arrayed from southern to west-central Illinois. The immigrant axis aligned along the expanding regional urban-transportation networks that integrated the Ohio-Wabash and Mississippi-Illinois corridors (figs. 3.3–3.7, 4.1).

A Wilderness Road branch connected Shawneetown with central and eastern Kentucky. A more significant road for extreme southern Illinois, the Nashville-Saline Trail, funneled Upland Southerners from western Kentucky, central Tennessee, and the piedmont of North Carolina. The trunk line split in western Kentucky and crossed the Ohio River at Ford's Ferry in Hardin County and Golconda (Lusk's Ferry) in Pope County. Tennesseans, like their Kentuckian brothers, floated the Tennessee and Cumberland Rivers to reach southern Illinois. At this juncture, they had the flexibility of available land routes or the opportunity to

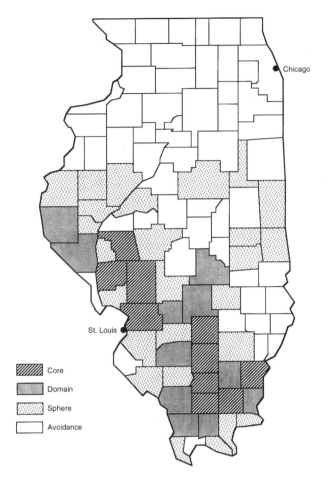

Fig. 6.2. Tennessee Immigrants in Illinois, 1850 (*Seventh Census Population Schedules, 1850*)

continue by water to west-central or east-central Illinois. Directional-bias of Tennesseans was influenced by the northward-penetrating navigable waterways and entwined road networks in southern and central Illinois.

Prior to statehood, the timbered, rolling topography in extreme southern Illinois received the earliest Tennessee immigrants. Chain migration perpetuated the clustering of individuals and groups along the north-trending immigrant axis. These Tennesseans desired the type of timbered hill country from which they emigrated (Meyer 1976c). Channelized migration flows produced a spillover of Tennesseans into adjacent counties. Others opted for the attractiveness of southwest

Illinois and Sangamon Country. Step-by-step migration patterns operated as Tennesseans who had lived in southern Illinois chose to migrate northwest to more fertile lands and, they hoped, greater opportunities.

News of successful Tennessee settlements along this southeast-northwest migration spearhead filtered back home by way of visitations by relatives and friends, return trips back home, and letters. Tennesseans, like other Upland Southerners, en route to their Illinois Country destinations, visited with or stayed awhile with relatives and friends. Such social networks created and sustained a chain migration process through time. Intervening contacts kept the diffusion network interconnected between rural areas and urban places in transAppalachia. A safety-net effect functioned within the Upland South culture diffusion network as family, friends, ethnic groups, and people of similar traditions and faith migrated in a stepwise migration fashion among Tennessean settlements.

Churches were organized everywhere in early-nineteenth-century Illinois. Religious affinity played an active and significant role in the spearheading of new settlements and the enlarging of older settlements on the frontier. Common to migration streams from the Upland South, New England, and Midland culture regions and foreigners who molded the cultural pluralism of Illinois were the information flows occurring within religious networks. Family and parish formed critical covenant bonds within the hierarchy of religious ties. Gjerde contends that the addition of regional or provincial bonds and ethnicity or nationality relationships produce a four-tier hierarchy within immigrant covenant communities (1979). Churches within dispersed rural settlement areas or urban places furnish a focus for individual, family, and group participation in and commitment to community ties. Channelized migrations that link social networks forge persistence of communal bonds. Past effects of religious affinity on community are evident in the landscape today with isolated spires of country churches, church towers punctuating village and town tree lines, and lofty, twin-tower, cathedral-like edifices in city ethnic neighborhoods.

Protestantism in Illinois originated with immigrant families from Tennessee and Kentucky (Stock 1919, 1). Scotch-Irish Tennesseans actively promoted the expansion of churches. "The first Baptist Church was organized in New Design, Monroe County, February 29, 1795. . . . This was the first Protestant Church in Illinois" (Landis 1923, 137). James Lemon, founder of the New Design settlement, and his sons were instrumental as itinerant evangelists in the founding of the first eight Baptist churches in Illinois (Stock 1919; Thrapp 1911). John Mason Peck, who was commissioned by the American Baptist Foreign Missionary Society, was a classic, circuit-riding preacher who emerged as one of the "Church Fathers of Illinois" (Stock 1919, 1–2). Peck "preached, organized Sunday Schools, argued the missionary cause, pleaded the temperance case, and collected money in the interest of education" (3). He founded Rock Spring Seminary and Shurtleff College in

Alton, where they merged in 1835, published the first religious newspaper in Illinois, authored and published a number of historically significant Illinois gazetteers, and organized anti-slavery societies (Babcock 1965; Stock 1919).

Other evangelical churches, Presbyterians and Methodists, sent their missionaries in the late eighteenth and early nineteenth centuries to organize churches in southern and central Illinois (Eller 1987; Harker 1925; Hayter 1936; Landis 1923; Lentz 1927; Patterson 1881; Short 1902; Stock 1919). The diffusion of the Presbyterian church symbolized a spatial cue of Scotch-Irish within the eighteenth- and early-nineteenth-century westward-expanding American frontier (Mitchell 1966). Tennesseans' dispersal influenced the location of Presbyterian and Cumberland Presbyterian churches in Illinois (Allen 1916; MacMillan 1919; Landis 1923). Presbyterian missionaries arrived in 1797 at Kaskaskia, and Cumberland Presbyterians appeared around the time of statehood. The first Presbyterian church was organized at Sharon in White County in 1816 (Short 1902, 60). Benjamin F. Spilman, who arrived in Golconda on the Ohio River in 1823, was to Presbyterianism what Peck was to Baptists in Illinois (Short 1902, 60; Stock 1919, 13). The Massachusetts and Connecticut Missionary Societies stimulated Presbyterian New Englanders' interest in Illinois Country by the early 1820s (Stock 1919, 12–13).

The first Methodist preacher from Kentucky arrived in Illinois in 1793. In 1803, a regular missionary was assigned by the Western Conference in Kentucky to ride a circuit in the American Bottom and its upland verge (Barnhardt 1919, 153). The preaching stations included Kaskaskia, New Design, Shiloh, Goshen, and Wood River (Stock 1919, 8–11). Three years later, the first Methodist church was built at Goshen in Madison County. The early influential Methodist circuit rider who held camp meetings in southwest Illinois beginning in 1807 was Jesse Walker. Walker, born in Virginia, preached in Tennessee and Kentucky and was affectionately known as the "Daniel Boone of the Methodist Church" (Barnhardt 1919, 175). Having been appointed to the Chicago Mission, he was instrumental in building the first Methodist church in Chicago in 1833 (179–80).

Another key Methodist preacher in Illinois was the Virginia-born Peter Cartwright. He left the slave state of Kentucky in 1823, making Pleasant Plains in Sangamon County his base of operations. He was an effective preacher, an outspoken anti-slavery proponent, and a strong supporter of the Methodist system of itinerant, circuit-riding preachers and camp or revival meetings. In time, he presided over a district stretching from the Ohio River to Galena (Stock 1919, 10). His ministerial career embraced twenty years in the South and forty-five years in Illinois, where he repeatedly served as the presiding elder of the Illinois Conference (Chamberlin 1902; Harker 1925). Barnhardt argues that the strength of the Methodist church on the Illinois frontier was the ability of its itinerant preachers to provide "the scattered settlers a religious life, a church organization, its worship and instruction" (199). Barnhart (1939) and Hayter (1936) stress the role of the

Methodist, Baptist, and Presbyterian churches in directing the southern element from the lower classes, not the aristocracy, into the Ohio Valley borderlands.

The Tennessee immigrant region formed bipolar migration clusters. In contrast to the west-east alignment of Kentuckians, Tennesseans formed a southeast-northwest settlement axis. The older migration cluster in southern Illinois, about one-third of the state total, developed domain counties around the core counties that spread a northward wedge that bifurcated at the National Road (figs. 3.4–3.7). Domain counties straddling the National Road linked the Tennessean migration clusters of southern and central Illinois. The substantial growth of the larger migration cluster during the 1830s and 1840s embraced channelized migration flows that tied southern Illinois with eastern, central, and western Tennessee. The core counties of Williamson, Franklin, Jefferson, and Marion arrayed along the major south-north road in the interior of southern Illinois by the 1840s. All the county seats became primary market centers for small hinterlands. The old road linkage for these settlement beads evolved as Illinois 37. Today, Interstate 57 follows this early Tennessean movement-settlement corridor.

The early emergence of Tennessean and North Carolinian migration clusters in the Shawnee Hills of southern Illinois possibly relates to land set aside for veterans, "The Old Soldiers' Reservation." "In October 22, 1787, the Continental Congress prescribed an area in the Northwest Territory where a discharged soldier of the Revolutionary War would receive 100 acres of his choice. Beginning at the mouth of the Ohio River; thence up the Mississippi to the mouth of the Au Vase [Big Muddy]; thence up that stream to a line running straight west from the mouth of the Little Wabash; thence east along that west line to the Wabash; thence down the Wabash and the Ohio, to the beginning" (Moyers 1931, 26). Environmental attributes of forested hills and valleys in the Shawnee Hills were very attractive to Upland Southerners during the territorial and early statehood periods.

The west-central Illinois cluster of core and domain counties included about one-fifth the state total of Tennesseans. At the National Road crossroads location, Tennessean settlement choices were between migrating northward to colonize the Shelbyville Moraine area or angling westward to the Edenic settlements in the Military Tract, Sangamon Country, and American Bottom (Goshen). The migration decision-making process was made easier as Tennessean social networks reinforced destination choices. Tennesseans joined with the migration flows that intermingled in west-central Illinois. The hills and timberlands akin to their home environments in Tennessee were especially attractive in the counties on either side of the lower Illinois River Valley. Perhaps the more important reason for settling in the interstice between the Mississippi-Illinois Rivers was that the land—the Military Tract—had been set aside for veterans of the War of 1812 (Landis 1923; Carlson 1951; D. K. Meyer 1980).

Tennesseans paralleled Kentuckians' northward dispersion into west-central and east-central Illinois (figs. 6.1, 6.2). Tennesseans were outnumbered but generally out-migrated greater distances than Kentuckians. The northward migration thrust of Tennesseans into central Illinois was greatly reduced. There emerged a northern peripheral settlement zone of sphere concentration counties far north of the Shelbyville Moraine and the National Road. Upland South immigrant groups uniformly agreed in their avoidance of Yankee northern Illinois and the Grand Prairie setting in east-central Illinois.

Virginia Immigrant Region

Virginians were the ninth largest immigrant group, 5.9 percent, and the third largest Upland South group in Illinois (tables 6.1, 6.2). Their immigrant surface delineates greater dispersion than Kentuckians or Tennesseans (figs. 6.1–6.3). Why were Virginians more spatially dispersed? Virginians embraced complex ethnic, social, economic, and cultural backgrounds. Potential Midland, Lowland South, and Upland South heritage expresses the cultural diversity of Virginia settlers. These attributes enhanced the greater lateral spread of the Virginia settlement surface. A stepwise migration from Virginia proffered a filtering and fusion process of new culture traits acquired in the regional way stations of southwest Ohio and central Kentucky (Mitchell 1978). In addition, distance-decay, social behavior, and environmental perception possibly influenced the Virginians to associate with diverse population origins. Potential economic and social advancements were probably a stronger pull factor than the safety-net bond of immigrant cohesion. Virginians reveal a more widespread diffusion in avoidance counties than other southerners, northerners, and foreigners (table 6.3).

The Virginia immigrant region embraced fragmented migration clusters. The Virginian core and domain concentration type counties configured a horseshoe-shaped immigrant surface. Stretching from the Wabash-Embarras Valleys to the Mississippi-Illinois Valleys were four Virginian core concentration areas linked with domain counties across central Illinois. Two Virginia migration clusters evolved in the Military Tract. One centered on the Mississippi Valley core county of Adams with Quincy. The other Virginia core focused on the middle Illinois Valley counties of Fulton and Peoria. Peoria emerged as the key riverside node in the Illinois Valley corridor with a marketplace hinterland that stretched east-west with the regional road network and upstream and downstream on the waterway (figs. 3.4–3.7, 4.1).

The Sangamon Country core of Morgan and Sangamon Counties with Jacksonville and Springfield integrated westward with the Military Tract. Trade connections developed southward via water and land routes with the Goshen and Turkey Hill settlements in southwest Illinois. Riverside Alton in Madison County and upland Belleville in St. Clair County and their mercantile hinterlands were

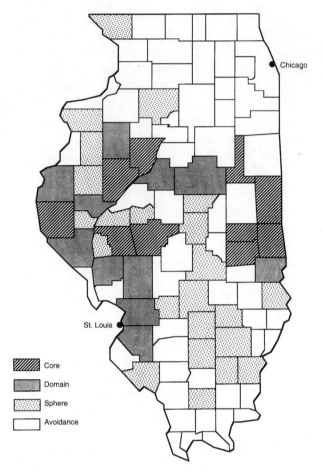

FIG. 6.3. Virginia Immigrants in Illinois, 1850 (*Seventh Census Population Schedules, 1850*)

attractive destinations tied to the entrepôt of St. Louis. The east-central Illinois core, adjacent to Terre Haute, comprised Edgar, Vermilion, and Coles Counties. Virginian core and domain counties north of the National Road embraced almost 50 percent of the state total. Sphere counties did not develop in contiguous fashion between Sangamon Country and the Wabash Valley corridor. Instead, they disclose a south-north alignment with the evolving interregional road network linking southern and central Illinois.

Sangamon County had the largest concentration of Virginians in Illinois, 4.5 percent. The overall spatial structure of Virginians hints at strong attachments for settling in counties with vigorous, urban places within the road-steamboat networks.

Subregional nodes (Quincy, Peoria, Jacksonville, Springfield, Alton, and Terre Haute) and lower-level nodes (Galesburg, Rushville, Pittsfield, Carrollton, Carlinville, Belleville, Bloomington, Danville, Charleston, Paris, and Marshall) were connected within the expanding urban road networks in east-central, west-central, and southern Illinois. Each lower-level node was a courthouse, market, agricultural processing, and distributive center for a small hinterland.

In this respect, the Virginia immigrant structure interspersed within the other Upland Southerners' settlement frameworks. Combining the number of Virginians in core and domain counties documents the Virginian migration cluster with the greatest migration pull. In west-central Illinois, the combined Military Tract cluster, 18.6 percent of the state total, had a substantially larger number of Virginians than its rival Sangamon Country with its southwest Illinois extension, 15.1 percent. The east-central Illinois cluster encompassed one out of ten Virginians. Their destination choices and northward penetration into central Illinois were similar to those of the largest Upland South group, Kentuckians (figs. 6.1, 6.3).

The Virginia immigrant region represents an end product of a migration flow that segmented into a number of micro-scale channelized migration flows. The individual routes that were traveled bifurcated the channelized migration streams of Virginians across central Illinois. Virginians' immigrant structure evolved within the framework of an Upland South diffusion network expanding across continental America. Its northward settlement spearheads hurdled beyond the Ohio Valley corridor and National Road but ended abruptly as a cultural divide at the physical-perceptual-cultural barrier of expansive prairies and Yankeeland.

North Carolina Immigrant Region

North Carolinians, the eleventh-largest immigrant group in Illinois, 3.4 percent, were about half the immigrant group size as Tennesseans and Virginians in 1850 (table 6.1). They were the fourth-largest Upland South immigrant group (table 6.2). Concentration type counties and immigrant patterns infer distinctive North Carolinian characteristics (table 6.3, fig. 6.4). The percentage of North Carolinians in core counties, 21 percent, was the least for any major native-born immigrant group, but they created more domain counties (table 6.3). Over one-fourth of them resided in domain counties, the highest percentage of the major native-born groups. Almost 36 percent of the North Carolinians settled in sphere concentration counties, showing their widespread dispersion.

Midland–Upland South material culture traditions characterized North Carolinians who out-migrated from piedmont rather than lowland plantation traditions. They participated in a stepwise migration through Tennessee and Kentucky, as evidenced from children's birthplaces. Figure 6.4 documents the discrete, segmented clusters of North Carolinians in west-central and southern Illinois. Intervening sphere counties linked the bipolar migration clusters of core and domain counties.

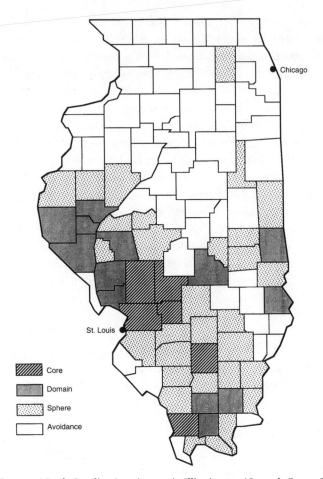

FIG. 6.4. North Carolina Immigrants in Illinois, 1850 (*Seventh Census Population Schedules, 1850*)

The North Carolinians' immigrant surface reveals a dispersion along a southeast-northwest settlement axis, similar to the Tennesseans (figs. 6.2, 6.4). The fragmented settlement structure hints at differences in North Carolinians' cultural traits.

North Carolina was settled by English, Scotch-Irish, Irish, and Germans. Immigrants arriving in Illinois during the early 1800s particularly out-migrated from the North Carolina piedmont counties of Iredell, Cabarrus, and Rowan (Monaghan 1945; Wooten 1953). Piedmont Carolinians descended from German Lutherans, German Reformed, German Baptist Brethren (Dunkers), Moravians, Quakers, and Scotch-Irish Presbyterians who had emigrated from southeast Pennsylvania through the Great Valley before the Revolutionary War (Bernheim

1872; Elbert 1985; Eller 1987; Harkey 1866; Haupert 1922; Monaghan 1945; Sifferd 1911; Wooten 1953). The Scotch-Irish and Irish tended to disperse widely in small family farm groups. Various German groups, known as Pennsylvania Germans, generally established small agricultural, ethnic enclaves.

Harkey (1866) and Bernheim (1872) argue the significant role of covenant communities on the Illinois frontier formed by German Americans from North Carolina who were descended from colonial Germans. Ethnic church communities were influenced by the processes of chain and cluster migration at their origins and destinations. An early German American covenant network linked piedmont North Carolina with central and southern Illinois. They created both dispersed, church-related rural communities and nucleated covenant communities in marketplace centers. Channelized migration flows persisted through a diffusion network of German Lutheran, Reformed, and Moravian settlements that developed small ethnic pockets in the North Carolina immigrant region. A sense of ethnic cohesion was reinforced with their German language usage in worship services and schools (Bernheim 1872, 180).

The propensity of German Americans to cluster in a social-religious context increased the effectiveness of the social networks driving the chain migration process. Individuals and groups with German backgrounds out-migrated from particular churches and rural communities. Such closed channelized migration flows preserved the essential elements of the covenant community in the insular frontier. Ethnic, covenant destinations fostered less risk, better security, and greater permanence for migrating family units. Channelized flows engendered kinship networks the means to disperse into the fertile lands of the New West, but facilitated within religious-social-cultural-ethnic constraints and bonds.

Monaghan argues that Tar Heels settled in small family groups, mixed with diverse groups, and were not organizers of colonies or towns (1945). Environmental affinity played a role in their destinations: "On the Wabash, the western boundary of Indiana, a belt of timber girded the stream. This was typical 'North Carolina Country'" (448). Anti-slavery Quakers were micro-scale flows within the North Carolinian migration stream. Quakers refrained from proselytizing pioneer families and moved into the Old Northwest at a slow pace. Their covenant communities of Friends or "meetings" were primarily in southern Indiana by 1830 (Monaghan 1945; Rose 1986a). Monaghan contends, "The next generation of Quakers coming from North Carolina settled among their friends and relatives instead of going on to Illinois" (421). Indiana had almost three times as many North Carolinians as Illinois in 1850.

A circuitous migration route originating in southeast Pennsylvania by the early eighteenth century replicated stepwise settlements through the Great Valley of Virginia and to the piedmont of North Carolina. By the late 1700s, North Carolinians dispersed into Tennessee and Kentucky. Numerous push factors influenced the growing North Carolinian out-migration. Agricultural-related forces were significant in the migration decision: growth of commercialized cotton farming, declining soil productivity, increasing soil erosion, decreasing crop yields, and inadequate markets. Growth in cotton production encouraged the small yeoman farmer to leave his land for the New West. Social-cultural-economic push factors created an urgency to migrate (Wooten 1953). The price received for agricultural products and the costs of necessities at distant markets were out of balance. Population pressures and a shift from self-sufficiency to marketplace agriculture placed undue stress on the land and people. Compelling social and religious issues also plagued the Carolina piedmont and would not disappear: the pros and cons of slavery and distilling grain. The use of slave labor in cotton production was not in universal agreement. Social disagreement "arose as to whether distilling grain and manufacture of liquor was right or wrong" (Wooten 1953, 70). Large amounts of cheap, fertile land, location on navigable rivers, and increased employment opportunities in growing communities were powerful pull factors. By 1850, the out-migration of North Carolinians left a visible landscape of abandoned houses and farm lands.

By the early 1800s, a dynamic North Carolinian diffusion network dispersed migration-stimulating information concerning potential destinations in central and western portions of Tennessee and Kentucky, southern Indiana, and southern Illinois. Letters and visits were exchanged among friends and relatives. This filtering of information promoted a chain migration process between origins and destinations. Families, singly or in groups, followed a westerly and northwesterly stepwise migration pattern to old and new destinations deeper in the continental interior. Intervening visits with relatives and friends eased the burden, risk, and stress of traveling and softened the adjustment to new lands. Information obtained enlarged and strengthened an expanding Upland South culture region system as it became interwoven with channelized migration flows that shaped immigrant diversity in midcontinent.

North Carolinian diffusion networks spatially configured bipolar primary destination areas in Illinois by 1850. The smaller North Carolinian migration cluster of core and domain counties accounted for 13 percent of the state total. This oldest migration cluster focused on the southern Illinois core county of Union (fig. 6.4). Arriving from the North Carolina piedmont in 1807, German-speaking Lutheran pioneers were attracted to the hunting and farming potential of the Mississippi floodplain and especially the Shawnee Hills habitat in Union County (Elbert 1985, 97–98; Meyer 1976c, 156). These woodland frontiersmen were followed shortly by a chain migration of relatives and friends. A channelized migration flow operated for a few decades and spilled over into contiguous counties.

A strong covenant-ethnic factor (Lutheran, Reformed, and Brethren) contributed to these early North Carolinians' clustering tendency. Whether descendants of

Pennsylvania Germans who migrated from North Carolina to Union County or who migrated directly from Pennsylvania to Jackson County, people of German heritage located in close proximity to other German-speaking settlements (Buck 1967, 107; Elbert 1985; Eller 1987). Illinois Lutheranism originated in 1807 in Union County with the North Carolinian settlements. The oldest Lutheran congregation, St. John's Church at Dongola near Jonesboro, was organized in 1816. Several congregations existed by 1834 in Union County (Elbert 1985, 97–98, 107).

By 1830, another North Carolinian destination was established in Montgomery County in west-central Illinois. Centering around Hillsboro, St. Paul's Evangelical Lutheran Church, with thirty-five members, was founded by Rev. Daniel Scherer, who emigrated from St. John's Church in Cabarrus County (Elbert 1985, 100–101, 111). Being the only Lutheran pastor in Illinois for a number of years, Reverend Scherer rode a circuit that included congregations in Hillsboro, St. John's in Union County, Mt. Carmel in Wabash County, and Shelbyville in Shelby County. A German American settlement network emerged as a micro-linkage in the larger North Carolina migration flow that operated in a spreading Upland South culture region system.

New Lutheran congregations (later affiliated with the Lutheran Church–Missouri Synod, the Lutheran Church of America, and the American Lutheran Church) were organized in west-central and southwest Illinois during the 1840s by German Americans from North Carolina, Pennsylvania, and Ohio. These migration clusters centered on church as community. They often became the rural ethnic enclaves and ethnic neighborhoods of cities that welcomed the incoming flood of Old World Germans in the 1840s, but especially after the Civil War (Elbert 1985, 109–12). The vast majority of North Carolinians who settled Illinois were German Reformed, "Far Western" Brethren or Dunkers, Moravians, or Quakers and of Scotch-Irish and English descent. A map of Far Western Brethren Congregations, 1810–50, emphasizes the growing attractiveness of west-central Illinois in configuring North Carolinians' immigrant surface (Eller 1987, 89).

The rolling, forested lands with interspersed small grassland areas stretching across southwest and west-central Illinois developed as the focus of the largest North Carolinian migration cluster of core and domain counties, about 28 percent of the state total. This magnetic migration cluster spread a full array of immigrant county concentration types (fig. 6.4). Besides the allure of large amounts of cheap, fertile land on either side of the lower Illinois River Valley, the land had been painted as an environmental ideal between northern and southern Illinois (Mitchell 1837, 19–22, 25–28). The settlement area included the northern part of the American Bottom, the Military Tract, and Sangamon Country. Stretching eastward from the core counties evolved a linear migration cluster astride the Wabash River and east-central Illinois road network that included about 8 percent of the North Carolinians (figs. 3.5–3.7). A micro-scale, channelized migration flow of kith and kin settled Kane County in Yankee northern Illinois. This isolated anomaly of North Carolinians materialized principally in townships bordering the Fox Valley.

Another petite cluster of North Carolinians formed in southeast Illinois. An ethnic-covenant bond distinguished the Edwards County Moravian settlement. Albert P. Haupert, pastor of the Moravian church in West Salem, noted that this German American community originated in 1830 (1922). Named "New Salem" because the inhabitants were from "Old Salem" in North Carolina, the community changed its name in 1854 in deference to New Salem in Menard County (82). The settlement grew for two decades, owing to channelized migration flows from the colonial Moravian settlement of Salem, North Carolina, and of German Moravians from Saxony in 1849. For nearly ten years, the North Carolinian Moravians had their services in English and the German Moravians in German. Each congregation division had its own minister and officers but utilized the same church edifice and cemetery. Finally, two independent congregations formed in 1858 in a village of two hundred individuals, only to be reunited in 1915 (Haupert 1922, 84–85).

North Carolinians tended to settle in sphere counties (table 6.3). This greater tendency to disperse configured intervening surfaces of contiguous sphere counties that connected major migration clusters. These sphere counties were astride the southeast-northwest-aligned road networks that linked southern, southwest, and west-central Illinois. Located within this intermediate sphere area was an isolated core county. Early trunk and bridging roads that dispersed Upland South immigrants between the Ohio-Wabash and Mississippi-Illinois corridors intersected at Mt. Vernon, the courthouse and market center of Jefferson County. The connectivity of this crossroads community was attractive to North Carolinians (fig. 6.4) and Tennesseans (fig. 6.2). The structure of the North Carolina immigrant region paralleled other primary Upland South groups (figs. 6.1–6.4). Given the smaller group size and distance-decay from their places of origin, their northward settlement thrust remained in the southern tier of central Illinois counties.

Why did Tennesseans (fig. 6.2) and North Carolinians (fig. 6.4) mold similar immigrant surfaces? As noted, their immigrant regions reveal migration clusters in southern, southwest, and west-central Illinois. In both cases, the southern Illinois core originated first as the immigrants were attracted to the rocky hills and bluffs, forested areas, numerous springs, river valleys, and similar climate of their former homeland (Smith 1940, 41). The Tennessean migration cluster in southern Illinois experienced significant infilling and lateral spread into contiguous counties during the 1830s and 1840s; by contrast, the North Carolinian migration cluster remained relatively small. The micro-scale channelized migration flow comprising German Americans from the piedmont region persisted in the core county of Union. North Carolinians were the largest immigrant group in only one

Illinois county. The core counties of Jefferson and Union existed as anomalies within the south-north wedge of Tennesseans across southern Illinois.

For the later North Carolinians and Tennesseans, environmental affinity and social-cultural cohesion factors that made southern Illinois initially attractive appear not as powerful determinants for their destinations. The primary reason for the polarity of the Tennessee and North Carolina immigrant structures (figs. 6.2, 6.4) identifies with what Smith calls "an alluring temptation coming from the great prairies in the central part of the state" (1940, 41). Many early Upland Southerners who settled the prairie margins of central Illinois were probably discouraged by a few cold winters, difficulties in breaking the prairie sod, limited availability of firewood, and isolated social-religious community existence. They frequently returned to previous destinations within the diffusion networks of their kinfolk and the hospitable hills of southern Illinois. Yet by 1850, the North Carolina and Tennessee immigrant structures substantiate a different story. The lure of large amounts of available, cheap, and fertile lands, water accessibility of destinations, and initial adoption of the extensive forested areas of the interstream hill areas and bluffs and valleys of the Mississippi-Illinois Rivers made west-central Illinois the settlement destination of choice by the late 1830s. The timber margins of the smaller prairies of west-central Illinois adjacent to the lower Illinois River Valley increasingly formed pioneer settlement intrusions.

Cultural adaptations to the mixed woodland–prairie environs served as a training ground for the utilization of the larger interior prairies (McManis 1964). The Grand Prairie in east-central Illinois, the extensive prairies in northern Illinois, and the prairies in the northern Military Tract were still empty by 1850 (figs. 5.5, 5.6). McManis argues that Upland Southerners, like many immigrants of the 1840s, "were either unwilling or technically unable to settle outside timbered land" (87). The "trial and error" evaluation of the smaller prairies and emerging subregional nodes in southwest Illinois, the Military Tract, and Sangamon Country enhanced these magnet settlement areas.

Secondary Upland South Immigrant Patterns

By 1850, lifetime out-migration from Lower South states included 186,479 South Carolinians, 122,954 Georgians, and 83,388 Alabamians. South Carolinians outmigrated principally to Georgia (28.0 percent), Alabama (26.1 percent), Mississippi (15.0 percent), Tennessee (8.2 percent), and Illinois (2.2 percent). Georgians emigrated primarily to Alabama (48.0 percent), Mississippi (14.2 percent), Florida (9.2 percent), Texas (6.2 percent), Arkansas (5.2 percent), Louisiana (4.8 percent), Tennessee (4.0 percent), and Illinois (1.1 percent). Alabamians migrated to Mississippi (40.8 percent), Texas (14.4 percent), Arkansas (13.5 percent), Louisiana (8.8 percent), Tennessee (7.7 percent), and Illinois (1.6 percent). Southerners settling

Illinois from South Carolina, Georgia, and Alabama were of upland, rather than lowland, origins. Micro-scale migration flows dispersed via Upland South diffusion paths established by the macro-scale migration streams. Secondary immigrant groups, South Carolinians (2,223), Georgians (646), and Alabamians (435), comprised only 2.2 percent of the native-born adult males in Illinois by 1850 (table 6.2). They generally mirrored the structure patterns of primary immigrant groups.

South Carolina Immigrant Region

The South Carolina immigrant surface depicted an Upland South regional settlement pattern from southeast-northwest (fig. 6.5). The structural patterns parallel all four primary Upland South immigrant groups (figs. 6.1–6.4). The early South Carolinian colonizing elements formed a migration cluster of core and domain counties in southern Illinois. The settlement growth was molded by the parameters established by the expanding regional road networks shortly after statehood in 1818 (figs. 3.3–3.4). Of the four core counties, three unfolded in the southern portion of the migration cluster. Randolph County, with 9.4 percent of the South Carolinians, had almost double those in Perry County and triple those in Hamilton County. Pioneers of Irish and Scotch-Irish descent frequented the margins of colonial, transAppalachian, and midcontinental settlement frontiers. The disproportionate number of South Carolinians in Randolph County were from the South Carolina piedmont. "The Plum Creek settlement east of the Kaskaskia River in Randolph County was a vigorous and influential Irish community, from which have sprung many of the leading citizens of the county. They came from Abbeyville, South Carolina, and were known in Randolph County as the 'South Carolina Irish'" (McGoorty 1927, 60).

An isolated anomaly emerged in Yankeeland. The core county of Kane had 5.0 percent of the South Carolinians. Channelized migration centered on township destinations in the Fox Valley. Almost half of the South Carolinians resided in Aurora Township (fig. 6.5). As noted earlier, North Carolinians created an isolated sphere county (fig. 6.4). North Carolinians were slightly less in number in Kane County. They were more dispersed but still concentrated in the Fox Valley, with St. Charles Township having almost one-fourth of the North Carolinians. The South Carolina immigrant surface periphery corresponded to the northwest lateral spread of dispersing Upland Southerners. A contiguous cluster of sphere counties unfolded north of the National Road in west-central Illinois. South Carolinians focused their settlements in southwest Illinois, Sangamon Country, and the Military Tract. Their destinations linked within the expanding road networks of the late 1830s and 1840s (figs. 3.5–3.7). Almost 60 percent of the Illinois counties were avoided (table 6.3). Yankee northern Illinois and prairie east-central Illinois characterized the primary avoidance areas.

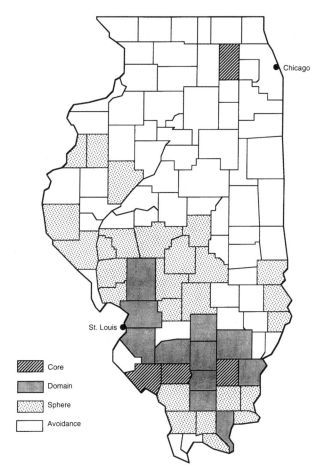

FIG. 6.5. South Carolina Immigrants in Illinois, 1850 (*Seventh Census Population Schedules, 1850*)

Georgia and Alabama Immigrant Regions

Although a diminutive immigrant group, the Georgian immigrant surface conformed to the typical southeast-northwestward dispersal pattern of Upland Southerners (table 6.2, fig. 6.6). The contiguous migration cluster of core and domain counties superimposed the expanding regional road and waterway networks. Both Clinton and Madison Counties within the core area had 5 percent of the Georgians, respectively. Peripheral areas displayed the two-prong, northward thrust of Georgians on either side of the state. Pocket-size immigrant destinations formed on opposite sides of northern Illinois. Small Upland South immigrant groups culturally avoided the Yankee North.

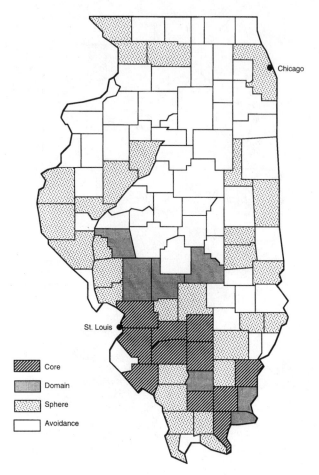

FIG. 6.6. Georgia Immigrants in Illinois, 1850 (*Seventh Census Population Schedules, 1850*)

Alabamians were the smallest Upland South secondary group (table 6.2, fig. 6.7). Their immigrant surface delineates fragmented core and domain counties, with the largest contiguous migration cluster concentrated in extreme southern Illinois. The largest number of Alabamians resided in the core counties of Union and Williamson, each with about 5 percent of the total. Alabamians dispersed north of the National Road by 1850 but principally in a northwesterly direction toward Sangamon Country in west-central Illinois. Georgia and Alabama immigrants dispersed among other Upland Southerners.

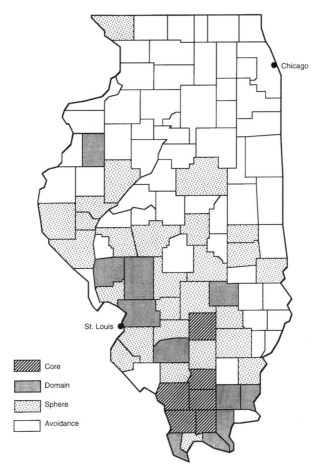

FIG. 6.7. Alabama Immigrants in Illinois, 1850 (*Seventh Census Population Schedules, 1850*)

Making Maps of Culture Regions

Synthesizing the ninety-nine county migration fields, which included twenty-three native-born immigrant groups, documents the Upland South, New England, and Midland-Midwest culture regions in Illinois at mid-nineteenth century. A geographical analysis differentiates the structural components of the culture regions: cores, peripheries, boundaries, divides, and mixtures. I explore four general assumptions: (1) a large number of American immigrants from a particular population source region create a spillover effect, causing contiguous counties to evolve similar discrete migration fields within a settlement region; (2) principal route-ways and entryways spawn directional-biases of selected migration streams that foster distinctive migration field regions; (3) the structure of migration field regions consist of core, domain, sphere, and avoidance type counties; (4) finally, Upland South and New England migration flows configured a distinct north-south polarity in the state.

Each county's migration field consisted of all birthplace states, except those excluded owing to insignificant numbers or grouped under the heading of "other." A native-born birthplace field contained those states from which a county's immigrants were born and used as a surrogate for a county's native-born migration field. To analyze the structure of the culture regions at the time of first effective settlement, I employed a factor analytic approach. I analyzed the data for each county's native-born migration field by the principal component method, with the resulting factors having eigenvalues greater than unity rotated to a varimax solution (Dixon 1973). Factors were rotated by means of both orthogonal and oblique solutions. Because the oblique solution exhibited very low correlations among the factors and both solutions evidenced the same basic factor structure, the factor loadings resulting from orthogonal rotations were employed. Despite questions raised concerning Q-mode factor analysis, factor loadings were mapped (Rummel 1970).

Of the six factors, only the strongest three were used. They account for 88.1 percent of the total variance in the original structure. These factors also represented the three primary native-born migration flows peopling Illinois. The Upland South factor emerged as the strongest, with New England and the Midland-Midwest comprising the second and third factors. Illinois' discrete culture regions integrated within an expanding American culture region system. As noted earlier, Meinig furnishes a useful typology for delimiting the structure of culture regions (1965, 1969). Three zones of concentration—core, domain, and sphere—emerge when regional culture groups diffuse unhindered. Such a condition did not exist when migration streams dispersed across the interior during the early 1800s. The basic concept of decreasing concentrations is appropriate for studying the structure of native-born migration field patterns that serve as a surrogate of the developing culture regions at the closing of the Illinois frontier.

Core concentrations represent a central zone portraying the greatest density of occupancy by a regional culture group. Factor loadings greater than 0.65 designated counties within the core or center of a culture region. Factor loadings ranging from 0.65 to 0.33 depict domain concentrations where a regional culture group is dominant. By contrast, sphere concentrations (0.33–0.00 loading) of a regional culture group delimit the zone of outer influence and, thereby, are peripheral in location and acculturation (Meinig 1965). This study incorporates a fourth zone, called avoidance areas. Not all potential destinations in a settlement surface were attractive to immigrants. Avoidance areas designate county factor loadings with a negative value.

Upland South Culture Region

The spatially extensive Upland South culture region in Illinois evolved as a convergence zone within an integrated American culture region system (fig. 6.8). A mixture of backwoods pioneers and yeoman farmers from the Upland South spread across southern and central Illinois. Midland–Upland South adaptive cultural strategies and traditions formed a versatile farming-hunting-gathering

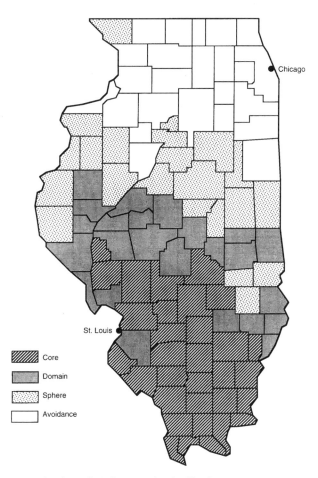

FIG. 6.8. Upland South Culture Region in Illinois, 1850

complex of traits that dispersed across the American backwoods frontier (Jordan and Kaups 1989, 8–9, 29–35). Jordan and Kaups argue that the cultural preadaptive strategy of Midland America diffused by Upland Southerners to the temperate woodlands enhanced their rapid occupation of interior environments (32).

The coherence of primary and secondary immigrant structures hint at shared cultural traits among Upland Southerners (figs. 6.1–6.7). Their widespread destinations demonstrate the versatility and success of their cultural strategy. The Upland South culture region represents a time-space summation of this powerful migration stream. As the earliest wave of American immigrants arriving in Illinois, they molded a contiguous culture region with decreasing concentrations arrayed from south to north. The Upland Southerners initiated the distinctive cultural dichotomy engraved into the state's regional settlement structure (fig. 6.8). Prior to 1830, they formed a riverine settlement pattern in southern Illinois with an outlier in Sangamon Country (fig. 5.5). In the ensuing two decades, they infilled southern Illinois and rapidly settled central Illinois. This dispersion into the state's interior meant that a spillover effect caused contiguous counties in southern Illinois to emerge as the Upland South core.

The Upland South immigrant structures indicate a hegemony in the culture region core. The structure of the Upland South core counties masks other state groups in the overwhelming numbers of Kentuckians, Tennesseans, Virginians, and North Carolinians. New England and Midland-Midwest immigrant patterns, with their repeated southern avoidance areas, appear to spatially corroborate their meager influence in southern Illinois. County migration fields in southern and central Illinois, where Upland South core counties evolved instead, reflect considerable differentiation. Inland and fringing riverine core counties reveal subtle heterogeneity in their population origins.

The Upland South core counties bordering the Ohio River and in the southern interior had a trace of New Englanders and an influx of Midwesterners and Midlanders. Southern Illinois core counties adjacent to the Mississippi and Wabash Rivers had substantially larger numbers of Yankee New Yorkers and even greater numbers of Midwesterners from Ohio and Indiana and Midlanders from Pennsylvania. A cultural linkage developed in the fringing Upland South core counties on both sides of the state. Equivalent numbers of Ohioans and Pennsylvanians existed in most counties. The core counties astride the Mississippi River that had greater accessibility to or were contiguous to St. Louis witnessed a substantial cultural mix of Upland South, New England, and Midland-Midwest immigrants. Upland Southerners were not as lopsided in their dominance as in inland core counties.

The Upland South core counties bisected by the National Road had substantial proportions of Midwesterners and Midlanders. Cultural heterogeneity prominently emerged in the southern tier core counties in central Illinois peripheral to

Sangamon Country in west-central Illinois. With improved accessibility to the Illinois Valley and a denser road web, the proportions of Midwesterners, Midlanders, and New Englanders increased significantly in the Upland South core counties. The relative location of the Upland South core in southern Illinois and its northward penetration into central Illinois was expected, with immigrant dispersion operating in vigorous migration flows. Yet the subtle cultural mixings in the core counties attest to diversity rather than a cultural homogeneity in regional settlement expansions.

The domain counties adjacent to the northern Upland South core counties typify an extraordinary immigrant pluralism in transitional central Illinois. An array of domain counties stretched between the Wabash and Mississippi riverine corridors. The greater northward spread of domain counties in the Illinois Valley corridor in west-central Illinois was influenced by waterborne accessibility. The early Upland South destinations in Sangamon Country and the southern margins of the Military Tract in the 1820s and 1830s was confirmed. Kentuckians were the largest state group in most domain counties, but Virginians were generally second- or third-largest. But what distinguishes the domain counties' migration fields in central Illinois was the dominant role of Midwesterners from Ohio and Indiana and increased numbers of Midlanders from Pennsylvania and Yankee New Yorkers. The small cluster of domain counties in east-central and southeast Illinois in the Wabash Valley corridor mirrored the migration streams of central Illinois. A true cultural mixing area epitomizes the east-to-west Upland South domain zone in central Illinois.

Immigrant diversity in central Illinois could have developed as either core, domain, or sphere counties in one of the three potential culture regions. Sangamon Country emerged as the only magnetic settlement area that failed to unravel as a core area of any culture region. Instead, its counties originated as domain counties of the Upland South and Midland-Midwest culture regions and sphere counties of the New England culture region. Representing a quintessential settlement platform, Sangamon Country personifies midwestern cultural mixing. Zelinsky (1973) and particularly Hudson (1984b) argue that cultural mixing in the Middle West was a late-nineteenth-century settlement development. The cultural vitality and regional settlement convergence promoted by "Illinois fever" in the 1830s and 1840s confirms a dynamic cultural mixing area in west-central Illinois by 1850.

Northward penetration of Upland Southerners via the Mississippi, Illinois, and Wabash Rivers and the expanding road networks created an extensive sphere area (fig. 6.8). A surge in Midwesterners, Midlanders, and New Englanders won the settlement competition with Upland Southerners. Ohioans were generally the largest county population source, with Pennsylvanians and New Yorkers second or third. Kentuckians and Virginians in the migration field rankings of sphere counties were now in fourth through sixth place. If the southern half of central

Illinois was characterized by the dominance of Upland South elements in the domain counties, the northern half marks a cultural reversal. West-central Illinois sphere counties had a substantially larger pluralistic immigrant influx from the primary American migration streams than the Grand Prairie–dominated east-central Illinois. Given their diffusion pathways, New Englanders were not as prevalent in east-central Illinois as in the Illinois Valley corridor in west-central Illinois. Jo Daviess County in northwest Illinois emerged as the only northern Upland South anomaly.

Yankee northern Illinois was avoided by large numbers of Upland Southerners. The northern boundary for avoidance counties did not abruptly emerge adjacent to domain counties, which would have indicated a strong cultural divide. Rather, the avoidance boundary abuts with periphery sphere counties aligned east-west. Upland Southerners' peripheral settlement spearheads were considerably farther north in Illinois than previously recognized by scholars. The northern array of Upland South sphere counties demarcates a cultural transition zone. The Upland South settlement edge was not a latitude-specific boundary. Two Yankee penetrations thrust southward into central Illinois. In west-central Illinois, they extended to Peoria and its extensive hinterland astride the Illinois River. In east-central Illinois, they probed southward by way of the road network that connected Chicago with Danville.

The convergence of migration flows in the state's midsection, particularly west-central Illinois, generated competitive settlement expansions in this cultural borderland. The sequential Upland South culture region patterns demonstrate a strong core/periphery framework. Upland Southerners behaviorally experienced a real and perceived sense of inclusion within a distinctive material culture group that spread into midcontinent. Legible, diagnostic Upland South landscape elements were etched into the rural and urban landscapes in southern and central Illinois. Place images imprinted in the cultural landscape included houses, barns, fences, pioneer log structures, a Midland-southern dialect, foodways, a diverse stockman-farmer-hunter economy, and Shelbyville courthouse square types (Jordan and Kaups 1989; Meyer 1975; Mitchell 1978; Newton 1974; Price 1968; Zelinsky 1973). Remnant Upland South traditions persist in the twentieth-century landscape.

7

New England Immigrant Regions

That portion of Illinois, situated in the northern part of
the state ... is known by the appellation of the Rock River
Country. It is a fertile agricultural region, combining all the
advantages of a rich and fruitful soil, a healthy and temperate
climate, a fine navigable river, and clear perennial streams, affording
excellent mill-seats.
—Mitchell 1837

Western boosterism perceived Illinois as a potential "garden spot" (Mitchell
1837; Peck 1836, 1837). Numerous attractive destinations emerged in the expanding growth areas of northern and west-central Illinois. Rock River Country
emerged as a key settlement area for New Englanders in northern Illinois (Buckingham 1942). An early traveler romanticized the valley: "The country bordering
on Rock River, in nearly its whole length, is one of the most beautiful that can be
imagined" (Farnham 1846, 284). The Illinois Valley corridor and Illinois and
Michigan Canal formed a bridge corridor to west-central Illinois' Military Tract
and Sangamon Country. According to Mathews, easterners' penetration southward extended as far as a line east-west above Springfield (1909, 215).

Arriving in northern Illinois, Yankees replicated a New England model landscape with its Congregational and Presbyterian village churches. Kofoid argues
that New England missionary societies influenced the spread of Presbyterianism
in southern Illinois in the early pioneer years and the later transplantings of Congregational churches in northern Illinois (1906). Congregationalism originated in
Illinois in 1833 (Savage 1910, 79). Heinl noted that Congregationalism and New
England attitudes and values influenced the religious, educational, social, and cultural life of Jacksonville in Morgan County in west-central Illinois (1935).

Congregational ministers functioned as dominant personalities in fashioning
covenant communities in the New England settlement scheme in northern Illinois (Savage 1910). Twenty-two Yankee colonies were planted primarily in northern Illinois in the 1830s (Mathews 1909, 214). Many Yankee groups out-migrated

from New England "fully equipped with pastor, schoolmaster, and eastern ways of life" (Billington 1950, 32). "The northern part of the State was settled in the first instance by wealthy farmers, enterprising merchants, millers, and manufacturers. They made farms, built mills, churches, school-houses, towns, and cities; and made roads and bridges as if by magic" (Ford 1854, 280).

Power asserts that religion was the spearhead of Yankee imperialism in the Upper Middle West (1953a, 5–7). Geographical propinquity as a mechanism of cohesion was important to New Englanders. "Yet it is not intended to say that only the Yankees saw the advantages of migrating in such numbers as to afford a congenial concentration. The Germans often went in force to rural as well as city destinations. Presbyterians from Kentucky and Quakers from the Carolinas concentrated on certain counties in Ohio, Indiana, and Illinois" (13). Whether because of social, cultural, and religious institutions or because of a tendency to mass-migrate, Power argues that Yankee areas were more homogeneous (34).

New Englanders were not common in early southern Illinois. Brown observed, "It was rare to meet an individual who claimed a birthplace east of the mountains, and still more rare to find a family who had emigrated from the Eastern States" (1881, 82). Immigrants from eastern States were differentiated "from their Western neighbors by their 'Yankee notions and Yankee fixings'" (82). Southerners "formed the opinion that a genuine Yankee was a close, miserly, dishonest, selfish getter of money, void of generosity, hospitality, or any of the kindlier feelings of human nature. . . . The northern man believed the southerner to be a long, lank, lean, lazy, and ignorant animal, . . . one who was content to squat in a log-cabin, with a large family of ill-fed and ill-clothed, idle, ignorant children. The truth was, both parties were wrong" (Ford 1854, 280–81). These stereotyped images of Yankees versus southerners were often perpetuated by later writers. Buck concluded that New England influences on Illinois politics prior to the Black Hawk War of 1832 were generally greater than previously thought (1912–13). He addressed the interpretation of many early writers that southerners directed strong animosity toward the few Yankees in the southern and central portions of the state. Buck argued that Yankees "were held in aversion by certain classes, but the idea that this feeling was universal or even widespread, among the small farmer class which make up the bulk of the Southern element fades away in the light of the extent to which these same 'Yankees' were elected to office in nearly every part of the State" (61).

Yankee immigrant regions portray a strong tendency for spatial convergence in Illinois by 1850. Structural patterns depict the southern extent of northernness in Illinois. New Englanders dispersed westward across northeast America within an American diffusion system (fig. 3.8). I hypothesize the genesis of a New England culture region and a cultural core. As an essential element of a new regional way station, it fused with spreading four-tier urban-transport and culture region systems.

Yankees dispersing into the Upper Middle West achieved a mobility level that earlier Upland Southerners required decades to develop. The mercurial spread of midwestern canal building and improvements in steam navigation were taken advantage of by New Englanders. Increasing ease and decreasing time and cost of traveling via the Great Lakes–Erie Canal trunk route reduced the likelihood of New Englanders' westward stepwise migration pattern. Yankees left directly from farms, villages, and towns in New England and regional way stations in the expanding New England culture region. Their social networks stretched eastward to the regional way stations in northeast Ohio (Western Reserve) and western New York, secondary areas within the periphery of New England, and the culture hearth of southern New England (Mitchell 1978, 74–78).

Prior to 1850, a north-south polarity of Yankee modernizers and Upland South traditionalists was etched in the Illinois landscape (Jensen 1978). Power notes the importance of the written word: "Letter writing and the diffusion of print explain why the Yankees knew more about the West in advance of migration than the Uplanders evidently knew. Recourse to print and script also made the Yankees more deliberate and selective in deciding where to migrate than were the men who came westward through the Cumberland Gap" (1953a, 42). Illinois typifies the diverse migration streams settling the Middle West during the Great Migration. Yankee migration fields concentrated in northern Illinois by 1850 (Meyer 1976b). Yankees dispersed farther southward in the Lower Midwest than scholars have acknowledged.

Primary New England Population Sources

New Englanders rapidly settled the northern half of the Old Northwest in the two decades prior to 1850 (Anderson 1943; Holbrook 1950; Hudson 1984a, 1986, 1988; Mathews 1909; Stilwell 1948; Turner 1897, 1906, 1920, 1935). Westward drift was channeled via the northern movement corridor (Mathews 1910). Yankees converged on northern Illinois, which also included Midlanders and foreigners (Hudson 1986, 1988; Meyer 1976b, 1976c). Lifetime out-migration of emigrants from primary New England states and New England extended comprised 547,218 from New York, 199,582 from Massachusetts, 154,891 from Connecticut, and 145,655 from Vermont by 1850. Disproportionate numbers of Yankees in northern states suggest a westward population spearhead. During colonial times, Yankee cultural traditions dispersed from a southern New England hearth area into northern New England and westward to the Mohawk corridor in upstate New York. With the Erie Canal's emergence, a New England extended region expanded into continental America with a strong latitude-specific shift.

Southern New England origins dominated the formation of regional way stations in western New York and the Western Reserve in northeast Ohio (Hudson

1986, 1988; Mitchell 1978). Hudson stresses that the next Yankee generational shift westward was dominated by New Yorkers. A stepwise migration pattern linked southern Michigan in the 1830s, southeast Wisconsin and northeast Illinois in the 1840s, and southern Minnesota in the 1850s. A narrow Yankeeland arrayed across the Upper Midwest. Lifetime state destinations of New Yorkers in 1850 support the sequential nature of Yankee movements: Michigan (24.4 percent), Ohio (15.4 percent), Wisconsin (12.5 percent), Illinois (12.3 percent), Pennsylvania (10.8), Indiana (4.4 percent), and New Jersey (3.8 percent). Michigan and Wisconsin emerged as "daughter states" of New York (Fuller 1935; Rose 1986b; Alexander 1946).

The second-largest Yankee group in the New West was from the New England culture hearth. Emigrants from Massachusetts transferred to New York (27.9 percent), Indiana (11.7 percent), Ohio (9.4 percent), New Hampshire (9.3 percent), Maine (8.3 percent), Vermont (7.6 percent), Rhode Island (6.0 percent), Connecticut (5.7 percent), Illinois (4.6 percent), Michigan (4.1 percent), and Wisconsin (3.2 percent). Powerful community conformity espoused in the religious-political-educational values of the New Englanders emerged as symbolic icons. Distinctive Yankee cultural imprints—churches, meeting halls, common houses, barns, and agricultural practices—were replicated across the Upper Middle West.

Out-migrants from Connecticut created a narrow directional-bias to their state destinations: New York (42.7 percent), Ohio (14.8 percent), Massachusetts (10.1 percent), Pennsylvania (6.0 percent), Illinois (4.5 percent), and Vermont (2.9 percent). Vermonters' lifetime out-migration was directed to New York (36.1 percent), Massachusetts (12.1 percent), Ohio (9.8 percent), Illinois (7.8 percent), New Hampshire (7.7 percent), Michigan (7.6 percent), and Wisconsin (7.0 percent). The pivotal role of western New York as an adaptive, replicated regional way station within New England extended is substantiated by its proportion of New Englanders. New York furnished a large pool of second-generation New Englanders to the Middle West. The increasing mercantile hegemony of the northern waterway trunk line connecting New York with gateway lake ports spatially compressed Yankee migration flows.

Primary New England Immigrant Patterns

Yankees from New England and New England extended embraced 25.9 percent of the native-born immigrants in Illinois in 1850 (table 7.1). Geographical propinquity was strongly influenced by place, cultural, and historical consciousness. The primary Yankee groups clustered a larger proportion of their population in a few core and domain counties, over 60 percent, than the other native-born migration flows (table 7.2). A smaller proportion of Yankees created sphere counties. East-central and southern Illinois comprised a large contiguous area that Yankees spatially shunned.

TABLE 7.1 Birthplaces of Adult Male New Englanders in Illinois,
1850

Birthplace	Number	Percentage of Native-Born
New York	23,054	15.11
Vermont	5,000	3.28
Massachusetts	4,370	2.86
Connecticut	3,134	2.05
New Hampshire	2,074	1.36
Maine	1,195	.78
Rhode Island	479	.31
Michigan	220	.14
Total native-born	152,591	25.89

Source: Seventh Census Population Schedules, 1850

Similarity of cultural heritage, spread of migration stimuli, and dynamic settlement processes spawned a dispersing ripple effect in destinations. I suggest that New Yorkers, the largest immigrant group within the New England migration stream, fixed the predominant structural patterns that smaller groups mirrored. Spatial expressions of the four levels of immigrant concentration types corroborate the structural patterns of the primary New England groups and their southward penetration.

New York Immigrant Region

In the 1840s, the number of New Yorkers swelled in Illinois, supplanting Kentuckians as the largest adult male group, 11.7 percent (table 6.1). New Yorkers were the largest Yankee New Englander group in the state by 1850 (table 7.1). Dispersing northwestward, westward, and southwestward from Chicago, they established a large, contiguous migration cluster in its developing hinterland (fig. 7.1). Almost 60 percent of the New Yorkers resided in the core and domain counties of this pivotal northern sector. A full range of immigrant concentration types emerged straddling the radiating roads extending to the Mississippi-Illinois corridors (figs. 3.5–3.7). A secondary migration cluster in the Military Tract comprised about 8 percent of the New Yorkers.

Yankees read and heard attractive place image descriptions of this northern Illinois habitat. Improved transportation was a primary factor in the rapid growth of northern Illinois (Lee 1917). The appeal of the Fox and Rock River Valleys attracted large numbers of New Englanders. Norris and Gardiner sketched a quintessential picture of these Yankee destinations:

TABLE 7.2 New England Immigrants' Concentration Patterns in Illinois, 1850

Birthplace	Core Concentrations		Domain Concentrations		Sphere Concentrations		Avoidance Areas	
	No. Counties	% Migrants	No. Counties	% Migrants	No. Counties	% Migrants	No. Counties	% Migrants
New York	9	47.5	7	19.1	18	21.0	65	12.4
Vermont	7	41.6	5	13.7	27	34.1	60	10.6
Massachusetts	11	46.5	7	16.7	20	24.4	61	12.4
Connecticut	8	38.8	10	24.6	19	23.6	62	13.0
New Hampshire	10	45.3	4	10.0	27	35.2	58	9.5
Maine	10	44.0	9	22.5	22	23.5	58	10.0

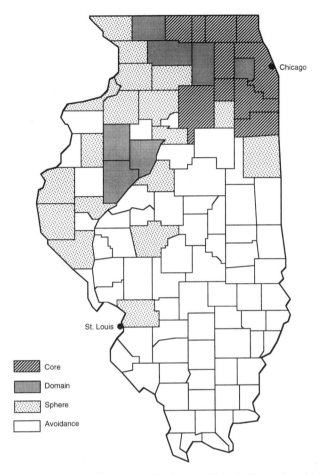

Fig. 7.1. New York Immigrants in Illinois, 1850 (*Seventh Census Population Schedules, 1850*)

The Fox and Rock River Valleys, including the northern tier of counties, have become justly celebrated, and are fast being occupied by an industrious and enterprising population. These are fertile agricultural regions, rejoicing in a rich soil, generally an abundant supply of timber, clear streams with gravelly bottoms, and an unlimited supply of waterpower; every part of these valleys being convenient of access to the Lakes and the Mississippi, the market is sure and steady. Flourishing manufacturing towns are springing up along the Fox and Rock Rivers, and in a few years it will become the richest agricultural and manufacturing region in the country. (1847, 18)

A decade earlier, Peck (1836, 1837) and Mitchell (1837) fabricated Edenic Fox and Rock River Valleys.

After the Black Hawk War of 1832, Kentuckians and Tennesseans predominated in the Rock River Valley (Buckingham 1942). Buckingham notes that "in the Rock River Country the southerner came farther north than anywhere else to colonize side by side with the later advancing Yankee" (241). By the late 1830s, Yankee waves arrived. The building of the Illinois-Michigan Canal was opposed by those who feared that Yankees would overwhelm the state. Tyler suggests that immigrants of Scotch-Irish and English stock by the early 1800s emerged as New England families on the Illinois frontier (1942).

Migration stimuli contrived by a generation of western promoters diffused through New England social networks. Their effectiveness integrated the structure of the New York immigrant region (fig. 7.1). Nearly 50 percent of the New Yorkers settled in the contiguous core counties in northeast Illinois. A disproportionate one in ten New Yorkers resided in Cook County, with two-thirds concentrated in Chicago. Almost 12 percent of the New Yorkers settled in the fringing Fox River core counties of McHenry and Kane. The settlement axis aligned with a vectored demographic thrust along the Chicago-Galena Road. Other diverging roads to the Mississippi River engendered contiguous domain and sphere counties.

Within the core and domain counties, flourishing commercial, agricultural processing, and distributive centers had emerged by 1850, such as the lower-level nodes of Elgin, St. Charles, Geneva, Aurora, Rockford, Oregon, and Freeport. Each courthouse and market center connected with Chicago and the eastern seaboard via the Great Lakes–Erie Canal trunk route. The upper Illinois Valley and Illinois and Michigan Canal became a movement-settlement corridor for New Yorkers. Will and La Salle Counties emerged as core counties. New Yorkers were concentrated in the townships with the canal towns of Lockport, Joliet, Ottawa, and La Salle and the river town of Peru. Other favorite destinations were those townships with access to Chicago or bordering the canal and the Illinois, Fox, and Du Page Rivers.

The immigrant dispersion process fashioned a lateral extension of connected sphere counties southwest into west-central Illinois. Almost 8 percent of the New Yorkers settled in the domain counties of Peoria, Fulton, and Knox in the Military Tract. The county seat and market centers of Fulton and Knox Counties were linked via roads to the riverside subregional node of Peoria. The intervening areas between the Mississippi-Illinois Rivers, lower-level nodes, such as Princeton and Pittsfield, and the subregional node of Quincy were attractive destinations for New Yorkers. In east-central Illinois, the New Yorkers failed to develop an extensive southern transitional settlement area. A rather abrupt perceptual-physical-cultural barrier appeared to the south with the large Upland South imprint; extensive, poorly drained prairies; and inaccessible markets. Avoidance areas spread to the Ohio Valley in eastern Illinois. Twelve percent of the New Yorkers dispersed in the avoidance areas, which included two-thirds of the counties (table 7.2).

Northern Illinois embraced a number of Yankee colonies as distinctive covenant communities. Hubbard described the role of Congregational pastors in fostering "western fever" in the Genesee Country of western New York. A religious awakening blossomed in the 1830s in Genesee Country. The missionary, revival spirit warranted the creation of Yankee covenant communities in the New West and centered on religious-educational institutions. In the quiet, western New York community of Bergen, Rev. Jairus Wilcox of the local Congregational church emerged as the initial propangandizer of "western emigration fever," conceived in 1831. In 1836, forty individuals traveled the difficult overland mud routes across Ontario, Canada, southern Michigan, and northern Indiana, through the Illinois Valley corridor to Princeton in Bureau County, then to Henry County and prairie isolation (1937).

An earlier exploring committee had selected a location, purchased farm land, and surveyed a town plat with particular reference to the church and school. The Geneseo colony acquired two thousand acres of "fine, rich, rolling land suitable for the homes of a small agricultural community" at the Galena government land office (Hubbard 1937, 410). The Geneseo colony of Yankees was established near the center of Henry County. Coinciding with the Geneseo colony were the Yankee colonies of Andover, fifteen miles to the south, and Wethersfield, twenty miles to the southeast. This triangle of New England colonies imprinted the prairie landscape with a distinctive Yankee appearance.

New Yorkers etched a legible New England material culture stamp in the rural and urban landscapes in northern Illinois. To a lesser degree, the Yankee cultural imprinting was replicated in Peoria on the Illinois River and in Quincy on the Mississippi River. The river towns were integrated to St. Louis and New Orleans to the south, but the linkage of Peoria via Ottawa to Chicago improved significantly with the Illinois and Michigan Canal opening. Two isolated sphere counties, Sangamon with the state capital and Madison with riverside Alton, show the New Yorkers' southward penetration.

In west-central Illinois, Peoria, the linchpin node of the Illinois Valley, was attractive to New Yorkers and New Englanders. A fertile agricultural hinterland, central crossroads location, and hustling mercantile, manufacturing, and service activities nurtured Peoria as a secondary New Yorker cluster (Barrows 1910, 88). The river town embodied a New England landscape ambience. "Peoria is the most beautiful town on the river. . . . The town is neatly laid out in rectangular blocks, the streets being wide and well graded. A public square has been reserved near the present center. The place wears quite a New England aspect; its schools and churches are prosperous, and its society is good" (Curtiss 1852, 317).

Vermont Immigrant Region

Vermonters were the largest adult male group from nuclear New England and the thirteenth-largest immigrant group in Illinois (tables 7.1, 6.1). Among the four primary Yankee New England groups, Vermonters were more dispersed in sphere counties (table 7.2). The Vermont immigrant region parallels the dominant New York immigrant structure (figs. 7.1, 7.2). A prominent north-south avoidance area in eastern Illinois was typical of Yankees. Settlement timing, push-pull factors, and dispersion patterns unfolded a large, contiguous migration cluster. Almost 55 percent of the Vermonters concentrated in the core and domain counties in northeast Illinois. Their spread promoted a westward spillover of contiguous sphere counties extending to the Mississippi River in northwest Illinois. Vermonters' dispersion into the Illinois Valley corridor fostered an areally extensive penetration into west-central and southwest Illinois.

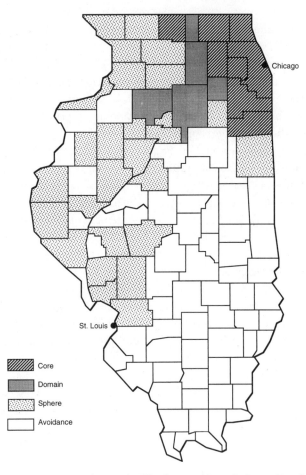

FIG. 7.2. Vermont Immigrants in Illinois, 1850 (*Seventh Census Population Schedules, 1850*)

Vermonters portray decreasing immigrant concentrations from a northeast migration cluster. Core-periphery relationships developed a northeast-southwest alignment. The contiguous nature of the decreasing structural patterns, with the largest number of sphere counties stretching beyond the magnetic Vermont core and domain counties, hint at the spread of farmers in search of cheap, fertile lands (fig. 7.2). West-central Illinois, with its alluring Military Tract and Sangamon Country, fit this need. This conterminous Vermonter surface structure was not shaped by other Yankees.

The navigable waterways aided the earlier northward settlement thrust of the Upland South migration stream far beyond the National Road in west-central Illinois. In the 1840s, improved steamboat navigation on the Illinois River increased the greater southward spread of Yankees. The intersecting road networks in northern and central Illinois linked the lower-level node of Rockford and the subregional nodes of Springfield, Jacksonville, Quincy, Peoria, and Alton (figs. 3.5–3.7). Lower-level nodes were connected to evolving regional urban-transport networks. Accessible trading hinterlands of these centers encouraged the formation of New England settlements deep into west-central and southwest Illinois.

Improved New England connections between origins and destinations coincided with regular Great Lakes steam navigation service. It dramatically reduced the frictional effect of distance, cost, and time. The increasing pace of the chain migration process formed numerous micro-scale, channelized migration flows that brought about rapid out-migration from Vermont to the Upper Middle West. Stilwell characterizes Vermont out-migration of the 1830s as the "Great Migration" and of the 1840s as "A Sequel with a Climax" (1948). The Great Lakes–Erie Canal movement corridor emerged as a channelized trunk line for the westward-expanding New England culture region system. Cheap, fertile, rolling timberlands, small prairies, and mill sites reinforced the numerous destination choices in northern and west-central Illinois.

Northern Illinois was the primary objective of Vermonters who, like other Yankees, organized colonies. Colony formations created channelized migration flows between origins and destinations within the larger New England migration stream. Covenanted communities and organized societies, such as Benson, Vermont, to DuPage County in 1832, tended to be extremely cohesive, micro-channelized flows of Puritan enthusiasm (Mathews 1909, 212; Stilwell 1948, 190). They evolved from small population pools that ebbed in a short time and rural villages, towns, or particular Congregational churches in nuclear and extended New England (Mathews 1909, 212–16). Yankee place consciousness is evident in such replicated township names as Rutland, Burlington, and Genoa and such village names as Vermont, Geneseo, and Woodstock.

Massachusetts Immigrant Region

Massachusetts settlers were the third-largest group within the Yankee migration stream but the fourteenth-largest immigrant group (tables 7.1, 6.1). They dispersed northwestward, westward, and southwestward from gateway Chicago (fig. 7.3). Like other New Englanders, they were most numerous in Cook County. Chicago served as the regional entrepôt for the evolution of settlement and commercial agriculture in northeast Illinois. It had a greater proportion of Yankees than rural Cook County: Vermont, 51.2 percent; New Hampshire, 58.4 percent; Rhode Island, 60.5 percent; Massachusetts, 66.6 percent; New York, 67.2 percent; Maine, 67.3 percent; and Connecticut, 71.6 percent. The four levels of immigrant concentration were similar to other Yankee immigrant groups (table 7.2). The Massachusetts immigrant region was fragmented. The immigrant structure did not develop a regular sequence of decreasing concentration zones from a central cluster of core and

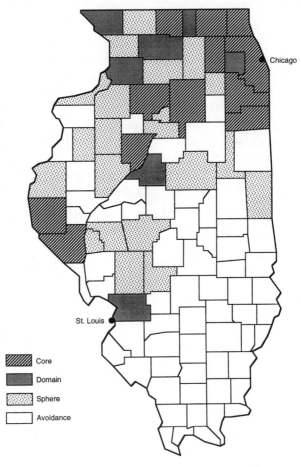

FIG. 7.3. Massachusetts Immigrants in Illinois, 1850 (*Seventh Census Population Schedules, 1850*)

domain counties in northeast Illinois. Avoidance counties were splintered, but the largest areas were in east-central and southern Illinois.

Almost 50 percent of the Massachusetts immigrants settled in northern Illinois. The elongated northeast-southwest settlement axis underscored the increasing influence of the Illinois Valley corridor and recently opened Illinois and Michigan Canal. The valley served as a major dispersion artery linking northeast Illinois with the Military Tract and Sangamon Country in west-central Illinois. The movement-settlement corridor functioned as a homogenizer rather than a segregator of spatial interaction. As a centrifugal movement system, land routes and waterways were connected to a New England culture region diffusion network (figs. 3.5–3.7). As a centripetal movement system, Chicago effectively connected its agricultural-mercantile hinterlands with radiating bridge and feeder routes.

The attractiveness of thriving urban centers is implicit in the segmented structure of the Massachusetts immigrant region, six core clusters and two isolated domain counties. Massachusetts represented a New England state where the spatial dynamics of early industrialization were already producing manufactured goods for both regional and national markets. The magnetism for many Massachusetts adult males of the emerging regional marketplace and incipient manufacturing centers, such as Chicago, Rockford, Galena, Ottawa, Peoria, Quincy, and Alton, was expected. Dynamic urban centers normally attracted 25 to 50 percent of the Massachusetts immigrants in a county.

Individuals, groups, and colonies contributed to the Massachusetts immigrant surface. In 1831, the Hampshire colony organized in Northampton, Massachusetts. It assembled in Albany, New York, for its westward Great Lakes–Erie Canal journey to Princeton in Bureau County, an early Yankee colony with "Illinois fever" (Dodge 1932; Mathews 1909, 213; Pooley 1968, 411). Earlier, in 1820, a few settlers from Pittsfield, Massachusetts, established Pittsfield in Pike County in the southern portion of the Military Tract. The net result was the emergence of a chain migration of friends and relatives (Mathews 1909, 211).

The domain county of Tazewell across from Peoria in the Illinois Valley corridor appealed to New Englanders. A Massachusetts Yankee colony organized Tremont in 1836. At the time, the county seat was nearly in the center of Tazewell County and almost equidistant from the river towns of Pekin and Peoria. The New England symbolic landscape did not just typify communities in northern Illinois. Abner D. Jones described Tremont as "beautifully laid off in squares, with streets of an hundred feet in width, running at right angles with each other. . . . In the centre of the town ten acres are thrown into a public square. . . . [T]hey have planted ornamental trees along the lines of these squares. . . . The buildings are frame, and generally painted white, which gives an exceedingly neat and pleasant aspect, as contrasted with the deep and brilliant green of the prairie which embosoms it. . . . The character of the place is New England, there being three quarters of the population from that section of our country" (1838, 72–73).

Numerous Yankee colonies settled Henry County in the northern Military Tract in the 1830s. The Andover colony characterized those colonies with a strong religious motivation. New Englanders from Andover, New York, did not settle in large numbers (Pooley 1968, 409). The earlier diffusion of the Andover place name into northern New England and then westward forms a toponym clue to Yankee place consciousness. It appears that the town name from Hampshire, England, became an American place name with the founding of Andover, Massachusetts, in 1646 (Rooney, Zelinsky, and Louder 1982, 143). The Andover toponym marks a trans-generational, continental stepwise shift.

Connecticut Immigrant Region

Emigrants from Connecticut were the smallest of the four primary New England immigrant groups in Illinois (table 7.1). The immigrant surface reveals the typical Yankee settlement array from northeast to southwest. The fragmented structure of the Connecticut immigrant region (fig. 7.4) was more like the Massachusetts immigrant region (fig. 7.3) than the more uniform immigrant surfaces articulated by New Yorkers (fig. 7.1) and Vermonters (fig. 7.2). Structural patterns indicate that Connecticut immigrants tended to disperse and form a greater number of domain counties than other Yankees (table 7.2). New Englanders avoided the extensive Grand Prairie of east-central Illinois and Upland South–dominated southern Illinois.

The arrangement of core and domain counties created two primary migration clusters with 63.4 percent of the Connecticut immigrants. First, a northeast sector integrated with Chicago. This dominant Connecticut migration cluster possessed about 41 percent of the adult males. Attractive urban opportunities in Chicago lured a lopsided 71.6 percent of the Connecticut immigrants in Cook County. In other core and domain counties, Connecticut immigrants were similar to other Yankees who primarily settled in the rural environs, since sizable urban places at this time were few in number. In Rockford in Winnebago County and Quincy in Adams County, urbanites comprised only 5 to 30 percent of the county total of Connecticut immigrants. Yankees were inclined to have a higher proportion in an urban setting.

A second Connecticut migration cluster formed in the Military Tract. Rival Quincy and Peoria emerged as urban growth poles that bifurcated the migration cluster. This smaller cluster possessed one-fifth of the Connecticut immigrants. The attraction of these subregional nodes and their hinterlands provided alternative Yankee destinations to northeast Illinois. Improvements in steamboats and road ties with St. Louis and Chicago enhanced the settlement-commercial advantages of these Mississippi-Illinois foci. Both river towns had comparable

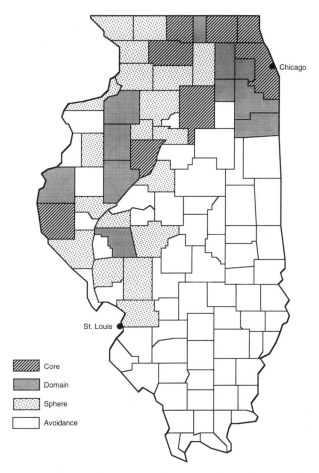

FIG. 7.4. Connecticut Immigrants in Illinois, 1850 (*Seventh Census Population Schedules, 1850*)

connections with southern trade markets. Peoria configured a larger Connecticut immigrant hinterland than Quincy. The centrality of Peoria within the expanding road network in west-central Illinois provided greater accessibility with lower-level nodes and Yankee colonies in the Military Tract's northern part (figs. 3.3–3.5). The northward-penetrating road network tied the core county of Peoria with the adjacent south-north alignment of the domain counties of Fulton, Knox, and Henry.

The religious zeal of the Wethersfield colony in Henry County was initiated by a Congregational minister from Wethersfield, Connecticut. An association of sixty men from New England formed a colony and acquired twenty thousand acres. By the Panic of 1837, only ten families had arrived on the prairies. Only four of the original association members migrated to Wethersfield. Pooley concluded that Wethersfield marked one more Puritan experimental failure (1968, 409–10). Yankees settling southeast Henry County formed a Congregational church in 1839. The railroad town of Kewanee perpetuated a Yankee imprint.

In Sangamon Country, rivals Jacksonville and Springfield and their hinterlands were attractive destinations for New Englanders. Morgan County emerged as an isolated Connecticut domain county (fig. 7.4). Yankees included almost 11 percent of the county's adult males, with almost one-third of them in Jacksonville, the county seat. New Englanders gave the frontier town a Puritan caste (Doyle 1978; Heinl 1935). The founding of Illinois College in 1829 was particularly appealing to Yankee ideals. Sangamon County existed as a sphere county in the Connecticut immigrant surface, but Yankees were almost 13 percent of the adult males in the county. The state capital and courthouse and market center of Springfield attracted 38 percent of the New Englanders in Sangamon County.

Why were the Connecticut and Massachusetts immigrant regions similar? A discrete Yankee cluster in northeast Illinois, fragmented clusters of core and domain counties, and sphere counties linking segmented migration clusters were shared structural traits (figs. 7.3, 7.4). The New England culture hearth evolved along the northeast seaboard in Massachusetts and Connecticut. Given this powerful southern New England hearth area, it is not surprising in the diffusion of New England cultural traditions that the immigrant structures of these two Yankee groups might be similar in Illinois.

Secondary New England Immigrant Patterns

The dispersion of secondary Yankee groups discloses a delayed continental penetration, a different settlement history, and a strong historical-cultural proclivity to persist near the New England hearth area. Smaller New England immigrant groups migrating to the New West also employed the northern commercial gateway. Their mobility conformed to the developing interregional road networks connecting lakeside nodes. Lifetime out-migration in 1850 from these secondary source areas involved 109,878 from New Hampshire, 67,193 from Maine, 43,300 from Rhode Island, and 12,409 from Michigan.

New Hampshirites relocated to the hearth area of Massachusetts (36.0 percent), Vermont (17.9 percent), New York (13.2 percent), Maine (12.3 percent), Ohio (4.4 percent), Illinois (3.9 percent), and Michigan (2.5 percent). The allure of the Middle West did not dominate. Emigrants from Maine portray a similar geographic mobility. They settled in Massachusetts (43.9 percent), New Hampshire (14.3 percent), New York (6.7 percent), Illinois (5.5 percent), Ohio (4.9 percent), Wisconsin (4.8 percent), and California (4.0 percent). Rhode Islanders refrained from making great leaps into the interior, going to New York (30.3 percent), Massachusetts

(26.4 percent), Connecticut (15.9 percent), Ohio (4.5 percent), Pennsylvania (4.5 percent), Illinois (2.4 percent), and Michigan (2.4 percent). Yankee predilections to persist near the hearth area and regional way station in western New York mark the powerful reinforcement of place and historical consciousness.

Michigan represented a New England extended area. First-generation Michiganders illustrate a mobility that was not always westward nor short-distance migration. They relocated to Ohio (18.0 percent), Illinois (17.4 percent), New York (15.5 percent), Wisconsin (15.3 percent), Indiana (14.6 percent), Iowa (4.2 percent), Missouri (2.4 percent), and California (2.3 percent). New England extended configured a Yankeeland fringing the Great Lakes (Hudson 1986, 1988).

The structural patterns of the secondary Yankee groups in Illinois should be similar to New Englanders from the hearth area of Massachusetts and Connecticut. The adult males in the secondary groups included 2,074 from New Hampshire, 1,195 from Maine, 479 from Rhode Island, and 220 from Michigan. These small Yankee groups constituted only 2.6 percent of the native-born adult males. The overwhelming majority arrived from northern New England, which was settled in the last half of the 1700s.

New Hampshire Immigrant Region

The New Hampshire immigrant surface extended from northeast to west-central Illinois via the Illinois Valley corridor (fig. 7.5). The segmented core and domain county structures were similar to Massachusetts and Connecticut immigrants (table 7.2; figs. 7.3, 7.4). The largest migration cluster of seven core counties with 28.9 percent of the New Hampshirites straddled the diverging roads from Chicago (figs. 3.3–3.5). The interstice areas between the roads became attractive destinations for Yankee farmers. Courthouse and market centers and mill sites in the Fox River Valley were appealing to Yankee tradesmen, professionals, and artisans. Lineaments of settlement expansions were linked to the expanding road networks in the late 1830s and 1840s (Boylan 1933; Lee 1917; Ramey 1949).

The primary roads were the Chicago-Galena Road and Chicago-Ottawa Road. The Rock River Country in Winnebago County, midway in northern Illinois, developed as a core concentration of Yankees. The mill site, market, and county seat center of Rockford spawned settlement and economic growth. La Salle County in the upper Illinois River Valley, with its river town of Peru and canal towns of La Salle and Ottawa and their respective hinterlands, functioned as a Yankee destination. La Salle County generally emerged as a core county of New Englanders. With increased steamboating on the Illinois River, Peru emerged as the head of navigation (Hunter 1949, 46). La Salle was designated the Illinois and Michigan Canal terminus (Coard 1941; Putnam 1918).

Ottawa had locational advantages over its downstream rivals of Peru and La Salle (Conzen 1987; Conzen and Morales 1989). During high water, Illinois River

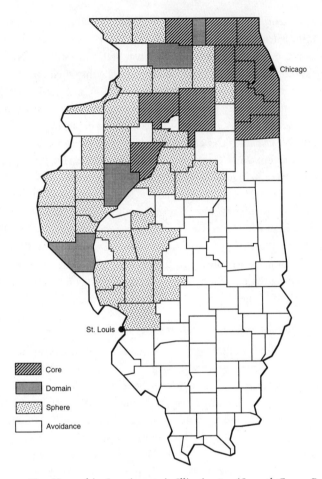

Fig. 7.5. New Hampshire Immigrants in Illinois, 1850 (*Seventh Census Population Schedules, 1850*)

steamboats served Ottawa. It developed as a county seat and market center near the middle of La Salle County. Ferry crossings evolved in proximity to Ottawa for roads that connected Ottawa with Chicago, Galena, and Peoria in the 1840s (King 1982). Ottawa emerged as an important canal town just east of the terminus at La Salle. It had the advantage of being located at the confluence of the Fox-Illinois Rivers. The north-south-flowing Fox River emerged as a Yankee ribbon settlement west of Chicago. Roads integrating Ottawa to the entrepôt enhanced the accessibility of Ottawa, the county, the bordering canal townships, and the lower Fox River Valley.

The periphery of the New Hampshire immigrant region conforms to the westward-southwest dispersion of Yankees. A contiguous cluster of sphere counties formed in northwest Illinois. The Illinois Valley corridor funneled New Hamp-shirites into adjacent Sangamon Country and the Military Tract. Small colonies of Yankees settled within this extensive sphere periphery. Mathews noted that a colony from Gilmanton, New Hampshire, established Hanover in Woodford County in 1835 because of its attractiveness for farms (1909, 211). The destination lured other Yankees from Rhode Island, Vermont, and Massachusetts. When Hanover became the county seat, the village changed its name to Metamora in 1843 (Pooley 1968, 380). The core county of Peoria, domain counties of Pike and Fulton, and contiguous sphere counties attracted Yankee farmers. Eastern Illinois persisted as an avoidance area.

Maine Immigrant Region

Almost half the size of New Hampshirites in Illinois, immigrants from Maine molded a discrete, northeast-southwest settlement axis (table 7.1, fig. 7.6). Seg-mented migration clusters comprising core and domain counties were linked by sphere counties. Maine immigrant patterns were similar to the Massachusetts, Connecticut, New Hampshire, and Rhode Island immigrant structures. Regional consciousness of cultural brethren engendered a geographical affinity to cluster. New Englanders frequently employed Massachusetts as an interim settlement to migrating to the Midwest. In the 1840s, Illinois was transforming into a space-economy with the evolution of regional agricultural-economic growth. Yankees desired two of the most accessible regional settlement areas that furnished an op-portunity for marketplace agriculture: northeast and west-central Illinois. Their settlement requirements were driven by a need for road networks, accessibility to waterborne routes, and convenient subregional and lower-level nodes integrated to mercantile regional nodes (figs. 3.6, 3.7, 4.1).

Maine immigrants dispersed southwest into west-central Illinois rather than fo-cusing in the Chicago-Yankee hinterland. Two-thirds of them resided in the frag-mented core and domain counties. The northern tier of Illinois counties had 34.9 percent of the total Maine adult males. The principal migration cluster evolved in the north-central counties of La Salle and Winnebago. Rockton in the Rock River Valley of Winnebago County originated in 1837 as a Maine colony. A circuitous route ensued for the colony, led by Ira Hersey: Portland to Boston by ship, to Providence by railroad, and to New York and Philadelphia by water. The immi-grants traversed Pennsylvania by rail to Pittsburgh, utilized the Ohio-Mississippi-Illinois Rivers to Ottawa in La Salle County, and then went northward by road to Rockton. The covenanted community established its Congregational church at the time of initial settlement (Mathews 1909, 213–14).

West-central Illinois core and domain counties attracted 31.6 percent of the Maine immigrants. The Military Tract between the Mississippi-Illinois Rivers was the principal destination area. The structural pattern of the Maine core

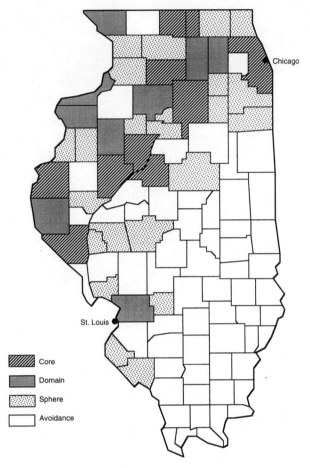

Fig. 7.6. Maine Immigrants in Illinois, 1850 (*Seventh Census Population Schedules, 1850*)

counties depicts the drawing power of the Illinois Valley corridor as a discrete riparian settlement region. With its five core counties stretching from La Salle to Pike County, slightly over one-fifth of the Maine adult males settled the fringing valley counties, a higher proportion than for any other New England immigrant group in Illinois.

Sphere counties, which included almost one-fourth of the Maine immigrants, connected migration clusters comprising core and domain counties. A small cluster of sphere counties and one domain county in southwest Illinois marks a colonizing effort as Maine immigrants were lured by the advantages of proximity to St. Louis and Alton markets. The long north-south array of avoidance counties in eastern Illinois symbolizes the Yankees' extensive, negative perceptual region.

Rhode Island Immigrant Region

Rhode Islanders were less than half the population size of Maine adult males (table 7.1). The structure of the Rhode Island immigrant region mirrors both primary and secondary Yankee groups in Illinois by 1850 (figs. 7.1–7.7). This coherence of destinations and settlement structures proffered a cultural umbrella for new arrivals. Yankees' shared sense of regional and place identity meant linking emotional bonds, common experiences, and values. As a distinctive culture group, their continuity stretched back East to regional way stations and a seaboard hearth area.

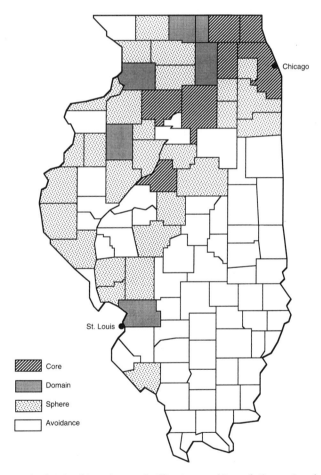

Fig. 7.7. Rhode Island Immigrants in Illinois, 1850 (*Seventh Census Population Schedules, 1850*)

Rhode Islanders configured a contiguous cluster of core and domain counties, principally in northern Illinois (fig. 7.7). The three core counties of Bureau, Cook, and Tazewell combined for almost one-fourth of the state total. In Bureau and Tazewell Counties, they were associated with colony experiments. Ten miles southwest of the Massachusetts colony of Princeton in Bureau County, a colony originating in Providence, Rhode Island, purchased seventeen thousand acres in 1836 (Pooley 1968, 411–12). Marketplace-oriented farmers formed a colony that created Delavan in the southern part of Tazewell County in 1837. An association purchased twenty-three thousand acres of primarily prairie land in the surrounding hinterland (378). Successful colonies meant west-central Illinois counties offered alternative destinations. Tazewell County was a cultural outpost of Yankees (figs. 7.1–7.8).

Sphere counties of Rhode Islanders aligned in a southwesterly direction across west-central Illinois toward Alton and St. Louis. Rhode Islanders dispersed, like other New Englanders, farther southward in Illinois than generally recognized by scholars. Both the Military Tract and Sangamon Country were equally attractive settlement areas. Avoidance areas conformed to the general Yankee pattern.

Michigan Immigrant Region

Michiganders were a tiny New England extended immigrant group in Illinois. The structural pattern of the Michigan immigrant surface discloses adult males highly concentrated in only a few core and domain counties (fig. 7.8). The few Michiganders would have been very isolated in sphere counties. They made a stepwise migration transfer to Illinois. Their migration decision-making process illustrates narrowly defined destinations. Almost 25 percent of them opted for Cook County, with 94 percent selecting gateway Chicago for a place of residence.

New England Culture Region

New Englanders disembarked westward and southwestward from lakeside Chicago (Meyer 1976b). The New England culture region evolved a large, contiguous block of northern tier core counties (fig. 7.9). Sequential patterns with decreasing levels of settlement concentrations were not as well developed for the New England versus the Upland South culture region (figs. 6.8, 7.9). New England domain and sphere counties did not embrace an orderly north-south peripheral array into central Illinois that bordered the northern Yankee culture core. But the Yankee culture region still substantiates a discrete core/periphery framework. The available land routes in northern Illinois, particularly the Chicago-Galena Road and the roads connecting Chicago with Ottawa and Peoria that paralleled the upper Illinois Valley and emerging Illinois and Michigan Canal, functioned as principal diffusion routes.

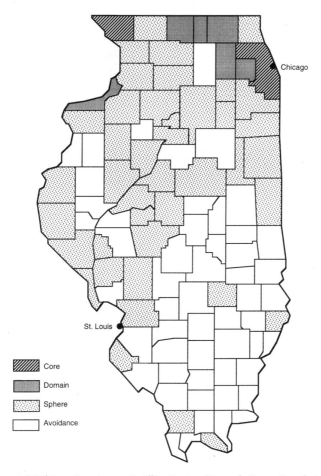

FIG. 7.8. Michigan Immigrants in Illinois, 1850 (*Seventh Census Population Schedules, 1850*)

The correspondence of primary and secondary immigrant structures implies common cultural traditions among New Englanders (figs. 7.1–7.8). The New England immigrant structures corroborate a Yankee hegemony in the culture region core (fig. 7.9). The structure of the New England core counties is obscured by the overpowering size of the New York migration flow. New Yorkers emerged as the largest immigrant group in northern Illinois counties. The total number of immigrants in a core county from New England states was usually surpassed by the number of New Yorkers. Likewise, the structure of Upland South and Midland-Midwest immigrant regions inferred minimal settlement influences in northern Illinois. County migration fields in northern Illinois attest to greater immigrant mixing within the New England core counties than previously recognized.

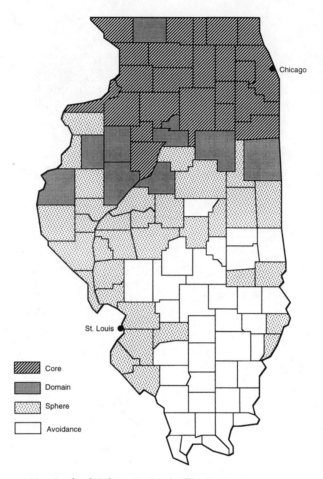

FIG. 7.9. New England Culture Region in Illinois, 1850

The New England core areally divided into two sectors on opposite sides of the state and an inland core area less accessible to waterborne travel. The New England core bordering Lake Michigan and in the immediate Chicago hinterland revealed county migration fields where New Yorkers were generally double the number from New England states. Northeast Illinois core counties usually had equivalent numbers of Midlanders from Pennsylvania and Midwesterners from Ohio and Indiana. Hidden in this salient Yankee core were substantial numbers of Upland Southerners in Cook, Kane, McHenry, and Will Counties. As previously discussed, Virginians were more widely dispersed in the state. Virginians outnumbered Kentuckians in this northeast Yankee core, but channelized migration flows had also brought South and North Carolinians to the Fox River Valley townships in Kane County.

Inland core counties possessed distinctive migration field differences with the verge core counties. Boone, Winnebago, and De Kalb witnessed the same migration field composition and proportions as the northeast core district, with the exception of a trace of Upland Southerners. The southern counties of Bureau and La Salle in proximity to the Illinois Valley corridor were different. Immigrants from New York and New England states and Midland-Midwest states were equivalent in size, with significant numbers of Upland Southerners from Virginia and Kentucky in Bureau County. The migration field of La Salle County revealed a slightly different character: Yankees were twice the size of Midlanders and Midwesterners, and Upland Southerners were fewer in number. Bureau and La Salle Counties document cultural mixing in the southern tier Yankee core counties. Transitional core counties stretching from east to west across northern Illinois generally included Ohio and Pennsylvania as their second- or third-largest state, not a New England state as in the northeast core area.

Another distinctive migration field pattern evolved among the interior New England core counties (fig. 7.9). A south-north axis emerged with Lee and Ogle Counties mirroring the Pennsylvania anomaly of Stephenson County in northwest Illinois, the largest state concentration. In Stephenson County, Midlanders outnumbered New Yorkers and other New Englanders two to one. Midlanders from Pennsylvania, Maryland, and New Jersey outweighed Midwesterners from Ohio and Indiana five to one. In Ogle County, Yankees, Midlanders, and Midwesterners were equivalent in numbers. Lee County was similar in immigrant composition to northeast Illinois. All three counties had few Upland Southerners. Inland Yankee core areas were characterized as having substantially more Midlanders and Midwesterners, particularly Pennsylvanians and Ohioans, than the northeast Yankee core.

Northwest Illinois counties disclose selective heterogeneity in their county migration fields. In this Mississippi riverine region, Jo Daviess County and the hinterland of Galena attracted comparable numbers from all three American migration streams. Upland Southerners almost equaled New Yorkers. Kentuckians outnumbered Virginians, but North Carolinians and Tennesseans also penetrated to this far northwest corner. Magnet destinations, like the lead mining district, contributed to regional cultural mixing. This peripheral New England core area, with its waterborne accessibility, formed a cultural mixture that was similar to the Military Tract's northern portion rather than to northeast Illinois. County migration fields varied with equivalent numbers of New Englanders and Midlanders and Midwesterners, to Yankees predominating, or to Midlanders and Midwesterners dominating. Pennsylvanians usually outnumbered Ohioans. Upland Southerners accounted for 10 to 15 percent of the adult males in these Yankee core counties. Increases in Upland Southerners distinguished this New England core sector. Kentuckians and Virginians were similar in total numbers in this riverine New England settlement strip.

Penetration of New Englanders into west-central Illinois aligned with the Illinois Valley corridor (fig. 7.9). Yankee core counties evolved in the Military Tract's northern part with its water highway boundaries. The core counties of Stark and Peoria formed a southward Yankee thrust. Midlanders and Midwesterners were definitely larger in population numbers than New Yorkers and New Englanders. Considerable numbers of Upland Southerners penetrated the middle Illinois Valley, with Virginians outnumbering Kentuckians. In Peoria County, Upland South immigrants comprised almost one-fifth of the adult male population. The regional road network in west-central Illinois converged on the crossroads mercantile river town of Peoria (figs. 3.5–3.7). As the dominant New England settlement outpost in the Military Tract, Peoria County was situated in a Yankee hinterland of contiguous domain counties.

The New England culture region did not develop regular decreasing concentration zones. A broad, orderly array of Yankee domain counties from east to west or north to south adjacent to the New England core counties failed to form. Being late arrivals in Illinois, New Englanders moved within rapidly expanding regional circulation networks. It is not surprising that the narrow band of Yankee domain counties that abuts the Yankee core area hints at the possible formation of a cultural divide because of significant shifts in cultural origins. County migration field compositions were distinctively different for west-central and east-central Illinois. Midwesterners substantially exceeded the number of Midlanders on both sides of the state. Together, the Midwest-Midland migration flows predominated over almost equivalent numbers of Yankees and Upland Southerners in west-central Illinois. In east-central Illinois, New Englanders did not infill the Grand Prairie in significant numbers.

The structure of the New England culture region exhibited two settlement surprises (fig. 7.9). A broader zone of Yankee sphere counties arrayed across central Illinois than anticipated. New Englanders' competitive spread with Midwest-Midland and Upland South migration flows engendered an areally extensive cultural borderlands in the midsection of the state. In central Illinois, New England peripheral sphere counties connected the Wabash, Illinois, and Mississippi Valleys. The vast majority of these Yankee sphere counties comprised Midland-Midwest core counties. Atypical Sangamon County emerged as a domain area for both Upland Southerners and Midlanders-Midwesterners but was for the New Englanders only a sphere area.

Numerous destinations attracted New Englanders to east-central, west-central, and southwest Illinois. Slicing through west-central Illinois, the Illinois Valley corridor expanded as a salient movement channel and as a competitive settlement region. The expanding regional road networks interconnected river towns and vital Peoria and Quincy in the Military Tract, Jacksonville and Springfield in Sangamon Country, and Alton in the American Bottom (figs. 3.5–3.7, 4.1). Crossroads market and courthouse nodes and intervening areas between the roads became attractive to immigrants of all persuasions. Serving as a cultural mixing area, west-central Illinois interspersed with New Englanders, Upland Southerners, Midlanders, Midwesterners, and foreigners.

The southward penetration of the Yankee sphere counties was far greater into the Upland South cultural core in southern Illinois than expected (figs. 6.8, 7.9). Contiguous New England sphere counties straddling the Illinois and Mississippi Rivers extended to the St. Louis hinterland in southwest Illinois. On the east side of Illinois, New Englanders encroached southward from Chicago and northward via the Wabash River. The Wabash Valley corridor did not have the lure or the accessibility of the Illinois Valley corridor for Yankees. The segmented sphere pattern extended southward from the New England core across east-central Illinois into southeast Illinois. The Grand Prairie counties of Champaign and Vermilion, the National Road counties of Cumberland and Clark, and the Wabash River counties of Lawrence and Wabash were diminutive Yankee destinations.

Within central Illinois, the contiguous sphere pattern exposed a hollow frontier with the avoidance area of De Witt County. Extensive wet-dry prairies fail to explain New Englanders' circumventing the county during their spread across east-central Illinois. Isolation and inaccessibility to markets for agricultural products retarded the growth of many inland counties. Yankees refrained from peopling the interior counties of southern Illinois with substantial numbers. The Upland Southerners' backwoods strategy had engraved a large, contiguous Upland South core area. Diverse population origins focused on the midsection of the north-south state lineation. Regional settlement and transport processes encouraged cultural mixing rather than cultural discontinuities.

The New England culture region in Illinois transformed a settlement area not unlike any previous habitat back East. Cultural and agricultural trait adaptations to the new timber-prairie environment enhanced the expansion of the New England culture region across the Mississippi River in the antebellum period. Yankee geographical propinquity was influenced by a strong feeling of cultural and place consciousness. Affective bonds, common experiences, and shared values meant "community as experience and community as place were one" (Wood 1982, 333). The idiosyncratic New England cultural impress dispersed swiftly across Illinois in the 1840s. Material culture elements imprinted northern and west-central Illinois landscapes. Place image signatures were inscribed in rural and urban landscapes. Essential landscape elements originating in southern New England and modified in western New York were engraved into the common landscape: houses, barns, church architecture, village greens, northern dialect, and foodways (Mitchell 1978; Price 1968; Zelinsky 1973). New England landscape traditions survive as relic cultural artifacts.

8

Midland-Midwest Immigrant Regions

Taking all the Bounty Tract together . . . there is no region
of country in the west more eligibly situated for all the purposes of agriculture and commerce. The lands everywhere, with
but few exceptions, are of the best quality, and in a manner surrounded by a sheet of navigable waters; and the country exhibits a
climate of great variety.
—Mitchell 1837

Expanding navigable waterways and regional road networks improved immigrants' opportunities to participate in marketplace-agrarian economies. A
rush of Pennsylvanians, Ohioans, and Indianans employed trunk line routes: the
National Road, the Ohio-Mississippi River system, and the Great Lakes–Erie
Canal system. Terre Haute on the Wabash River in Indiana and Marshall in Clark
County, Illinois, some fifteen miles west on the National Road, served as points of
entry for Midland-Midwest immigrants. Road networks connected east-central
and west-central Illinois. Water movement corridors formed alternative trunk
routes to western Illinois. Midlanders and Midwesterners configured complex migration patterns north of the National Road.

Midland-Midwest immigrant regions exhibited a propensity for widespread
dispersion and segmentation in Illinois by 1850. Structural patterns reveal dispersion northward and southward from a midstate base. Midlanders and Midwesterners dispersed westward across the Middle West within an American diffusion
system (fig. 3.8). I argue the formation of a cultural core in a Midland-Midwest
culture region. As a fundamental segment of a new regional way station, it linked
with enlarging four-tier urban-transport and culture region systems.

In a recent reappraisal of the Pennsylvania culture area, Pillsbury postulated a
secondary American regional culture hearth (landscape formation zone) in central and western Pennsylvania (1987, 51). Earlier, Mitchell argued that replicated
Midland regional way stations formed in southwest Pennsylvania in the late 1700s
and in southwest Ohio and southeast Indiana in the early 1800s (1978). Adaptive

cultural strategies evolved in the Midland regional way stations that shaped distinctive cultural landscapes (Mitchell 1978; Pillsbury 1987; Zelinsky 1973). Hudson (1988) and Rose (1988c) suggest a Pennsylvania extended across the Lower Midwest. Discrete Midland-Midwest migration fields unfolded in central Illinois as a wedge between Upland Southerners and New Englanders at either end of the state by 1850 (Meyer 1976b).

Primary Midland-Midwest Population Sources

Midlanders spread slowly westward from their southeast Pennsylvania hearth area into central and western Pennsylvania and southwestward through the Great Valley into the Carolina piedmont (Anderson 1943; Barnhart 1937b; Buck and Buck 1939; Chaddock 1908; Jordan and Kaups 1989; Mitchell 1978; Pillsbury 1987; Rose 1985a, 1986a, 1986c, 1988a, 1988c; Turner 1897, 1906, 1920, 1935; Wilhelm 1982). Southwest movements of Midlanders of German, Scotch-Irish, Irish, and English backgrounds conformed to colonial population spearheads between 1725 and 1775. By 1800, their descendants transferred their Midland–Upland South backwoods frontier culture across transAppalachia (Jordan and Kaups 1989; Newton 1974; Mitchell 1978; Mitchell and Newton 1988). Midwestern cultural diversity unfolded north of the Ohio River.

Lifetime out-migration of emigrants from the primary Midland-Midwest states by 1850 numbered 422,055 Pennsylvanians, 295,453 Ohioans, 92,038 Indianans, and 45,889 Illinoisans. Pennsylvanians were the cultural vectors of Midland material culture from the hearth area in southeast Pennsylvania. They migrated to Ohio (47.5 percent), Indiana (10.5 percent), Illinois (9.0 percent), New York (6.2 percent), Maryland (3.8 percent), New Jersey (3.6 percent), and Iowa (3.5 percent). The Midland culture region had spread into the adjacent Middle Colonies. Later movements westward meant that Ohio evolved as the "daughter state" of Pennsylvania and as Midland extended (Chaddock 1908; Rose 1988c; Wilhelm 1982).

State destinations of Ohioans and Indianans were directional-biased. Ohioans out-migrated to Indiana (40.7 percent), Illinois (21.7 percent), Iowa (10.4 percent), Michigan (5.0 percent), Missouri (4.3 percent), Wisconsin (3.9 percent), Kentucky (3.4 percent), and Pennsylvania (2.6 percent). Indianans emigrated to Illinois (33.6 percent), Iowa (21.7 percent), Missouri (13.9 percent), Ohio (8.0 percent), Kentucky (6.4 percent), and Wisconsin (3.0 percent). Both Ohio and Indiana emerged as cultural mixing areas. Their state destinations mark the immigrant diversity spreading across midcontinent.

Illinoisans lifetime out-migration reflected other Midwesterners with diverse cultural backgrounds. They primarily settled contiguous states: Missouri (23.8 percent), Iowa (15.8 percent), Wisconsin (11.5 percent), Indiana (9.1 percent), Arkansas (7.1 percent), Texas (6.2 percent), California (5.9 percent), Kentucky

(3.6 percent), Ohio (3.1 percent), Utah (2.8 percent), and Oregon (2.2 percent). Illinoisans with a Yankee cultural heritage shifted north. Those with an Upland South cultural legacy relocated to Missouri, Arkansas, and Texas. In the Far West, they participated in the California Gold Rush, the settling of the Willamette Valley of Oregon, and the Mormon exodus from Nauvoo to the Wasatch Oasis.

Population origins in the Old Northwest were not homogeneous (Swierenga 1989). Upland Southerners, New Englanders, Midlanders, Midwesterners, and foreigners molded midwestern cultural pluralism. Diversity, not uniformity, characterized heartland immigrant origins (Hudson 1984b, 1988; Swierenga 1989; Zelinsky 1973). Ohio Valley corridor states experienced stepwise westward and northwestward migration. Return migration was commonplace: Ohioans to Kentucky and Pennsylvania, Indianans to Ohio and Kentucky, and Illinoisans to Indiana, Kentucky, and Ohio.

Primary Midland-Midwest Immigrant Patterns

The Midland-Midwest migration stream represented the largest native-born adult male group in Illinois by 1850, 38.6 percent (table 8.1). Given their diverse cultural origins—Middle Atlantic, Upland South, and New England—the primary Midland-Midwest immigrant patterns were dominated by fragmentation. Upland Southerners (figs. 6.1–6.4) and New Englanders (figs. 7.1–7.4) formed, instead, large, contiguous clusters of core and domain counties. Midlanders and Midwesterners, however, disproportionately settled in sphere counties (tables 6.3, 7.2, 8.2). Their increasing cultural contacts with Upland Southerners, New Englanders, and foreigners in Illinois fostered cultural fusions and adaptations. In the antebellum period,

TABLE 8.1 Birthplaces of Adult Male Midlanders-Midwesterners
in Illinois, 1850

Birthplace	Number	Percentage of Native-Born
Pennsylvania	13,451	8.82
Ohio	17,069	11.19
Indiana	6,180	4.05
Illinois	14,319	9.38
New Jersey	2,899	1.90
Maryland	2,891	1.89
Missouri	1,333	.87
Delaware	650	.43
District of Columbia	131	.09
Total native-born	152,591	38.62

Source: Seventh Census Population Schedules, 1850

TABLE 8.2 Midland-Midwest Immigrants' Concentration Patterns in Illinois, 1850

Birthplace	Core Concentrations		Domain Concentrations		Sphere Concentrations		Avoidance Areas	
	No. Counties	% Migrants	No. Counties	% Migrants	No. Counties	% Migrants	No. Counties	% Migrants
Pennsylvania	6	25.2	6	13.2	41	46.6	46	15.0
Ohio	8	29.4	7	14.0	33	36.9	51	19.7
Indiana	10	30.6	7	13.9	31	35.6	51	19.9
Illinois	7	29.6	4	8.1	39	48.5	49	13.8
New Jersey	6	31.8	6	15.0	34	40.5	53	12.7
Maryland	4	26.9	6	13.8	39	44.0	50	15.3

cultural processes were creating a "mainstream" marketplace-agrarian society in midcontinent. Spatial variations of the four immigrant concentration types confirm the distinctive structural patterns of the primary Midland-Midwest groups.

Pennsylvania Immigrant Region

Pennsylvanians were the sixth-largest immigrant group (6.8 percent) by 1850 (table 6.1). They dispersed across central and northern Illinois, but north of the National Road (fig. 8.1). A northeast-southwest alignment emerged between the Mississippi-Illinois riparian corridors. Four segmented migration clusters unfolded in west-central and northeast Illinois. A fifth migration cluster formed in northwest Illinois in proximity to the Chicago-Galena Road (figs. 3.5–3.7). Only 38.4 percent of the Pennsylvanians resided in the core and domain counties of the fragmented migration clusters (table 8.2). This was the smallest proportion in core and domain counties among the largest immigrant groups. They established the largest number of sphere counties, the largest percentage of immigrants in sphere counties (almost 50 percent), and the fewest number of avoidance counties.

Rock River Country in northwest Illinois was sketched in Edenic place images:

> The fertility of most of the Rock river and Upper Mississippi bottoms is indestructible. On such a soil, under proper cultivation, 100 bushels of corn and 40 bushels of wheat to the acre could be raised with facility. . . . There are thousands of situations in the Rock river country, where plenty of timber in proximity to prairies will give settlers the advantages of timber and prairie united. . . . The products of this region are the same as those of the adjoining districts, and are raised with the same facility as in the most favoured parts of the state. . . . There can be no doubt of this region being eminently healthy. The country is supplied bountifully with water from good springs, and the air is second only to mountain air in purity. . . . Easy access to market will always insure to the farmer the rewards of industry; and a rich agricultural community ever promotes the steadiest and purest prosperity to all other classes. (Mitchell 1837, 23–25)

The core counties of Stephenson and Ogle and domain county of Jo Daviess in northwest Illinois composed the largest Pennsylvanian migration cluster (12.8 percent). Stephenson County had a disproportionate number of Pennsylvanians (7.4 percent). Pennsylvania Germans arrived as individuals, families, small groups, and colonies. Pooley quotes a newspaper extract of a typical Pennsylvania Dutch colony in 1843: "On Wednesday May 31, a company of about sixty emigrants passed through this place [Clarion, Pennsylvania] on their way . . . to Stephenson county, Illinois. They had fourteen wagons, each drawn by an elegant span of horses. . . . They were all from one neighborhood, had plenty of cash and appeared in fine spirits" (1968, 436). Marketplace-oriented farmers were attracted to the small hinterlands of Freeport in Stephenson County on the Chicago-Galena Road and Oregon in Ogle County on the Rock River. These county seat and market

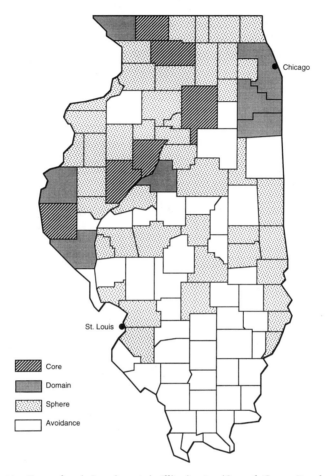

FIG. 8.1. Pennsylvania Immigrants in Illinois, 1850 (*Seventh Census Population Schedules, 1850*)

centers connected with the subregional node of Galena, the lower-level node of Rockford, and the regional node of Chicago. Each courthouse center evolved hinterlands with tiny settlements three to six miles apart. The density of this rural settlement hierarchy suggests the evolution of a commercial agricultural system entwined in an expanding regional urban-transport network.

Geographical propinquity was influenced by strong feelings of group identity and cohesiveness. Midlanders, particularly those with Germanic roots, shared ethnic bonds, common traditions, attitudes, and values. Pennsylvania Germans established settlement enclaves, such as Buckeye and Lancaster Townships, and fixed tiny market centers, such as German Valley in Ridott Township in Stephenson County. Here, a sense of belonging and ethnic consciousness persisted with

German language usage in home, social, business, and church functions. German worship services in Lutheran, Catholic, Methodist, and Reformed churches and Lutheran and Catholic church-related schools perpetuated Germanness into the early twentieth century in rural agricultural communities. German Americans and Germans who settled among them psychologically and socially recognized experience and place as community.

The second-largest migration cluster of Pennsylvanians (10.5 percent) developed in the core counties of Fulton and Peoria and the domain county of Tazewell (fig. 8.1). Fulton County had the second-largest Pennsylvanian concentration after Stephenson County. Peck described Fulton County's potential settlement and agricultural success in glowing attributes: "Nearly one half of Fulton county is heavily timbered with the varieties that abound on the military tract; and . . . its prairie and timbered land, is of an excellent quality. It is in general well watered; the streams usually flow over a gravelly bottom and furnish many good mill seats. . . . [T]he Illinois and Spoon rivers will afford facilities to market. This whole region on the Illinois must shortly become a wealthy agricultural country" (1837, 104). Peoria was centrally located in the Illinois Valley corridor and eastern Military Tract. These riverine counties lured Midlanders, Midwesterners, New Englanders, Upland Southerners, and foreigners.

The Military Tract counties astride the Mississippi Valley corridor in proximity to the subregional node of Quincy were the third-largest concentration of Pennsylvanians (7.9 percent). The core county of Adams and the domain counties of Hancock and Pike formed a riparian migration cluster. Peck said of Adams County: "For quality of soil, well proportioned into timber and prairie, it is second to none in the state" (1837, 91). Quincy was a market, distributive, service, and manufacturing center linked to the entrepôt of St. Louis. Gem City's centrality made it the key river town between Alton and Galena. The fourth-largest Pennsylvanian migration cluster (4.2 percent) comprised the domain counties of Will and Cook in northeast Illinois. Lured to lakeside Chicago, 77 percent in the city, they were primarily laborers, artisans, merchants, and professionals. Marketplace-biased Pennsylvania farmers in Will County settled townships astride roads that linked with the Illinois and Michigan Canal and the courthouse and canal town of Joliet.

The final Pennsylvania migration cluster emerged as an isolated core county at the head of steamboat navigation on the Illinois River and terminus of the Illinois and Michigan Canal. Their numbers in La Salle County were slightly less than the fourth migration cluster. Favored township locations were astride the upper Illinois Valley and Illinois and Michigan Canal. Ottawa Township and the courthouse and canal town of Ottawa attracted the largest number of Pennsylvanians. Salisbury Township, with the terminus canal town of La Salle and river town of Peru a few miles away, was close behind as a destination. Other destinations included potential agricultural areas and tiny hamlets adjacent to or in the regional road network's interstice. The Pennsylvania immigrant structure was distinctive in that almost half of the immigrants settled in sphere counties. Sphere counties connected the fragmented migration clusters and straddled the major regional roads, the National Road, and roads paralleling the Wabash Valley corridor. Avoidance areas coincided with the Upland South core in southern Illinois and extensive open prairie areas.

Pennsylvanians symbolize an overlay of Germanic traditions. Descendants of colonial Germans, German Americans originated from ethnic enclaves in the Midland hearth area and the pre–Revolutionary War frontier. They sequentially replicated communities from southeast Pennsylvania through the Great Valley to the piedmont. After the Revolutionary War, like the Scotch-Irish, Irish, and English, German Americans dispersed in a stepwise, clockwise fashion northwestward. Their network of facsimile settlements connected across Tennessee and Kentucky to north of the Ohio Valley. Another stepwise expansion of German Americans extended westward from the Midland core area. During the late 1700s, they dispersed into the valleys of central and southwest Pennsylvania. This expanding Midland culture region met its counterpart of German Americans from the transAppalachian Upland South in the early 1800s in the Lower Middle West during the Great Migration. Germanic Upland Southerners and Midlanders converged on Ohio, Indiana, and Illinois.

German American enclaves that formed both north and south of the Ohio Valley increasingly integrated destination communities within the westward-spreading American culture region system. Rural enclaves and city neighborhoods, such as Cincinnati, Louisville, St. Louis, and Chicago, received large numbers of Germans directly from Europe in the decades prior to the Civil War. For many of these German communities, the chain migration from the fatherland persisted into the late 1800s. The substantial numbers increase contributed to the reinforcement of Germanic traditions in the Midwest. Sense of community persisted owing to German cultural linkages of heritage, language usage, and religion.

German Americans from North Carolina and Pennsylvania transplanted communities in their respective immigrant structures (figs. 6.4, 8.1). Covenant, ethnic communities with their rural hinterlands developed cohesive bonds for cultural survival. The United Brethren Church, which originated in the Midland culture region hearth area, spread westward from Virginia, Pennsylvania, Ohio, and Indiana into Illinois (Turner 1940, 41–42). The stepwise movements of this German American group focused on central Illinois, where the Wabash Valley Conference formed in 1835. Itinerant ministers served the Embarras, Kankakee, Sangamon, Spoon, and Rock River Valleys. Elbert dispels the popular notion that American roots of German Lutheranism in Illinois was synonymous with later German and Scandinavian immigrants (1985). German American Lutherans who were descendants of

Pennsylvania Germans out-migrated from the North Carolina piedmont in 1807 to the Shawnee Hills of Union County in southern Illinois. By 1830, a second covenant settlement of North Carolina Lutherans had transplanted to Montgomery County in west-central Illinois. Lutheran pastors' letters and returned visits served as stimuli that caused social networks to foster micro-scale channelized migration flows.

Pennsylvania German Lutherans migrating from Pennsylvania arrived in Jackson and Wabash Counties on opposite sides of southern Illinois in the 1830s. Although ethnicity, language, and religion in these covenant communities encouraged cultural survival, these affective bonds failed in later years to attract large numbers of Germans to these destinations. The continuity of Germanic traditions surviving as cultural expressions was also influenced by the German Baptist Brethren, also known as Dunkers (Eller 1987). As another Pennsylvania German element, they duplicated covenant communities in the westward-expanding Midland extended. The "Far Western" Brethren initiated their settlement near Jonesboro in Union County, shortly after the North Carolina German Lutherans. By 1850, congregations were established in the counties of Bond, Macoupin, Fulton, Hancock, and Adams. Eller stresses that Brethren accommodated the wider social-political order of frontier society (90). Both Elbert (1985) and Eller (1987) argue the pivotal role of pastors as dominant personalities: Daniel Scherer, a Lutheran, from Cabarrus County, North Carolina, and George Wolfe, a Dunker, from Lancaster County, Pennsylvania. These resourceful pastors maintained multiple covenant communities as frontier circuit-riders in southern and west-central Illinois. Pastors Scherer and Wolfe fashioned important connections within the dynamic ethnic-social-church networks.

Ohio Immigrant Region

Ohioans were the third-largest immigrant group (8.7 percent) and the largest Midland-Midwest population element in Illinois by 1850 (tables 6.1, 8.1). Arriving via the National Road and the Ohio-Mississippi River system after the mid-1830s, they principally located north of the National Road (figs. 3.5–3.7, 4.1, 8.2). An array of core and domain counties formed an expansive east-west Ohioan migration cluster across central Illinois, with almost 45 percent of the total (table 8.2). They dispersed into a large number of sphere counties, 37 percent of the Ohioans in one-third of the counties. Like Virginians and Indianans, Ohioans were more dispersed in avoidance counties (about 20 percent) than other immigrants (table 8.2). This greater dispersion probably relates to their diverse material culture, given their settlement and migration histories. The cultural mixture was particularly composed of Midland and Upland South heritage. Virginians settling Illinois were rarely from tidewater or plantation population origins. Ohioans and Indianans included a smaller proportion of New England cultural legacy. The major avoidance areas of Ohioans developed as a bifurcated pattern in southern and northern Illinois.

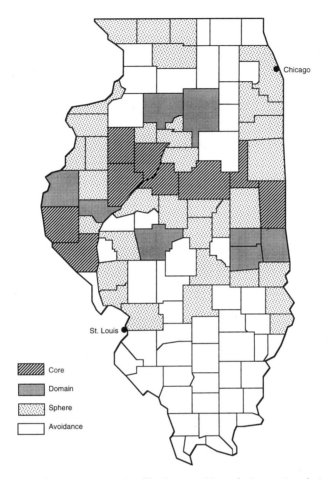

Fig. 8.2. Ohio Immigrants in Illinois, 1850 (*Seventh Census Population Schedules, 1850*)

An east-west array of Ohio core and domain counties in the state's midsection was a complex immigrant structure. Almost one-fourth of the Ohioans settled in the Military Tract. One large concentration included the core counties of Pike and Adams and the domain county of Hancock linked to the mercantile center of Quincy on the Mississippi River. The domain county of Schuyler served as a bridge linkage, with the largest concentration of Ohioans bordering the Illinois Valley corridor. These eastern Military Tract counties connected with the commercial center of Peoria. The core county of Fulton attracted the largest number of Ohioans (6.5 percent). Spoon River, a tributary of the Illinois River, traversed Fulton County. Peck described Spoon Valley: "Large bodies of timber of the best quality line the banks of this stream, and the soil in general is inferior to none.

The main river and several of its tributaries furnish excellent mill seats. The prairies adjacent are generally undulating, dry and fertile" (1837, 295).

Marketplace-biased Ohioans found Peck's descriptors of Fulton County's linkages favorable to their settlement predispositions: "Its productions are and will continue to be similar to this region of country; and the Illinois and Spoon rivers will afford facilities to market. This whole region on the Illinois must shortly become a wealthy agricultural country" (1837, 104). Market accessibility entwined in a three-level urban hierarchy made destinations appealing to commercial agriculture–oriented settlers. The expanding regional road network in west-central Illinois focused on the river towns of the Mississippi-Illinois Rivers with their increased steamboat movements. Immigrants were tied to the regional marketplaces of St. Louis and Chicago and a national and world space-economy. The core counties of Fulton, Peoria, and Knox comprised 13.7 percent of the Ohioans in Illinois.

Four smaller Ohio migration clusters developed in central and northern Illinois (fig. 8.2). Sangamon Country, east of the Illinois River, lured the earlier migration flow of Upland Southerners, particularly Kentuckians. The destination area was not popular for Pennsylvanians, but the domain county of Sangamon with the state capital was attractive to Ohioans. The smallest concentration of Ohioans was located in the domain counties of La Salle and Bureau. These Ohioans, who possibly mirrored New England traditions, selected destinations in the northern tier of Yankee counties. They disembarked from gateway Chicago because of the northern commercial corridor's linkages.

Another small Ohio migration cluster consisted of the core counties of Tazewell and McLean. These north-central Illinois counties served as bridging settlements for dispersing Midlanders and Midwesterners. In the 1840s, the evolving regional road network connected the county seat and market centers of Tremont and Bloomington with the river nodes of Pekin and Peoria. The migration cluster straddled the bridging road network that integrated the middle Wabash Valley with the middle Illinois Valley. An Ohioan migration cluster unfolded in east-central Illinois fringing the Wabash Valley corridor. This slightly larger concentration of Ohioans included the core county of Vermilion and domain counties of Coles and Edgar. The regional road network connected with the subregional node of Terre Haute in western Indiana on the National Road. The bustling courthouse and market centers and their hinterlands served as attractive destinations, thus fostering the northward-penetrating cultural mixing zone.

Sphere counties filled the intervening space between and contiguous with the primary Ohio migration clusters. The interwoven regional road networks in east-central and west-central Illinois functioned as a powerful settlement process that shaped the immigrant structure of the Ohioans in the 1830s and 1840s. Yet the Military Tract evolved as the "siren" destination, given its greater accessibility at this time to the entrepôt of St. Louis for marketplace-biased farmers. An extensive

Ohio avoidance area in southern Illinois corresponded to the strong northward thrust of the Upland Southerners. In northern Illinois, it coincided with inland isolation, prairies, and Yankee expansion.

Indiana Immigrant Region

Immigrants from Indiana represented about a third of the Ohioans and about one-half the number of Pennsylvanians in Illinois by 1850 (table 8.1). Indianans utilized similar pathways and entryways as other Midland-Midwest immigrants (fig. 8.3). Their primary migration clusters also concentrated north of the National Road. County concentration types of Indianans were almost identical with the Ohioans (table 8.2). Core and domain counties comprised 44.5 percent of the Indianans. Sphere counties comprised almost one-third of the counties with slightly over one-third of the Indianans. They possessed Midland and Upland South traditions. Those with a New England heritage would have been a small minority.

The Indiana immigrant region structure was segmented with primary migration clusters situated in east-central and west-central Illinois. Sequential ordering of core and domain county clusters spawned south-north alignments on opposite sides of the state. Two small, detached migration clusters formed in the interstice. Each Indiana migration cluster—the Military Tract and Wabash Valley corridor— had about one-fifth of the Indianans. The structure of the western Illinois Indiana migration cluster was similar to the spatial configurations of Pennsylvanians and Ohioans. Spatial linkages of the immigrant cultural mixtures in the mesopotamian Military Tract tied to the rival river towns of Quincy and Peoria. During the 1840s, the northern domain counties of Warren and Mercer became better connected in the expanding regional road network integrating Rock Island with Quincy on the Mississippi River and Peoria on the Illinois River.

Within the Military Tract, Fulton County had the largest number of Indianans. It also had the largest concentration of Ohioans and second-largest number of Pennsylvanians. Midlander ancestry abounded, but Upland South and Yankee farmers were also lured by an attractive environmental habitat and entwined regional urban-transport web. In the 1830s and 1840s, Indianans arrived overland on the coalescing network of roads that spread northwest from the National Road and northward from the Ohio River (figs. 3.5–3.7, 4.1). Numerous Military Tract settlements along the fringing Mississippi-Illinois Rivers, steamboat landings, and small river towns encouraged immigrant dispersal into the bordering river bluffs and the uplands between Quincy and Peoria.

On the east side of Illinois, a south-north settlement axis fringed the Wabash River by 1830 (figs. 5.4, 5.5). Compared with the Illinois movement-settlement corridor, the riparian Wabash Valley corridor failed to captivate immigrants, except for the earlier-arriving Upland Southerners. With improved steamboat navigation

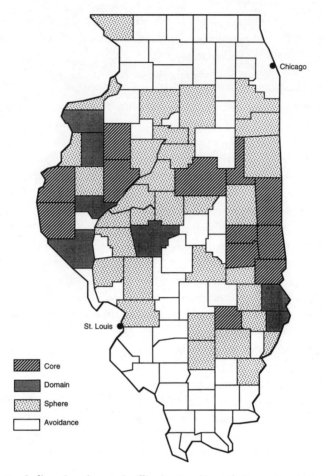

FIG. 8.3. Indiana Immigrants in Illinois, 1850 (*Seventh Census Population Schedules, 1850*)

on the Wabash River and expansion of the eastern Illinois road network, Wabash Country emerged as a more appealing destination area by 1850 (figs. 5.6, 5.7). The east-central Illinois road network thrust bridging roads westward and northward that connected with Sangamon Country and the Military Tract in west-central Illinois and the upper Illinois Valley and Chicago in northeast Illinois.

A south-north array of contiguous core and domain counties paralleled the Illinois-Indiana border (fig. 8.3). Indianans' stepwise migration pattern and available transport modes in eastern Illinois fashioned the linear structure. The Wabash Country Indiana migration cluster was slightly smaller than the Military Tract cluster. Five core and two domain counties were joined by a road network linking courthouse and market centers. In extreme southeast Illinois, Crawford and Lawrence emerged as domain counties. Vincennes on the Wabash River served as the exit point from Indiana and tied to Louisville. Lawrenceville in Lawrence County was the paired Illinois entry point.

Terre Haute on the National Road, the Wabash River, and the Wabash and Erie Canal functioned as the major disembarkation point into central Illinois for Indianans, Ohioans, and Midlanders. The magnitude of this subregional node as an entry-and-exit point is evident from the twin gateway foci on the Illinois side of the movement-settlement corridor. These lower-level nodes were connected via the interwoven urban-transport network to a number of destinations. Fifteen miles west of Terre Haute on the National Road was situated the courthouse and market center of Marshall in Clark County. Paris in Edgar County, to the northwest, evolved as a county seat and mercantile node. A south-north road paralleled the Wabash River. Marshall and Paris linked with Vincennes to the south and with Danville and Chicago to the north.

The crossroads location of Paris provided excellent linkages with the Indiana core county of Coles to the west, which straddled the Shelbyville Moraine and was traversed by the Embarras River. Within the road circulation network of east-central Illinois and its connections with west-central Illinois, numerous courthouse and market centers, such as Charleston, Shelbyville, and Decatur, were linked with the subregional nodes of Springfield, Jacksonville, Peoria, and Alton. Edgar County was within the commercial hinterland of Terre Haute to the southeast. Peck endorsed the economic rewards of Edgar County: "The soil in general is rich, adapted to the various productions of this state. Pork and beef—especially the former—are its chief exports, which find a ready market at Terre Haute and Clinton, Indiana" (1837, 100). Tiny Clinton was due east about fifteen miles on the Wabash River and the canal. Commercial agriculture developed within ten to fifteen years of the initial settlement of the Paris hinterland.

Danville in Vermilion County and Covington, Indiana, functioned as paired dispersal nodes. Indianans migrating from central and southeast Indiana to Illinois Country headed west on the National Road to Terre Haute. Another option was to travel northwest from Indianapolis to Crawfordsville, Covington, and Danville. During the 1840s, Covington's role as a market center for east-central Illinois was enhanced by its crossroads location and traversing waterway. Its strategic location on the Wabash and Erie Canal, which paralleled the Wabash River, increased its influence as a distribution and disembarkation center. Farmers in this south-north settlement axis who were driven by marketplace agriculture had accessibility to national markets in New York and New Orleans. The relative location of Covington in the northern apex of the riverine movement-settlement corridor was augmented by its position near the great bend of the Wabash and Erie Canal. Covington and its paired gateway of Danville were integrated northeastward with Fort Wayne and Toledo, the terminus of the canal. To the west,

Danville was situated at a crossroads location with accessibility to Chicago, Peru, and Ottawa on the Illinois and Michigan Canal. More importantly, it connected northwestward with Bloomington and Peoria and westward to Sangamon Country and the Military Tract. The Indiana core county of Vermilion, with its courthouse and market center of Danville, had slightly fewer Indianans than Fulton County in the Military Tract, which had the largest number.

Peck addressed the hinterland situation and accessibility of Danville: "The exports are pork, beef, corn, salt, etc., which find a convenient market at the towns on the Wabash, and down river to New Orleans. In due time much of the produce of the Vermilion country will pass by the way of Chicago and the lakes; and up the Wabash, and through a canal to Lake Erie. It would be no difficult matter to open a water communication between the Wabash and Illinois rivers, and thus furnish an outlet for the productions of this part of the state in every direction" (1837, 138). The intervening area between Danville and the Wabash River was oriented to commercial agriculture.

In the Wabash Valley corridor, paired dispersal points in west-central Indiana and east-central Illinois emerged approximately a day's travel apart by wagon or ten to twenty miles on the existing road networks (figs. 3.5–3.7). Immigrants utilizing the National Road not only traveled on a vastly improved road but also gained important disembarkation options for their trek to west-central Illinois. The westward extension and upgrading of the National Road to Vandalia, the Illinois capital between 1821 and 1839, occurred during the 1830s (Hardin 1967). In the 1830s, two key exit points on the National Road proffered greater accessibility northwestward to the mesmeric Sangamon Country and Military Tract in west-central Illinois.

Greenville in Bond County and Vandalia in Fayette County were the two primary egress points on the National Road. Both operated as important bridge points between the expanding southern and central Illinois urban road networks. Each crossroads courthouse and market center connected with the southern Illinois road network gateways of Shawneetown, Golconda, and Ft. Massac on the Ohio River and Vincennes on the Wabash River. In providing bridge and exit point ties, Vandalia on the Kaskaskia River emerged with greater connectivity. Immigrants who utilized the National Road had the option to continue westward, even though it was never completed to the Mississippi River. The role of Greenville, slightly less than twenty miles west, emerged as a key route bifurcation with greater accessibility to the river towns of St. Louis and Alton. Greenville was connected by the late 1820s with these rival riverside nodes and their hinterlands, which developed as important destinations.

Finally, the internal differentiation of the Indiana immigrant region reveals an isolated core and domain county (fig. 8.3). The core county of Clay probably formed as a result of a micro-scale channelized migration flow, given that most of the immigrants' children were born in Indiana. The domain county of Sangamon had three attractive destination characteristics: (1) political functions of the third state capital in 1839, Springfield; (2) "siren" place image status of Sangamon Country; and (3) a subregional node that also functioned as a county seat and market center. Sphere counties served as intervening linkages between the two major Indianan migration clusters on opposite sides of the state. They also functioned as Indiana settlement spearheads into destination areas dominated by New Englanders in the north and Upland Southerners in the south. The northward penetration probably associated with Indianans of Midlander heritage and the southward thrust reflected Indianans of Upland South traditions. Variant cultural backgrounds contributed to Indianans' greater dispersion across Illinois than most other major immigrant groups. Avoidance counties correlated with the culture polarization just mentioned. A south-north avoidance area evolved between the two major migration clusters. This inland avoidance area lay the greatest distance from accessible markets via the Wabash-Illinois-Mississippi navigable channels.

Illinois Immigrant Region

The Illinois immigrant region structure marks the length of lifetime migration of adult males, early evolution of premier destinations, vital early road arteries, and significance of riparian movement-settlement corridors. Of the major native-born groups, Illinoisans ranked fifth in size and second among the Midlanders and Midwesterners by 1850 (tables 6.1, 8.1). Where should Illinoisans be placed among the American regional culture groups? They are not similar to the migration patterns of New Englanders, slightly similar to Midlanders and Midwesterners, and most similar to Upland Southerners. Why place Illinoisans with Midlanders and Midwesterners rather than Upland Southerners? Illinois immigrant patterns unfold the northward penetration of early-arriving Upland Southerners. The spatial ordering of settlement frontiers in 1830 (fig. 5.5) proximates the Illinois immigrant structure (fig. 8.4). Later Illinoisans' interstate migration patterns exemplify their mixed cultural backgrounds. Mobile immigrants from heartland America embraced a growing regional consciousness perceived as midwestern (Shortridge 1989). Illinoisans comprised a fusion of Upland South, New England, Midland-Midwest, and foreign cultural customs that became lost in the cultural transformations in the Midwest (Swierenga 1989).

Only 37.7 percent of the Illinoisans dwelled in core and domain counties (table 8.2). Of the major immigrant groups settling Illinois, only Pennsylvanians (38.4 percent) were as minimally concentrated in core and domain counties. The structure of the Illinois (fig. 8.4) and Pennsylvania (fig. 8.1) immigrant regions reveals a propensity to disperse widely across the state, creating sphere counties, 48.5 and 46.6 percent, respectively. Sphere counties in both cases equaled almost 40 percent of the counties. Why were immigrant concentration types so similar? Their immigrant

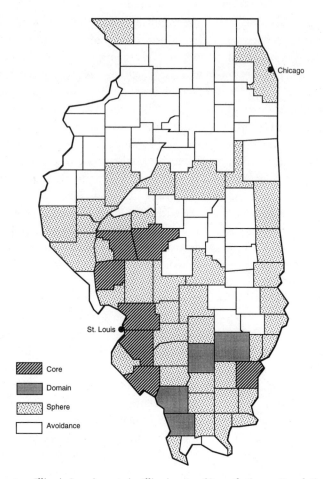

FIG. 8.4. Illinois Immigrants in Illinois, 1850 (*Seventh Census Population Schedules, 1850*)

spatial configurations appear dichotomous, a south-north polarity. In actuality, they are reversed immigrant patterns. The similarity of immigrant structures possibly associates with a cultural link between Upland Southerners who settled early Illinois and Midlanders. Transgenerational mobility from the Pennsylvania culture hearth had spread southwest into the Great Valley and later westward across the Lower Midwest. In the early nineteenth century, a convergence zone of like-minded people emerged in the Ohio Valley Country. Newton (1974) and Jordan and Kaups (1989) argue that their preadaptive traits made it possible for a Midland–Upland South culture to preempt the New West east of the Mississippi Valley in a short time span.

A south-north array of Illinois core and domain counties bordered the Mississippi-Illinois Rivers. This large, elongated migration cluster in western

Illinois included almost one-third of the Illinoisans. The immigrant cluster segmented into destinations associated with three distinct settlement periods: French colonial, territorial, and early statehood. The Shawnee Hills of southern Illinois were popular with Upland South woodland frontiersmen, particularly Union County for the early-arriving North Carolinians. The American Bottom was trumpeted by early western image makers. It enclosed floodplains and bordering Mississippi bluffs extending from Randolph County northward to Madison County. Sangamon Country also emerged as a mesmeric destination.

The reduced attractiveness of the Shawnee Hills as a destination in extreme southern Illinois is evident from the absence of any Illinois core counties. Four processes explain why the core counties of St. Clair, Madison, and Randolph accumulated the largest concentration of individuals born in Illinois, over 15 percent. The early key French settlements—Kaskaskia in Randolph County and Cahokia in St. Clair County—plus smaller urban and rural enclaves were linked by road and river. Persistence of French families in this French colonial island meant an aggregation of Illinois place-of-birth individuals. The longevity of the American Bottom as a potentially rich agricultural area lured Upland Southerners along with New Englanders, Midlanders, Midwesterners, and foreigners, especially Germans. Marketplace-biased farmers who infilled this diverse cultural matrix opted for accessibility to local, regional, and national market opportunities. Nearby St. Louis furnished a vital market and effective downstream connections to New Orleans with ties to Baltimore, Philadelphia, New York, Boston, and Europe.

Early federal land offices opened at Kaskaskia and Edwardsville. The immediate hinterland area of Edwardsville became known as the land of Goshen. This potential land of milk and honey emerged as a key destination in the northern uplands bordering the American Bottom. Traversing these three counties were the early roads of developing networks that integrated southeast and southwest Illinois. Overland routes converged on the St. Louis hub. The northern segment of the American Bottom was characterized by cultural diversity. The southern sector was attached to the domain counties of Jackson and Union. These counties depicted cultural uniformity: the dominance of Upland Southerners.

At the northern apex of the south-north Illinoisan immigrant axis were the core counties of Sangamon, Greene, and Morgan. With almost 10 percent of the Illinois immigrants, the early settlement appeal of Sangamon Country was confirmed. Sangamon and Morgan Counties symbolized the blunted tip of a northward-thrusting Upland South settlement spearhead. The Military Tract to the west, improved steamboat navigation, and expanding regional road infrastructure in the 1830s and 1840s perpetuated and intensified the attractiveness of west-central Illinois. These settlement processes shaped a large settlement area bifurcated by the Illinois Valley corridor.

The nuclei of Illinois immigrants in southeast Illinois comprised the core county of White and domain counties of Wayne and Jefferson (fig. 8.4). The population distribution map of 1820 reveals the attractiveness of the interstice area between the Little Wabash and Wabash Rivers during the territorial period (fig. 5.4). Within the expanding road network of southern Illinois in the 1820s and the 1830s, three important crossroads county seat and market centers evolved. These dynamic lower-level nodes included Carmi in White County, Fairfield in Wayne County, and Mt. Vernon in Jefferson County. Their surrounding hinterlands emerged as enticing destinations for Upland Southerners. All three crossroad nodes served as small distributive centers and disembarkation foci to other destinations in southern and central Illinois (figs. 3.4–3.6). Carmi was centrally located within the lower Little Wabash River settlements. In southeast Illinois, it benefited from being situated on a route between Shawneetown and the English colony in Edwards County. But Fairfield and Mt. Vernon had the advantage of emerging as settlement clusters on old bridging roads linking gateway nodes on the verge of the state.

Of these early lower-level nodes, the ascendancy of Mt. Vernon within the interior of southern Illinois was enhanced because of its centrality. It was astride the key bisecting south-north road connecting southern Illinois with the second state capital of Vandalia and west-central Illinois. Being at the crossroads of a number of well-worn immigrant pathways, Mt. Vernon was almost midway between the primary points of entry for immigrants and the American Bottom and Sangamon Country. It developed successful crossroads activities, therefore emerging as a pivotal destination within the Upland South culture region (fig. 6.8).

Illinoisans were different from other large immigrant groups in that sphere counties included almost half the Illinoisans (table 8.2, fig. 8.4). Sphere counties formed in the intervening areas between the major migration clusters. The Shawnee Hills area of southern Illinois did not emerge as a remnant magnet cluster of Illinoisans, given its appeal to early Upland South pioneer-hunters (Meyer 1976c). Footloose, woodland frontiersmen were not stayers; instead, their inclinations fostered stepwise movements to other parts of Illinois, the Ozarks of Missouri and Arkansas, and the hill country of Texas (Jordan 1967, 1969, 1970). They were replaced by later-arriving Upland South yeoman farmers.

The broad expanse of contiguous sphere counties straddled the expanding road network of the 1820s and early 1830s (figs. 3.3–3.5). A southeast-northwest trend dominated this road network that connected the points of entry on the Ohio River, particularly Shawneetown, Golconda, and Ft. Massac, with the American Bottom and Sangamon Country. The array of sphere counties in the Wabash Valley corridor portray northward-penetrating Upland Southerners in the eastern margins of the state. The Military Tract sphere counties illustrate the early desirability of the southern section of this attractive destination. The Illinois Valley corridor as an attractive settlement ribbon sequentially advanced northeastward during the 1820s and 1830s. Bridging sphere counties formed astride the north-central Illinois road network that traversed Tazewell and McLean Counties. They connected the crossroads river town of Peoria in the middle Illinois Valley with Danville in the northern part of Wabash Country. Early lead mining in Jo Daviess County contributed to its sphere county status, and Chicago captivated Illinoisans from the southern state margins to settle in Cook County.

By 1850, the northern boundary of the sphere counties in the Illinois immigrant region paralleled a cultural divide created by the Upland South, New England, and Midland-Midwest migration streams. The northern avoidance area corresponded primarily to Yankeeland. The large, contiguous block of avoidance counties in central Illinois associated with interior areas with limited access to regional and national markets and extensive open prairies. Two smaller Ohio Valley avoidance areas conformed to easily inundated floodplains and rugged uplands with limited agricultural potential. These heavily dissected bluff areas were not particularly attractive to yeoman farmers.

Secondary Midland-Midwest Immigrant Patterns

The lifetime state destinations of secondary Midland-Midwest immigrants suggest delayed movements into midcontinent from the eastern seaboard. The out-migration patterns mirror the cultural diversity of the Middle Atlantic coast and interior regions, owing to a strong historical-cultural propensity to persist in place. All three of the traditional seaboard culture hearths and interior secondary areas formed by late colonial times imprinted Midland-Midwest sending states to varying degrees: Pennsylvanian (Midland), New England, Lowland South, and Upland South (Mitchell 1978). Emigrants from the "Show Me State" of Missouri were not coaxed in great numbers to leap westward. A powerful immigrant directional-bias coexisted with the upgrading of the National Road and Ohio-Wabash-Mississippi-Illinois River system. Midlanders and Midwesterners followed channelized waterborne and overland pathways. Developing regional road networks connected river towns, crossroads courthouse and market centers, and lakeports to mesmeric destinations engraved in "Illinois fever." By 1850, lifetime out-migration comprised 133,381 New Jerseyites, 127,799 Marylanders, 37,824 Missourians, and 31,965 Delawareans.

New Jerseyites' state destinations attest to their mixed Midland, Yankee, and Dutch cultural traditions: New York (26.5 percent), Pennsylvania (21.8 percent), Ohio (17.6 percent), Virginia (8.6 percent), Indiana (5.9 percent), Illinois (5.1 percent), and Michigan (4.2 percent). The New West overshadowed the attractiveness of the domain areas in the eastern seaboard culture regions. Marylanders' ethnic-cultural mix and their appeal for eastern domain areas were also corroborated by state destinations. But their mobility documents the impress of Pennsylvanian and Lowland South cultures on Maryland and the fusion of Upland South culture in the Great Valley of western Maryland and Virginia during colonial times. Marylanders relocated to Ohio (28.7 percent), Pennsylvania (16.4 percent), Virginia (8.1 percent), Indiana (8.0 percent), District of Columbia (7.2 percent), Illinois (5.4 percent), Kentucky (5.1 percent), Delaware (3.4 percent), Missouri (3.3 percent), and New York (3.1 percent).

Short-distance migration to adjacent states, great leaps to the Pacific rim, return migration to Upland South origins, and movements counter to the dominant American predilections were prominent Missourian migration patterns. Missourians relocated to Illinois (19.1 percent), California (15.6 percent), Arkansas (14.1 percent), Texas (13.6 percent), Iowa (10.1 percent), Oregon (5.8 percent), Kentucky (3.9 percent), Wisconsin (2.7 percent), Indiana (2.6 percent), Tennessee (2.4 percent), and Louisiana (2.4 percent). Appalachian mountain culture was a pivotal settlement element in the forested eastern United States (Jordan 1970; Newton 1974). For over a century, they persisted in their circuitous stepwise migration patterns, which penetrated deeper into the continent. Pioneer-hunters from Missouri, Illinois, Indiana, and Ohio represented a continuum of Midland–Upland South backwoods frontier culture that traversed transAppalachia, the Midwest, and the Ozarks. They fought at the Alamo, mined gold at Sutters Mill, and established kinfolk enclaves in the coniferous forests of Oregon.

State destinations of Delawareans typify their Midland cultural ties. Although few in number, Delawareans followed initial shifts into the Midland hearth and domain area before transgenerational filterings into the Old Northwest: Pennsylvania (39.3 percent), Ohio (14.8 percent), Maryland (13.7 percent), Indiana (8.6 percent), Illinois (4.4 percent), New Jersey (4.3 percent), and New York (2.8 percent). Micro-scale channelized migration flows connected origins in the Midland hearth and domain areas back East with Midland regional way stations and new destinations in Illinois. Social networks within the small, secondary groups of Midlanders and Midwesterners operated within the expanding Midland-Midwest culture region diffusion network established by the macro-scale migration streams. The structural patterns of their immigrant regions in Illinois should parallel Midlanders originating from Pennsylvania and Midland extended Ohio. The four adult male secondary groups numbered 2,899 from New Jersey, 2,891 from Maryland, 1,333 from Missouri, and 650 from Delaware (table 8.1). These small Midland-Midwest immigrant groups constituted only 5.1 percent of the native-born adult males.

New Jersey Immigrant Region

The structure of the New Jersey core and domain counties replicates the stellar destination that attracted the primary Midland-Midwest migration streams (figs. 8.1–8.3, 8.5). Forty-three percent of the New Jerseyites settled in a bifurcated migration cluster straddling the Illinois Valley corridor with sphere counties linking the core cluster polarity in west-central Illinois. They were about equally divided between the Military Tract and Sangamon Country. Only the core county of Cook emerged outside the pivotal migration cluster. Almost 70 percent of the New Jerseyites in Cook County resided in Chicago. The sphere counties, with about 40 percent of the New Jerseyites, spread across the northern half of west-central and northern Illinois (table 8.2). A large, contiguous area of avoidance counties, about 13 percent of the New Jerseyites, formed a north-south axis linking east-central and southern Illinois. The New Jersey core counties in west-central Illinois were not contiguous, except for Adams and Pike Counties. The structure of the New

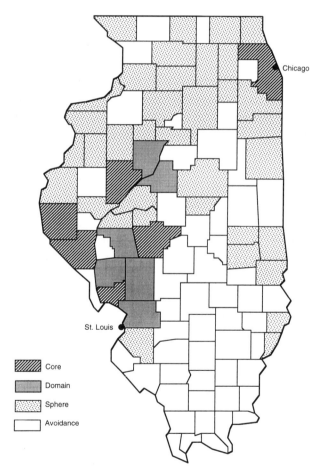

FIG. 8.5. New Jersey Immigrants in Illinois, 1850 (*Seventh Census Population Schedules, 1850*)

Jersey migration cluster reflects strong, micro-scale, channelized migration patterns to place-specific destinations. Disproportionate numbers of New Jerseyites settled three core counties: Fulton, Jersey, and Sangamon. Agrarian marketplace Midlanders were captivated with the accessibility and fertility of Fulton County. It had the largest concentration of Ohioans, Indianans, and New Jerseyites and second-largest cluster of Pennsylvanians in Illinois. One in ten New Jerseyites located in Fulton County. New Jerseyites of Midlander background were also intrigued with urban settings. Twenty-eight percent of the Jerseyites in Jersey County resided in Jerseyville, the courthouse and market center. Springfield, the state capital, attracted 30 percent of the New Jersey immigrants in Sangamon County.

Maryland Immigrant Region

Almost equal in size to the New Jerseyites, the immigrant surface configured by Marylanders paralleled their destinations (table 8.1, figs. 8.5, 8.6). Four fragmented core counties had slightly over 25 percent of the Marylanders (table 8.2). Three core counties were located in west-central Illinois: Fulton, Adams, and Sangamon. Immigrants of similar cultural backgrounds and agricultural motivations were inclined to settle in equivalent favorable locations. Marylanders disproportionately settled in the northwest Illinois core county of Ogle, with one-eighth of the state total. They spilled over into the contiguous domain county of Carroll. Ogle County was adjacent to Stephenson County, with the largest concentration of Pennsylvanians (figs. 8.1, 8.6). The primary Maryland migration cluster spread southwest-northeast on the west side of the Illinois Valley corridor in the Military Tract. Two core and three domain counties had 16.7 percent of the Marylanders in the state. In the isolated Sangamon core county, 38 percent of the Marylanders opted to live in Springfield. Marylanders in Illinois primarily represented Midland cultural traditions. Their settlement choices were quite different in the two detached domain counties of Madison and Vermilion. In Vermilion County, they were primarily pioneer-hunters and yeoman farmers, since they ignored Danville as a destination. Riverside Alton was appealing to laborers, artisans, and professionals. One-third of the Marylanders in Madison County dwelled in the river town with its manufacturing, processing, distributive, financial, and market center activities.

Marylanders dispersed across the expansive, featureless plains of Illinois. Forty-four percent of the Marylanders resided in the thirty-nine sphere counties (table 8.2). Of the macro- and micro-scale Midlander migration flows, 40 to 47 percent of the Marylanders, New Jerseyites, and Pennsylvanians scattered into sphere counties. Sphere counties emerged in east-central, west-central, and northwest Illinois. The common thread among these Midlanders from the East was their preoccupation with a traditional agrarian marketplace focus. West-central Illinois, with its movement-settlement corridor, developed the broadest expanse of

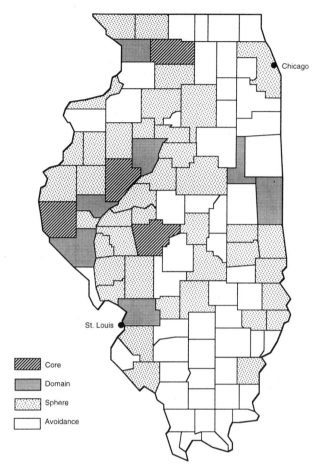

FIG. 8.6. Maryland Immigrants in Illinois, 1850 (*Seventh Census Population Schedules, 1850*)

sphere counties. On opposite sides of southern Illinois were southward penetrations of Marylanders bordering the Wabash-Mississippi corridors. In southwest Illinois across from St. Louis, these Marylanders probably reflect a Pennsylvania German heritage, because their destinations were etched in the primary German migration cluster. Finally, about 15 percent of the Marylanders were dispersed in avoidance counties in southern, central, and northern Illinois.

The segmented Maryland immigrant structure parallels the Pennsylvania, Ohio, Indiana, and New Jersey immigrant structures (figs. 8.1–8.3, 8.5, 8.6). This regional congruity in destinations attests to the continuity and persistence of cultural-economic bonds. Regional settlement growth in the 1840s modified the frontier into a commercial agrarian economy. Midlanders and Midwesterners, like

New Englanders and Upland Southerners, settled accessible riparian corridors in western Illinois. Crop-livestock export products moved within a four-tier urban-market hierarchy. Improved roads meant that lower-level and subregional nodes in west-central Illinois were more accessible as market centers. Steamboats on the Illinois-Mississippi Rivers furnished downstream access to St. Louis and a world space-economy. The Illinois and Michigan Canal and a railroad network short-circuited the southward Mississippi trade flow.

Missouri Immigrant Region

Stepwise, short-distance migration meant bordering states witnessed substantial exchanges in population. By mid-nineteenth century, 10,917 Illinoisans (23.8 percent) stepped westward across the Mississippi River into Missouri. At the same time, 7,228 Missourians (19.1 percent) stepped back eastward across "Old Man River" into Illinois. During the Great Migration, directional movements were far more complex than a generalized westward-bias. Missourians' immigrant structure diverged from the primary and secondary Midland-Midwest groups. A contiguous Missouri migration cluster emerged in western Illinois bordering the Mississippi upstream and downstream from St. Louis (fig. 8.7). This linear cluster of core and domain counties included over 40 percent of the Missourians. Pike and Adams Counties had a disproportionate number, about 20 percent, evenly divided. Two isolated core counties associated with attractive destinations: the lead mining region of Jo Daviess County and Cook County. The lure of urban opportunities occurred in both instances. In Jo Daviess County, 42.3 percent of the Missourians settled in Galena. Chicago attracted 96.9 percent of the Missourians in Cook County. One-third of the Missourians were dispersed in sphere counties. The largest concentration of sphere counties was adjacent to the primary migration cluster. Sphere counties formed upstream in the Illinois Valley corridor, Sangamon Country, and inland from the Mississippi River in southern Illinois. Avoidance counties comprised a contiguous array stretching across northern and eastern Illinois.

The riverine migration cluster of Missourians discloses underlying cultural processes. The core counties of Calhoun, Pike, and Adams in the southern Military Tract and the domain county of Greene in Sangamon Country probably included Missourians with predispositions for settling among Upland Southerners. The core counties of Madison and St. Clair and the domain counties of Monroe and Randolph delineate an area within the mercantile hegemony of St. Louis. Southwest Illinois represents three distinctive cultural-immigrant mixtures. First, a small residual of French descendants persisted in St. Clair and Madison Counties. Second, Upland Southerners established a regional way station impress (fig. 6.8). Third, a primary German migration cluster bordered German concentrations in St. Louis and the lower Missouri River Valley. Many Missourians were

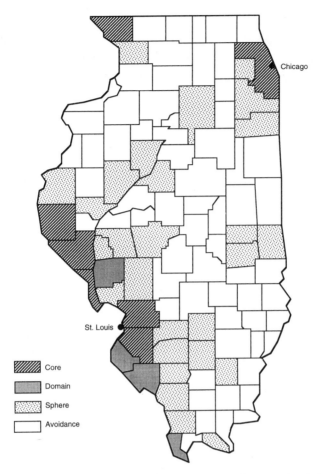

FIG. 8.7. Missouri Immigrants in Illinois, 1850 (*Seventh Census Population Schedules, 1850*)

possibly of German background, electing to live amid German brethren in the free state of Illinois.

Delaware Immigrant Region

Delawareans were a very small Midland-Midwest immigrant group in Illinois (table 8.1). Their immigrant region structure exhibits strong similarities with the primary and secondary Midland-Midwest immigrant groups (figs. 8.1–8.8). A south-north aligned, riparian migration cluster with inland extensions emerged in western and west-central Illinois (fig. 8.8). This contiguous cluster of core and domain counties had a disproportionate half of the Delaware immigrants. Adams County in the Military Tract had the largest concentration of Delawareans. Of the five core counties, Adams and Fulton on opposite sides of the Military Tract attracted a considerable cultural mix. Scott County bordering the Illinois River in Sangamon Country and Madison and St. Clair Counties across from St. Louis developed agricultural marketplace activities. A small migration cluster evolved in the Wabash Valley corridor. Sphere counties linked the small concentration of Delawareans in east-central Illinois with the larger cluster in west-central Illinois. The greater width of the sphere counties occurred upstream in the Illinois Valley and the Illinois and Michigan Canal corridor. As was common with many Midland-Midwest immigrant regions, the avoidance areas for Delawareans were bifurcated with a north-south polarity.

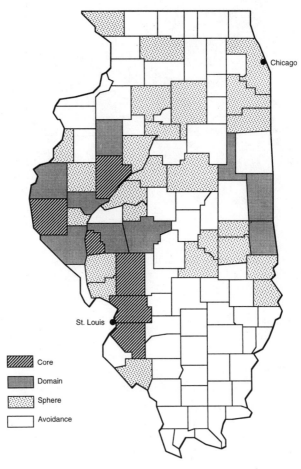

FIG. 8.8. Delaware Immigrants in Illinois, 1850 (*Seventh Census Population Schedules, 1850*)

Midland-Midwest Culture Region

The Midland-Midwest culture region in Illinois symbolizes the dynamic cultural-agricultural adaptations and fusions emerging in midcontinent by 1850 (fig. 8.9). A distinctive Pennsylvania extended floundered in spreading west of Ohio across Indiana, Illinois, and Iowa in the 1800s. I propose that a subtle, mixed version of Midland–Upland South cultural-agricultural traditions was integrated at the core of the expanding Midwest culture region. Prior to the Civil War, marketplace-motivated farmers, whether from Pennsylvania, Ohio, Indiana, or Illinois, transplanted an incipient Corn Belt legacy across the American heartland (Bogue 1968; Power 1953a). After the Civil War, the expanding midwestern railroad networks engendered an expansion of the Corn Belt family farms' steer-hog-corn amalgam.

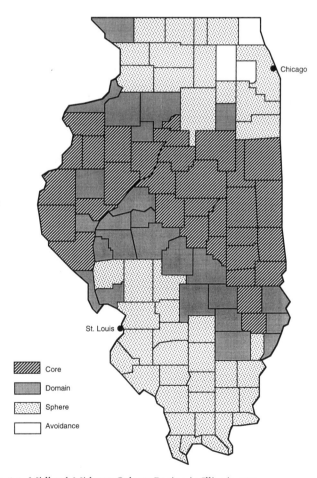

FIG. 8.9. Midland-Midwest Culture Region in Illinois, 1850

Midlanders and Midwesterners transplanted in mixed-settlement enclaves westward across the interior. During the late 1830s and 1840s, migration ebbed and flowed from origins in the eastern Midwest and the Middle Atlantic states (Hudson 1988; Mitchell 1978; Pillsbury 1987; Rose 1988c). The upgrading of trunk roads and more flexible regional road networks and improvements in steamboat navigation and inland canal shipping inundated Illinois with Ohioans, Pennsylvanians, and Indianans. Population elements from Midland-Midwest sources in central Illinois were not acknowledged as a distinct regional culture group like Upland Southerners and New Englanders by early writers, observers, or immigrants. Southerners stereotyped anyone from an eastern state or state north of the Ohio River as a "Yankee."

The congruity of primary and secondary immigrant structures hints at equivalent cultural traditions among Midlanders and Midwesterners (figs. 8.1–8.8). Universal dispersal symbolizes the flexibility of their cultural settlement strategy. The Midland-Midwest immigrant structures suggest a hegemony in the culture region core (fig. 8.9). The Midland-Midwest core counties formed a broad east-west belt across central Illinois. Ohioans predominated the northern tier core counties, whereas Kentuckians dominated in the southern tier. County migration fields in central Illinois typify a primary trend emerging in the midwestern cultural terrain: cultural mixing. The structure of Midland-Midwest core counties discloses distinctive shifts in regional immigrant composition. These regionalization changes were affected by the cultural integration of diverse migration streams in west-central Illinois.

The configuration of the Midland-Midwest core counties corroborates the influence of the National Road as a principal dispersing route. The westward-tapering Midland-Midwest core pattern in east-central Illinois confirms the powerful northward thrust of Upland Southerners and the impact of the expanding regional road web (figs. 6.8, 3.5–3.7). Roads radiated into the interior from the Wabash Valley corridor. Terre Haute, Danville, and dispersal foci along the National Road were primary exit points during the late 1830s and 1840s. Roads converged on Springfield and Jacksonville in Sangamon Country and Peoria in the Military Tract. Midlanders and Midwesterners sought out courthouse and market centers and their tiny tributary areas situated like beads in the evolving urban-transport networks. Infilling occurred in the interstices between the diverging routes to the "siren" settlement platforms.

The mesopotamian Military Tract in west-central Illinois possessed a natural, dispersing funnel shape between the Mississippi and Illinois Rivers. The triangular Midland-Midwest core wedge attests to the Military Tract's popularity. The movement channels quickened the settlement of riverine counties and penetration of inland counties. Quincy became the focal hub of the Mississippi Valley corridor in western Illinois. The Illinois Valley corridor, however, bisected and

integrated the Military Tract and Sangamon Country. Roads dispersed from numerous river towns, thus generating a denser road network in the riparian counties in west-central Illinois. Midway Peoria served as the fulcrum link for the two
triangular-shaped Midland-Midwest core areas. The crossroads linchpin, riverside node consolidated an extensive mercantile hinterland that extended upstream and downstream in the movement-settlement corridor between Chicago
and St. Louis. Only Peoria County integrated into two different culture region
cores: New England and Midland-Midwest (figs. 7.9, 8.9).

The migration fields of the Midland-Midwest core counties in east-central Illinois depict a cultural borderlands. Midwesterners and Midlanders predominated
over Upland Southerners in the northern tier counties. In the southern tier counties astride the Wabash Valley corridor, a northward spearhead of Upland Southerners displayed an affinity to mix. County migration fields extending from Coles
and Edgar southward typify those Midland-Midwest core counties where Upland
Southerners substantially outnumbered Midwesterners and Midlanders. The expansive east-central Illinois Midland-Midwest core symbolizes a regional convergence zone where immigrants shared subtle cultural roots.

Central Illinois embraced a transplanted amalgamation of Midland–Upland
South cultural heritage. Jordan and Kaups argue the preadaptive strategy of Midland America as the most successful farming-hunting-gathering complex adapted
to the temperate woodlands (1989, 30). The Midland–Upland South cultural mix
arrived in Illinois by different, sequential diffusion routes. Many Upland Southerners originated from southeast Pennsylvania German, Scotch-Irish, Irish, and
English colonial stock. Their geographic mobility shifted in a clockwise fashion
through the Great Valley, the Piedmont, and transAppalachia to the Nashville and
Bluegrass Regions (Mitchell 1978; Newton 1974). Their progeny arrived as Virginians, North Carolinians, Tennesseans, and Kentuckians north of the Ohio River.
Midlanders from southeast Pennsylvania successively moved westward to south-
central and southwest Pennsylvania and to southwest Ohio and southeast Indiana
(Jordan and Kaups 1989; Mitchell 1978; Pillsbury 1987; Zelinsky 1973). These two
strands of Midland–Upland South traditions reunited and mixed in the Ohio Valley corridor. These diverse Midland–Upland South immigrants revealed both
backwoods frontier culture and yeoman marketplace culture as they intermingled
in central Illinois (fig. 8.9).

The more significant regional convergence zone comprising Upland Southerners, New Englanders, Midlanders, Midwesterners, and foreigners formed in west-
central Illinois. With the Military Tract and Sangamon Country, west-central
Illinois developed as a dynamic, quintessential midwestern settlement platform. It
was centrally located and highly accessible with the fringing Mississippi and traversing Illinois Rivers. The cultural diversity in the Military Tract uniquely portrays a north-south polarity similar to the entire state and a cultural mixing zone

(D. K. Meyer 1980). In the Midland-Midwest core's northern half in the Military Tract, the county migration fields composed a distinctive proportional mix of Upland Southerners, Midlanders, Midwesterners, and New Englanders. The pattern holds for counties adjacent to Peoria County on the east side of the Illinois Valley corridor. At first glance, the Midland-Midwest core's southern half in the Military Tract appears similar in county migration fields. Instead, Upland Southerners were overweighted in numbers as these counties evolved as Upland South domain counties. This trend is not surprising, since it was settled initially by an Upland South intrusion. The Midland-Midwest subculture in its diverse migration forms predominated. The Military Tract in west-central Illinois emerged with a stronger Pennsylvanian imprint than east-central Illinois.

The southern fringe of the Midland-Midwest core abutted a strong northward wedge of Upland Southerners. I argue that a larger number of domain counties emerged along the southern verge as immigrants of diverse Midland–Upland South cultural backgrounds interacted. The Midland-Midwest domain area formed a concave arc around the northward Upland South settlement push. Within this cultural transition zone, Sangamon Country counties formed the apex of this cultural mixing zone. They embraced both Midland-Midwest and Upland South domain characteristics but also emerged as a New England sphere area. A prominent northern cultural mixing zone adjacent to the New England core did not emerge, owing to their hegemony in northern Illinois. Instead, the northern boundary of the Midland-Midwest core abruptly ends. Core counties were even situated next to sphere counties, which suggests a sharp migration field gradient between contiguous counties. The isolated lead mining area of Jo Daviess County evolved in anomalous fashion in Yankeeland as a Midland-Midwest domain county.

Midland-Midwest immigrants dispersed into more sphere counties than Upland Southerners or New Englanders (figs. 6.8, 7.9, 8.9). Their sphere counties extended northward into the New England core and southward into the Upland South core. Their material culture and agricultural traits adapted to the mixed timber–prairie habitats in central Illinois. These cultural processes supported an expansion of this immigrant cultural mixture across the Mississippi River. Immigrants deeply rooted in Pennsylvanian traditions recognized their inclusion within a distinctive migration stream. An idiosyncratic, contiguous Pennsylvania extended subculture region failed to evolve in the Old Northwest's western margins. Instead, a culturally mixed Midland-Midwest culture region with a midstate core area expanded its periphery to Illinois' southern and northern verge.

Tradition-bound Pennsylvania Germans planted farming enclaves where language and religion persisted. Preservation of Germanic cultural traditions sharpened a sense of community in rural villages. Legible Midland material culture traits in the landscape were highly localized. Distinctive Pennsylvanian landscape elements intertwined in a common landscape: houses, barns, agricultural complexes, farming methods, pioneer log structures, Midland-northern dialect, foodways, and diamond courthouse squares or Lancaster squares (Jordan and Kaups 1989; Mitchell 1978; Pillsbury 1987; Price 1968; Zelinsky 1973). Pennsylvania German place image signatures were engraved in rural and urban landscapes. Today in the rural landscape, the relic Midland artifact icon remains the large Pennsylvania bank barn with forebay. These cultural vestiges symbolize both the rootedness of built forms in the agrarian landscape and successful marketplace agricultural complexes. Pennsylvania barns exemplify the attitudes and values of commercially oriented Pennsylvania German farm families. Pennsylvanian landscape traditions persist as residual cultural contrivances.

9

Foreign-Born Immigrant Regions

The Irish homes of Illinois,
The happy homes of Illinois,
  No landlord there
  Can cause despair,
Nor blight our fields in Illinois!
  —McGee c. 1850 (in Barry 1902)

Atlantic Europe was driven by a westward impulse (Hansen 1961). Promoters, immigrants, and British travelers influenced Europeans' migration to the American interior in the early nineteenth century. Midcontinental Illinois, with its open spaces and frontier communities, offered fertile soil, cheap land, jobs, and freedom. Personal letters and visits from relatives and friends from America formed a powerful bond in social networks linking origins and destinations. Potential emigrants' mental maps were affected by social networks as long-distance migration emerged as a vigorous topic of village intercourse. Information fields were critical to the formation and effectiveness of chain and channelized migration patterns within "American fever." By 1850, Europeans' segmented patterns were interwoven among Upland South, New England, and Midland-Midwest immigrant structures in Illinois.

Travel books and letters concerning America and Illinois shaped a "siren's illusion" of the New West (Rodman 1947). Morris Birkbeck's *Letters from Illinois* (1818a) and *Notes on a Journey in America* (1818b) were the earliest influential European promotional literature for the new state. The latter volume went through eleven editions and the former seven editions in three years (Rodman 1947, 333). English travelers' impressions proliferated into the 1840s (Buckingham 1842; Hoffmann 1835; Latrobe 1835; Martineau 1837; Shirreff 1835; Stuart 1833; Woods 1822). First-hand impressions of travelers and American emigrants were widely accepted in Europe. Vivid place and landscape images portrayed the prairies' beauty, peoples' customs and life, and opportunities in frontier Illinois (Jones 1954).

Birkbeck promoted emigration to his southern Illinois English colony. Speaking of the colony site, Birkbeck noted: "The land is rich natural meadow, bounded by timbered land, within reach of two navigable rivers, and may be rendered immediately productive at a small expence. The successful cultivation of several prairies has awakened the attention of the public, and the value of this description of land is now known; so that the smaller portions, which are surrounded by timber, will probably be settled so rapidly as to absorb, in a few months, all that is to be obtained at the government rate, of two dollars per acre" (1818b, 129–30). The location was supposedly favorable: "The Big Wabash, a noble stream, forming its eastern boundary, runs a course of about four hundred miles, through one of the most fertile portions of this most fertile region" (130). Shawneetown served as an egress and ingress gateway with America and Europe (153). Cheap, fertile land was contrasted with the "worn-out soils in England" that required twice as much capital for cultivation (Birkbeck 1818a, 18).

Handlin argues that "immigrants were American history" (1973, 3). Foreigners comprised 11 percent of the almost twenty million Americans in 1850. Native- and foreign-born immigrants were a continuous settlement process in the eastern United States (Hansen 1961, xvii). Illinois was settled by 736,931 native-born immigrants or 86.6 percent, 110,593 foreign-born immigrants or 13.0 percent, and less than half a percent with unknown birthplaces. The 196,896 adult males comprised a slightly different origin snapshot (table 6.1). Native-born adult males principally from the states due east and southeast accounted for 77.5 percent of the total. Foreign-born adult males, who included 22.5 percent of the total, were from northwest Europe. A higher proportion of foreigners were adult males than native-born, 40.1 percent and 20.7 percent, respectively. Young adult males and husbands preceding their families generally participated in the transatlantic migration.

The ebb and flow of a diverse Great Migration spread an immigrant "lumpy stew" across midwestern plains and Illinois. "In no other State in the Union, I believe, is the population of so variously composite a character. . . . In our blood there is, more or less, a strain of that of the chivalric, pleasure and art loving French; the picturesquely aggressive Scotch-Irish—itself, by the way, a composite racial type; the sturdy, undying tenacity of the Anglo-Saxon; the brave, prudent, thoughtful, fore handed German; the stubborn, freedom loving, astute Dutchman; the alert, active, resourceful, tireless Yankee; the canny Scot; the free handed, hot blooded, gamecock of all the races, the Irishman" (McConnel 1902, 75).

Some foreign groups' segregated clusters emerged as "mother areas" for replicated settlements in midcontinent and later in the northern plains (Qualey 1976). "Mother areas" functioned as dispersion points that duplicated new ethnic enclaves. Foreign-born immigrants competed with native-born groups for the remaining lands and community sites. Infilling of previously settled attractive areas was a universal settlement process as foreigners acquired land that had not been occupied or purchased earlier-cultivated acreage. Selectivity of immigration, destinations, American ethnic structure, and availability of cheap, fertile lands influenced the transplanting of foreign enclaves across the eastern United States (Conzen 1980, 8–9). Segregated foreign-born clusters were expected, given immigrants' fundamental need for social-cultural imperatives, living in a community setting, and survival in a new world. Numerous individuals and families were satisfied with being isolated or receiving mutual cultural support from only a few individuals or families. Such foreigners were comfortable with their isolation, as they carried out their existence amongst a diversity of immigrants or in another ethnic cluster.

Foreign-born immigrant regions document foreigners' predisposition for creating distinctive, fragmented clusters in Illinois by 1850. Segregated immigrant patterns concentrated in southwest, west-central, northwest, and northeast Illinois. Foreigners dispersing westward and northward into the Middle West migrated within an expanding four-tier urban-transport and culture region system (fig. 3.8). I posit that a foreign-born culture region, with segmented cultural cores that emerged, integrated within the evolving urban-transport networks of Illinois.

Primary Foreign-Born Population Sources

Europeans' settlement predilections focused on the northern half of the eastern United States. The over 2.2 million foreigners concentrated in seven states in 1850: New York (29.5 percent), Pennsylvania (13.3 percent), Ohio (9.9 percent), Massachusetts (7.7 percent), Illinois (5.0 percent), Wisconsin (4.8 percent), and Missouri (3.3 percent). The largest European sources were Ireland (43.5 percent), Germany (26.4 percent), and England (12.6 percent), for a lopsided 82.5 percent of the total. Numerous destinations developed in the Midwest, almost one-quarter of the total foreign-born. Germans outweighed the Irish in midcontinent, in contrast to northeast America, where the Irish dominated. Availability of large tracts of cheap, fertile land and accessibility of the northern, middle, and southern commercial gateways engendered a rapidly expanding, diverse European population in the interior.

Lifetime European migration in the United States in 1850 included 961,719 Irish, 584,720 Germans, and 278,675 English. Germans comprised German-speaking immigrants from the German states, 573,225; Prussia, 10,549; and Austria, 946. The proportions from Ireland, Germany, and England in their respective destination states reflect the incipient stage of large population shifts from northwest and northern Europe. This diverse ethnic imprinting in the rural and urban environs presaged the massive population redistributions of southern and eastern Europeans. They were attracted to the mining and manufacturing centers in America prior to World War I.

The Irish settled New York (35.7 percent), Pennsylvania (15.8 percent), Massachusetts (12.1 percent), Ohio (5.4 percent), New Jersey (3.2 percent), Illinois (2.9 percent), Connecticut (2.8 percent), and Wisconsin (2.2 percent). Germans migrated to New York (20.1 percent), Ohio (19.2 percent), Pennsylvania (13.5 percent), Missouri (7.7 percent), Illinois (6.6 percent), Wisconsin (6.5 percent), Indiana (5.0 percent), Maryland (4.6 percent), Louisiana (3.1 percent), and Kentucky (2.4 percent). The English emigrated to New York (30.4 percent), Pennsylvania (13.7 percent), Ohio (9.2 percent), Wisconsin (6.8 percent), Illinois (6.7 percent), Massachusetts (6.0 percent), New Jersey (4.1 percent), Indiana (2.0 percent), and Missouri (2.0 percent). Rival Middle Atlantic gateways of New York and Philadelphia functioned as important destinations along with their respective states. Ohio, the initial state settled in the Old Northwest, infilled with Irish, Germans, and English (Wilhelm 1982). Foreigners' settlements were an integral part of a geographical growth system that was thrusting deeper into the heartland of America during the Great Migration.

Primary Foreign-Born Immigrant Patterns

Europeans tended to segregate within a region, because they were the "filler-in" in previously settled or bypassed areas by American pioneers (Ostergren 1981a, 30). If the ethnic enclave grew substantially beyond a particular township, foreigners spilled over into conterminous townships or even contiguous counties. Larger foreign groups formed discrete core-periphery structures. Europeans did not assume significant proportions in Illinois until the two decades prior to 1850 (Pooley 1968, 491). Germans (35.9 percent or 15,889), Irish (27.3 percent or 12,075), and English (17.9 percent or 7,911) predominated with 81.1 percent of the total foreign-born adult males of 44,305 (table 9.1). Their distribution among immigrant concentration type counties were similar to the Americans but had some distinctive differences (tables 6.3, 7.2, 8.2, 9.2). Germans reveal a tendency toward geographical clustering (table 9.2). A larger proportion of Germans, over 60 percent, settled in a few fragmented core and domain counties. Germans, Irish, and English shaped small ethnic pockets embedded in sphere counties. Their avoidance counties accounted for over half the counties.

Europeans entered America at one of four gateway, national nodes: New York, Philadelphia, Baltimore, or New Orleans. Each seaboard entrepôt was integrated with a trunk line, movement corridor into the interior: northern, northeastern or middle, and southern commercial gateway (Walton 1987, 230–34) (fig. 3.1). Historical-geographical conditions in Europe and America influenced the directional- and destination-biases of Europeans. Riverside St. Louis and lakeside Chicago emerged as key interior gateways for Europeans dispersing into Illinois. Expanding road networks in the 1840s increasingly converged on and diverged

TABLE 9.1 Birthplaces of Adult Male Foreigners in Illinois, 1850

Birthplace	Number	Percentage of Foreign-Born
Germany	15,889	35.86
Ireland	12,075	27.25
England	7,911	17.86
Canada	2,436	5.50
Scotland	2,109	4.76
France	1,442	3.25
Norway	823	1.86
Switzerland	610	1.38
Sweden	331	.75
Wales	256	.58
Portugal	116	.26
Netherlands	85	.19
Poland	56	.13
Denmark	52	.12
Italy	27	.06
Belgium	15	.03
Other	72	.16
Total native-born	44,305	

Source: Seventh Census Population Schedules, 1850

from the regional nodes of St. Louis and Chicago (figs. 3.5–3.7). Regional three-tier urban hierarchies emerged as attractive destinations. Segmented German, Irish, and English immigrant structures focused on regional and subregional nodes.

German Immigrant Region

The German lower middle class participated in the transatlantic migration to America prior to 1850 (Walker 1964, 42–69). Neither great landowners nor harvest hands, they were small, landowning farmers. Neither apprentices, unskilled laborers, nor wealthy merchants, they were village shopkeepers and artisans. Few were from major cities or larger towns, but they were self-assured because of a reliance on their own skills and a desire to continue to do so. Their property could be transferred into cash, so emigration was generally based on their own resources. They perceived their economic worth atomizing because of social, economic, and political forces. A marketplace agricultural economy literally was being destroyed from under them. Small merchants and craftsmen experienced the economic decline of small farmers and villages.

Kamphoefner maintains that German peasants were motivated by two universal pull factors: "the land of plenty and freedom" (1987, 68). Arriving in Illinois, they were not preoccupied with establishing "New Germanys" or colonization

TABLE 9.2 Foreign Immigrants' Concentration Patterns in Illinois, 1850

Birthplace	Core Concentrations		Domain Concentrations		Sphere Concentrations		Avoidance Areas	
	No. Counties	% Migrants	No. Counties	% Migrants	No. Counties	% Migrants	No. Counties	% Migrants
Germany	5	51.3	3	10.5	30	32.0	61	6.2
Ireland	3	38.4	5	18.8	37	37.2	54	5.6
England	4	30.7	7	20.5	32	38.5	56	10.3
Canada	3	38.1	6	20.9	27	34.4	63	6.6
Scotland	6	44.3	4	12.8	27	32.9	62	10.0
France	6	56.9	5	17.4	15	18.6	73	7.1

schemes, as in some states (Hawgood 1940). Walker argues that Germans desired to recover and preserve a deep-rooted way of life that a new Germany appeared destined to extinguish. They were insistent in traveling the difficult journeys "to keep their roots, their habits, their united families and the kind of future they wanted for their families" (1964, 69). Culturally and physically, Germans transplanted conservative traditions in order to perpetuate their sense of identity and community. Their enclaves formed astride interior navigable waterways. For many German rural enclaves and urban neighborhoods, immigration from the fatherland persisted into the late 1800s. Community cohesiveness remained strong because of traditions, language, religion, and Turnverein societies. Preserving Germanness was a priority in midwestern and Illinois destinations.

German "Illinois fever" began in the 1820s and increased with each decade as peasant farmers, merchants, laborers, and craftsmen sought new homes and opportunities. The political and professional refugees from the 1830 and 1848 German revolutions added to the German social mix in established, rural ethnic islands and urban neighborhoods (Wittke 1952, 1967). By the 1840s, the number of Germans swelled in Illinois. Germans emerged as the largest foreign-born element in the state, over a third of the adult male foreigners (table 9.1). They comprised the fourth-largest immigrant group, 8.1 percent (table 6.1).

Germans settled in proximity to regional and subregional nodes interwoven in the expanding three-level urban infrastructure. Dispersing from St. Louis, Germans molded a spatially discrete settlement pattern in southwest Illinois (fig. 9.1). Spreading from Chicago, Germans established a smaller migration cluster in northeast Illinois. A disproportionate number of Germans, 61.8 percent of the total, were concentrated in less than 10 percent of the counties, five core and three domain counties (table 9.2). A German riparian ethnic island tied to the subregional node of Peoria formed between the regional nodes. Pooley noted the larger influx of German farmers who preferred fertile agricultural districts with access to a marketplace economy (1968, 491). Two secondary German migration clusters emerged in conjunction with the subregional nodes of Quincy and Galena.

The German immigrant region was segmented into four primary migration clusters. The northeast Illinois German migration cluster fringed the interior terminus of the northern movement corridor. Almost two-thirds of the adult male immigrants in Cook County were foreign-born, with 73.1 percent living in Chicago. The German core county of Cook possessed the largest concentration, 17.9 percent, of adult male Germans in the state. Gateway Chicago had almost two-thirds of the Cook County Germans. They included slightly less than one-third of the foreigners in the city but almost half of those in the surrounding rural townships. The core county of Cook, domain county of DuPage, and five collar sphere counties configured a German ethnic island that included 26 percent of the Germans in Illinois.

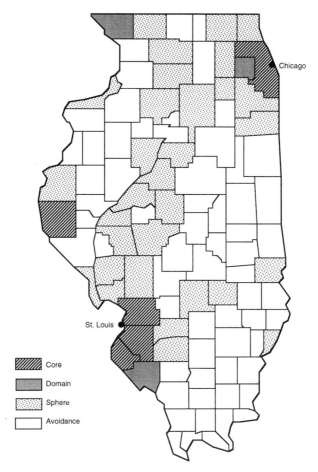

FIG. 9.1. German Immigrants in Illinois, 1850 (*Seventh Census Population Schedules, 1850*)

The largest German migration cluster was situated in southwest Illinois fringing gateway St. Louis. The riverside node emerged as a pivotal interior terminus of the southern movement corridor. This dynamic German migration cluster offered an alternative settlement choice for anti-slavery Germans who desired not to reside in the slave state of Missouri. A German riparian ethnic enclave had been forming astride the Mississippi-Missouri Rivers and tied to the German cultural hearth of the middle Mississippi Valley. A German spillover forged an Illinois German culture hearth that linked with the large German communities of St. Louis and Chicago and the upstream German enclaves in the Illinois-Mississippi Valley corridors.

The German migration cluster formed a north-south axis of three core counties and one domain county fringing the Mississippi River (fig. 9.1). The German core county of St. Clair was second in German concentration to Cook County. The proportion of adult male Germans residing in the four contiguous counties included 6.3 percent in Madison, 15.1 percent in St. Clair, 5.2 percent in Monroe, and 3.6 percent in Randolph. With the addition of the five abutting sphere counties, the German ethnic island comprised 35.5 percent of the Illinois Germans. Farmers, laborers, artisans, merchants, professionals, and some political refugees from the 1830 and 1848 German revolutions were attracted to Germanic southwest Illinois. The Missouri-Mississippi-Illinois riverine German enclaves interconnecting with St. Louis emerged as the largest German ethnic island in the interior. A Germanic overlay of vernacular architectural forms, landscape elements, and landscape traditions intensified with increased German infilling in the late 1800s. A material culture landscape that "read" German emerged in time and place in the Missouri-Illinois German region (Meyer 1988).

The courthouse and market center of Belleville in St. Clair County unfolded as the German hearth area in southwest Illinois. The majority of the adult males, 57.1 percent, in St. Clair County were foreign-born, with Germans dominating, 78.5 percent. Germans especially settled in small covenanted, agricultural market centers, such as Red Bud in Randolph County, Waterloo and Columbia in Monroe County, Millstadt and Mascoutah in St. Clair County, and Highland in Madison County. Large numbers of Germans infilled the intervening frontier-agricultural areas between the tiny marketplaces. Rural settlement clusters centered around the dispersed German Lutheran and Catholic churches. The river towns of Chester in Randolph County and Alton in Madison County were attractive to laborers, merchants, and artisans. German farmers dispersed northward into Madison County and southward into Randolph County from the German core of Belleville and intervening area with Columbia and Waterloo. German settlements spread eastward into Clinton and Washington Counties. In the 1850s and postbellum period, Germans settled in hamlets and villages replicated in the railroad corridors of parallel rail lines converging on the growing rail hub. Rail lines connected St. Louis with Cincinnati, Louisville, and Nashville. Interstice lands mirrored an ethnic agrarian society.

Germantown in Clinton County marked the earliest German Catholic colony in Illinois. In 1833, Ferdinand Boehne and Friedrich Hemann emigrated from the Osnabruck area in Hanover, sailing from Bremen to Baltimore. Having worked in Philadelphia, they traveled west to St. Louis in 1834 and acquired fifty acres on Shoal Creek (Kelly 1939, 85–91). The pathfinders encouraged Low Country relatives and friends to join their colony. Between 1835 and 1837, single adult males and families arrived and purchased government land or previously occupied land. In 1837, the colonists purchased 120 acres for church purposes. Forty acres of the church lands were set aside for a town site with one-acre town lots. By 1838, sixty German families dwelt in the Shoal Creek colony and worshiped in the log edifice of St. Boniface. Outgrowing the place of worship, they built a frame structure in 1840 and the present stone church in 1856. Dispersed German settlements formed west of Germantown. Spires of rural Catholic parishes are visible today, approximately four to six miles apart.

A third German migration cluster originated upstream on the Mississippi River (fig. 9.1). The enclave, 8.1 percent of the adult male Germans, was considerably smaller than the two previous clusters. The core county of Adams included 6.8 percent of the Germans in Illinois. Almost two-thirds of the county's foreigners were Germans, and 68 percent resided in Quincy. German landscape and architectural imprints are still visible in the old ethnic neighborhood on the city's south side. The final German cluster formed in northwest Illinois as an urban destination with an agricultural periphery. The domain county of Jo Daviess and sphere county of Stephenson included 5.9 percent of the Germans. Germans, 23.5 percent of the foreign-born, were third in size. Almost two-thirds of the Germans resided in Galena, which was a higher percentage than for the Irish, 39.6 percent, and English, 20.6 percent. A higher proportion of Germans, 13.0 percent, were laborers, but a smaller proportion, 8.2 percent, were miners. One-fourth of the Germans were in artisan, manufacturing, and mercantile activities. German farmers were attracted to Stephenson County, which had the largest concentration of Pennsylvania Germans in Illinois (figs. 8.1, 9.1).

The structure of sphere counties mirrors German farmers' desire for accessibility to a marketplace economy and the attraction of market centers for German laborers, artisans, and merchants. They settled adjacent to the traversing waterway of the state and key overland routes. Subtracting the twelve contiguous sphere counties to the four German migration clusters from the thirty sphere counties in the German immigrant region reveals that the remaining eighteen sphere counties possessed 18.4 percent of the total adult male Germans (table 9.2). Distinctive sphere county patterns emerged: connecting, penetrating, and scattered.

The dominant connecting sphere pattern joined St. Louis and Chicago. In the lower and middle Illinois Valley, Germans straddled the accessible upstream steamboat channel. The Germans, 9.2 percent of the state total, settled in six key counties with vigorous local markets and ties to regional and national markets: Sangamon, Cass, Mason, Tazewell, Woodford, and Peoria. Five of them were situated in this riparian enclave's eastern margins. Half the Germans in Sangamon County resided in the state capital of Springfield. In Cass County, the Germans, 55.1 percent, congregated in the riverside market, manufacturing, and distributive center of Beardstown. Tazewell County attracted the largest number of Germans in the valley, with about one-third in the small river town of Pekin, ten to twelve miles downstream from Peoria. Woodford County adjacent to Peoria appealed to marketplace-oriented German farmers. Peoria County was second to Tazewell County in number of Germans, with almost two-thirds lured to the diverse urban opportunities of Peoria.

In the upper Illinois Valley, the sphere pattern bifurcated at La Salle County (fig. 9.1). The counties of La Salle and Stephenson were terminal clusters of this German settlement sphere that penetrated northwest, linking Ottawa and Peru on the Illinois River, Freeport, and Galena. The larger German clusters tended to align with the expanding road network that thrust northwest from the Illinois Valley and westward from Chicago to Galena. The German settlement sphere coincided with the Illinois and Michigan Canal and included Will County with its Germans in Joliet and Frankfort Townships. Chicago, the lakeside and canal terminus, emerged as the German culture hearth in northeast Illinois.

Germans penetrated the transitional area of southern and central Illinois. Sphere counties aligned with the National Road. Fayette and Effingham Counties were settled by German colonies in the second state capital of Vandalia and Teutopolis. Stroble stresses the role of the entrepreneur and land speculator who organizes, funds, and conducts another type of covenant community, the ethnic colony (1987). Ferdinand Ernst, one such dominant personality, transplanted a German colony of one hundred individuals to Vandalia on the Kaskaskia River in 1820. Push factors ranged from the effects of the Napoleonic Wars, economic and social disruptions, and crippling crop failures and inflation. Because the covenant community lacked the bond of faith, cultural survival of the German settlement disintegrated after members met their indentured financial obligations to Ernst and after his death in 1822. Without leadership and social ties, the Rhinelanders dispersed, and the German colony emerged as a failure of the past (108–9).

A larger, successful German colony was established at the "City of the Teutons." The cohesive German community formed a distinctive cultural affinity, tiny market center, and rural hinterland that persists today. Teutopolis typifies the struggles and dissensions of a German Catholic colonization scheme in the isolated frontier. On the National Road, it was founded by a Cincinnati German land company for the specific purpose of creating a German Catholic colony west of the Wabash River (Kelly 1939, 133–42; Rothan 1946, 44–45). Physical, social, economic, and psychological stresses often related to loose colony organizations, thus, a priest's ministrations were a necessity for cultural survival.

A committee from Cincinnati, including land agent Henry Roennebaum, who platted Oldenburg, Indiana, was selected to examine potential interior colony lands (Kelly 1939, 133–34). Ten thousand acres of land were purchased in eastern Effingham County and recorded in the Superior Court at Cincinnati on September 21, 1839. Each member of the colony was entitled to one front lot, one back lot, and one garden lot along with forty acres outside of town for fifty dollars. The covenant town was laid out with forty-eight blocks with nine lots each and fifty-foot street frontage. Lots were set aside for church, cemetery, and marketplace activities. The National Road, or Main Street, eighty feet in width, was distinguished from the remaining sixty-foot wide streets (134). The colony received support for their spiritual welfare from the bishop of Cincinnati, who sent Reverend Masquelet to the diocese's outer edge in November 1839 (135–36). Members were dissatisfied with the priest, since he spoke High and not Low German. A priest who could provide their children with religious instruction in Low German was requested from the bishop of Vincennes. By 1842, 141 Germans owned four-acre town lots. Within seven miles of the village, ninety German families resided in the mixed forest–prairie borderlands.

Scattered German sphere counties bordered riverine corridors. Germans tended to locate in or near small riverside nodes: Rock Island in Rock Island County, Mt. Carmel in Wabash County, and Darwin in Clark County. Small German clusters closely linked with potential marketplace agriculture centers and Pennsylvania German settlement patterns. German and Pennsylvania immigrant structures were spatially related (figs. 8.1, 9.1). Pennsylvania Germans and Germans recognized their identity, culture, religion, language, and attachment to the fatherland. Wilhelm substantiates a similar proximity of Germans and Pennsylvania Germans in Ohio (1982). Three fragmented German avoidance areas formed across Illinois. Two north-south avoidance zones were the Grand Prairie through the southern Illinois woodlands and northern prairies to the southern forests in the Military Tract. A small area formed in the prairie interior of northern Illinois.

Direct German migration duplicated small and large ethnic enclaves in the Illinois regional settlement web by 1850. F. W. Bogen advised Germans wishing to settle in Missouri, Iowa, western and southern Illinois, or southern Indiana to employ New Orleans as the gateway to the Mississippi Valley. If using New York as the port of entry for the interior, he admonished them not to be swayed by Germans living in the great eastern seaboard cities to stay in those national nodes (1852, 45). Successful ethnic communities derived growth, survival, and prosperity from geographical-cultural propinquity. "If you have relations or acquaintances in the interior, who have written you, travel to them. If you were accustomed to a country life in Germany, and like it, a country life in America will please you, as many thousands of your countrymen are very much pleased with it, and are doing very well. Never buy land, which you have not seen with your own eyes" (51).

By the 1830s and the 1840s, German ethnic-religious, covenant communities emerged as attractive destinations in Illinois for Germans migrating across the Atlantic. Lalor argued that "[t]he Germans in this country are clannish, gregarious in their instincts . . . that is, with his own countrymen. . . . The Lutheran German builds a Lutheran school-house next to his Lutheran Church, and then sends his children to be brought up Lutherans" (1873, 461, 466). He also stressed Germans' attachment to physical training, particularly the Turnverein gymnastic societies. Finally, Lalor noted: "A German community without music is unthinkable; as well talk of a German community without a language or a brewery" (467).

Gustave Koerner noted the influence of social networks on German destinations (McCormack 1909). The Koerner, Abend, and Engelmann families arrived in New York from Havre, France, in 1833. They traveled by steamer upstream on the Hudson River, traversed the Erie Canal, crossed Lake Erie from Buffalo to Cleveland, journeyed on the Erie and Ohio Canal to Portsmouth on the Ohio River, floated downstream on the Ohio River to the Falls of the Ohio at Louisville, and changed steamboats for St. Louis on the Mississippi River (1:266–86). The Engelmann family discovered that friends and acquaintances who had left Havre ten days earlier had arrived in St. Louis about a week before via New Orleans. Their destinations were place-specific: settle among Germans in the lower Missouri River Valley or in Illinois adjacent to St. Louis. The migration routes were well defined and offered a number of settlement options. The Koerner party notified relatives who had emigrated a few years earlier and settled east of St. Louis in St. Clair County of their arrival. Turkey Hill, southeast of German Belleville, became an important destination (1:286–93). Being an original member of the intellectual elite in Shiloh Valley, Koerner acquainted himself with his adopted country: he read Peck's history of Illinois and Missouri, Flint's *History and Geography of the Mississippi Valley*, and the *Missouri Republican* newspaper. He concluded "that advertisements are the very best teachers of a people's character" (1:302).

German influences in Illinois occurred as direct transplantings from the fatherland and indirect German American migrations from Pennsylvania and North Carolina. Early colonial German seaboard settlements and post–Revolutionary War, secondary, interior German enclaves furnished immigrants. A German migration flow lasting into the late 1800s emerged from the Old World shortly after statehood. The majority of the Germans represented the poorer social classes of farmers, laborers, and artisans. Beinlich noted the early formation of a small German group from the highly cultured and scholarly classes in the Belleville area (1909). After the German revolution of 1830, numerous university-educated Germans from the middle and professional classes emigrated for political, religious, and social reasons.

Shiloh Valley, northeast of Belleville, unfolded as a unique ethnic pocket of "Latin farmers." Beinlich argues that these young, energetic, cultured men "formed the basis for German life and power, and quickly influenced farming, commerce, journalism and trade" (1909, 213). The name "Latin farmers" associated with their high educational level, knowledge of Latin, and classical training. Both Villard (1942) and Klett (1947) noted the significant role of German intellectuals, professionals, and upper-class individuals in southwest Illinois. Well-to-do Germans left much in the fatherland. They followed relatives and friends to the Belleville area as part of a micro-scale channelized migration from the Rhineland.

Immigrant mixture stereotypes in southwest Illinois characterizes Kern's perceptions: "There are many native Americans in Randolph County whose ancestors came from Virginia and Kentucky, the same sturdy and superior element which joined the French in St. Clair County, and soon outstripped and outnumbered them as they themselves were later superseded and outnumbered by the efficient, the patient, the plodding, the thoughtful, frugal and hard-working Germans" (1916, 38). Germanic heritage in Belleville was clearly evident in the spoken or written language of Negro servants, pastors' sermons, school teachers, business clerks, and newspapers (Villard 1942). Germanness was rooted in the humanizing bonds of language, religion, social cohesion, and customs. Socially, politically, and visually, Germanness was mirrored in the rural and urban landscape. Englemann, an influential German community member, wrote in 1837: "Life in this settlement is only very slightly modified by the influence of the American environment. Different in language and customs, the Germans isolate themselves perhaps too much from the earlier settlers and live a life of their own, entirely shut off" (Hawgood 1940, 37–38). Recognition of the need to establish German communities was fundamental to the reinforcement and perpetuation of the German spirit in a new land, but it failed to evolve spatially as a "New Germany" (104–5).

Irish Immigrant Region

The Irish, the largest American foreign group in 1850, were predisposed to the eastern seaboard. Their enclaves were adjacent to primary waterways where urban centers required large numbers of laborers. Frontiersmen of Irish ancestry from Pennsylvania and Virginia who had fought with George Rogers Clark in 1778 settled in Illinois Country (Barry 1902). In the Midwest and Illinois, Irish settlements integrated with an expanding continental urban-transport system. Irish laborers were attracted to lakeside and riverside nodes, the Illinois and Michigan Canal, and the lead mining country (fig. 9.2). The Irish immigrant structure emerged similar to the Germans (fig. 9.1) but was different in several ways. Comprising slightly over one-fourth of the foreign adult males, the Irish were second to the Germans (table 9.1). In the 1840s, Irish numbers mushroomed with the need for laborers in the transport, mining, processing, manufacturing, and distributive sectors of rapidly growing subregional and regional nodes. They constituted the eighth-largest immigrant group, 6.1 percent (table 6.1). Almost 60 percent of the Irish settled in three core and five domain counties (table 9.2). Scattered Irish clusters aligned in the upper and middle Illinois Valley. Less than 6 percent of the Irish dispersed in the avoidance counties in eastern Illinois.

The Irish immigrant region was splintered into three primary and two secondary migration clusters. Dispersing from gateway Chicago, the Irish configured a fragmented structure in northern Illinois. The largest Irish migration cluster in northeast Illinois was peripheral to the western terminus of the northern movement corridor. Almost a fourth of the Irish were situated in the core county of Cook. Lakeside Chicago had a disproportionate number of the Irish in Cook

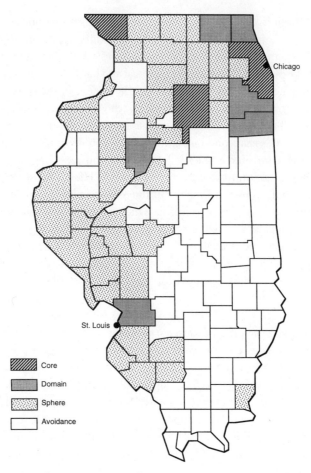

FIG. 9.2. Irish Immigrants in Illinois, 1850 (*Seventh Census Population Schedules, 1850*)

County, 83.5 percent. They comprised the largest foreign-born group in Chicago, with 39.8 percent of the total. The core county of Cook, the domain counties of Lake, Will, and McHenry, and the six fringing sphere counties marked a key interior Irish enclave that included 43.5 percent of the state total.

Irish settlement pockets formed in the peripheral domain counties. In Lake County, the Irish, 41.1 percent of the total foreign-born, were double the size of the English and Germans. They dispersed throughout the inland townships, but Waukegan Township and its lakeport possessed 22 percent of the Irish in the county. Inland McHenry County, adjacent to Lake County, also witnessed the Irish dominating, 51.0 percent or almost three times the English element. Located in all the townships, the Irish again clustered in one township, Hartland, with 30 percent of the county total. The Illinois and Michigan Canal traversed the northwest portion of Will County. The Irish included 31.0 percent of the foreign element in Will County, which portrayed an incredible foreign diversity. They were attracted to the canal towns and farmlands bordering or in proximity to the movement corridor, with over a third being laborers. Three canal townships, Joliet (24.6 percent), Lockport (21.1 percent), and Channahon (12.8 percent), contained the key Irish settlement pockets in Will County. Farmers' accessibility to Chicago, eastern seaboard, and world markets improved with the canal's opening in 1848. Irish farmers were not an anomaly.

In the bordering sphere counties of Kane and Grundy, Irish preferences for canal, river, and mill site town locations and adjacent fertile farmlands were commonplace (Maguire 1868; O'Hanlon 1976; Onahan 1881). In Kane County, the Irish represented the largest foreign element, 42.1 percent of the total, and laborers, 45.4 percent. The north-south-flowing Fox River experienced 42.2 percent of the Irish in townships with mill sites and junctures of roads radiating from Chicago. Yet one-fourth of the Irish, principally farmers, settled in Rutland Township, traversed by the Chicago-Galena Road. In Grundy County, the Irish dominated the foreign element, with 54.1 percent of the total. Morris Township, with its canal town namesake and Aux Sable Township, bisected by the canal corridor, had over half of the Irish in the county, with 29.7 percent laborers.

The Irish were clustered in two segregated locations that linked with specialized economic activities on the Illinois frontier: mining and waterborne traffic. The Irish were concentrated in the core counties of Jo Daviess (8.4 percent) and La Salle (7.3 percent). Neither core county spawned a large Irish spillover into contiguous counties, although sphere counties were peripheral (fig. 9.2). The Irish predominated over Germans and English in both counties, 38.2 percent in Jo Daviess and 45.6 percent in La Salle. In the lead mining county of Jo Daviess, the Irish were distributed throughout the townships but were particularly concentrated in Galena and the immediate vicinity, with 53.4 percent of the county total. Another 22.3 percent of the Irish resided in the adjacent precincts of Irish Hollow and Vinegar Hill. The Irish were in two nonfarming occupations: laborers, 11.0 percent, and miners, 17.6 percent. Irish also spread eastward into Stephenson County, 26.3 percent of the foreign-born. Germans were almost double the Irish numbers in Stephenson County, given their settlement affinity for Pennsylvania Germans.

The Irish located in the northern La Salle County townships in the Illinois Valley corridor. They had been involved in the spade and pick construction of the canal. Numerous canal laborers had switched their tools for the plough and harrow of farming the canal scrip land from Bridgeport to La Salle. Farm acreage and town lots had been offered for payment of work during the state banking system's failure in the early 1840s (Onahan 1881, 159). Onahan contends that many Irish

laborers who "took up" farming were discontented because there were no alternatives (160). Irish farm settlements and pockets in canal towns formed the nuclei of
colonies and social networks that attracted immigrants from Ireland to settle in
the movement corridor from Chicago to La Salle and downstream to Peoria (160).
Over half the Irish, almost equally divided, concentrated in Ottawa Township,
with the canal town of Ottawa, and in Salisbury Township, with the twin nodes of
La Salle, the western terminus canal town, and Peru, the head of steamboat navigation. Laborers made up 43.4 percent of the workers in the county.

Aligned along the movement corridor connecting Chicago and St. Louis were
two Irish domain counties, Peoria and Madison. Settlement and economic activities reverberated around their respective riverside, subregional nodes and substantial tributary areas. Peoria, the steamboat center of the middle Illinois Valley,
attracted an almost equal number of Germans and English and slightly more
Irish. A larger proportion of Irish, 57.6 percent, than the Germans, 36.8 percent,
settled in the rural townships in contrast to the market center of Peoria. Almost
45 percent of the Irish in the county were laborers. Riverside Alton, with its transshipment, processing, distributive, and manufacturing activities, evolved as the
Illinois terminus of the Illinois Valley corridor. Germans outnumbered Irish almost three to one and congregated in the rural townships, 83.4 percent. By contrast, the Irish slightly outnumbered the Germans in Alton, but 53.0 percent of
the Irish were dispersed in Madison County. Almost two-thirds of the Irish were
laborers.

Sphere counties contained over one-third of the Irish, who formed small agricultural and urban communities with their signature Roman Catholic parishes
(table 9.2, fig. 9.2). Irish pockets emerged in northern, west-central, and southwest
Illinois. A contiguous surface of sphere counties straddled the Illinois Valley corridor and diverging roads from Chicago. Irish laborers located in Quincy, Jacksonville, and Springfield. Segregated Irish farm pockets formed in Randolph and
Monroe Counties. Fifty percent of the Irish in Monroe County clustered in the
upland New Design Township with tiny Burksville.

Sixty percent of the Irish in Randolph County located in the uplands, bisected
by the Kaskaskia River. The majority of Irish farmers, a mix of Irish from Ireland
and Scotch-Irish from Ulster, settled with their earlier brethren from the South
Carolina piedmont (figs. 9.2, 6.5). Early in the nineteenth century, a micro-scale
channelized migration flow originated in the Abbeville area backcountry of South
Carolina. The Plum Creek settlement, east of the Kaskaskia River, centered around
Preston. The Irish and Scotch-Irish mixtures in this enclave were simply referred
to as the "South Carolina Irish" (McGoorty 1927, 60; *Combined History of Randolph, Monroe and Perry Counties* 1883, 69). Immigrants of shared ancestry and
traditions were lured from Ireland, Ulster, the South Carolina piedmont, and the
Upland South to southwest Illinois.

Numerous push factors in the stormy, tragic environment of Ireland precipitated emigration: opposition to British control over Ireland, religious problems, oppressive tithes, absentee landlords, high rents, poor wages, extreme poverty, and, particularly, crop failures and famines (Miller 1985; Pooley 1968, 499; Wittke 1956; Wyman 1984, 19–39). Money was scarce, travel was difficult and slow, illiteracy was widespread, mail service was virtually nonexistent, and American destinations were terrae incognitae in early-nineteenth-century Ireland. Counterpart to burial in a grave, the night before the exodus of relatives or friends from an Irish village epitomized a terminal physical and emotional separation (Miller 1985, 557). "American wakes" replicated traditional Irish deathwatches in their physical appearances and symbolic importance: "Both were held to gather together relatives and neighbors to honor the 'departed,' to share and assuage the grief of the bereaved, and to express at once communal sorrow and a reaffirmation of communal continuity in the face of potentially demoralizing disruptions" (558). The last night at home was an important break from their Irish roots. Yet it also bonded the social networks' integrating origins and destinations in the chain migration process (Wyman 1984, 44).

Wyman notes the importance of American funds for paying passage (1984, 39–44). Optimistic "America letters" to relatives and friends and newspaper articles in Ireland that pictured a new life, dreams, and hopes were essential pull factors. Life in America and Illinois was not an easy adjustment and was filled with disappointments for most European immigrants. O'Hanlon stressed in his emigrant guide that "Irishmen living in this country and writing to their friends at home, should by all means avoid giving over coloured pictures of what they see and experience.... Exaggeration and extenuation are as opposite to trust, as direct misrepresentation; but we conceive it only necessary to warn our countrymen against the former in epistolary correspondence" (1976, 255, 257). Social networks were critical to successful settlement adaptations as the Irish left their homeland to avoid starving to death from the potato famine in the 1840s.

English Immigrant Region

English, Irish, and Germans shared many push factors for leaving their homelands. The early English colony and writings of British travelers and immigrants were widely known in Europe concerning the promise of prosperity in Illinois (Erickson 1969, 1972; Foreman 1941; Jones 1954; Rodman 1947, 1948; Salter 1981). Foreman concluded that "America letters" from Illinois to relatives and friends in England were fundamental to social networks that formed chain and channelized migration patterns (1941). Letters were frequently reprinted "in provincial English newspapers, for the contents had an irresistible appeal to land-hungry and food-hungry tenantry. They all told of the abundance and cheapness of food in Illinois, a subject the writers never tired of, and which they knew would hold spellbound the incredulous readers they hoped would follow them to this land of plenty" (306).

The English were the third-largest foreign group in the United States and Illinois by 1850 (table 9.1). They represented the tenth-largest adult male group in Illinois, 4.0 percent (table 6.1). The English made up 17.9 percent of the foreigners, or about half the size of the Germans. In the early 1800s, they were attracted to two early English settlements: the English colony in Edwards County and the lead mining entrepôt of Galena. Dispersing westward from Chicago and eastward from St. Louis, the English attached their settlements to the expanding urban-transport webs. Small English enclaves dispersed across northern, west-central, and southwest Illinois (fig. 9.3). In the late 1830s and 1840s, the English typified the Germans and Irish destinations but with some definite differences.

Half the English were concentrated in four core and seven domain counties (table 9.2). The smaller proportion of English in core and domain counties, in contrast to the Germans and Irish, suggests an inclination to settle among native-born English-speaking immigrants. Only in northeast Illinois adjacent to Chicago were English concentration type counties—core, domain, and sphere—situated at regular decreasing intervals. The Illinois Valley corridor emerged as a salient pattern with regularly spaced English enclaves. A southwest Illinois tributary to St. Louis lured average concentrations of English, who infilled among the large urban and rural settlements of Germans and Upland Southerners in this culturally diverse settlement area. A larger percentage, 10.3 percent, of the English diffused into avoidance counties.

The English immigrant region was fragmented with four primary and five secondary migration clusters by 1850. The largest English cluster in northeast Illinois abutted lakeside Chicago. Almost half the English congregated in Cook County. Two-thirds of the English in Cook County located in the regional node. The English, Irish, and German adult males disproportionately worked as laborers in Cook County, 21.9 percent, 23.3 percent, and 16.8 percent, respectively. The English emerged as the third-largest foreign group in Chicago, with 12.2 percent of the total. The core county of Cook aggregated a disproportionate 13.4 percent of the English in the state. Along with the domain counties of Lake and Will and four fringing sphere counties, this English migration cluster included 28 percent of the Illinois total.

English constituted about half the size of the Irish in Will and Lake Counties. The English were lured to canal towns and farmlands in verge townships of the Illinois and Michigan Canal. Two canal townships, Joliet, 19.5 percent, and Lockport, 16.6 percent, comprised the primary English enclave in Will County. The English were farmers, with laborers comprising only 7.5 percent in Lake County and 13.4 percent in Will County. In the sphere counties, the English were either the second- or third-largest foreign group. Kendall County was an anomaly, where

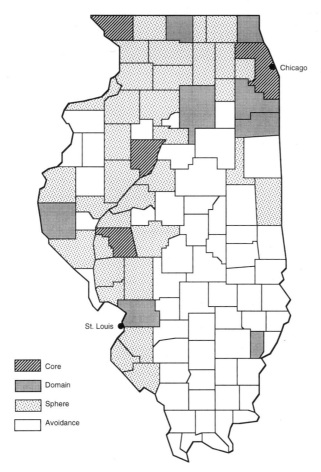

FIG. 9.3. English Immigrants in Illinois, 1850 (*Seventh Census Population Schedules, 1850*)

the English were the largest foreign group, 30.1 percent. Attached to the soil, English farmers dispersed throughout the sphere counties. Generally, two townships had about 30 percent of the English population in each sphere county. In Kane and DuPage Counties, about one in five English were laborers in townships with excellent mill sites on the Fox and DuPage Rivers.

English enclaves emerged in three segmented core counties: Jo Daviess, Peoria, and Morgan (fig. 9.3). The respective core counties situated astride waterways with dynamic market centers and with access to regional and national space-economies. Jo Daviess County required labor specialization tied to lead extraction. The English, second to the Irish, comprised 27.5 percent of the foreigners in Jo Daviess County. Like the Irish, the English were concentrated in Galena, its immediate hinterland, and the lead mining townships. They comprised the largest number of miners, 39.3 percent, and were lopsidedly concentrated in mining as an occupation, 34.6 percent. A smaller proportion of English, 6.4 percent, were laborers, in comparison with Germans, 13.0 percent, and Irish, 11.0 percent. Like Mineral Point in southwest Wisconsin, Cornish miners were a specialized labor element in Galena (Copeland 1898).

English immigrants, 70 percent, in comparison to the Irish, 57.6 percent, and the Germans, 36.9 percent, were more inclined to settle the countryside than riverside Peoria. At the midsection of the Illinois Valley corridor, Peoria included 37.0 percent foreigners. The English, 18.7 percent, were third among the city's foreign-born, substantially behind the Irish, 29.1 percent, and Germans, 39.6 percent. By contrast, foreigners in the county's population were considerably less, 26.3 percent. The English were the largest foreign element outside the city. In the lower Illinois Valley, Morgan County and Jacksonville were an early English destination. The English, 46.7 percent, were the largest foreign group with only one-sixth lured to the county seat and market center.

Smaller enclaves formed in five scattered domain counties, with a total of 14.2 percent of the English. Three domain counties were intertwined in riverine transport networks. La Salle County, with its riverside and canal transshipment centers, witnessed 35.7 percent of its English located in the townships with Peru, La Salle, and Ottawa. Almost two-thirds of the English in Adams County, with the river town of Quincy, resided in the countryside. Madison County, with riverfront Alton, was a magnet for English desiring either an urban or an agricultural setting. Alton attracted 40.2 percent of the English in the county, who accounted for one-fifth of the foreigners in the city, whereas both the Germans and Irish embraced one-third. In the countryside of Madison County, Germans overwhelmed, 51.3 percent of the foreigners.

Astride the Chicago-Galena Road, English immigrants, 34.2 percent, emerged as the largest foreign element in Winnebago County (fig. 9.3). One-fourth of the adult males were foreigners. The English were dispersed in the county but formed English pockets in three Rock River townships: Rockton, Roscoe, and Rockford. These townships possessed half of the English, with Rockford Township and county seat by the same name with a disproportionate number of English, 29.5 percent.

Southeast Illinois was not attractive to foreigners, who avoided the isolated inland areas dominated by Upland Southerners. Yet there persisted a remnant "mother area" in Edwards County, with 2.7 percent of the English in the state. The process of chain migration to the English colony surrounding the courthouse and market center of Albion had sustained itself through three decades of sluggish infilling. Edwards County was an anomaly in extreme southern Illinois where foreigners represented 39.1 percent of the total adult males. English accounted for a lopsided 80.1 percent of the foreigners, and Germans were 12.3 percent. Albion attracted only 18.5 percent of the English, since the majority were farmers.

The Birkbeck-Flower English settlement marked the most prominent foreign enclave established at the time of statehood. "Farmers of England, miners of Cornwall, drovers of Wales, mechanics of Scotland, planters of the West Indies, of the Channel Isles, and of Ireland were attracted to Wanborough, founded by Birkbeck and named for his old home in England, and Albion, founded by Flower and named for his native county" (Strawn 1910, 52). Separated by two miles, the villages in the uplands between the Big and Little Wabash Rivers grew to almost seven hundred people in two years. Almost sixteen thousand acres were purchased. Language, religion, and kinship networks were essential bonds of frontier ethnic enclaves.

Morris Birkbeck's published letters and books made him famous in America. His writings planted seeds that promoted emigration to his English colony (Rodman 1947, 343; 1948, 64). It was a classic example of a philanthropic experiment in transplanting agricultural laborers and providing hope for the common man. His propaganda enticed almost four hundred English settlers the first year (1948, 67). Rodman suggests that the English colony furnished "a haven for distressed farmers and mechanics who saw no future hope of prosperity in England. The founders themselves did not prosper too well in the New World" (1947, 360–61). The colony was fairly successful by the mid-1820s. Rampant land speculation had not emerged, so small farmers were able to purchase land at reasonable prices. Prairies were better suited for English farmers than dense woodlands, and a diverse group of Englishmen were attracted (361). Travelers' descriptions of the environ niche were a composite of two landscape extremes: earthly paradise versus a miserable, unhealthy swamp (361). Like most pioneer settlements, imagined and real success or failure probably lay midway between the extremes.

Social networks affected the propensity to migrate to ethnic islands. Letters and personal visits spawned effective channelized migration flows. Flower describes the English colony's information field in the 1820s:

Having done well themselves, and by a few years of hard labor acquired more wealth than they ever expected to obtain, they wrote home to friend or relative an account of their success. These letters handed round in the remote villages of England, in which many of them lived, reached individuals in a class to whom information in a book form was wholly inaccessible. Each letter had its scores of readers, and passing from hand to hand, traversed its scores of miles. The writer, known at home as a poor man, earning perhaps a scanty subsistence by his daily labor, telling of the wages he received, his bountiful living, of his own farm and the number of his live-stock, produced a greater impression in the limited circle of its readers than a printed publication had the power of doing. His fellow-laborer who heard these accounts, and feeling that he was no better off than when his fellow-laborer left him for America, now exerted every nerve to come and do likewise. (1882, 287–88)

Almost 40 percent of the English settled in sphere counties (fig. 9.3). A large block of contiguous sphere counties stretched across northern Illinois and straddled the Illinois Valley corridor. Small English pockets interspersed peripheral to the Mississippi River. English sphere counties tied to the urban-transportation networks. Contiguous blocks of avoidance counties, with one out of ten Englishmen, formed in two principal areas. A small area emerged in the Military Tract's northwestern part. A larger area avoided by English, Germans, and Irish developed in eastern Illinois.

Nineteenth-century English and Scotch were invisible immigrants in the eastern United States (Erickson 1969, 1972). Their quest for cheap land enticed them into the Old Northwest. Their adaptability to subsistence or marketplace agriculture did not produce major innovations in American farming. Yet they contributed to the economic growth of regions, given their preoccupation with diversification (1969, 356). First-generation families and friends embraced their most-valued social relationships (1972, 70). "America letters" reveal remarkably individualistic and self-reliant settlers who cherished independence. Frontier existence was sustained by kinship "comfort and companionship from family life and a circle of immigrant friends, and from their religious faith" (78). Despite their English language and Protestant faiths, participation in American life was not easy.

Secondary Foreign-Born Immigrant Patterns

By 1850, the secondary foreign groups' lifetime out-migration included 147,711 Canadians, 70,550 Scotch, and 54,069 French. Canadians crossed the border into northeast America: New York (32.0 percent), Massachusetts (10.7 percent), Vermont (9.8 percent), Maine (9.6 percent), Michigan (9.5 percent), Illinois (7.2 percent), Wisconsin (5.6 percent), and Ohio (4.0 percent). The Scotch emigrated to New York (33.2 percent), Pennsylvania (10.3 percent), Ohio (7.4 percent), Illinois (6.6 percent), Massachusetts (6.3 percent), Wisconsin (5.0 percent), New Jersey (3.2 percent), and Connecticut (2.7 percent). French destinations reflect a distinct polarity: New York (23.1 percent), Louisiana (21.4 percent), Ohio (13.6 percent), Pennsylvania (7.6 percent), Illinois (6.3 percent), Indiana (4.2 percent), Missouri (4.0 percent), California (2.9 percent), and Kentucky (2.0 percent). The three secondary groups, Canadians (2,436 or 5.5 percent), Scotch (2,109 or 4.8 percent), and French (1,442 or 3.3 percent), aggregated 13.6 percent of the foreign-born adult males (table 9.1). Their proportions to the total adult males were minuscule (table 6.1). Their immigrant patterns conformed to the primary foreign groups' structural patterns and reveal a preference for the regional and subregional nodes and their tributary areas and the Illinois Valley corridor.

Canadian Immigrant Region

Numerous French place names are scattered across Illinois but few relic artifacts of the fur trading episode (Kantowicz 1982). During the early 1800s, French Canadian coureurs de bois cabins were still adjacent to northern Illinois' rivers. American Fur Company traders inhabited these lonely sentinel outposts (Pooley 1968, 505). In the two decades prior to 1850, French Canadian ethnic enclaves primarily were created, rather than English Canadian. French Canadians particularly settled in the three core counties in northern Illinois (fig. 9.4). The core county of Will possessed a disproportionate number of French Canadians (Campbell 1906;

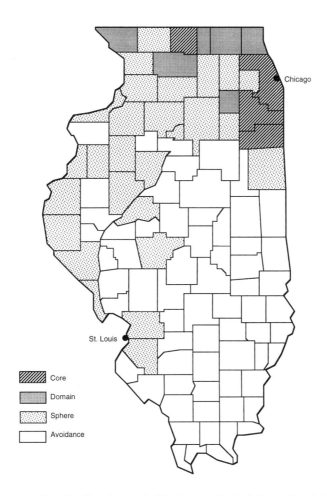

FIG. 9.4. Canadian Immigrants in Illinois, 1850 (*Seventh Census Population Schedules, 1850*)

Kantowicz 1982). Those lured to Cook County resided in Chicago, 71.6 percent. In Winnebago County, two-thirds of the French Canadians were in Rock River townships.

Canadians were concentrated (59.0 percent) in nine counties, three core and six domain (table 9.2). A full array of immigrant concentration types—core, domain, and sphere counties—formed in northeast Illinois. A contiguous block of sphere counties straddled the Chicago-Galena Road, which connected the antipodal urban growth poles in northern Illinois. If the contiguous sphere counties are included with the core and domain counties, the Canadian migration cluster possessed a lopsided 77.6 percent of the total. In the domain county of Kendall, half the French Canadians segregated in an ethnic pocket situated in the Fox Valley Township of Oswego. Other sphere counties formed a discontinuous array west and north of the Illinois Valley corridor. Southwest Illinois emerged with an average concentration of Canadians. French Canadians in St. Clair County clustered with their French brothers in the American Bottom village of Cahokia and its environs. Avoidance counties, accounting for less than 7 percent of the Canadians, predominated between the Illinois and Michigan Canal and Ohio Valley.

French Canadians' contiguity in Will County reveals a number of key migration processes influencing immigrant structural patterns. Three important migration factors molded the geographical propinquity at Bourbonnais on the Kankakee River. French Canadians from Lower Canada segregated in an ethnic, covenant enclave comprising the township surrounding the village with the same name. Relatives and friends followed colonizing pioneers, thus contriving an efficient chain migration. Social networks between origins and destinations forged a sustainable, channelized migration flow. The French Canadian core at Bourbonnais resulted from a pathfinder's colonization plan. The motivator spread "Illinois fever" among habitants who sought a better future.

The large cluster of French Canadians, 17.6 percent of the state total, dispersed throughout Yankee-impressed Will County. About 41 percent of Will County's adult males formed a diverse group of foreigners. Irish and Canadians comprised over half the total foreign-born, 30.9 percent and 25.6 percent, respectively. Germans, English, and Scotch embraced the other largest foreign elements, 17.9 percent, 14.7 percent, and 7.3 percent, respectively. French Canadians were not attracted to the opportunities of the Illinois and Michigan Canal. Instead, the permanent colony sought isolation upstream on the Kankakee River in Bourbonnais Township. The settlement contained 62.4 percent of the Canadians in Will County. Because French Canadians included 97.8 percent of the foreigners in the township and outnumbered Americans four to one, a strong French cultural imprint emerged. In 1853, Bourbonnais Township, with other southern tier townships in Will County, incorporated as a part of Kankakee County.

Francois Bourbonnais, a French fur trader, was the first white settler in the area. Noel Le Vasseur, employed by Astor's American Fur Company, initiated around 1837 the promotion of trade and settlement in the Kankakee vicinity (Kantowicz 1982). He promoted the beauty and serenity of the Bourbonnais area during a trip to Lower Canada in search of a wife and a visit with his parents. Accounts of low land prices, excellent soil, and good climate fell on receptive listeners in the province of Quebec. Family and friends increased the emigration of French Canadians to Bourbonnais in the 1840s (Campbell 1906, 70–71; Houde and Klasey 1968, 33; Wassen 1973, 12–16). Others arrived from Maine, Vermont, Massachusetts, Connecticut, New York, and Michigan (Kelly 1939, 193–94). By 1850, Bourbonnais prospered as the largest French Canadian enclave in Illinois and a miniature "Petit Canada" (Shea 1879, 597–98).

The ethnic island did not stagnate but experienced a resurgence in its microscale channelized migration flow. It served as the parent for other satellite communities, St. Anne, St. Mary, Le Arable, and Papineau (Kelly 1939, 194). Impetus for the growth focused on the apostate priest Father Charles Chiniguy. He traveled to Bourbonnais in 1851 and upon his return to Quebec encouraged emigration (Chiniguy 1886, 535–41; Kantowicz 1982; Kelly 1939, 194–97; Hansen and Brebner 1940, 128–30; Houde and Klasey 1968, 54). St. Anne, southeast of Bourbonnais, became the focal point of his colonization plan. Numerous distorted newspaper accounts were written that intensified out-migration. The perceived relative comfort of Kankakee County described by Father Chiniguy and "America letters" contrasted with the potential emigrants' general discontent over conditions in French Canada. About two hundred people inhabited St. Anne by December 1851, but during the spring of 1852, a thousand families arrived, which prompted the establishment of other villages (Chiniguy 1886, 541; Houde and Klasey 1968, 54).

Father Chiniguy was censured by the Roman Catholic church hierarchy for his attacks on church officials, as he had been earlier in Canada. Emigration from French Canada by the mid-1850s was further stifled by restrictions initiated by the government and the Canadian Catholic church. Immigration to Kankakee County and eastern Illinois was now being influenced by the Illinois Central Railroad's settlement schemes in the Grand Prairie (Gates 1934; Wasson 1973). By 1860, 70 percent of the adult male French Canadians concentrated in three Kankakee townships: Bourbonnais, Kankakee, and St. Anne. Emigration to Kankakee County during the 1850s represented a substantial increase. The original enclave at Bourbonnais was joined by new "Petit Canada" islands in Kankakee and Iroquois Counties.

The French Canadian covenant villages of Bourbonnais and St. Anne integrated the cultural traits of the old French parishes on the St. Lawrence River: church and convent grouped together, French hospitality and language, and traditional customs (Shea 1879, 597–98). Kantowicz argues that this relic fragment of Lower

Canada on the Illinois prairies represented "a remarkable example of what French-Canadians call survivance—the survival of language, culture, and religion" (1982, 265). Existence of "Petit Canada" astride the Kankakee River symbolizes the persistence of ethnic, religious, and cultural identity in a rural setting. Fertile farmland, commercial agriculture, and manufacturing in Kankakee prior to World War I sustained a stable rural and small-town community life (267–68).

The Catholic church supported preserving the distinctive French Canadian communities. The Catholic parishes in Bourbonnais, St. Anne, and St. George originated in the 1840s. Kantowicz contends that survival and growth of the French Canadians' spiritual and cultural health linked to the Clerics of St. Viator's arrival in Bourbonnais (1982, 268). This order of French preaching, teaching priests and lay brothers arrived from Quebec and established St. Viator's College in 1868 to provide classical education for priests, doctors, and lawyers. As a model of Quebec *colleges classiques,* it was the first institution established outside of Canada. It persisted for seventy years, training a small, elite leadership for the French Canadian enclave and as a seminary for the Archdiocese of Chicago (268–72).

Bourbonnais was a fertile setting for the preservation of Quebecois religious customs, Catholic schools, and French cultural heritage (Kantowicz 1982, 274, 276). Rural ethnic, covenant enclaves, particularly German Catholic and Lutheran, all across the Midwest and Great Plains sustained cultural traditions longer than in the large cities (Conzen 1980). Rural churches and schools were endorsers of cultural survival and ethnic identity rather than melting pots of Americanization (Kantowicz 1982, 274, 276). Rural, ethnic communities reinforced and perpetuated cultural survival of religion, language, and customs.

Scotch Immigrant Region

The Scotch were early pathfinders in transAppalachia, the Old Northwest, and Illinois Country. Pioneer descendants from Virginia, the Carolinas, and Georgia transplanted to Tennessee and Kentucky, then transferred to the Ohio Valley corridor in the Lower Middle West. From Daniel Boone to George Rogers Clark, frontiersmen in the interior during the early pioneer period were frequently of Scottish ancestry (Gray 1904; Leyburn 1962; MacMillan 1919, 34). Economic conditions precipitated push factors for the Scotch emigration. The expansion of the wool industry pressured farmers to emigrate in the 1830s, as did the famine of 1847. By the mid-1830s, Scotch immigrants settled northern Illinois. As citizens and farmers, their frugality, sobriety, and industry were deemed qualities of successful pioneers (Pooley 1968, 504). Scotch immigrant structure reflects a northeast Illinois bias, but also a southwest Illinois inclination.

Of the Scotch immigrants, 57.1 percent were segmented in six core and four domain counties (table 9.2, fig. 9.5). Nearly equivalent numbers of Scotch located in four domain counties as in sixty-two avoidance counties. Juxtaposed sphere counties stretched across northern Illinois and into the Illinois Valley corridor. Southwest Illinois evolved a Scotch cluster that infilled this diverse settlement area. Avoidance counties were scattered and fragmented. A smaller bifurcated block of avoidance counties formed in the Military Tract along with the Grand Prairie and southern Illinois.

The structure of the Scotch immigrant surface reveals a proclivity for concentrating in the tributary area of lakeside Chicago. The largest Scotch migration cluster of five core, one domain, and six sphere counties in northeast Illinois included a disproportionate half of the Scotch adult males. Tiny kith-and-kin Scotch settlements dispersed throughout many townships. The core county of

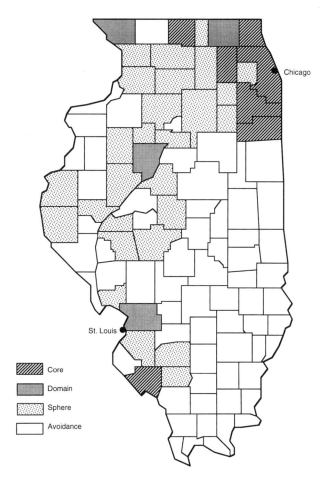

FIG. 9.5. Scotch Immigrants in Illinois, 1850 *(Seventh Census Population Schedules, 1850)*

Cook attracted a lopsided number of Scotch, 16.7 percent of the state total. They were mesmerized by Chicago, which had 74.8 percent of the Scotch in Cook County.

In northern Illinois, Scotch settled in three townships. In the core county of Winnebago, 40.3 percent of the Scotch segregated in Harlem Township. On the township's east side, John Greenlee, the pathfinder of the Argyle Scotch settlement, settled on the county line between Winnebago and Boone Counties in 1836. A micro-scale channelized flow persisted into the 1840s. Argyllshire in Scotland, the out-migration shire of many of the first Scotch, furnished the name for the village and surrounding ethnic pocket (MacMillan 1919, 63–66). A Presbyterian church formed in Argyle in 1844. The Argyle Scotch spilled over into adjacent Boone County. Caledonia Township, contiguous to Winnebago County, possessed 76.3 percent of the Scotch in the sphere county of Boone. The township was situated just north of Belvidere on the Chicago-Galena Road. In the core county of Kane, a Scotch ethnic pocket, 41.2 percent of the Scotch, formed in the Fox River Valley township of Dundee. In 1837, the village of Dundee was named after Alexander Gardiner's native town in Scotland (MacMillan 1919, 61).

Two Scotch domain counties were isolated. Jo Daviess County attracted early Scotchmen before Chicago was an enterprising town. Over one-fourth of the Scotch resided in Galena. Peoria County in the middle Illinois Valley enticed a slightly larger number of Scotch. The city of Peoria captivated the Scotch, 37.3 percent of the county total, with its diverse job opportunities. In the sphere county of La Salle, the Scotch were located in river and canal towns. Sphere counties in northern Illinois and the Illinois Valley revealed tiny Scotch pockets. In Sangamon County, 83.3 percent of the Scotch resided in the capital.

Peripheral to St. Louis in southwest Illinois, a Scotch migration cluster developed a structure of one core, one domain, and four sphere counties, with 12.2 percent of the state total (fig. 9.5). In the domain county of Madison, half the Scotch were lured to riverside Alton. The Scotch ethnic pocket in the core county of Randolph focused on a mixed Scotch-Irish and Irish settlement. Upland Southerners of Irish and Scotch-Irish heritage had out-migrated from the South Carolina piedmont (*Combined History of Randolph, Monroe and Perry Counties* 1883, 69). Randolph County, a core county of the South Carolina immigrant region, had a lopsided number of South Carolinians (fig. 6.5). The Irish in Randolph County, a sphere county of the Irish immigrant region, were of Scotch-Irish ancestry from Ulster (fig. 9.2). The Scottish farmers who sought Randolph County were probably comfortable with shared cultural roots and the Presbyterian faith of the Scotch-Irish. The pioneers from South Carolina, Ulster, and Scotland settled in the Plum Creek area. Irish, Scotch-Irish, and Scotch ancestry outnumbered the Germans settled in the county.

MacMillan exaggerated Scottish genealogy, means of livelihood, and impact on Illinois settlements (1919). Some twenty counties and a hundred communities reflect Scottish names, such as Elgin and Dundee in Kane County and a Scotland Township in McDonough County. Cyrus McCormick of Ulster-Scotch ancestry and Scotch Chicago bankers marked an impact beyond their small numbers. Scotch immigrant patterns reveal hidden agendas influenced by diverse settlement-economic processes.

French Immigrant Region

Eighteenth-century colonizers from France and Lower Canada were the earliest Europeans in Illinois Country. Connected to the continental fur trade, a French colonial, riparian settlement was established as a remote agricultural and political outpost. Settlements aligned in the American Bottom of the middle Mississippi Valley, Cahokia, Prairie du Rocher, and Kaskaskia. Because of unstable political conditions in Illinois Country after British occupation in 1765, the French transferred across the Mississippi River to Spanish Territory, especially St. Louis. Pooley asserts that the French were few in number, with most of them arriving after 1845 (1968, 505). By 1850, French adult males were nearly equivalent to the French population at the time of statehood, about 1,500 (Buck 1967, 93) (table 9.1).

Of the six largest foreign groups, the French were more segregated in Illinois. Their settlement proclivities produced a disproportionate number, 74.3 percent, in the six core and five domain counties (table 9.2, fig. 9.6). As with Germans, over half of the French clustered in the core counties. They were similarly concentrated in the five domain and fifteen sphere counties. The French also avoided a greater number of counties. The French immigrant region was characterized by five segmented clusters formed in southwest Illinois, northeast Illinois, the middle Illinois Valley, and Hancock and Jasper Counties. French ethnic pockets were discontinuously linked by a narrow riverine settlement pattern that connected Lake Michigan and the Mississippi River. Jasper and Hancock Counties emerged as scattered, isolated ethnic clusters that epitomized the fragmentation of the French.

The largest French migration cluster emerged in southwest Illinois, 27.3 percent of the state total. The original French colonial settlement hearth in the American Bottom persisted as a remnant that was attractive for adult males from France. The French concentration focused on Cahokia in St. Clair County rather than the old political center of Kaskaskia in Randolph County. The core county of St. Clair had a lopsided number of Frenchmen, 18.8 percent. Almost three-fourths of them resided in the American Bottom between Cahokia and French Village, with nearly half of them in Cahokia and its vicinity. The French were widely dispersed in the domain county of Madison, but in the sphere county of Randolph, their locus persisted in the villages of Kaskaskia and Prairie du Rocher.

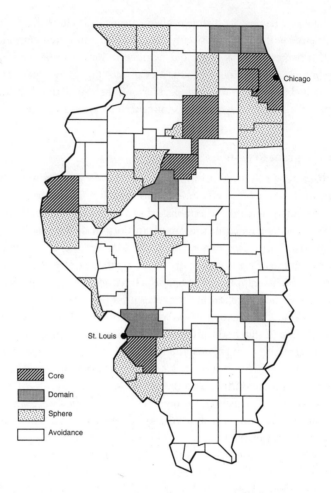

FIG. 9.6. French Immigrants in Illinois, 1850 *(Seventh Census Population Schedules, 1850)*

The second-largest French migration cluster emerged in northeast Illinois in proximity to Chicago, 25.9 percent of the state total. The core county of Cook included almost half the French population of St. Clair County. Two-thirds of the French resided in Chicago and were scattered throughout the city. In the core county of DuPage, almost 80 percent of the French settled in the contiguous townships of Lisle and Napierville astride the DuPage River. In the domain counties of Lake and McHenry, they segregated in tiny ethnic pockets in two juxtaposed townships. In Lake County, 64.5 percent of the French settled in Ela and Vernon Townships, whereas in McHenry County, 86 percent of the French were fixed in Greenwood and Seneca Townships. In the sphere county of Will, slightly

over 50 percent of the French settled in Joliet Township. In the sphere county of
De Kalb, all the Frenchmen congregated in Somonauk Township.

The third-largest French cluster, 20.9 percent, stretched northeast-southwest,
straddling the middle Illinois Valley (fig. 9.6). The French, 16.5 percent, located in
the two core counties of La Salle and Woodford and the domain county of
Tazewell. In La Salle County, the French settled in the Illinois River township of
Ottawa, 32.1 percent, and the Fox River township of Northville, 40.6 percent. In
the sphere county of Peoria, over half the French resided in the city of Peoria. The
French in the domain and sphere counties reflected tiny ethnic pockets in one or
two townships, not a continuous riverine settlement corridor. The fourth-largest
French cluster bordered the Mississippi River, about half the population size of
the Illinois Valley corridor. In the sphere county of Adams, Quincy attracted 78.3
percent of the French. The segregated French enclave in the core county of Hancock represented a micro-scale channelized migration flow. The ethnic pocket was
spawned by a colony of socialistic French Icarians.

Icarian tenets stressed removing self-interest, establishing common ownership
of property, tolerating religious freedom, the equality of men and women, and
creating an egalitarian society (Pooley 1968, 532). M. Etienne Cabet of Dijon,
France, founder of the Icarian colony, attempted a practical test of his communistic doctrine in the Red River Valley of Texas in 1848. It failed, and Cabet with his
diehard followers transplanted to Nauvoo in Hancock County in 1849. The Mormon exodus in 1846 had left an abandoned landscape of fields, houses, and businesses that Brigham Young was interested in selling. Eight hundred acres of
farmland were rented. In order to implement their utopia, a mill, a distillery, and a
few houses were acquired. The colony prospered for a few years under the Icarians
before financial problems and dissension caused dissolution (Miller 1906; Pooley
1968, 415–16, 505, 531–34).

Pooley stressed that the Icarian colony was simply another socialistic experimental failure on the Illinois prairies (1968, 534). Utopian social and religious experimental communities were etched into westward expansion. The frontier offered
favorable locations because of remoteness from mainstream American society. Numerous isolated locations were available in Illinois that furnished the desired spatial separation for social freedom, but the peril of the frontier verge was absent
(Pooley 1968, 534). Porter and Lukermann argue that "the frontier as state-of-mind,
as a journey of purification and as a preparation for the millennium, figured
strongly in the thinking of members of experimental communities" (1976, 201).

The smallest French enclave was situated in the domain county of Jasper in
southeast Illinois. It persisted as an anomalous foreign cluster because of a tiny
channelized migration flow with Alsace, France. This isolated colony of German-
speaking French was established by the Picquet brothers in 1837 at St. Marie on
the Embarras River. In 1836, Joseph Picquet, only nineteen years of age, traveled

extensively throughout the Old Northwest and selected the site (*Jasper County, Illinois* 1988, 16–17; Pooley 1968, 447; *Sainte Marie, Illinois, Sesquicentennial* 1987, 3–7). Joseph was charged by his father and elders "to select a region where they could get sufficient land to establish large estates, enjoy the pleasures of the chase and above all, practice the Catholic religion unmolested" (*Sainte Marie, Illinois, Sesquicentennial* 1987, 3).

Place images that described large amounts of virgin timber, rich, rolling country, and a bisecting river in frontier America meshed with their homeland images surrounding the town of Haguenau in Alsace (*Jasper County, Illinois* 1988, 16–17). Desire to migrate, destination selection, and colonization strategy involving a contract of sixteen articles of association were not hasty decisions (*Sainte Marie, Illinois, Sesquicentennial* 1987, 3–4). Joseph Picquet, leader of the French German colony, emigrated with twenty-five people, all blood- and marriage-related. The Picquets, a well-to-do family, acquired about twelve thousand acres at the Palestine land office in September 1837. On October 28, the tiny group took formal possession of the land and dedicated the village to the Virgin Mary. Because the colonists were related, the new settlement was "named Colonie des Freres or Colony of Brothers." The zealous Catholics, with their crucifix, candles, and vestments from Alsace, implanted their cultural-religious heritage astride the Embarras River. Traditional social bonds, ethnicity, language, and religion were critical to the survival of old customs in this tiny frontier covenant community (Robins 1938, 24–25; *Sainte Marie, Illinois, Sesquicentennial* 1987, 3–4). The first chapel was built in 1842, but in 1850, a red brick church and parsonage were constructed. The first store, saw and grist mill, church, free school, and post office were established in St. Marie, the cultural-commercial center in this wilderness area. Joseph returned a number of times to Alsace to bring additional colonists.

By 1850, the French disproportionately resided, 78.3 percent, in St. Marie. Yet adjacent Newton Township, with the county seat and market center of Newton, had almost 20 percent of the French. Where small foreign enclaves formed in the Illinois frontier, the inclination was to cluster in adjacent townships where potential farmland and cultural ties were available. French-German Alsatians attracted a small contingent of Germans, who settled in the two townships. The French grew 50 percent during the 1850s. Almost 85 percent of the French persisted in St. Marie Township. The emigration from Alsace to Jasper County virtually ceased by the time the railroads came in the 1870s.

Finally, isolated sphere counties reveal French attractions to frontier farming environs and the urban settings of Springfield and Galena (fig. 9.6). Half the French resided in the market center of Galena in Jo Daviess County. The French avoided settling in three-fourths of Illinois' counties. Extensive avoidance areas emerged on opposite sides of the Illinois Valley corridor. The smaller area extended northeast-southwest across northern and west-central Illinois. The larger area coincided with extensive prairie landscapes and the earlier-settled forested habitats in eastern Illinois.

Minor Foreign-Born Immigrant Patterns

A number of smaller foreign groups forged distinctive ethnic enclaves in Illinois that were sustained by micro-scale channelized migration flows. Transplanting into midcontinent, they created colonies located near accessible commercial markets or in peripheral frontier locations. By 1850, lifetime out-migration patterns of these minor European groups—29,868 Welsh, 13,358 Swiss, 12,678 Norwegians, and 3,559 Swedes—depicted a tendency to locate in a few destinations. Scandinavian numbers significantly increased during the late 1800s in the Upper Midwest and northern Great Plains. The Welsh, frequently of mining background, located in the eastern states of Pennsylvania (30.0 percent) and New York (25.4 percent) and interior states of Ohio (19.6 percent), Wisconsin (14.5 percent), and Illinois (1.9 percent). Swiss settled in the Old Northwest rather than northeast America: Ohio (24.6 percent), New York (13.9 percent), Illinois (12.2 percent), Wisconsin (9.3 percent), Pennsylvania (6.8 percent), Missouri (7.4 percent), Indiana (5.4 percent), Kentucky (2.1 percent), and Tennessee (2.0 percent). Norwegians primarily located in the western portion of the Old Northwest. New York was their entry point as they transplanted to Wisconsin (68.2 percent), Illinois (19.1 percent), New York (3.1 percent), Iowa (2.9 percent), and Missouri (1.2 percent). Swedes concentrated in Illinois (31.6 percent) and New York (21.2 percent), but also settled in Massachusetts (7.1 percent), Louisiana (7.0 percent), Iowa (6.5 percent), California (4.6 percent), Pennsylvania (3.7 percent), Wisconsin (2.5 percent), Ohio (1.5 percent), and Maine (1.5 percent). Illinois emerged as a key destination for three of the four minor European groups, which included 823 Norwegians (1.9 percent), 610 Swiss (1.4 percent), 331 Swedes (0.7 percent), and 256 Welsh (0.6 percent) (table 9.1). Other tiny European groups from Portugal (116), the Netherlands (85), Poland (56), Denmark (52), Italy (27), and Belgium (15) added to the ethnic diversity.

Norwegian Immigrant Region

The largest Scandinavian element in the United States in 1850 were Norwegians. Three small, fragmented clusters, with a disproportionate 85.2 percent of the Norwegians, formed in four core counties, La Salle, Cook, Boone, and Kendall, and one domain county, Grundy, in northeast Illinois (fig. 9.7). Chicago served as disembarkation point. With the addition of four sphere counties, Winnebago, Jo Daviess, Stephenson, and Sangamon, 94.5 percent of them resided in nine counties. They were rare in the avoidance counties and totally absent from sixty-nine counties.

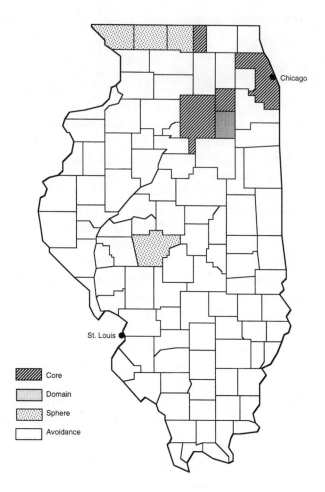

FIG. 9.7. Norwegian Immigrants in Illinois, 1850 *(Seventh Census Population Schedules, 1850)*

The sphere counties' structure marked the attractiveness of Springfield, Galena, and tiny, isolated ethnic pockets where language provided a shared tradition. Almost half the Norwegians in Sangamon County resided in the state capital. The sphere counties in extreme northwest Illinois linked with the core county of Boone. Three-fourths of the Norwegians in Jo Daviess County settled in Galena and its hinterland. In Stephenson County, 81.3 percent of the Norwegians segregated in Rock Run Township in the eastern verge. The "New Norway" settlement of Rock Run spilled over into adjacent Laona and Howard Townships in Winnebago County, where 83.9 percent of the Norwegians clustered. This Norwegian ethnic pocket astride the Stephenson and Winnebago county line comprised almost five percent of the state total. It served as a dispersion point northward into Wisconsin.

The largest Norwegian cluster focused on the core counties of La Salle and Kendall and domain county of Grundy, with their lopsided 43.7 percent of the state total. Almost 30 percent of the Norwegians settled in the Illinois Valley corridor county of La Salle, where they constituted 12.5 percent of the foreigners. Scandinavian migration to the Upper Midwest remained small prior to 1850. "New Norways" and "New Swedens" were inevitable in the fertile, inexpensive prairie lands of northern Illinois and along the Illinois and Michigan Canal (Babcock 1914). Stepwise migration of Quaker Norwegians from Orleans County adjacent to Lake Ontario in New York to the Fox River Valley north of Ottawa in La Salle County occurred in 1834. Most Norwegians from the New York colony had transplanted to Illinois by 1836. Original colonizers refrained from moving farther west, thus, the Norwegian cluster developed continuity over time (Babcock 1914, 27–29). Channelized migration flows with Norway enlarged the Fox River Valley Norwegian enclave (Anderson 1975; Babcock 1914; Blegen 1969; Qualey 1934, 1938).

The Norwegian settlement structure in La Salle County became highly segregated as fertile farmlands were the primary objective (fig. 9.7). They concentrated, 87.6 percent, in five Fox River Valley townships. Mission Township included almost half the Norwegians in this riverine ethnic enclave. They spilled over into the adjacent townships of Fox and Big Grove, almost 80 percent of the Norwegians, in Kendall County. They disproportionately settled in Big Grove Township, 58.6 percent. Norwegians comprised 13.4 percent of the county's foreigners. The ethnic pocket spread into the contiguous townships of Nettle Creek and Saratoga in Grundy County, which contained almost 100 percent of the Norwegians. The Fox River Valley in the bordering counties evolved as a discrete Norwegian enclave.

Kendall in Orleans County, New York, was the first Norwegian settlement in America. Between 1825 and 1833, the immigrants' economic situation markedly improved over that in Norway (Blegen 1969, 59). Beginning in 1834, the New York colony started to break up as it transferred to the Fox River Valley, the first interior Norwegian enclave (61). Cleng Peerson, the "pathfinder," directed Norwegians from the older frontier in western New York to the unoccupied promised land of Illinois (Babcock 1914; Blegen 1931, 1969; Qualey 1934, 1938). Peerson founded the Fox River Valley settlements, established a colony in northern Missouri, and contributed to settlements in Iowa. Besides trips to the Norwegian colony in New York, he returned to Norway in 1843 to encourage emigration to midcontinent.

Chain migration from Norway commenced in 1836 to the Norwegian enclave. Letters heralded potential prosperity available from the cheap, fertile prairie lands in northern Illinois. Economic expansions were expected to increase rapidly in those areas in proximity to the Illinois and Michigan Canal. Upward movement in land prices and accessible markets in west-central New York were credited to the

earlier Erie Canal. The argument followed that Norwegian farmers and speculators would reap greater rewards in the Fox River Valley in northeast Illinois (Babcock 1914, 27–28; Blegen 1969, 62–63). Emigrants reading "America letters"
experienced another reason for destination propinquity—the safety of the social
network. Newcomers knew they could seek instruction, advice, and encouragement in Norwegian.

Blegen notes that letters "were copied and recopied, sent among the parishes
from neighbor to neighbor, carried by lay preachers from parish to another" in
western Norway (1969, 64–65). "America fever" dispersed widely among individuals, families, and parishes. In the late 1830s and 1840s, "America letters" served as
migration spoors falling like seeds on potential emigrants to the Fox River Valley
(Babcock 1914; Blegen 1969; Qualey 1934, 1938). Social networks enhanced the
chain migration process between Norway and the Illinois prairies. The infilling of
the Norway colony in La Salle County spilled over into Kendall and Grundy
Counties (Babcock 1914, 29–30).

Additional social network pull factors were those who had personally visited
America and then returned to their origins (Babcock 1914; Blegen 1969; Qualey
1934, 1938). Babcock argues that "young men who had prospered in the new life
returned to the homesteads of their fathers and became, temporarily, missionaries
of the new economic gospel, teaching leisurely but effectively by word of mouth
and face to face, instead of by written lines at long range" (1914, 31). "America
fever" merged with "Illinois fever." Place image seeds of a promised land fell on
fertile soil because of hard economic times, fluctuating money value, poor crop
yields, and weak demand for peasant labor. Life in many rural districts of Norway
was becoming worse, not better (Babcock 1914, 30).

Hudson maintains that Norwegians and Swedes found newspapers printed in
their native languages in America extremely valuable (1976). The newspapers
functioned as information clearinghouses, since they furnished news from home
and from their countrymen who migrated farther westward. Norwegian social
networks followed typical sequences that engendered and constrained mobility.
Small groups colonized distant locations in response to a pathfinder's encouragement, advertising, or traveler's account in a native language newspaper. Infilling of
immigrants at new destinations from previously transplanted ethnic enclaves in
response to personal or published correspondence encouraged Norwegians to follow. Stepwise sequences of small groups, families, and friends created Norwegian
ethnic pockets in northern Illinois, the Upper Midwest, and the northern Great
Plains (Hudson 1973, 1976; Qualey 1934, 1938).

Common among foreigners was out-migration from dispersion points or
"mother areas" (Qualey 1976, 16). The Norwegian enclave in the Fox River Valley
emerged as the initial midcontinent mother settlement (Babcock 1914; Blegen 1969;
Qualey 1934, 1938, 1976). Dispersing from the nucleus, they colonized contiguous

northern tier counties. Later, sequential Norwegian enclaves spread to northeast Iowa, southwest Wisconsin, southeast Minnesota, and the Dakotas. By 1870, persistence, substantial infilling, and dispersion in the three counties of the Fox River Valley enclave characterized the Norwegian nucleus (Qualey 1938, 31). Persistence and growth also marked the Norwegian settlements in Chicago and northern Boone County (35).

The second-largest Norwegian cluster emerged in Cook County, with 26.3 percent of the adult males (fig. 9.7). Chicago comprised a disproportionate 95.4 percent of the Norwegians in Cook County, but they accounted for only 3.6 percent of the foreigners. A Norwegian ethnic pocket evolved in Boone County, with 15.2 percent of the state total. Norwegians, one-fourth the foreigners in the county, located in two segregated townships. Boone (52.8 percent) and Manchester (39.2 percent) were adjoining townships north of the Chicago-Galena Road.

Norwegian migration must be viewed in a larger social, economic context. Early Norwegians from the valleys and fjords found town and city life strange, dangerous, and hostile; plus, they were part of a conservative movement. Their sense of place warranted the planting and survival of familiar homeland traditions. Cultivating land and transferring a social organization similar to the home parish—but with fewer stones and more bread—were attractive pull factors of community life in the midwestern frontier. "Stock effect," the influence of earlier emigration through letters, returned emigrants, prepaid tickets, emigrant guides, and newspapers, were effective when Norwegians were comfortable and achieved a degree of economic success in the new destinations (Semmingsen 1976, 8–9).

Recent transatlantic chain migration studies by Gjerde (1979, 1985), Ostergren (1979, 1981b, 1988), and Rice (1977) stress the pivotal role of family, friends, and community identity among Norwegians and Swedes in their replication of transplanted communities in the Upper Middle West. Social network bonds remained fundamental to the effectiveness and persistence of the willingness to migrate to new homes. The success of the essential processes of migration and settlement were connected to interwoven social networks (Ostergren 1988, 330). Emigrants were constrained by the interplay of community life and affective bonds, both at their origins and destinations. Their encounters with physical, social, and economic milieus conformed to similar sequences of pioneering experiences as they fashioned their individual and collective well-being within deep-rooted community frameworks.

Wisconsin emerged as the destination state for Norwegians, with slightly over two-thirds of all Norwegians in America in 1850. "New Norways" in south-central Wisconsin bordering the Rock River formed as northward extensions from "mother areas" in northern Illinois. Southwest Wisconsin was then transplanted with Norwegian settlements. These enclaves functioned as dispersion foci for the westward spread across the Mississippi River to the "greener pastures" of Iowa and

Minnesota (Qualey 1938, 76–129). Upper Midwest Norwegian clusters emerged as "mother areas" for the westward progression of land-hungry Norwegians, who spread to the Big Sioux Valley of South Dakota and the Red River Valley of North Dakota (Hudson 1976; Qualey 1938, 130–171). Decadal processions of Norwegian Americans and Norwegians replicated "mother areas" in the Midwest to "New Norways" in the northern plains. The Fox River Valley was recognized as the interior Norwegian hearth area.

Swiss Immigrant Region

The Swiss were highly segregated in the Prairie State (fig. 9.8). The core county of Madison and domain county of Jo Daviess had almost two-thirds of the Swiss adult males. The Swiss typify the propensity of smaller foreign groups to be extremely selective in their destinations and channelized in their geographic mobility. Madison County, with 54.3 percent of the Swiss, marks the early "mother area" of Swiss settlements in midcontinental America (von Grueningen 1940, 24). One-fifth of the Swiss were settled in the sphere counties. They were absent in almost half the avoidance counties.

A Swiss enclave emerged in the Highland area of Madison County but entwined in the German migration cluster in southwest Illinois (figs. 9.1, 9.8). The Swiss comprised 15.5 percent of the foreigners in the county but were far outnumbered by Germans. They were overwhelmingly concentrated, 91.8 percent, in the townships of Highland, Saline, Marine, and Looking Glass (St. Jacob). The village of Highland possessed a disproportionate 43.8 percent of the county's Swiss. The townships also attracted a sizable German population, one-fifth of the county total. The pathfinders of the German-speaking Swiss colony were Dr. Kaspar Koepfli, a medical doctor, and his nephew Joseph Suppiger, from a textile business family, both from the town of Sursee in the Canton of Luzerne (Abbott 1987; Bettis 1968; Newbauer 1904; Spahn 1978; Spencer 1937). Wealthy, well-educated, and liberal Swiss, the Koepfli family members considered their decision to emigrate for over a decade (Abbott 1987). They read about America and formed a strategy for settling the Mississippi Valley. Their financial well-being permitted escaping political and religious conditions in Switzerland. In 1830, the families acquired a copy of Duden's Report, which had affected German emigration to Missouri. The economic attractions of "the land of plenty" sealed their exodus decision. It was used as a guide in their journey to the midcontinent frontier.

In the spring of 1831, fourteen relatives and friends disembarked from Havre, France, for New York. After arriving in St. Louis, Koepfli was disenchanted with the broken, timbered uplands of Missouri. Exploring east of St. Louis, the woodland verge of Looking Glass Prairie near the later site of Highland proffered a desirable location for a Swiss German colony. Slightly over a thousand acres were purchased for a "New Switzerland" on the Illinois prairies. Highland, some 32

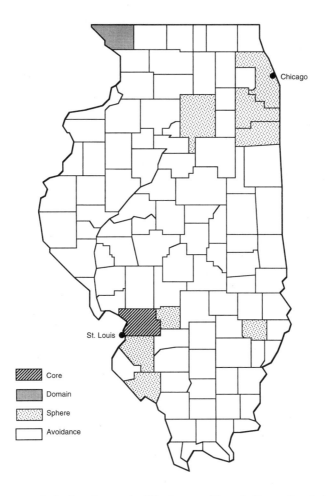

FIG. 9.8. Swiss Immigrants in Illinois, 1850 *(Seventh Census Population Schedules, 1850)*

miles or two days' distance from St. Louis, was platted as a colony town in 1836 and functioned as the Swiss dispersion point into adjacent townships. The accessibility of Highland improved with a stagecoach route in 1843 between Vandalia and St. Louis. The event marked a long-delayed, permanent extension of the National Road to the Mississippi River.

"America letters" to relatives and friends and monographs written by Koepfli and his nephew were sent for the specific purpose of initiating a chain migration. The size, quality, and cheapness of the land described attracted seventeen Swiss in 1833 and some fifty additional ones in 1835. The preferred migration route linked Havre, New Orleans, and St. Louis. Swiss filtered in from other German- and

French-speaking cantons in the 1840s. Swiss French settled in the Sugar Creek area east of Highland. Return visits by leaders contributed to perpetuating the channelized migration flow. Koerner noted a key trait of the founders and a successful resource adaptation: "Both of these families had considerable means and, what was more, real, practical, Swiss common-sense. . . . But raising cattle on these large prairies was one of the principal and profitable pursuits of these families" (McCormack 1909, 1:327–28).

In northwest Illinois, the lead country of Jo Daviess emerged as the only domain county, with almost nine percent of the Swiss (fig. 9.8). Slightly over half the Swiss settled in Galena. In northeast Illinois, they were minuscule as a foreign-born group in Cook County. Almost two-thirds of them located in Chicago. The Illinois and Michigan Canal counties of Will and La Salle attracted a few Swiss. Their settlement inclinations were the canal towns of Joliet and Ottawa. The Swiss in the isolated sphere county of Richland in southeast Illinois embraced primarily German surnames. With a slightly greater number of Germans, both foreign groups were probably attracted to the northeast township of German, which abutted the French German-speaking colony at St. Marie in Jasper County. The three remaining sphere counties, with 9.3 percent of the Swiss, were situated in or contiguous to the German migration cluster in southwest Illinois. Given the safety net of propinquity, the Swiss in Bond County probably settled near the Swiss enclaves in Highland and Saline Townships in Madison County. In St. Clair County, they congregated in the precinct of Ridge Prairie, 42.3 percent, between Belleville and Edwardsville, which was thickly populated with Germans. The few Swiss in Randolph County dispersed throughout the county.

Dr. Kaspar Koepfli's letter of May 1833 described the Highland habitat:

The part of the prairie on which New Switzerland is located lies between Silver Creek and Sugar Creek, both of which are bordered by a band of woods. The distance between the two creeks averages two to three miles and never exceeds six miles. . . . Most of our woods are in the northwest part of our acreage. Settlers usually choose a site on grassland as close as possible to woods. It should be land that lies high enough so that it drains well and will be ready for cultivation as soon as spring comes. Most of the earliest immigrants chose level land on which to settle because they believed its soil was richer. . . . Swiss farmers can best come to understand the ideal conditions for agriculture here by picturing a meadow, not under cultivation for years, that now is to be used for growing wheat. It can continue to be used for growing wheat for some years with a good chance that the yield will increase in the two years immediately following and with less expenditure of effort. After two to three years of growing wheat, however, it would be well to rotate with another crop such as rye, oats, corn. (Abbott 1987, 175–76, 178, 180)

Their marketplace agricultural strategy focused on St. Louis:

Potatoes are plentiful and excellent. Sweet potatoes do well here and are a favorite of new arrivals. Both kinds of potato are popular in the St. Louis market. Like most other staples they increase drastically in price as spring approaches, and during the spring they often disappear completely from the market place. . . . The important business of raising livestock can be accomplished with much less effort than in the old country. Because of the tremendous amount of prairie land here, it can be used freely by all, for only a part of it is under cultivation, for one thing because of the lack of wood for fencing. . . . What should be evident from all this is how effortless, inexpensive, and profitable it is to raise livestock here. (Abbott 1987, 181, 182, 184)

Swiss colony promoters desired that emigrants recognize the potential for economic success. "The stories told in Europe about the difficulties of marketing one's products if one lives inland are very erroneous. . . . Of course, if he considered it too much trouble to take the two or three days' time to load a wagon with his products and have his horses or oxen haul it to the daily market in St. Louis, where such products can be sold readily and profitably, he could find persons willing to do it, of course for pay. We have learned already how the principal products, wheat, salted meat, etc. find a ready market" (Abbott 1987, 189).

Why was "New Switzerland" not transplanted to a Missouri river?

We had come to the Mississippi Valley with the intention of farming and raising livestock, and we found after investigation that Illinois with its prairies was more suitable than Missouri. We found the prairie land of Illinois not only more practical for growing crops but better suited for raising cattle than the woodland which first would have had to be cleared, as would have been the case in Missouri. . . . What influenced us the most was the richness of the soil on the prairie as compared with that of land in Missouri, which is wooded, and its greater suitability for the growing of important crops like wheat. . . . We did not settle on a navigable stream, because the rivers in the Midwest do not have steep banks, and there are frequent floods. (Abbott 1987, 188–89)

Swedish Immigrant Region

Swedes in Illinois represented almost one-third of the total in America in 1850. The Swedish immigrant structure embraced only three core counties, Henry, Cook, and Knox, and two sphere counties, Rock Island and Stark. Two small ethnic enclaves formed on opposite sides in northern Illinois (fig. 9.9). Swedes were absent from 73 of the 94 avoidance type counties stretching from border to border. The stray Swede who settled in a few avoidance counties still accounted for almost 15 percent of the state total.

The smallest Swedish ethnic pocket emerged in the core county of Cook, with 22.4 percent of the state total. They were highly concentrated, 97.3 percent, in gateway Chicago with its job opportunities. But they were a minuscule proportion, less than 1 percent, of the city's foreigners. The regional node developed by the mid-1840s as a key Swedish destination and embarkation point into northern

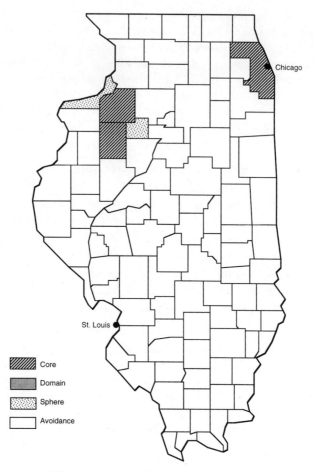

FIG. 9.9. Swedish Immigrants in Illinois, 1850 (*Seventh Census Population Schedules, 1850*)

Illinois (Babcock 1914). Their neighborhoods were closely linked with the availability of the Gospel in Swedish. Gustaf Unonius, a Lutheran Swede, emigrated in 1841 to New York and traveled to Milwaukee and settled in the Pine Lake area near Delafield. The ethnic enclave attracted other Swedes through personal letters and newspaper reports (Bergendoff 1948; Janson 1931). By 1845, Unonius was ordained an Episcopal minister and in 1849 transferred his ministry to Chicago. He formed a Swedish Episcopal congregation, owing to a schism in a Lutheran church where Norwegians outnumbered Swedes. Norwegians had been emigrating to Chicago since 1836. Swedish migration was initiated in 1845 with fifteen families. In late 1846, a group arriving in Chicago opted not to settle at Bishop Hill. Forty more families arrived in Chicago in 1847, a hundred in 1848, four hundred families in 1849, and five hundred in 1850.

The largest Swedish enclave included Henry, Knox, Rock Island, and Stark Counties in the northern Military Tract, almost two-thirds of the state total. Scattered in tiny family clusters and small communities, Swedes concentrated in Henry County, 35.3 percent, and neighboring Knox County, 19.3 percent. In Knox County, they represented almost one-fourth of the foreigners. They settled Victoria, Knoxville, and Galesburg but primarily dispersed into family clusters in the village hinterlands. Swedes comprised one-half the foreigners in Henry County. The Bishop Hill colony, the Jansonists' experimental settlement on the border between Weller and Galva Townships, accounted for almost three-fourths of the Swedes. The remainder of the Swedes were mostly in Andover and neighboring vicinity.

The dominant personalities of Jonas and Olof Hedstrom influenced the tiny Swedish family clusters at scattered destinations in the "New Sweden" of early Illinois (Babcock 1914; Bergendoff 1948; Erdahl 1925). Jonas, a blacksmith turned Methodist preacher, settled in Victoria northeast of Knoxville in 1838. In 1845, his brother Olof, a Methodist preacher to Scandinavian sailors in New York harbor, wrote Jonas that he anticipated future Swedish emigrants arriving at the port of entry. Olof Olson, a Swedish farmer, arrived in New York in the fall of 1845 as a scout for a site the persecuted Jansonists could settle in America. Olof Hedstrom informed Olson of Victoria in Knox County, Illinois. He visited the isolated frontier and selected a colony site sixteen miles north of Victoria in Henry County.

Andover, Galesburg, Knoxville, Wataga, Victoria, Rock Island, and Moline in northwest Illinois and Chicago developed well-worn migration channels. The utopian Swedish colony at Bishop Hill failed to unfold as the "mother area" for Swedish settlements. Its fame degenerated because of its schism from mainstream Swedish religious and community life and its internal problems. Numerous Swedes destined for the colony refrained from settling amongst the Jansonists. Alternatively, they located in the dispersed family pockets and tiny communities scattered in the prairies adjacent to the Mississippi River. Other followers disenchanted with the Jansonists' communistic experiment sought refuge in Andover, Galesburg, and Victoria and their hinterlands (Janson 1931, 132). Of the rural communities, the Andover settlement, about sixteen miles northwest of Bishop Hill, infilled with a colony of Swedes in 1849. In 1850, some 180 Swedes, led by their pathfinder, Pastor Esbjorn, organized the first Swedish Lutheran church in the Midwest. Andover emerged as the nucleus of the Swedish Lutheran movement (Janson 1931, 188). The focus of Swedish settlement shifted from Bishop Hill to the slowly growing villages. They were initially linked by a circuit-riding Jonas Hedstrom and emerged as the Swedish "mother area." Bergendoff argues that tiny farm communities and isolated farmsteads characterized the rural Swedish enclaves, and laborers, machinists, and carpenters identified the urban, ethnic neighborhoods (1948, 26).

In the 1840s, personal letters published in the press were potent pull factors in stimulating out-migration to America (Janson 1931, 127). "America letters" influenced the growth of the Swedish "mother area" in northwest Illinois. As a settlement-dispersion area, the enclave with its scattered destinations infilled with the later Swedish influx. With dissension over religious practices and disintegration of various economic enterprises promoted by the Bishop Hill colony in the mid-1850s, many families and individuals left the communal setting for the nearby Swedish ethnic island (Babcock 1914, 54–61; Bergendoff 1948; Erdahl 1925; Janson 1931; Mikkelsen 1892).

A Swedish infrastructure materialized as denominations, particularly the Swedish Lutheran church, grew substantially and established colleges in the upper Mississippi Valley. Augustana College and Theological Seminary at Rock Island, the oldest Swedish American educational institution, represents the prototype college: small beginnings, financial difficulties, uncertain location, and expansion (Ander 1933; Stephenson 1969, 136–37). Stephenson argues that "the role of the educational institutions in stimulating and keeping alive Swedish, as a spoken language, was in a sense forced upon them by the necessity of training pastors for congregations that worshiped in the language of Sweden" (138). The publication houses operated by the churches furnished what their members demanded and desired.

Ethnic church bodies—Swedish, Norwegian, and German Lutheran churches—were powerful instruments in the promotion of cultural survival in the dominant American society. The fundamental components of ethnic denominations, like the Swedish Lutherans, were their churches, colleges, theological seminaries, Sunday schools, parochial schools, and publishing houses (Stephenson 1969; Uppvall 1969). Ethnic churches, fraternal organizations, and Swedish American presses were dynamic cultural-social phenomena. The institutional church in the late nineteenth and early twentieth centuries proffered immigrant children contact with the language, customs, and culture of their antecedent homelands. Language preservation was a community imperative for ethnic identity, cohesion, and pride in urban neighborhoods and particularly in rural communities prior to World War I.

An atypical Scandinavian settlement was the ill-fated Bishop Hill colony. The utopian site in Henry County was selected by the advance agent Olof Olson for the founder/prophet Eric Janson (Babcock 1914; Bigelow 1902; Erdahl 1925; Janson 1931; Mikkelsen 1892; Pooley 1968). Separation from the Lutheran church in Sweden was assured in 1844 when Janson proclaimed himself as the second coming of Christ, who would restore the purity and glory of Christianity. Restless peasants were enthusiastic, but church leaders and civil authorities were alarmed and sought to stamp out the heretics (Babcock 1914, 55). The colony was named after Biskopskulla Parish in Sweden, Janson's birthplace. Founded in 1846 with about five hundred followers and 750 acres, the communistic agricultural colony became a place of refuge. With emigrants primarily from Norrland, the colony grew to slightly over a thousand disciples and 1,400 acres in four years (Janson 1931, 132).

By 1856, the colony's population had dwindled to 780 followers, but it owned 8,500 acres, of which 3,250 were cultivated (Erdahl 1925, 557). For a brief time, Bishop Hill's economic prosperity and population size made it the key settlement between Peoria on the Illinois River and Rock Island on the Mississippi River. But religious instability, the cholera epidemic of 1849, the assassination of their dictatorial leader in May 1850, the establishment of celibacy for the colonists, and speculative economic investments all contributed to the disarray and demise of the Jansonist followers' hopes and economic fortunes. The dissolution of the religious-communistic experiment was almost complete by the Civil War.

Porter and Lukermann argue that the important components of utopian movements to the frontier were "preparation for a new life, visionary leadership, and the importance of an arduous journey" (1976, 201). As a new Eden, Bishop Hill had difficulty surviving, even though alternative ways of life were not in close proximity for the faithful (207). They were a persecuted religious society of refugees who experimented in practical communism. Mikkelsen asserts that what the Jansonists "sought in the New World was not wealth, but freedom to worship God after their own manner. They held views that were repugnant to the Church of Sweden" (1892, 5). An immediate concern of the covenant community was the erection of a sacred space for corporate worship. "Already before the arrival of the second party a large tabernacle has been erected. It was built in the form of a cross and was able to room about a thousand persons. The material consisted of logs and canvas, and the whole structure was intended merely as a temporary makeshift. Divine worship was held here twice a day on week days and three times on Sundays" (30). Virtual landscape abandonment had occurred by 1900, except for the artifact remnants of the Bishop Hill colony, now designated a state historic site.

The structure of foreign immigrant regions integrated with letters from relatives and friends that promoted America and Illinois (Janson 1931, 15–16). Many Swedish letters included prepaid passage tickets and a guaranteed job. Letters often exaggerated the opportunities and potential prosperity and neglected to outline the inherent hardships. Return visits by Swedes demonstrated the success story firsthand and assured the return of a number of relatives or friends with the visitor to his home in America. Social networks were fused with letters and personal visits across the Atlantic that spawned chain migration patterns. Given heavy taxation, numerous crop failures, religious and political intolerance, and desire among peasant folk for access to a better life, the written and spoken word spread "America fever" in Sweden (Janson 1931, 16, 140; Ostergren 1988, 190–92, 236).

"America letters" inspired adventuresome young Swedish men to seek their prairie, agricultural paradises (Janson 1931, 142). A letter from Knoxville in Knox County in 1850 spoke of the opportunities in the "New Sweden" settlements: "The soil here is good and fruitful. . . . The soil here looks like a cabbage patch, all loose black dirt about six feet deep. . . . A wonderful country it is . . . divided by many rivers which make possible transportation many hundreds of miles inland with sail boats, like the Mississippi" (Janson 1931, 141). Swedes arriving in Illinois were not the most impoverished people, given they financed the transatlantic voyage and provisioned their families for three to five months (147). The Swedish ethnic island in northwest Illinois served as an interior "mother area."

Welsh Immigrant Region

During the colonial period, individuals and families from Wales had settled the eastern seaboard and inland frontiers. Welsh emigrated from the rugged upland peninsula of western Britain. For centuries, they had resisted assimilation of their language and culture into an Anglicized society (Hartmann 1967). They were a distinctive, small ethnic group in the immigrant diversity of early-nineteenth-century America. Slightly over one-third of the Welsh settled in the Old Northwest. Farmers, miners, skilled and unskilled industrial workers, and laborers were the most frequent occupations (Hartmann 1967; Monaghan 1939).

British history in the 1840s was characterized as the "hungry forties" (Hartmann 1967, 61–100). Agricultural conditions in Wales were depressed. Farmers were oppressed by high land rentals, harassed by toll roads that taxed market produce, and living near starvation. Emigration to America offered a means for alleviating many problems. Welshmen settled temporarily in the older communities of Pennsylvania and New York. Later, they migrated to destinations in Ohio and Wisconsin. Welsh and Welsh Americans from the "mother settlements" back East settled southeast Wisconsin peripheral to Milwaukee. Besides farmers, miners were lured to the lead mining country in southwest Wisconsin. Those converted to Mormonism had settled at Nauvoo, but they had already escaped to the Great Salt Lake's shores by 1850.

The Welsh clustered, 62.1 percent, in three core counties, one domain county, and two sphere counties (fig. 9.10). Small ethnic enclaves formed in northern Illinois' verges, and diminutive ethnic pockets emerged in north-central and southwest Illinois. They were absent from two-thirds of the avoidance counties. The Welsh generally settled where English, Scotch, and Irish resided. The largest enclave emerged in northeast Illinois, with one-third of the Welsh in two core counties, 16.8 percent in Cook and 12.1 percent in Kane, and one sphere county, 3.9 percent in Lake. Welsh farmers located in five Cook County townships, but almost three-fourths dwelled in Chicago. Laborer and manufacturing jobs were available in the bustling lake port. Monaghan observed that they were linked by their common religion in the mid-1840s (1939). Methodist services in Welsh occurred in private homes. Hartmann noted that in 1900, the Chicago Welsh, 5,037, were almost one-half the state total, and their colony rivaled New York City's (1967). Their contributions as contractors and builders to the city's economy were out of proportion to their numbers. They tenaciously held to their language and their music (Monaghan 1939). In the core county of Kane, Welsh farmers were segregated, 58.1 percent, in Big Rock Township. In the sphere county of Lake, they settled in the inland Warren Township, 60 percent.

In northwest Illinois, a smaller Welsh enclave formed in the core county of Jo Daviess, 16.8 percent of the state total. A higher proportion of Welsh adult males,

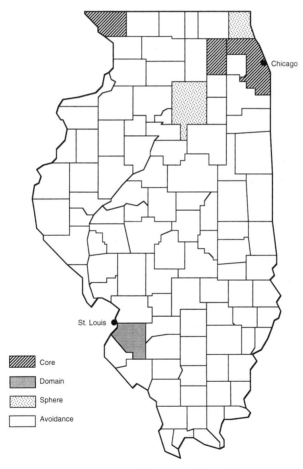

FIG. 9.10. Welsh Immigrants in Illinois, 1850 (*Seventh Census Population Schedules, 1850*)

41.9 percent, were miners than the other foreigners. They located on opposite sides of the county: 27.9 percent in Galena and 25.6 percent in the Millville Precinct, now Thompson Township. The Millville area was primarily settled by farmers in the rolling uplands of the Apple River Valley. Minuscule Welsh pockets emerged in the sphere county of La Salle, 5.1 percent, and the domain county of St. Clair, 7.4 percent. In La Salle County, they resided in Freedom Township, 53.8 percent. In St. Clair County, Welsh coal miners were sequestered, 84.2 percent, in Centreville Township. The township and the village of Millstadt were overwhelmingly German. Although Welsh numbers were meager, the immigrant structure reflected small, antecedent clusters in Chicago and Kane and La Salle Counties that grew in the late nineteenth century. The only new sizable Welsh settlement emerged in Will County.

Making a Foreign-Born Culture Region Map

Synthesizing the ninety-nine county migration fields, which included ten foreign-born immigrant groups, by means of factor analytic and cluster analysis techniques failed to delineate a foreign-born culture region structure. With few exceptions, the counties with primary concentrations of foreigners included distinctive blends of Germans, Irish, and English. Even the counties with fewer foreigners epitomized this ethnic mixing. Foreign immigrant groups were generally smaller in population size and tended to form segregated clusters in only a few townships or counties. To analyze the structure of the foreign-born culture region at the time of first effective settlement, I simply mapped the number of foreign-born adult males in each of the ninety-nine counties. County concentrations—core, domain, sphere, and avoidance—confirm the segmented cultural cores and peripheries. More than 1,000 foreign-born adult males in a county identify a core concentration. Two-thirds of the core counties had over 1,500 foreigners. Domain concentrations ranged from 375 to 1,000 foreigners and generally mark the lateral spread of immigrants from core areas into contiguous counties. Sphere concentrations, 65 to 374 foreigners, represent average immigrant dispersion. Avoidance counties, less than 64 foreigners, delineate minimal settlement interest and peripheral locations.

Foreign-Born Culture Region

Dispersing westward and northward, Europeans employed the expanding American transport system. Large amounts of fertile, cheap land, ease of communication and circulation, and divergent job opportunities in urban communities affected foreigners' destinations. Those with "Illinois fever" faced the difficult and expensive long-distance migration experience of crossing the Atlantic and penetrating the interior. In western and northern Europe, Illinois was a competitive "American fever" destination state in the 1840s. Several factors influenced foreigners' destination choices (figs. 9.1–9.10). Many foreign-born adult males, just as American pioneers with farming predilections, elected the better agricultural lands or districts. The hinterlands of regional nodes (St. Louis and Chicago), subregional nodes (Galena, Peoria, Quincy, Jacksonville, Springfield, and Alton), and lower-level nodes (county seat and market centers and river and canal towns) were attractive destinations for marketplace-oriented farmers. Some foreigners, such as the Irish, were disposed to the major urban nodes where the need for unskilled laborers predominated. Others with skilled labor backgrounds also selected the larger towns and cities. The lead mining district in northwest Illinois magnetized a diverse composition of foreigners who satisfied the unskilled and skilled labor needs of an extractive industry and a vital subregional node.

Foreign-born adult males, 44,305, were unevenly distributed across the regional spectrum of Illinois by 1850. Southern and central Illinois had equivalent numbers of foreigners, 10,258 and 10,547, respectively. Northern Illinois, the primary destination region, had more foreign-born immigrants, 23,500, than the other two regions combined. Foreign immigrants were highly selective in their settlement choices within the respective settlement regions. South of the National Road in the southern third, foreigners, 8,376, were lopsidedly concentrated in the American Bottom and inland tier of counties fringing St. Louis in southwest Illinois. Southeast Illinois, which included inland tier and riverine counties bordering the Wabash River, had a scattering of foreigners, 1,274. The extreme southern tip of Illinois, which embraced insular interior and riverine counties bordering the Wabash, Ohio, and Mississippi Rivers, had a minuscule number of foreigners, 608.

The central third of Illinois, wedged between the National Road on the south and the east-west corridor of the upper Illinois Valley and Illinois and Michigan Canal to the north, was fragmented into three distinctive settlement platforms. The Illinois Valley corridor bisected two mesmeric destination areas in west-central Illinois, the Military Tract and Sangamon Country. With the bordering Mississippi and Illinois riverine corridors and the dynamic, riverside verge foci of Quincy and Peoria, the Military Tract attracted a larger influx of foreigners, 5,692, than its rival settlement district. Sangamon Country, a settlement district east of the Illinois River, lured 4,270 foreigners to adjacent river counties and to inland hinterlands of Jacksonville and Springfield. In east-central Illinois, dominated by geographic isolation and the Grand Prairie, a diminutive number of foreigners located, 585.

A deluge of foreigners, 53 percent of the state total, were attracted to the northern third of Illinois. Yet the northern counties were not equivalent settlement destinations. A disproportionate number of foreigners, 17,178 or 38.8 percent, concentrated in the northeast sector juxtaposed to the evolving inland tributary counties of Chicago. The northwest corner of Illinois magnetized a substantial number of foreign immigrants, 6,322, who were enamored by the cheap, fertile government lands and the Lead Country mystic. The inland tier of counties embraced the magnetic Rock River Country. Foreigners penetrated this remote interior in northern Illinois with its evolving urban-transport web that connected Chicago, Galena, and the Illinois Valley corridor.

The foreign-born culture region (fig. 9.11) and Upland South (fig. 6.8), New England (fig. 7.9), and Midland-Midwest (fig. 8.9) culture regions in Illinois were interconnected within expanding regional and national urban-transport and culture region infrastructures. Europeans' clustering, dispersing, and mixing patterns engendered the culture region's fragmented structure. The nodes and hinterlands in the expanding three-tier urban hierarchies were primary destinations. The cultural cores attest to foreigners' settlement fixations and geographical propinquity. Foreigners' segmented structures formed focal settlement platforms within the spreading urban-transport networks in the late 1830s and 1840s (figs. 3.5–3.7). They transplanted in waves to northeast Illinois, the northern tier counties astride the Chicago-Galena Road, west-central Illinois, and southwest Illinois. The foreign-born periphery area arrayed from northeast to southwest, linking the fragmented cultural cores.

Europeans' destinations in midcontinental Illinois suggest an infilling of predisposed marketplace-oriented farmers and urban-oriented laborers, artisans, and merchants. County enclaves, dispersed farmsteads, tiny rural communities, and small urban neighborhoods exhibit an essential necessity for geographical clustering among ethnic groups. Dislocation from their European mother country, transatlantic separation, and culture shock of mainstream American frontier existence guaranteed a penchant among foreigners for geographical and social contact with their own kind. Clustering in compact and scattered ethnic rural and urban communities was integral to foreigners' transplantation, maintenance, and survival of their social well-being, customs, ethnicity, language, and religion. Persistence of sense of community for individuals, families, and groups was propagated in social and cultural bonds deeply rooted in old-world traditions, attitudes, and values. Shared memories, customs, and social guidelines assured sustainability and adjustment of one's personal and ethnic spirit in a new American and Illinois homeland.

In northeast Illinois, Cook County, with 17.8 percent of all foreign-born adult males in Illinois, emerged as the epicenter of an expanding foreign-born cultural core (fig. 9.11). A lopsided number of foreigners, 73.1 percent, in Cook County settled in the lake port and canal town of Chicago. Both Chicago and Cook County were diverse "foreign countries," with foreigners comprising 64.2 percent and 62.7 percent, respectively, of their total adult male populations. Will County, with the

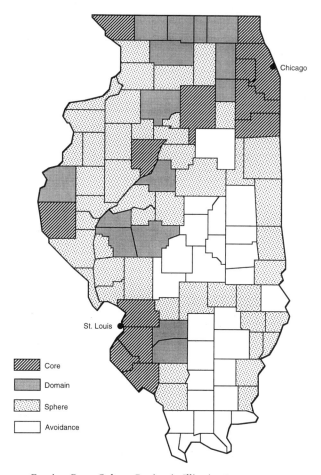

FIG. 9.11. Foreign-Born Culture Region in Illinois, 1850

traversing Illinois and Michigan Canal, was also attractive to foreigners with its settlement and economic potentials. Foreigners were very visible in the populations of Lake, DuPage, and Will Counties, 38.0 percent, 42.5 percent, and 40.5 percent, respectively. La Salle County, at the juncture of steam navigation and inland terminus of the canal, matured as a magnet foreign cluster. La Salle County witnessed a high proportion of foreigners, 41.3 percent. Northern tier domain counties emerged as an attractive European settlement thrust astride the Chicago-Galena Road. Recently, Cronon suggested that only large midwestern cities like Chicago, Milwaukee, and St. Louis were dominated by "foreignness" (1991, 104). Jo Daviess County formed the key foreign cluster in northwest Illinois. The county and Galena were pluralistic "foreign countries," with foreign-born immigrants embracing 55.7 percent and 62.0 percent, respectively. Because of out-lying lead mines, dispersed farmsteads, and tiny rural communities, foreigners were not as concentrated in Galena, 39.6 percent, as in Chicago.

Bisected by the Illinois Valley corridor, west-central Illinois unfolded three seg-mented foreign-born clusters in the Military Tract and Sangamon Country. The core counties of Peoria and Adams in the Military Tract, with rivals Peoria and Quincy, were the key destinations. Peoria County, with 20.7 percent of the Mili-tary Tract's foreigners, had the largest aggregation of foreigners in the middle and lower Illinois Valley. In Peoria County, foreigners comprised 26.3 percent of the diverse population. A larger proportion of foreigners, 36.9 percent, resided in the city. The domain county of Tazewell embraced 21.5 percent foreigners. One-third of the foreigners in the county resided in the courthouse-river town of Pekin. It included 27.5 percent foreigners, mostly Germans, 58.4 percent. Adams County had the largest cluster of foreigners in the Military Tract, 29.1 percent of the total. They accounted for 28.8 percent of the county's population. Riverside Quincy de-veloped as a "foreign country" like Galena and Chicago, with 56.4 percent foreign-ers. But its foreigners were not as diverse; almost two-thirds were Germans. The foreign mixture in Peoria County compared with northeast Illinois, where Irish predominated. Adams County paralleled German-dominated southwest Illinois.

East of the Illinois Valley in Sangamon Country, three domain counties formed a prominent foreign cluster of Cass with riverside Beardstown, Morgan with Jack-sonville, and Sangamon with Springfield. Cass County had a larger proportion of foreigners than Sangamon and Morgan Counties, 31.1 percent, 18.1 percent, and 12.7 percent, respectively. Foreigners were attracted to Beardstown, "hog butcher of Illinois," and Springfield, the state capital, 46.0 percent and 58.0 percent, re-spectively, of their county totals. The market center of Jacksonville lured one-fourth of the foreigners in its county. The community social fabric of Springfield and Jacksonville were distinctively foreign-born, 28.8 percent and 26.6 percent, re-spectively. Beardstown was a "foreign country," with 52.4 percent foreigners. Like Quincy, Beardstown had a strong German imprint, 68.3 percent of the foreigners.

The second-largest cultural core in the foreign-born culture region spread east-ward from the middle Mississippi Valley mercantile linchpin (fig. 9.11). The ripar-ian, foreign enclave forged a contiguous block of core counties straddling the road network that converged on St. Louis and Alton. Southwest Illinois revealed a mix-ture of Germans, Irish, and English but a lopsided number of Germans. French and Swiss also infilled these counties. Foreigners settled on dispersed farmsteads and in tiny rural communities. Belleville and Alton attracted a smaller percentage of their county's foreigners, 16.9 percent and 23.8 percent, respectively. The court-house and market center of Belleville had a higher proportion of foreigners, 70.4 percent, than Chicago. But this "foreign country" was overwhelmingly a "German city" in numbers and landscape ambience; 90.0 percent of the foreigners were

Germans. Alton had almost equal proportions of foreign- and native-born immigrants. Its foreign element was equally diverse, with Irish and Germans about one-third each and English one-fifth.

Foreigners were highly visible in the core counties of Monroe, St. Clair, Madison, and Randolph, with 58.9 percent, 57.1 percent, 39.0 percent, and 37.1 percent, respectively. They were heavily skewed towards a "German fatherland" transplanted to southwest Illinois, with 73.3 percent, 78.5 percent, 46.9 percent, and 51.6 percent, respectively, of the total foreigners. The inland tier of domain counties, Clinton and Washington, abutting St. Clair County, had substantial proportions of foreigners, 32.9 percent and 27.4 percent, respectively. Both counties were saturated with Germans, 80.6 percent and 68.3 percent of their foreign populations. German settlements had thrust eastward from a culture hearth base in the Belleville area. Monroe and St. Clair Counties in southwest Illinois joined Cook and Jo Daviess Counties in northern Illinois as "foreign countries" in Illinois.

In northern and west-central Illinois, the segmented core and domain counties were linked by contiguous sphere counties astride the Illinois Valley and Mississippi Valley corridors. Sporadic filterings of foreigners molded linear alignments of sphere counties in east-central and southern Illinois. The first one extended eastward straddling the National Road from the foreign-born cultural core in southwest Illinois. The second one extended northward from the Ohio River to the Illinois and Michigan Canal astride the Wabash Valley corridor in eastern Illinois. A few isolated foreign colonies transplanted in southern Illinois. The largest foreign cluster persisted in Edwards County, where the remnant English colony continued to attract English immigrants. The English comprised 80.6 percent of the foreigners in this sphere county. In this Upland South settlement area, foreigners were 39.1 percent of the county's adult males. Attached to the National Road was a German cluster in Effingham County, a lopsided 95.3 percent of the foreigners. They were 30.0 percent of the population in this Upland South–dominated county.

The interior counties in southern and east-central Illinois were foreign avoidance areas (fig. 9.11). The isolated Shawnee Hills and riparian counties bordering the Ohio-Mississippi Rivers in extreme southern Illinois experienced settlement restraints that precluded foreigners. There was difficulty in obtaining clear title to much of the land, given earlier squatter settlements. The fertile, alluvial floodplains frequently flooded. The rugged, forested Shawnee Hills were not viewed as an ideal settlement habitat. The better agricultural lands had been earlier settled in the forested, rolling plains of interior southern Illinois. Isolated farmsteads and tiny market and county seat centers were distant from waterborne channels, thus retarding commercial agriculture. Finally, Upland South woodland frontiersmen had inundated southern Illinois; thus, cheap government lands were less available.

In east-central Illinois, the less-dense road network was a major constraint to a large influx of settlers. Isolated farmers and rural communities between the

Wabash-Illinois commercial waterways were distant from steamboat river towns and regional, national, and world markets. Farmers with a marketplace-bias slowly settled the Grand Prairie, even though large amounts of cheap, fertile lands were available. A limited urban hierarchy developed other than the fringing riverside, subregional node of Terre Haute. Without larger market centers that offered labor and business opportunities, east-central Illinois remained unacceptable to many foreigners. With the building of the Illinois Central Railroad, the peripheral railroad lands and replicated railroad towns in the Grand Prairie fostered a ripple effect of destinations with marketplace accessibility. In the postbellum era, the spreading Illinois railroad network furnished accessible destinations for farmers, unskilled and skilled laborers, and merchants.

10

Conclusion

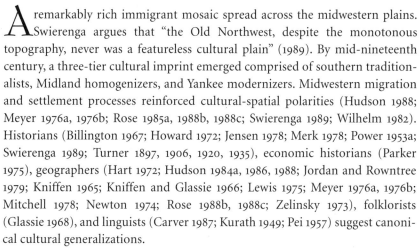

Whilst the population on the great rivers and other
thorough-fares is of a very mixed and doubtful character,
much of that on the prairies and purely agricultural districts
consists of decent people of simple manners, and is as unlike
that of the eastern states as if they were of different nations.
—Oliver 1843

A remarkably rich immigrant mosaic spread across the midwestern plains.
Swierenga argues that "the Old Northwest, despite the monotonous
topography, never was a featureless cultural plain" (1989). By mid-nineteenth
century, a three-tier cultural imprint emerged comprised of southern traditionalists, Midland homogenizers, and Yankee modernizers. Midwestern migration
and settlement processes reinforced cultural-spatial polarities (Hudson 1988;
Meyer 1976a, 1976b; Rose 1985a, 1988b, 1988c; Swierenga 1989; Wilhelm 1982).
Historians (Billington 1967; Howard 1972; Jensen 1978; Merk 1978; Power 1953a;
Swierenga 1989; Turner 1897, 1906, 1920, 1935), economic historians (Parker
1975), geographers (Hart 1972; Hudson 1984a, 1986, 1988; Jordan and Rowntree
1979; Kniffen 1965; Kniffen and Glassie 1966; Lewis 1975; Meyer 1976a, 1976b;
Mitchell 1978; Newton 1974; Rose 1988b, 1988c; Zelinsky 1973), folklorists
(Glassie 1968), and linguists (Carver 1987; Kurath 1949; Pei 1957) suggest canoni-
cal cultural generalizations.

Zelinsky's benchmark culture region map (1973) has formed the basis of other
scholars' identification and delimitation of subregions in the eastern United States
(Jordan and Rowntree 1979; Mitchell 1978). Mitchell's structure of early American
culture regions portrays Illinois as an unknown quantity in the genesis, development, and expansion of diffusion patterns and regional way stations (1978).
Crosscurrents of native- and foreign-born immigrants interspersed an extraordinary cultural diversity. I conclude with a retrospection of the population origins,
cultural borders, culture regions, and regional way stations in Illinois by 1850. But

283

first, a brief review is in order of geographers' suppositions within the framework of Zelinsky's seminal culture region structure.

Upland South Impress

Rapidly spreading Upland Southerners, with their adaptive woodland cultural strategy, duplicated settlements in the eastern United States (Hudson 1988; Jordan and Rowntree 1979; Jordan and Kaups 1989; Mitchell 1978; Newton 1974; Mitchell and Newton 1988; Zelinsky 1973). Moving deeper into the interior, they merged with other primary migration streams as areally extensive cultural mixing zones emerged. Hart maintains that migration flows remained segregated: "Each entryway served a migration stream from a distinctive source region, and these streams remained remarkably separate as they continued westward across the Middle West" (1972, 260). Trunk lines shaped directional-biases with sharp cultural divides developing between Pennsylvanians and Kentuckians. The National Road implicitly demarcated a cultural border between northerners and southerners (Hart 1972; Kurath 1949; Pei 1957; Rose 1988b; Turner 1920). Hudson argues, instead, that "transportation routes, whether water, road, or rail, are far more effective homogenizers than they are segregators" (1988, 410).

Zelinsky contends that the Midwest's distinctive subculture regions represent major fusions of regional cultures that make the "section most nearly representative of the national average" (1973, 118–19, 128–29). In his American culture region map, a first-order cultural boundary that borders the northern edge of the Ohio Valley corridor separates the Middle West and the South (fig. 10.1). In southern Illinois, the first-order cultural boundary more closely parallels the Vincennes–St. Louis Trace, not the National Road. Given greater southward latitudinal penetration and fringing rivers, Zelinsky speculates a larger Upland South areal extent in Illinois in contrast to Indiana and Ohio. Population sources of the Upland South (IIIc subculture area) embrace Midland, Lowland South, and Great Britain (Zelinsky 1973, 119). Northern portions of southern Illinois and central Illinois denote the Lower Middle West. Population origins in the Lower Middle West (IVb subculture area) include Midland, Upland South, New England extended, and nineteenth-century Europe (Zelinsky 1973, 119).

Hudson proposes that a midwestern Upland South zone formed principally south of the thirty-ninth parallel of latitude (1988). His dominant regional patterns depict a series of Upland South immigrant wedges thrusting northward, which closely parallels available Ohio and Mississippi tributaries (411). These Upland South settlement areas reveal birthplace origins principally from Kentucky and Virginia. The Upland South settlements extended into central Illinois and central Indiana. In extreme southern Illinois, Hudson notes Upland South

FIG. 10.1. Illinois Culture Regions According to Zelinsky (Zelinsky 1973)

birthplace origins from the Carolinas and Tennessee. The northern boundary of the Upland South corresponds to an irregular east-west settlement wave.

Broad population origin strokes have a number of weaknesses. Zelinsky's population origin generalizations and culture region substructures for the Midwest are primarily based on secondary sources rather than primary (1973). Hart's (1972) and Hudson's (1988) birthplace data were substantially removed from the period of first effective settlement; late-nineteenth-century census data and county histories were the population origin sources. In the case of Hudson's midwestern population origin study, the county histories were socially biased and ignored the large influx of ordinary immigrants (1988). These generalized regional migration patterns were also derived from a small sample of counties. In my opinion, the sample counties were too scattered and few in number to delineate detailed immigrant structures.

New England Impress

Yankees were late starting in comparison with Upland Southerners in planting settlements deep into the interior. The creation of an effective, cheap, all-water Great Lakes–Erie Canal trunk line after 1825 and steam navigation improvements were powerful migration mechanisms (Mathews 1909, 1910). Out-migration intensified from western New York and the New England states during the late 1830s and 1840s (Hudson 1986, 1988; Mathews 1909; Mitchell 1978). The National Road has been suggested as a more precise cultural divide than the Ohio River between North and South or Yankees and southerners in the Lower Midwest (Rose 1988b). An equivalent overland artery functioning as a cultural discontinuity between New Englanders and Midlanders has not been proposed. Yet numerous maps infer a cultural border between Yankees and Midlanders that extends westward from the southern shore of Lake Erie to the southern tip of Lake Michigan (Hart 1972; Hudson 1986, 1988; Jordan and Rowntree 1979; Kurath 1949; Mitchell 1978; Zelinsky 1973). Ford argued that southerners were hostile toward constructing the Illinois and Michigan Canal because they feared completion "would open a way for flooding the State with Yankees" (1854, 281).

Zelinsky divides the Midwest culture region into Upper Middle West, Lower Middle West, and Cutover Area (1973, 118–19, 128–29). His second-order cultural boundary delimits northern Illinois within the southern margins of the Upper Middle West (fig. 10.1). This subculture region extends as a fairly broad east-west belt across the northern sectors of Illinois, Indiana, and Ohio and the southern half of lower Michigan and southern Wisconsin. West of the Mississippi River, the Upper Middle West is not areally defined. The second-order cultural boundary separating the Upper and Lower Middle West appears as a latitude-specific cultural border. Upper Middle West population sources (IVa subculture area) include New England extended, New England, nineteenth-century Europe, and British Canada (Zelinsky 1973, 119). Midland-Midwest population origins were not posited as an integral component of his subculture region. Jordan and Rowntree's culture region map deviates from Zelinsky's map by showing a slight southwest skew in the subculture boundary corresponding to the upper Illinois River bend (1979).

Hudson's reinterpretations of Upper Midwest population origins delimit an east-west Yankeeland arrayed from southern Michigan across northeast Illinois and southeast Wisconsin (1984a, 1984b, 1986, 1988). A constriction occurs crossing the Mississippi River into Minnesota, then a rapid areal expansion of Yankee-dominated counties across Minnesota and into the Dakotas. In his midwestern population origin studies, he stresses a cultural mixing theme. The Upper and

Lower Midwest transitional area marks a Yankee-Midland cultural mixing zone (Hudson 1984b, 1986). Recently, Hudson redefined a Yankee-Midland mixture zone in the upper Illinois Valley and northwest Illinois (1988, 404–6, 411).

Midland-Midwest Impress

Pennsylvanians, New Jerseyites, and Marylanders commingled as Midland cultural elements in the Midwest. Ohioans and Indianans represent population origin mixtures of Upland South, Midland, and New England cultural traditions. Stepwise migration by Pennsylvanians created their "daughter state" of Ohio (Chaddock 1908; Mitchell 1978; Rose 1988c; Wilhelm 1982). Rose argues that pre-1850 settlers in southeast Ohio migrated from nearby southwest Pennsylvania and northwest Virginia (1988a). Indianans typified Midland–Upland South cultural traditions (Jordan and Kaups 1989; Rose 1985a, 1986a, 1986c, 1988c). In the interior, discrete Midland regional way stations were not replicated beyond southwest Pennsylvania, southwest Ohio, and southeast Indiana (Mitchell 1978). Midlanders-Midwesterners functioned as coalescing homogenizers in the Lower Midwest (Rose 1988c).

Cultural separation and divides, rather than cultural mixing and transitional borderlands, formed in the Midwest, according to Hart (1972). The Pennsylvania component of the Midland migration stream configured a spatially uniform sector "in the middle just north of the National Road" (Hart 1972, 260). The national diffusion pathway prescribed a directional-bias that developed as a cultural segregator between Pennsylvanians and Kentuckians. A Turner student perpetuated this cultural "fault line" interpretation of the national pike: "That road formed a line of demarcation between southern and northern population elements in the Old Northwest" (Merk 1978, 125). Implicit in the material culture and folk architecture traditions in the eastern United States has been a cultural edge separating North and South. With broad arrows marking diffusion vectors of building methods and architectural ideas, scholars presume a cultural discontinuity (Glassie 1968; Kniffen 1965; Kniffen and Glassie 1966; Lewis 1975).

Zelinsky perceives the Middle West, with its idiosyncratic subculture structure, as exemplifying a major cultural mixing region (1973, 118–19, 128–29). His second-order cultural boundary, IVb, depicts the Lower Middle West as a cultural transition zone (fig. 10.1). The cultural borderlands stretch as a broad swath across the midsections and southern portions of Ohio, Indiana, and Illinois, the northern half of Missouri, and the extreme southern portions of Iowa. He suggests a cultural mixing bowl that includes Midland, Upland South, New England extended, and nineteenth-century European population origins. Hudson (1988) and Rose (1988c) delineate the Lower Midwest as a region dominated by Midlanders who originated primarily from southwest, central, and southeast Pennsylvania. Hudson's northern

Midland boundary closely conformed to the forty-first parallel of latitude (1988, 411). A contributing factor to the irregularity of the southern Midland boundary linked to Pennsylvanians' shift southward from the National Road and northward from the Ohio Valley corridor via available road networks and navigable riverine channels.

Population Origins

Zelinsky's synoptic reference map of American cultural-genetic regions generalizes population origins (1973). The complex array of population origins interspersed across Illinois (figs. 6.1–6.7, 7.1–7.8, 8.1–8.8, 9.1–9.10) requires synthesis. Four native-born immigrant groups were widely dispersed: Kentuckians, New Yorkers, Tennesseans, and Ohioans (table 10.1, fig. 10.2). Kentuckians outnumbered New Yorkers in more counties because of their earlier settlement forays in the state. Tennesseans were half the number of New Yorkers but dominated the same number of counties. Ohioans diffused into the number of counties as expected for a large migration flow. Germans concentrated in more counties than their Pennsylvania German kinfolk from Pennsylvania. The Irish, English, North Carolinians, and New Jerseyites formed isolated cases of dominance.

TABLE 10.1 Migration Field Structure of Illinois, 1850

Birthplace*	Counties Where Largest	%	Counties Where 2d Largest	%
Kentucky	29	29.3	25	25.3
New York	18	18.2	7	7.0
Tennessee	18	18.2	11	11.1
Ohio	16	16.2	20	20.2
Germany	9	9.1	6	6.1
Pennsylvania	5	5.0	6	6.1
Ireland	1	1.0	7	7.1
England	1	1.0	4	4.0
North Carolina	1	1.0	4	4.0
New Jersey	1	1.0		
Virginia			4	4.0
Vermont			2	2.0
Indiana			1	1.0
Sweden			1	1.0
France			1	1.0
Total	99	100.0	99	100.0

Source: Seventh Census Population Schedules, 1850

*Excludes Illinois.

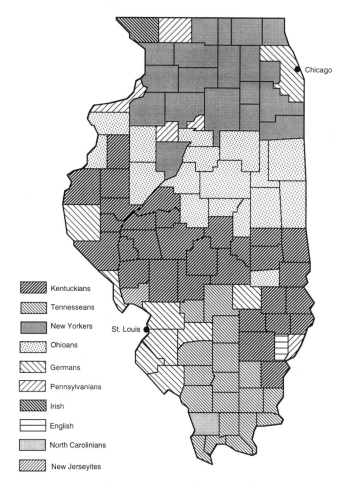

FIG. 10.2. Largest Immigrant Groups in Illinois, 1850 (*Seventh Census Population Schedules, 1850*)

Southern and central Illinois experienced an overlay of Upland Southerners, particularly from Kentucky and Tennessee (fig. 10.2). From southern Illinois gateways, Tennesseans dispersed northward, forming an elongated axis that paralleled a south-north road. Kentuckians spread over a greater area than Tennesseans, possibly revealing their large numbers, a stepwise migration across the Ohio Valley, and a propensity to diffuse northward. Upland Southerners' settlements extended far north of the National Road. North Carolinians in the western verge of the Shawnee Hills had migrated chiefly from the piedmont, thus typifying Upland South material culture rather than Lowland South (Meyer 1976c).

Pennsylvanians, Ohioans, and New Jerseyites who created scattered anomalies represent Midland heritage. The English anomaly perpetuated a remnant of the Birkbeck-Flower colony established at the time of statehood. For an anomalous county to go against a mainstream migration trend, channelized migration flows must evolve (Roseman 1977). The most atypical population origin pattern within the Upland South domination across southern and central Illinois was the emergence of Germans as the largest immigrant group. Germans were inclined to converge on particular places, thus engraving their distinctive ethnic enclaves (Meyer 1988). This German veneer replaced and modified an earlier Upland South settlement impress. Five contiguous counties formed in southwest Illinois adjacent to the German hearth of St. Louis and the lower Missouri River Valley German settlements (van Ravenswaay 1977). Scattered German counties included the interior county of Effingham, the Mississippi River counties of Calhoun and Adams, and lakeside Cook County.

New Yorkers dispersed from gateway Chicago across northern Illinois in the decade and a half prior to 1850 (fig. 10.2). Their uniform, compact pattern was modified with two foreign-born settlement intrusions. Powerful cultural mixtures converged at the antipodes of northern Illinois, Cook and Jo Daviess Counties. Germans were the largest adult male group in Cook County, but New Yorkers included almost half of the Americans. In remote Jo Daviess County, the Irish emerged as the largest immigrant group with New Yorkers comprising almost one-fourth the native-born immigrants. Pennsylvanians dispersed into northern Illinois. Stephenson County adjacent to Jo Daviess County possessed the largest number of Pennsylvanians.

Ohioans rivaled Kentuckians and New Yorkers for prominence as the largest immigrant group across central Illinois. A large block of counties tapered toward the Mississippi River. The interconnected road networks of east-central and west-central Illinois engendered the spatial ordering of Ohioans. They failed to disperse in large numbers south of the National Road.

An Upland South settlement spearhead progressed northwestward from the Ohio Valley corridor to Sangamon Country in west-central Illinois (fig. 10.3). Upland Southerners spread extensively across central Illinois from the Wabash to the Mississippi Rivers as they readily mixed with Midwesterners (Ohioans), Midlanders (Pennsylvanians and New Jerseyites), Yankees (New Yorkers), and foreigners (Germans). Midwesterners (Ohioans) diffused more widely throughout central and southeast Illinois than either Yankees (New Yorkers) or Midlanders (Pennsylvanians). Yankees and Midlanders limited their extensive settlement penetration to the northern counties in the Military Tract.

Foreign-born enclaves were forged in southwest, northeast, and northwest Illinois where Europeans dominated over Americans. A few scattered foreign-born

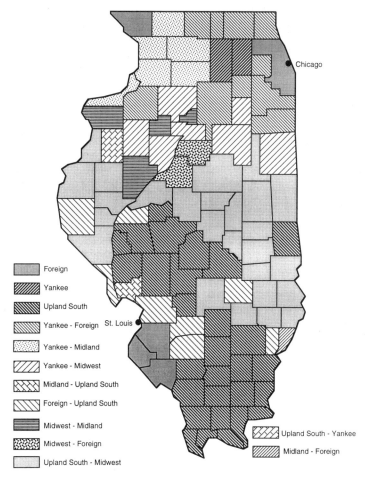

FIG. 10.3. Two Largest Immigrant Groups in Each County in Illinois, 1850
(*Seventh Census Population Schedules, 1850*)

counties existed in southern and west-central Illinois astride the Mississippi-
Illinois Rivers where foreigners mixed with Upland Southerners and Midwesterners. In northeast Illinois and bordering the Illinois and Michigan Canal, a block of
counties formed where foreigners mixed with Yankees. A Yankee core formed in
northeast Illinois. Yet between Lake Michigan, the Mississippi Valley, and the
upper Illinois Valley, the counties were dominated by a mixture of Yankees, Europeans, and Midlanders-Midwesterners. Northern Illinois was not a solid Yankeeland but disclosed a distinctive cultural diversity.

Redrawing Cultural Borders and Culture Regions

Zelinsky's hierarchical classification of the cultural-genetic subregions of his American culture area map requires confirmation or revision for Illinois (1973). Twenty-three native-born and ten foreign-born immigrant structural patterns (figs. 6.1–6.7, 7.1–7.8, 8.1–8.8, 9.1–9.10) and four culture regions' core-periphery frameworks (figs. 6.8, 7.9, 8.9, 9.11) confirm that Illinois emerged as an archetypal "historic test-strip" of midwestern cultural diversity. Immigrant migration patterns and cultural imprints were not ephemeral settlement episodes. Dynamic immigrant-cultural cores served as "mother areas" or dispersion points into contiguous townships and counties or adjacent states or deeper into the continent. Immigrant patterns were neither trendless nor simply broad latitudinal zones dispersed across the breadth of the state; instead, immigrants interrelated in watershed settlement platforms. Favorable place images and improving connectivity levels in northeast, northwest, west-central, and southwest Illinois consolidated immigrants' cultural mixing.

During the antebellum, American culture region and urban-transport systems expanded from the eastern seaboard to the Mississippi Valley. Scholars have postulated segmented cultural imprints and subculture regions for the Middle West. Figure 10.4 depicts a representative sample of cultural boundaries overlaid on Zelinsky's prototype Illinois subculture regions (1973). Over time, a North-South cultural border has been variously associated with the Ohio River and the National Road, the preferred midwestern cultural divide (Rose 1988b). Boundary lines on maps are frequently perceived as spatial separators or divides instead of as diacritic clues of transitional zones. Their attributes are implicitly interpreted as breaks or edges rather than as cultural mixing areas. Hudson contends that transport routes strongly influenced the heterogeneous arrangement of immigrant patterns inscribed in regional settlement development (1988, 410). Flexible national and regional transport networks molded intricate midwestern immigrant layerings. Instead of cultural segregation symbolizing regional settlement expansion, cultural mixing typified settlement regionalization in the interior's midsection (Hudson 1984b).

Immigrant orderings in Illinois mirror the cultural porosity and metamorphosis of Midwest subculture regions. The cultural borders of Zelinsky's benchmark culture region map require redrawing for Illinois (1973) (figs. 10.1, 10.4, 10.5). The first-order cultural boundary differentiating the Midwest and South (Upland South) reveals minimal congruence with Zelinsky's boundary. Zelinsky's cultural border reflects the accepted scholarly notions on the northward dispersion of southernness in the Middle West, which corresponds with the National Road and Vincennes–St. Louis Trace interstice. This investigation substantiates that an Upland South core diffused widely across southern Illinois and northwestward into

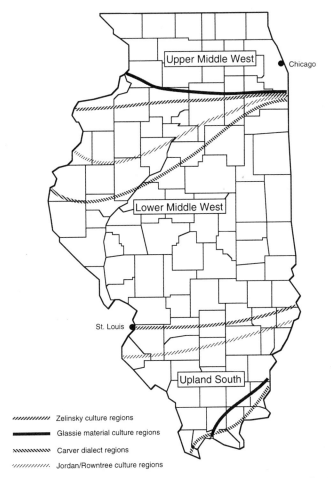

FIG. 10.4. Selected Culture Regions in Illinois (Zelinsky 1973; Glassie 1968; Carver 1987; Jordan and Rowntree 1979)

Sangamon Country and the southern Military Tract in west-central Illinois. The northward areal spread of Upland South periphery was greater than previously perceived by scholars (figs. 6.8, 10.1, 10.4, 10.5). Uniformity did not prevail in the Upland South subculture region; instead, core-periphery areas reveal extensive cultural mixing with Yankees, Midlanders-Midwesterners, and Europeans (figs. 6.8, 7.9, 8.9, 9.11, 10.5).

The second-order cultural boundary differentiating the Upper Middle West and Lower Middle West depicts basal correspondence with Zelinsky's boundary (figs. 10.1, 10.4, 10.5). His Yankee cultural border coheres with scholars' general perception that New Englanders' southward spread from gateway Chicago was

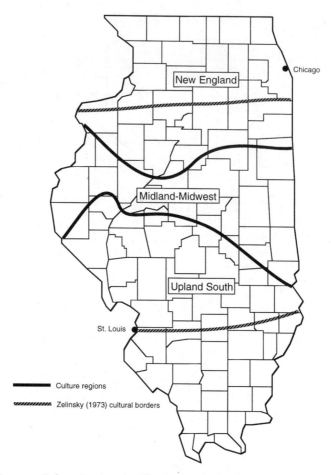

FIG. 10.5. Culture Regions in Illinois, 1850 (Zelinsky 1973)

spatially limited. Zelinsky's Yankee cultural border coincided with a line connecting the northern Military Tract and the upper Illinois River Valley. This study authenticates that not only was the New England core dominant in northern Illinois, but also it diffused southwestward. Yet the Yankee core was not culturally uniform; it experienced salient infillings of Europeans and Midlanders-Midwesterners. Yankees significantly dispersed along a northeast-southwest axis straddling the Illinois Valley corridor toward Peoria in west-central Illinois. New Englanders' dispersion spawned a more extensive areal spread than heretofore recognized by scholars (figs. 7.9, 10.1, 10.4, 10.5). The Yankee periphery extended across central Illinois astride the Illinois, Mississippi, and Wabash Rivers and the available road networks into southwest and southeast Illinois. Considerable cultural mixing developed with Upland Southerners, Midlanders-Midwesterners, and Europeans in the Yankee periphery (figs. 6.8, 7.9, 8.9, 9.11, 10.5).

The Upland South and New England subculture regions engendered a discrete polarity in Illinois by 1850. A constricted Lower Midwest geographical wedge evolved between the first-order cultural boundary distinguishing the Midwest and South and the second-order cultural boundary marking the Upper Midwest and Lower Midwest. The Midland-Midwest subculture region depicts minimal conformity with Zelinsky's Lower Middle West region (figs. 10.1, 10.4, 10.5). Zelinsky's Lower Middle West subculture region replicates accepted scholarly impressions. A broad latitudinal swath of distinctive Pennsylvania or Midland extended failed to emerge in Illinois. This research corroborates that the northward thrust of an Upland South impress and the southward thrust of a New England impress in Illinois were areally greater and more complex than previously posited. The geographical result was a contracted infilling of a mixed Midland-Midwest heritage in central Illinois. Midwestern elements from Ohio and Indiana included complex mixtures of Pennsylvanian, New England, and Upland South traditions. The Midland-Midwest subculture region in the Grand Prairie in east-central Illinois and in the northern margins of Sangamon Country and midsection of the Military Tract in west-central Illinois emerged constricted in the middle Illinois Valley corridor. The dispersion of culturally mixed Midland-Midwest immigrants crisscrossed Illinois from their midstate core (figs. 8.9, 10.1, 10.4, 10.5). This complex Midland-Midwest periphery molded greater areal diffusion than recognized by scholars. Cultural coherence was not the norm in the Midland-Midwest core; instead, a quintessential cultural mixing zone formed that included Upland Southerners, Yankees, and Europeans (figs. 6.8, 7.9, 8.9, 9.11, 10.5).

Regional Way Stations

As culture regions diffused across the eastern United States in the late eighteenth and early nineteenth centuries, cultural accretions and regionalizations emerged (Mitchell 1978, 74–90). Functioning as open systems, discrete regional way stations formed in settlement convergence areas. Mitchell argues that regional way stations originated where the "fusion and reconfiguration of traits and institutions" occurred in the subculture structure (90). I posit that Upland Southerners, New Englanders, Midlanders-Midwesterners, and foreigners forged regional way stations in Illinois that interrelated in expanding American culture region and urban-transport systems. Core concentration type counties of the four largest immigrant groups in each primary migration flow were aggregated to delimit the configuration of the regional way stations: Upland South (Kentucky, Tennessee, Virginia, North Carolina), New England (New York, Vermont, Massachusetts, Connecticut), Midland-Midwest (Ohio, Pennsylvania, Indiana, New Jersey), and foreign-born (Germany, Ireland, England, Canada). Regional way stations reflect immigrants' settlement proclivities that formed elemental regional settlement platforms in pre-railroad Illinois. Accessibility to primary migration pathways, urban-transport networks, and regional, national, and world space-economies enhanced these pivotal destination areas. Segmented regional way stations unfolded that were characterized by cultural mixing and interaction rather than by cultural uniformity and separation (figs. 6.8, 7.9, 8.9, 9.11, 10.6).

Southern Illinois emerged the closest to regional cultural conformity with its strong Upland South character (fig. 10.6). Yet its material culture traditions embraced a cultural mixture, given its entwined Midland–Upland South heritage (Jordan and Kaups 1989). Southwest Illinois, bordering gateway St. Louis, attracted

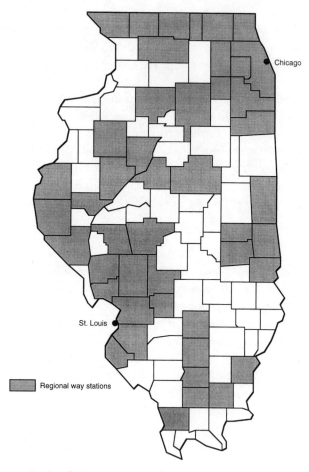

FIG. 10.6. Regional Way Stations in Illinois, 1850

large infusions of foreigners, particularly Germans, Upland Southerners, Midlanders-
Midwesterners, and smaller infillings of New Englanders. Searching for a commercially oriented economic settlement region, diverse immigrant groups converged
on this key midwestern regional way station. The regional way stations in central
Illinois developed distinct cultural mixing patterns. A small area in east-central
Illinois that integrated with west-central Indiana astride the Wabash Valley corridor marked the northward extension of Upland Southerners and the westward
spread of Midlanders-Midwesterners. Sangamon Country in west-central Illinois
lured large numbers of Upland Southerners, Midlanders-Midwesterners, and substantial infillings of foreigners and New Englanders. The mesopotamian wedge of
the Military Tract between the Mississippi and Illinois movement-commercial
channels significantly attracted all the major migration flows. A dynamic, culturally mixed, west-central Illinois regional way station straddled the Illinois Valley
corridor.

A regional way station stretched across northern Illinois that formed two an-
tipodal sections with different cultural mixtures and economic integration levels.
The hinterland of gateway Chicago in northeast Illinois attracted a flood of New
Englanders and foreigners. Significant numbers of Midlanders-Midwesterners
and a few Upland Southerners added to the cultural mixture in this vital midwest-
ern regional way station. Distant northwest Illinois, with its isolated interior areas,
Mississippi River verge, and Galena hinterland, revealed greater cultural mixing.
Larger proportions of Midlanders-Midwesterners, decreasing numbers of New
Englanders and foreigners, and larger infillings of Upland Southerners character-
ized this regional way station subcomponent.

Expanding regional urban-transport and marketplace networks spurred immigrant diversity and promoted cultural, social, and economic interactions and exchanges. The immediate hinterlands of the regional entrepôts of St. Louis and
Chicago developed as essential regional way stations where cultural mixtures intensified cultural adaptations and fusions (fig. 10.6). As culturally diverse economic-
settlement platforms, southwest Illinois, northeast Illinois, and west-central Illinois
expanded as quintessential midwestern settlement landscapes. The integration of
local, regional, national, and world economic systems accelerated immigrants'
cultural mixing.

The Military Tract in west-central Illinois emerged as a precursor of statewide
and midwestern immigrant and cultural diversity. Highly integrated between the
rival regional nodes of St. Louis and Chicago, Adams and Peoria Counties, with
their subregional nodes of Quincy and Peoria, represented prototypal midwestern
counties. All four primary migration flows—Upland Southerners, New Englanders, Midlanders-Midwesterners, and foreigners—established core concentrations
in these mesmeric destinations. Urban, economic, and transport processes encouraged commercial agricultural growth that connected with rapidly expanding

regional, national, and world markets and a maturing four-tier urban hierarchy. Successful farmers in the hinterlands of the lower-level and subregional nodes required and expected higher levels of specialized services, marketplace functions, and manufactured goods. Adaptations and fusions occurred among diverse immigrant groups in this evolving Corn Belt, crop-livestock, agricultural landscape.

The diverse cultural mixtures in the Military Tract engraved distinctive barns, houses, and agricultural complexes that were prototypal midwestern cultural, agricultural landscapes. The mix of double-crib, four-crib, and transverse crib barn types of the Upland Southerners, Pennsylvania bank barns with forebays and some Swiss bank barns with forebays of the Midlanders, and three-bay English barns of the New Englanders imprinted a material, cultural landscape rooted in the soil whose relic artifacts remain visible today. The disparate cultural groups built similar planform cottages (double-pen cottages) and houses (double-pile houses, "I" houses) rooted in inherited continental European and eastern seaboard traditions that were interwoven into national, regional, and local builders' traditions. But the "I" house variety, with gables to the side, at least two rooms in length, one room deep, and two full stories in height, emerged as a folk type widely distributed in rural eastern United States (Kniffen 1965, 555). As a rural dwelling, it became, as Kniffen argues, the symbol of economic achievement and social respectability in the post-frontier era of economic development (1965).

Yet distinctive mixtures of folk structure types were inscribed in the Military Tract by Upland Southerners ("I" houses with two-story porches, saddlebag cottages), Yankees (upright and wing houses, New England classic cottages, and gable-front houses), Midlanders (Pennsylvania four-over-four houses), and Germans (brick double-pile cottages) (Jakle, Bastian, and Meyer 1989; Kniffen 1965; Lewis 1975). The arrangement of settlement forms in the rural and urban landscapes substantiates the integral cultural pluralism of the land between the rivers. Courthouse and market centers, with their public square forms, possibly reflect regional culture heritage (Price 1968). The diversity of place and regional images remains legible in numerous landscape expressions today. The coinciding of the Great Migration and handcraftsmen's "Golden Era" molded distinctive regional patterns of art, crafts, and architecture in Illinois and the Middle West (Madden 1974, xii).

Powerful native- and foreign-born migration flows contrived quintessential place and regional images during the nineteenth century. In west-central Illinois, the Military Tract and Sangamon Country symbolized cutting-edge cultural diversity and marketplace motivations. Cultural convergence, mixing, and change were essential processes embraced in the agricultural, settlement, and cultural traditions implanted in west-central Illinois. West-central Illinois, bisected by the Illinois Valley corridor, demarcated a benchmark, midcontinental regional way station within the expanding American culture region system (fig. 10.6). At the micro-scale of regional cultural and settlement development, it mirrored the broader, complex macro-scale brush strokes replicated across Illinois and the Middle West.

Accessible Illinois witnessed the ebb and flow of immigrant crosscurrents that intensified the processes of cultural diffusion and integration. Cultural contacts and mixings developed as diverse migration streams integrated successful cultural-agricultural systems. The Prairie State developed as a pluralistic settlement seedbed for American societies moving deeper into the continental interior. These emerging Midwesterners in turn significantly contributed to the agricultural settlement of the Great Plains a generation later. As a new component of the expanding American culture region system during the nineteenth century, the Middle West metamorphosed its own traditional, spatially mixed, cultural identity (Shortridge 1989).

Bibliography / Index

Bibliography

Abbott, John C., ed. 1987. *Journey to New Switzerland.* Translated by Raymond J. Spahn. Carbondale: Southern Illinois University Press.

Abler, Ronald, John S. Adams, and Peter Gould. 1971. *Spatial Organization: The Geographer's View of the World.* Englewood Cliffs, NJ: Prentice-Hall.

Adler, Jeffrey F. 1991. *Yankee Merchants and the Making of the Urban West: The Rise and Fall of Antebellum St. Louis.* Cambridge: Cambridge University Press.

Agnew, John. 1987. *The United States in the World-Economy: A Regional Geography.* Cambridge: Cambridge University Press.

Alexander, Edward P. 1946. "Wisconsin, New York's Daughter State." *Wisconsin Magazine of History* 30:11–30.

Allen, Ira W. 1916. "Early Presbyterianism in East Central Illinois." *Transactions, Illinois State Historical Society* 22:71–78.

Allen, John L. 1976. "Lands of Myth, Waters of Wonder: The Place of the Imagination in the History of Geographical Exploration." In *Geographies of the Mind,* edited by David Lowenthal and Martyn J. Bowden, 41–61. New York: Oxford University Press.

Alvord, Clarence W. 1920. *The Illinois Country, 1673–1818.* Vol. 1. Springfield: Illinois Centennial History Commission.

Ander, Fritiof. 1933. "Some Factors in the Americanization of the Swedish Immigrants, 1850–1890." *Journal of the Illinois State Historical Society* 26:136–50.

Anderson, Arlow W. 1975. *The Norwegian-Americans.* Boston: Twayne.

Anderson, Russell H. 1929. "Agriculture in Illinois During the Civil War Period, 1850–1870." Ph.D. diss., University of Illinois.

————. 1943. "Advancing Across the Eastern Mississippi Valley." *Agricultural History* 17:97–104.

Babcock, Kendric C. 1914. *The Scandinavian Element in the United States.* Studies in the Social Sciences, vol. 3. Urbana: University of Illinois.

Babcock, Rufus, ed. 1965. *Memoir of John Mason Peck: Forty Years of Pioneer Life.* Carbondale: Southern Illinois University Press.

Barnhardt, John D., Jr. 1919. "The Rise of the Methodist Episcopal Church in Illinois from the Beginning to the Year 1832." *Journal of the Illinois State Historical Society* 12:149–217.

Barnhart, John D. 1935a. "Sources of Southern Migration into the Old Northwest." *Mississippi Valley Historical Review* 22:49–62.

————. 1935b. "The Southern Element in the Leadership of the Old Northwest." *Journal of Southern History* 1:186–97.

————. 1937a. "The Southern Influence in the Formation of Indiana." *Indiana Magazine of History* 33:261–76.

————. 1937b. "The Southern Influence in the Formation of Ohio." *Journal of Southern History* 3:28–42.

————. 1939. "The Southern Influence in the Formation of Illinois." *Journal of the Illinois State Historical Society* 32:358–78.

————. 1940. "Southern Contributions to the Social Order of the Old Northwest." *North Carolina Historical Review* 17:237–48.

————. 1941. "Frontiersmen and Planters in the Formation of Kentucky." *Journal of Southern History* 7:19–36.

————. 1951. "The Migration of Kentuckians Across the Ohio River." *Filson Club History Quarterly* 25:24–32.

————. 1970. *Valley of Democracy: The Frontier Versus the Plantation in the Ohio Valley, 1775–1818.* 1953. Reprint, Lincoln: University of Nebraska Press.

Barrows, Harlan H. 1910. *Geography of the Middle Illinois Valley.* Bulletin no. 15. Urbana: Illinois State Geological Survey.

Barry, P. T. 1902. "The First Irish in Illinois." *Transactions, Illinois State Historical Society* 7:63–70.

Beck, Lewis C. 1823. *A Gazetteer of the States of Illinois and Missouri.* Albany: Charles R. and George Webster.

Beinlich, B. A. 1909. "The Latin Immigration in Illinois." *Transactions, Illinois State Historical Society* 14:209–14.

Belcher, Wyatt W. 1947. *The Economic Rivalry Between St. Louis and Chicago, 1850–1880.* New York: Columbia University Press.

Benson, Adolph B., and Naboth Hedin, eds. 1969. *Swedes in America, 1638–1938.* New York: Haskel House.

Benton, Elbert J. 1903. *The Wabash Trade Route in the Development of the Old Northwest.* Studies in Historical and Political Science, vol. 21. Baltimore: Johns Hopkins Press.

Bergendoff, Conrad. 1948. "The Beginnings of Swedish Immigration into Illinois a Century Ago." *Journal of the Illinois State Historical Society* 41:16–27.

Bernheim, G. D. 1872. *History of the German Settlements and of the Lutheran Church in North and South Carolina.* Philadelphia: Lutheran Book Store.

Berthoff, Rowland T. 1968. *British Immigrants in Industrial America.* New York: Russell and Russell.

Bettis, Norman C. 1968. "The Swiss Community of Highland, Illinois: A Study in Historical Geography." Master's thesis, Western Illinois University.

Bidwell, Percy W., and John I. Falconer. 1925. *History of Agriculture in the Northern United States, 1620–1860.* Washington, DC: Carnegie Institution.

Bigelow, Hiram. 1902. "The Bishop Hill Colony." *Transactions, Illinois State Historical Society* 7:101–8.

Billington, Ray A. 1950. "The Frontier in Illinois History." *Journal of the Illinois State Historical Society* 43:28–45.

———. 1958. "The Garden of the World: Fact and Fiction." In *The Heritage of the Middle West,* edited by John J. Murray, 27–53. Norman: University of Oklahoma Press.

———. 1967. Westward Expansion: *A History of the American Frontier.* 3rd ed. New York: Macmillan.

Birkbeck, Morris. 1818a. *Letters from Illinois.* 3rd ed. London: Taylor and Hessey.

———. 1818b. *Notes on a Journey in America.* 3rd ed. London: Ridgway.

Blegen, Theodore. 1931. "Leaders in American Immigration." *Transactions, Illinois State Historical Society* 38:144–55.

———. 1969. *Norwegian Migration to America, 1825–1860.* 1931. Reprint, New York: Haskell House.

Bogen, F. W. 1852. *The German in America.* 3rd ed. Boston: B. H. Greene.

Boggess, Arthur C. 1968. *The Settlement of Illinois, 1778–1830.* 1908. Reprint, Ann Arbor: University Microfilms.

Bogue, Allan G. 1968. *From Prairie to Cornbelt: Farming on the Illinois and Iowa Prairies in the Nineteenth Century.* 1963. Reprint, Chicago: Quadrangle Paperbacks.

Bogue, Margaret B. 1959. *Patterns from the Sod: Land Use and Tenure in the Grand Prairie, 1850–1900.* Illinois Historical Collections, vol. 34. Springfield: Illinois State Historical Library.

Borchert, John R. 1987. "Maps, Geography, and Geographers." *Professional Geographer* 39:387–89.

Bowen, William A. 1972. "Migration and Settlement on a Far Western Frontier: Oregon to 1850." Ph.D. diss., University of California, Berkeley.

Boylan, Josephine. 1933. "Illinois Highways, 1700–1848." *Journal of the Illinois State Historical Society* 26:5–59.

Braderman, Eugene M. 1939. "Early Kentucky: Its Virginia Heritage." *South Atlantic Quarterly* 38:449–61.

Brown, Samuel R. 1817. *The Western Gazetteer; or Emigrant's Directory.* Auburn, NY: H. C. Southwick.

Brown, Thomas J. 1982. "The Age of Ambition in Quincy, Illinois." *Journal of the Illinois State Historical Society* 75:242–62.

Brown, William H. 1881. "Early History of Illinois." 1840. Reprint, *Fergus Historical Series* 14:81–102.

Buck, Solon J. 1912. "Pioneer Letters of Gershom Flagg." *Transactions, Illinois State Historical Society* 15:138–83.

———. 1912–13. "The New England Element in Illinois Politics Before 1833." *Proceedings, Mississippi Valley Historical Association* 5:49–61.

———. 1914. *Travel and Description, 1765–1865.* Illinois Historical Collections, vol. 9. Springfield: Illinois State Historical Library.

Buck, Solon J., and Elizabeth H. Buck. 1939. *The Planting of Civilization in Western Pennsylvania.* Pittsburgh: University of Pittsburgh.

———. 1967. *Illinois in 1818.* 2nd ed., rev. Urbana: University of Illinois Press.

Buckingham, Clyde E. 1942. "Early Settlers of the Rock River Valley." *Journal of the Illinois State Historical Society* 35:236–59.

Buckingham, J. S. 1842. *The Eastern and Western States of America.* 3 vols. London: Fisher.

Buley, R. Carlyle. 1950. *The Old Northwest: Pioneer Period 1815–1840.* 2 vols. Bloomington: Indiana University Press.

Burchard, Edward L. 1925. "Early Trails and Tides of Travel in the Lead Mine and Blackhawk Country." *Journal of the Illinois Historical Society* 17:565–604.

Busch, Francis X. 1922. "The French in Illinois." *Transactions, Illinois State Historical Society* 29:90–101.

Cammack, Eleanore A. 1954. "Notes on Wabash River Steamboating: Early Lafayette." *Indiana Magazine of History* 50:35–50.

Campbell, Charles B. 1906. "Bourbonnais; or the Early French Settlements in Kankakee County, Illinois." *Transactions, Illinois State Historical Society* 11:65–72.

Carey, H. C., and I. Lea. 1822. *Geographical, Statistical, and Historical Map of Illinois.* Philadelphia: H. C. Carey and I. Lea.

Carlson, Theodore L. 1951. *The Illinois Military Tract: A Study of Land Occupation, Utilization and Tenure.* Illinois Studies in the Social Sciences, vol. 32. Urbana: University of Illinois.

Carver, Craig M. 1987. *American Regional Dialects: A Word Geography.* Ann Arbor: University of Michigan.

Chaddock, Robert E. 1908. *Ohio Before 1850: A Study of the Early Influence of Pennsylvania and Southern Populations in Ohio.* Studies in History, Economics and Public Law, vol. 31. New York: Columbia University.

Chamberlin, M. H. 1902. "Rev. Peter Cartwright, D.D." *Transactions, Illinois State Historical Society* 7:47–56.

Chiniguy, Charles. 1886. *Fifty Years in the Church of Rome.* New York: Fleming H. Revell.

Clark, John G. 1966. *The Grain Trade in the Old Northwest.* Urbana: University of Illinois Press.

Coard, Helen C. 1941. "The Illinois and Michigan Canal as an Influence on Westward Migration." Master's thesis, University of Illinois.

Collot, Victor. 1908. "A Journey in North America: Extracts Describing a Visit to Illinois in 1796." *Transactions, Illinois State Historical Society* 13:269–98.

Combined History of Randolph, Monroe and Perry Counties, Illinois. 1883. Philadelphia: J. L. McDonough.

Conger, John L. 1932. *History of the Illinois River Valley.* 3 vols. Chicago: S. J. Clarke.

Conzen, Kathleen N. 1980. "Historical Approaches to the Study of Rural Ethnic Communities." In *Ethnicity on the Great Plains,* edited by Frederick C. Luebke, 1–18. Lincoln: University of Nebraska Press.

Conzen, Michael P. 1975. "A Transport Interpretation of the Growth of Urban Regions: An American Example." *Journal of Historical Geography* 1:361–82.

———. 1977. "The Maturing Urban System in the United States, 1840–1910." *Annals, Association of American Geographers* 67:88–108.

———. 1988. "The Historical and Geographical Development of the Illinois and Michigan Canal National Heritage Corridor." In *The Illinois and Michigan Canal National Heritage Corridor: A Guide to Its History and Sources,* edited by Michael P. Conzen and Kay J. Carr, 3–25. DeKalb: Northern Illinois University Press.

———. ed. 1987. *Focus on Ottawa: A Historical and Geographical Survey of Ottawa, Illinois, in the Twentieth Century.* Studies on the Illinois and Michigan Canal Corridor, no. 1. Chicago: Committee on Geographical Studies, The University of Chicago.

Conzen, Michael P., and Melissa J. Morales, eds. 1989. *Settling the Upper Illinois Valley: Patterns of Change in the I and M Canal Corridor, 1830–1900.* Studies on the Illinois and Michigan Canal Corridor, no. 3. Chicago: Committee on Geographical Studies, The University of Chicago.

Copeland, Louis A. 1898. "The Cornish in Southwest Wisconsin." *Collections of the State Historical Society of Wisconsin* 14:301–34.

Corliss, Carlton J. 1937. *Trails to Rails: A Story of Transportation Progress in Illinois.* 2nd ed. Chicago: Illinois Central System.

Cowperthwait, Thomas. 1850. *A New Map of the State of Illinois.* Philadelphia: Thomas Cowperthwait and Co.

Cronon, William. 1991. *Nature's Metropolis: Chicago and the Great West.* New York: W. W. Norton.

Curtiss, Daniel S. 1852. *Western Portraiture and Emigrants Guide.* New York: J. H. Colton.

Dana, Edmund. 1819. *Geographical Sketches of the Western Country: Designed for Emigrants and Settlers.* Cincinnati: Looker, Reynolds.

Danhof, Clarence H. 1969. *Change in Agriculture: The Northern United States, 1820–1870.* Cambridge: Harvard University Press.

Darby, William. 1818. *The Emigrant's Guide to the Western and Southwestern States and Territories.* New York: Kirk and Mercein.

Dixon, W. J., ed. 1973. *Biomedical Computer Programs.* Berkeley: University of California Press.

Dodge, Stanley D. 1932. "Bureau and the Princeton Community." *Annals, Association of American Geographers* 22:159–209.

Downs, Roger M., and David Stea. 1977. *Maps in Minds: Reflections on Cognitive Mapping.* New York: Harper and Row.

Doyle, Don H. 1978. *The Social Order of a Frontier Community: Jacksonville, Illinois, 1825–70.* Urbana: University of Illinois Press.

Drown, S. DeWitt. 1851. *Historical View of Peoria.* Peoria: E. O. Woodcock.

Earle, Carville. 1987. "Regional Economic Development West of the Appalachians, 1815–1860." In *North America: The Historical Geography of a Changing Continent,* edited by Robert D. Mitchell and Paul A. Groves, 172–97. Totowa, NJ: Rowman and Littlefield.

Eckenrode, H. J. 1918. "Virginia in the Making of Illinois." *Transactions, Illinois State Historical Society* 24:31–37.

Eighth Census, 1860, Population. 1864. Washington: Government Printing Office.

Elbert, E. Duane. 1985. "The American Roots of German Lutheranism in Illinois." *Illinois Historical Journal* 78:97–112.

Eller, David B. 1987. "George Wolfe and the 'Far Western' Brethren." *Illinois Historical Journal* 80:85–100.

The Emigrant's Guide, or Pocket Geography of the Western States and Territories. 1818. Cincinnati: Phillips and Speer.

Erdahl, Sivert. 1925. "Eric Janson and the Bishop Hill Colony." *Journal of the Illinois State Historical Society* 18:503–74.

Erickson, Charlotte. 1969. "British Immigrants in the Old Northwest, 1815–1860." In *The Frontier in American Development,* edited by David M. Ellis, 323–56. Ithaca: Cornell University Press.

————. 1972. *Invisible Immigrants: The Adaptation of English and Scottish Immigrants in Nineteenth Century America.* Coral Gables: University of Florida Press.

Faragher, John M. 1986. *Sugar Creek: Life on the Illinois Prairies.* New Haven: Yale University Press.

Farnham, Eliza W. 1846. *Life in the Prairie Land.* New York: Harper and Brothers.

Fishlow, Albert. 1965. *American Railroads and the Transformation of the Ante-Bellum Economy.* Cambridge: Harvard University Press.

Flint, Timothy. 1828. *Geography and History of the Western States.* 2 vols. Cincinnati: William M. Farnsworth.

Flower, George. 1882. *History of the English Settlement in Edwards County, Illinois.* Chicago Historical Society's Collection, vol. 1. Chicago: Fergus Printing Company.

Fogel, Robert W. 1964. *Railroads and American Economic Growth: Essays in Econometric History.* Baltimore: Johns Hopkins Press.

Ford, Thomas. 1854. *History of Illinois, from Its Commencement as a State in 1818–1847.* Chicago: S. C. Griggs.

Foreman, Grant. 1941. "English Settlers in Illinois." *Journal of the Illinois State Historical Society* 34:303–33.

Friis, Herman R. 1974. "The Importance of Canals, Roads, and Waterways in Establishing Paths of Migration in the United States Prior to 1861." Paper Read at Genealogists' Fair, May, Washington, DC.

Fuller, George N. 1935. "Settlement of Southern Michigan, 1805–1837." *Michigan History Magazine* 19:179–214.

Gates, Paul W. 1932. "Large-Scale Farming in Illinois, 1850–1870." *Agricultural History* 6:14–25.

————. 1934. *The Illinois Central Railroad and Its Colonization Work.* Cambridge: Harvard University Press.

————. 1945. "Frontier Landlords and Pioneer Tenants." *Journal of the Illinois State Historical Society* 38:13–20.

————. 1948. "Cattle Kings in the Prairies." *Mississippi Valley Historical Review* 35:379–412.

————. 1960. *The Farmer's Age: Agriculture 1815–1860.* New York: Holt, Rinehart and Winston.

Gerhard, Fred. 1857. *Illinois as It Is.* Chicago: Keen and Lee.

Gerlach, Russel L. 1986. *Settlement Patterns in Missouri.* Columbia: University of Missouri Press.

Gjerde, Jon. 1979. "The Effect of Community on Migration: Three Minnesota Townships, 1885–1905." *Journal of Historical Geography* 5:403–22.

————. 1985. *From Peasants to Farmers: The Migration from Balestrand, Norway, to the Upper Middle West.* Cambridge: Cambridge University Press.

Glassie, Henry. 1968. *Pattern in the Material Folk Culture of the Eastern United States.* Philadelphia: University of Pennsylvania Press.

Gray, Robert A. 1904. "The Scotch-Irish in America." *Transactions, Illinois State Historical Society* 9:308–13.

Haggett, Peter. 1966. *Locational Analysis in Human Geography.* New York: St. Martin's Press.

Haites, Erik F., and James Mak. 1970–71. "Ohio and Mississippi River Transportation, 1810–1860." *Explorations in Economic History* 8:153–80.

————. 1971. "Steamboating on the Mississippi, 1810–1860: A Purely Competitive Industry." *Business History Review* 45:52–78.

Haites, Erik F., James Mak, and Gary M. Walton. 1975. *Western River Transportation: The Era of Early Internal Development, 1810–1860.* Studies in Historical and Political Science, vol. 93. Baltimore: Johns Hopkins University Press.

Hall, James. 1828. *Letters from the West.* London: Henry Colburn.

————. 1831. "Hints to Emigrants." *Illinois Monthly Magazine* 14:49–55.

Handlin, Oscar. 1973. *The Uprooted.* 2nd ed. Boston: Little, Brown.

Hansen, Marcus L. 1961. *The Atlantic Migration, 1607–1860.* 1940. Reprint, New York: Harper Torchbooks.

Hansen, Marcus L., and John B. Brebner. 1940. *The Mingling of the Canadian and American Peoples.* 2 vols. New Haven: Yale University Press.

Hardin, Thomas L. 1963. "Vandalia, Illinois: Western Terminus of the National Road." Master's thesis, Eastern Illinois University.

————. 1967. "The National Road in Illinois." *Journal of the Illinois State Historical Society* 50:5–22.

Harker, J. R. 1925. "Progress in the Illinois Conference, 1824–1924." *Journal of the Illinois State Historical Society* 18:159–74.

Harkey, S. W. 1866. "The Early History of Lutheranism in Illinois." *Evangelical Quarterly Review* 16:526–46.

Hart, John F. 1972. "The Middle West." *Annals, Association of American Geographers* 62:258–82.

————. 1974. "The Spread of the Frontier and the Growth of Population." *Geoscience and Man* 5:73–81.

Hartmann, Edward G. 1967. *Americans from Wales.* Boston: Christopher Publishing House.

Haupert, Albert P. 1922. "The Moravian Settlement in Illinois." *Transactions, Illinois State Historical Society* 29:79–89.

Hawgood, John A. 1940. *The Tragedy of German-America.* New York: G. P. Putnam's Sons.

Hayter, Earl W. 1936. "Sources of Early Illinois Culture." *Transactions, Illinois State Historical Society* 43:81–96.

Heinl, Frank J. 1935. "Congregationalism in Jacksonville and Early Illinois." *Journal of the Illinois State Historical Society* 27:441–62.

Henlein, Paul C. 1959. *Cattle Kingdom in the Ohio Valley, 1783–1860.* Lexington: University of Kentucky Press.

History of St. Clair County, Illinois. 1881. Philadelphia: Brink, McDonough.

Hoffman, Charles F. 1835. *A Winter in the Far West.* 2 vols. London: Richard Bentley.

Holbrook, Stewart H. 1950. *The Yankee Exodus.* New York: Macmillan.

Houde, Mary J., and John Klasey. 1968. *Of the People: A Popular History of Kankakee County.* Chicago: General Printing.

Howard, Robert P. 1972. *Illinois: A History of the Prairie State.* Grand Rapids, MI: William B. Eerdmans.

Hubbard, Anson M. 1937. "A Colony Settlement: Geneseo, Illinois, 1836–1837." *Journal of the Illinois State Historical Society* 29:403–31.

Hudson, John C. 1969. "A Location Theory for Rural Settlement." *Annals, Association of American Geographers* 59:365–81.

———. 1973. "Two Dakota Homestead Frontiers." *Annals, Association of American Geographers* 63:442–62.

———. 1976. "Migration to an American Frontier." *Annals, Association of American Geographers* 66:242–65.

———. 1984a. "Cultural Geography and the Upper Great Lakes Region." *Journal of Cultural Geography* 5:19–32.

———. 1984b. "The Middle West as a Cultural Hybrid." *Transactions, Pioneer America Society* 7:35–46.

———. 1986. "Yankeeland in the Middle West." *Journal of Geography* 85:195–200.

———. 1988. "North American Origins of Middlewestern Frontier Populations." *Annals, Association of American Geographers* 78:395–413.

———. 1994. *Making the Corn Belt: A Geographical History of Middle-Western Agriculture.* Bloomington: Indiana University Press.

Hunter, Louis C. 1933–34. *Studies in the Economic History of the Ohio Valley.* Smith College Studies in History, vol. 19. Northampton, MA: Department of History of Smith College.

———. 1949. *Steamboats on the Western Rivers: An Economic and Technological History.* Cambridge: Harvard University Press.

Jakle, John A. 1977. *Images of the Ohio Valley: A Historical Geography of Travel, 1740 to 1860.* New York: Oxford University Press.

———. 1990. "Social Stereotypes and Place Images: People on the Trans-Appalachian Frontier as Viewed by Travelers." In *Place Images in Media: Portrayal, Experience, and Meaning,* edited by Leo Zonn, 83–103. Lanham, MD: Rowman and Littlefield Publishers.

Jakle, John A., Robert W. Bastian, and Douglas K. Meyer. 1989. *Common Houses in America's Small Towns.* Athens: University of Georgia Press.

Janson, Florence E. 1931. *The Background of Swedish Immigration, 1840–1930*. Social Service Monograph, no. 15. Chicago: University of Chicago Press.

Jasper County, Illinois. 1988. Vol. 1. Paducah, KY: Turner Publishing.

Jensen, Richard J. 1978. *Illinois: A Bicentennial History*. New York: W. W. Norton.

Jones, Abner D. 1838. *Illinois and the West*. Boston: Weeks, Jordan.

Jones, Dallas L. 1954. "Illinois in the 1830s: Impressions of British Travelers and Immigrants." *Journal of the Illinois State Historical Society* 47:252–63.

Jordan, Terry G. 1967. "The Imprint of the Upper and Lower South on Mid-Nineteenth Century Texas." *Annals, Association of American Geographers* 57:667–90.

———. 1969. "Population Origins in Texas, 1850." *Geographical Review* 59:83–103.

———. 1970. "The Texan Appalachia." *Annals, Association of American Geographers* 60:409–27.

Jordan, Terry G., and Matti Kaups. 1989. *The American Backwoods Frontier: An Ethnic and Ecological Interpretation*. Baltimore: Johns Hopkins University Press.

Jordan, Terry G., and Lester Rowntree. 1979. *The Human Mosaic*. 2nd ed. New York: Harper and Row.

Kamphoefner, Walter D. 1987. *The Westfalians from Germany to Missouri*. Princeton: Princeton University Press.

Kantowicz, Edward R. 1982. "A Fragment of French Canada on the Illinois Prairies." *Journal of the Illinois State Historical Society* 75:263–76.

Kelly, Mary G. 1939. *Catholic Immigrant Colonization Projects in the United States, 1815–1860*. New York: United States Catholic Historical Society.

Kern, Fred J. 1916. "The First Two Counties of Illinois and Their People." *Transactions, Illinois State Historical Society* 22:35–42.

King, Charles W., Jr. 1982. "Ferry Locations Enacted by the State of Illinois: 1819–1855." *Bulletin of the Illinois Geographical Society* 24:32–41.

Klett, Ada M. 1947. "Belleville Germans Look at America, 1833–1845." *Journal of the Illinois State Historical Society* 40:23–37.

Kniffen, Fred. 1965. "Folk Housing: Key to Diffusion." *Annals, Association of American Geographers* 55:549–77.

Kniffen, Fred, and Henry Glassie. 1966. "Building in Wood in the Eastern United States: A Time-Place Perspective." *Geographical Review* 56:40–66.

Knight, J. 1828. *Illinois and Missouri*. Philadelphia: Wm. Darby.

Kofoid, Carrie P. 1906. "Puritan Influences in the Formative Years of the Illinois History." *Transactions, Illinois State Historical Society* 10:261–338.

Kurath, Hans. 1949. *A Word Geography of the Eastern United States*. Ann Arbor: University of Michigan Press.

Lalor, J. J. 1873. "The Germans in the West." *Atlantic Monthly* 32:459–70.

Landis, Edward B. 1923. " The Influence of Tennesseans in the Formation of Illinois." *Transactions, Illinois State Historical Society* 30:133–53.

Lang, Elfrieda. 1954. "Southern Migration to Northern Indiana Before 1850." *Indiana Magazine of History* 50:349–56.

Latrobe, Charles J. 1835. *The Rambler in North America*. 2 vols. London: Seeley and Burnside.

Lawlis, Chelsea L. 1947a. "The Great Migration and the Whitewater Valley." *Indiana Magazine of History* 43:125–39.

———. 1947b. "Migration to the Whitewater Valley, 1820–1830." *Indiana Magazine of History* 43:225–39.

———. 1947c. "Settlement of the Whitewater Valley, 1790–1810." *Indiana Magazine of History* 43:23–40.

Lee, Judson F. 1917. "Transportation: A Factor in the Development of Northern Illinois Previous to 1860." *Journal of the Illinois State Historical Society* 10:17–85.

Lentz, E. G. 1927. "Pioneer Baptists of Illinois." *Transactions, Illinois State Historical Society* 34:122–31.

Lewis, Kenneth E. 1984. *The American Frontier: An Archaeological Study of Settlement Pattern and Process.* Orlando, FL: Academic Press.

Lewis, Marcus W. 1933. "The Development of Early Emigrant Trails East of the Mississippi River." *National Genealogical Society* 3:1–15.

Lewis, Peirce F. 1975. "Common Houses, Cultural Spoor." *Landscape* 19:1–22.

———. 1979. "Axioms for Reading the Landscape." *In The Interpretation of Ordinary Landscapes*, edited by Donald W. Meinig, 11–32. New York: Oxford University Press.

Leyburn, James G. 1962. *The Scotch-Irish: A Social History.* Chapel Hill: University of North Carolina Press.

Lindley, Harlow. 1912. "The Quakers in the Old Northwest." *Proceedings, Mississippi Valley Historical Association* 5:60–72.

Lynch, William O. 1943. "The Westward Flow of Southern Colonists Before 1861." *Journal of Southern History* 9:303–27.

MacMillan, Thomas C. 1919. "The Scots and Their Descendants in Illinois." *Transactions, Illinois State Historical Society* 26:31–85.

Madden, Beverly I. 1974. *Art, Crafts, and Architecture in Early Illinois.* Urbana: University of Illinois Press.

Maguire, John F. 1868. *The Irish in America.* London: Longmans, Green.

Mahoney, Timothy R. 1990. *River Towns in the Great West: The Structure of Provincial Urbanization in the American Midwest, 1820–1870.* Cambridge: Cambridge University Press.

Martineau, Harriet. 1837. *Society in America.* 3 vols. London: Saunders and Otley.

Mathews, Lois Kimbal. 1909. *The Expansion of New England.* Boston: Houghton Mifflin.

———. 1910. "The Erie Canal and the Settlement of the West." *Buffalo Historical Society Publications* 14:189–203.

Mayer, F. P., ed. 1960. *Alexis de Tocqueville: Journey to America.* New Haven: Yale University Press.

McConnel, George M. 1902. "Illinois and Its People." *Transactions, Illinois State Historical Society* 7:70–84.

McCormack, Thomas J. ed. 1909. *Memoirs of Gustave Koerner, 1809–1896.* 2 vols. Cedar Rapids, IA: Torch Press.

McDermott, John F. 1965. "Myths and Realities Concerning the Founding of St. Louis." In *The French in the Mississippi Valley*, edited by John F. McDermott, 1–13. Urbana: University of Illinois Press.

————. 1969. "Auguste Chouteau: First Citizen of Upper Louisiana." In *Frenchmen and French Ways in the Mississippi Valley,* edited by John F. McDermott, 1–15. Urbana: University of Illinois Press.

McGoorty, John P. 1927. "The Early Irish of Illinois." *Transactions, Illinois State Historical Society* 34:54–64.

McManis, Douglas R. 1964. *The Initial Evaluation and Utilization of the Illinois Prairies, 1815–1840.* Department of Geography Research Paper, no. 94. Chicago: University of Chicago.

McQuillan, D. Aidan. 1978. "Territory and Ethnic Identity: Some New Measures of an Old Theme in the Cultural Geography of the United States." In *European Settlement and Development in North America,* edited by James R. Gibson, 136–69. Toronto: University of Toronto Press.

Meinig, Donald W. 1965. "The Mormon Culture Region: Strategies and Patterns in the Geography of the American West, 1847–1964." *Annals, Association of American Geographers* 55:191–220.

————. 1969. *Imperial Texas: An Interpretive Essay in Cultural Geography.* Austin: University of Texas Press.

————. 1986. *The Shaping of America: Atlantic America, 1492–1800.* Vol. 1. New Haven: Yale University Press.

Merk, Frederick. 1978. *History of the Westward Movement.* New York: Alfred A. Knopf.

Meyer, Balthasar H. 1948. *History of Transportation in the United States Before 1860.* 1917. Reprint, Washington, DC: Carnegie Institution.

Meyer, David R. 1980. "A Dynamic Model of the Integration of Frontier Urban Places into the United States System of Cities." *Economic Geography* 56:120–40.

————. 1983. "Emergence of the American Manufacturing Belt: An Interpretation." *Journal of Historical Geography* 9:145–74.

————. 1989. "Midwestern Industrialization and the American Manufacturing Belt in the Nineteenth Century." *Journal of Economic History* 49:921–38.

Meyer, Douglas K. 1975. "Diffusion of Upland South Folk Housing to the Shawnee Hills of Southern Illinois." *Pioneer America* 7:55–66.

————. 1976a. "Illinois Culture Regions at Mid-Nineteenth Century." *Bulletin of the Illinois Geographical Society* 18:3–13.

————. 1976b. "Native-Born Immigrant Clusters on the Illinois Frontier." *Proceedings, Association of American Geographers* 8:41–44.

————. 1976c. "Southern Illinois Migration Fields: The Shawnee Hills in 1850." *Professional Geographer* 28:151–60.

————. 1979. "Types of Farming on the Illinois Frontier." *Bulletin of the Illinois Geographical Society* 21:9–17.

————. 1980. "Immigrant Clusters in the Illinois Military Tract." *Pioneer America* 12:97–112.

————. 1984. "Persistence and Change in Migrant Patterns in a Transitional Culture Region of the Prairie State." *Bulletin of the Illinois Geographical Society* 26:13–29.

————. 1988. "German Cottage Structure-Types of Southwestern Illinois." In *French and Germans in the Mississippi Valley: Landscape and Cultural Traditions,* edited by Michael Roark, 191–208. Cape Girardeau: Center for Regional History and Cultural Heritage, Southeast Missouri State University.

Mikkelsen, Michael A. 1892. *The Bishop Hill Colony: A Religious Communistic Settlement in Henry County, Illinois.* Johns Hopkins University Studies in Historical and Political Science, vol. 10. Baltimore: Johns Hopkins Press.

Miller, I. G. 1906. "The Icarian Community of Nauvoo, Illinois." *Transactions, Illinois State Historical Society* 11:103–7.

Miller, Kerby A. 1985. *Emigrants and Exiles: Ireland and the Irish Exodus to North America.* New York: Oxford University Press.

Mitchell, Robert D. 1966. "The Presbyterian Church as an Indicator of Westward Expansion in 18th Century America." *Professional Geographer* 18:293–99.

———. 1972. "The Shenandoah Valley Frontier." *Annals, Association of American Geographers* 62:461–86.

———. 1974. "Content and Context: Tidewater Characteristics in the Early Shenandoah Valley." *Maryland Historian* 5:79–92.

———. 1978. "The Formation of Early American Culture Regions: An Interpretation." In *European Settlement and Development in North America,* edited by James R. Gibson, 66–90. Toronto: University of Toronto Press.

Mitchell, Robert D., and Milton B. Newton. 1988. "The Appalachian Frontier: Views from the East and the Southwest." *Historical Geography Research Series* 21:1–64.

Mitchell, S. Augustus. 1837. *Illinois in 1837.* Philadelphia: Grigg and Elliot.

Monaghan, Jay. 1939. "The Welsh People in Chicago." *Journal of the Illinois State Historical Society* 32:498–516.

———. 1945. "North Carolinians in Illinois History." *North Carolina Historical Review* 22:418–59.

Moore, Frank. 1902. "Kaskaskia Road and Trails." *Transactions, Illinois State Historical Society* 7:125–28.

Morse, Jedidiah. 1812. *The American Universal Geography.* Vol. 1. Boston: Thomas and Andrews.

Morse, Sidney E., and Samuel Breese. 1844. *Illinois.* N.p.

Moses, John. 1889. *Illinois, Historical and Statistical.* Vol. 1. Chicago: Fergus Printing Company.

Moyers, William N. 1931. "A Story of Southern Illinois." *Journal of the Illinois State Historical Society* 24:26–104.

Muller, Edward K. 1976. "Selective Urban Growth in the Middle Ohio Valley, 1800–1860." *Geographical Review* 66:178–99.

———. 1977. "Regional Urbanization and the Selective Growth of Towns in North American Regions." *Journal of Historical Geography* 3:21–39.

Nelson, Peter. 1930. "A History of Agriculture in Illinois with Special Reference to Types of Farming." Ph.D. diss., University of Illinois.

Newbauer, Ella C. 1904. "The Swiss Settlements of Madison County, Illinois." *Transactions, Illinois State Historical Society* 11:232–37.

Newton, Milton. 1974. "Cultural Preadaptation and the Upland South." *Geoscience and Man* 5:143–54.

Norris and Gardiner, eds. 1847. *Illinois Annual Register and Western Business Directory.* Chicago: Geer and Wilson.

North, Douglass C. 1961. *The Economic Growth of the United States, 1790–1860*. Englewood Cliffs, NJ: Prentice-Hall.

———. 1974. *Growth and Welfare in the American Past: A New Economic History*. 2nd ed. Englewood Cliffs, NJ: Prentice-Hall.

O'Hanlon, John. 1976. *The Irish Emigrant's Guide for the United States*. 1851. Reprint, New York: Arno Press.

Oliver, William. 1843. *Eight Months in Illinois*. Newcastle Upon Tyne, England: William Andrew Mitchell.

Onahan, William F. 1881. "Irish Settlements in Illinois." *Catholic World* 33:157–62.

Ostergren, Robert C. 1979. "A Community Transplanted: The Formative Experience of a Swedish Immigrant Community in the Upper Middle West." *Journal of Historical Geography* 5:189–212.

———. 1981a. "Geographic Perspectives on the History of Settlement in the Upper Middle West." *Upper Midwest History* 1:27–39.

———. 1981b. "Land and Family in Rural Immigrant Communities." *Annals, Association of American Geographers* 71:400–411.

———. 1982. "Kinship Networks and Migration." *Social Science History* 6:293–320.

———. 1988. *A Community Transplanted: The Trans-Atlantic Experience of a Swedish Immigrant Settlement in the Upper Middle West, 1835–1915*. Madison: University of Wisconsin Press.

Owsley, Frank L. 1945. "The Pattern of Migration and Settlement on the Southern Frontier." *Journal of Southern History* 11:147–76.

Parker, William N. 1975. "From Northwest to Midwest: Social Bases of a Regional History." In *Essays in Nineteenth Century Economic History*, edited by David C. Klingaman and Richard K. Vedder, 3–34. Athens: Ohio University Press.

Patterson, Robert W. 1881. "Early Society in Southern Illinois." *Fergus Historical Series* 14:103–31.

Paullin, Charles O. 1932. *Atlas of the Historical Geography of the United States*. New York: American Geographical Society and the Carnegie Institution of Washington.

Paxson, Frederic L. 1911. "The Railroads of the 'Old Northwest' Before the Civil War." *Transactions, Wisconsin Academy of Sciences, Arts, and Letters* 17:243–74.

Pease, Theodore C. 1918. *The Frontier State, 1818–1848*. Vol. 2. Springfield: Illinois Centennial Commission.

Peck, John M. 1831. *A Guide for Emigrants*. Boston: Lincoln and Edmands.

———. 1836. *A New Guide for Emigrants to the West*. Boston: Gould, Kendal and Lincoln.

———. 1837. *A Gazetteer of Illinois*. 2nd ed. Philadelphia: Grigg and Elliot.

———. 1839. *The Traveller's Directory for Illinois*. New York: J. H. Colton.

Peet, J. Richard. 1969. "The Spatial Expansion of Commercial Agriculture in the Nineteenth Century: A von Thünen Interpretation." *Economic Geography* 45:283–301.

———. 1970–71. "Von Thünen Theory and the Dynamics of Agricultural Expansion." *Explorations in Economic History* 8:181–201.

Pei, Mario. 1957. *Language for Everybody*. New York: Devin-Adair.

Perrin, J. Nick. 1902. "The French in Illinois." *Transactions, Illinois State Historical Society* 7:129–32.

316 BIBLIOGRAPHY

Petersen, William J. 1937. *Steamboating on the Upper Mississippi: The Water Way to Iowa.* Iowa City: State Historical Society.

Pierce, Bessie L. 1937. *A History of Chicago: The Beginning of a City, 1673–1848.* Vol. 1. New York: Alfred A. Knopf.

———. 1940. *A History of Chicago: From Town to City, 1848–1871.* Vol. 2. New York: Alfred A. Knopf.

Pierson, George W. 1954. "The Moving Americans." *Yale Review* 44:99–112.

———. 1962. "The M-Factor in American History." *American Quarterly* 14:275–89.

———. 1964. "A Restless Temper . . ." American Historical Review 69:969–89.

Pillsbury, Richard. 1987. "The Pennsylvania Culture Area: A Reappraisal." *North American Culture* 3:37–54.

Poggi, Edith M. 1934. *The Prairie Province of Illinois.* Illinois Studies in the Social Sciences, vol. 29. Urbana: University of Illinois Press.

Pooley, William V. 1968. *The Settlement of Illinois from 1830 to 1850.* 1908. Reprint, Ann Arbor: University Microfilms.

Porter, Philip W., and Fred E. Lukermann. 1976. "The Geography of Utopia." In *Geographies of the Mind,* edited by David Lowenthal and Martyn J. Bowden, 197–223. New York: Oxford University Press.

Porterfield, Neil H. 1969. "Ste. Genevieve, Missouri." In *Frenchmen and French Ways in the Mississippi Valley,* edited by John F. McDermott, 141–77. Urbana: University of Illinois Press.

Power, Richard L. 1953a. *Planting Corn Belt Culture: The Impress of the Upland Southerner and Yankee in the Old Northwest.* Indianapolis: Indiana Historical Society.

———. 1953b. "Settlers on Corn Belt Soil." *Indiana Magazine of History* 49:161–72.

Pred, Allen R. 1966. *The Spatial Dynamics of United States Urban-Industrial Growth, 1800–1914.* Cambridge: MIT Press.

———. 1973. *Urban Growth and the Circulation of Information: The United States System of Cities, 1790–1840.* Cambridge: Harvard University Press.

Price, Edward T. 1968. "The Central Courthouse Square in the American County Seat." *Geographical Review* 58:29–60.

Putnam, James W. 1918. *The Illinois and Michigan Canal: A Study in Economic History.* Chicago Historical Society Collection, vol. 10. Chicago: University of Chicago Press.

Quaife, Milo M. 1923. *Chicago's Highways Old and New.* Chicago: D. F. Keller.

Qualey, Carlton C. 1934. "The Fox River Norwegian Settlement." *Journal of the Illinois State Historical Society* 27:133–77.

———. 1938. *Norwegian Settlement in the United States.* Northfield, MN: Norwegian-American Historical Association.

———. 1976. "Norwegians in the Upper Midwest: Immigration and Acculturation." In *Norwegian Influence on the Upper Midwest,* edited by Harald S. Naess, 16–20. Duluth, MN: Continuing Education and Extension, University of Minnesota.

Ramey, Nell H. 1949. "History of the Early Roads in Illinois." Master's thesis, University of Illinois.

Rennick, Percival G. 1935. "The Peoria and Galena Trail and Coach Road and the Peoria Neighborhood." *Journal of the Illinois State Historical Society* 27:351–431.

Reynolds, John. 1879. *My Own Times.* Chicago: Chicago Historical Society.

Rice, John G. 1977. "The Role of Culture and Community in Frontier Prairie Farming." *Journal of Historical Geography* 3:155–75.

Robins, Martha. 1938. *Historical Development of Jasper County Illinois.* N.p.: Martha Robins.

Rodman, Jane. 1947. "The English Settlement in Southern Illinois, 1815–1825." *Indiana Magazine of History* 43:329–62.

———. 1948. "The English Settlement in Southern Illinois as Viewed by English Travelers, 1815–1825." *Indiana Magazine of History* 44:37–68.

Rogers, Tommy W. 1968. "Origin and Destination of Tennessee Migrants, 1850–1860." *Tennessee Historical Quarterly* 27:118–22.

Rohrbough, Malcom J. 1978. *The Trans-Appalachia Frontier: People, Societies, and Institutions, 1775–1850.* New York: Oxford University Press.

Rooney, John F., Wilbur Zelinsky, and Dean R. Louder, eds. 1982. *This Remarkable Continent.* College Station: Texas A and M University Press.

Rose, Greg S. 1983. "Major Sources of Indiana's Settlers in 1850." *Transactions, Pioneer America Society* 6:67–76.

———. 1985a. "Hoosier Origins: The Nativity of Indiana's United States–Born Population in 1850." *Indiana Magazine of History* 81:201–32.

———. 1985b. "Information Sources for Nineteenth Century Midwestern Migration." *Professional Geographer* 37:66–72.

———. 1986a. "Quakers, North Carolinians and Blacks in Indiana's Settlement Pattern." *Journal of Cultural Geography* 7:35–48.

———. 1986b. "South Central Michigan Yankees." *Michigan History* 70:32–39.

———. 1986c. "Upland Southerners: The County Origins of Southern Migrants to Indiana by 1850." *Indiana Magazine of History* 82:242–63.

———. 1987a. "The County Origins of Southern Michigan's Settlers: 1800–1850." *East Lakes Geographer* 22:74–87.

———. 1987b. "The Origins of Canadian Settlers in Southern Michigan, 1820–1850." *Ontario History* 79:31–52.

———. 1988a. "The County Origins of Migrants to Eastern Ohio Before 1850." *Ohio Geographers* 16:24–41.

———. 1988b. "The National Road Border Between the North and the South in the Midwest by 1870." *Geoscience and Man* 25:159–67.

———. 1988c. "The Southern Midwest as 'Pennsylvania Extended.'" *East Lakes Geographer* 23:53–70.

———. 1991. "The Distribution of Indiana's Ethnic and Racial Minorities in 1850." *Indiana Magazine of History* 87:224–60.

Roseman, Curtis C. 1977. *Changing Migration Patterns Within the United States.* Resource Papers for College Geography, no. 77-2. Washington, D.C.: Association of American Geographers.

Rothan, Emmet H. 1946. *The German Catholic Immigrant in the United States, 1830–1860.* Washington, DC: Catholic University of America Press.

Rummel, R. J. 1970. *Applied Factor Analysis.* Evanston: Northwestern University Press.

Sainte Marie, Illinois, Sesquicentennial. 1987. N.p.

Salter, Mary A. 1981. "Morris Birkbeck's Empire on the Prairies—Speculation, Philanthropy, or Mania?" *Selected Papers in Illinois History* n.v.:1–6.

Sauer, Carl O. 1976. "Homestead and Community on the Middle Border." *Landscape* 20:44–47.

Savage, G. S. F. 1910. "Pioneer Congregational Ministers in Illinois." *Journal of the Illinois State Historical Society* 3:78–93.

Schieber, Harry N. 1969. "The Ohio-Mississippi Flatboat Trade: Some Reconsiderations." In *The Frontier in American Development,* edited by David M. Ellis, 277–98. Ithaca: Cornell University Press.

Schnell, J. Christopher. 1977. "Chicago Versus St. Louis: A Reassessment of the Great Rivalry." *Missouri Historical Review* 71:245–65.

Schockel, Bernard H. 1916. "History of Development of Jo Daviess County." In *Geology and Geography of the Galena and Elizabeth Quadrangles,* Bulletin no. 26, by Arthur C. Trowbridge and Eugene Wesley Shaw, 173–228. Urbana: Illinois State Geological Society.

Semmingsen, Ingrid. 1976. "Norwegian Immigration in Nordic Perspective: Recent Migration Research." In *Norwegian Influence on the Upper Midwest,* edited by Harald S. Naess, 6–12. Duluth: Continuing Education and Extension, University of Minnesota.

Seventh Census Population Schedules, 1850. 1971. Microfilm Publication M432, Illinois Rolls 97-134. Washington: National Archives and Records Service.

Shea, John G. 1879. "The Canadian Element in the United States." *American Catholic Quarterly Review* 4:581–604.

Shirreff, Patrick. 1835. *A Tour Through North America.* Edinburgh, Scotland: Oliver and Boyd.

Short, W. F. 1902. "Early Religious Methods and Leaders in Illinois." *Transactions, Illinois State Historical Society* 7:56–62.

Shortridge, James R. 1989. *The Middle West: Its Meaning in American Culture.* Lawrence: University Press of Kansas.

Sifferd, C. W. 1911. "The Lutheran Church in Southern Illinois." *Lutheran Quarterly* 41:412–23.

Smith, George W. 1940. "Egypt's Cultural Contribution." *Papers in Illinois History* n.v.:40–58.

Smith, Page. 1966. *As a City upon a Hill: The Town in American History.* New York: Alfred A. Knopf.

Spahn, Raymond J. 1978. "German Accounts of Early Nineteenth-Century Life in Illinois." *Papers on Language and Literature* 14:473–88.

Sparks, William H. 1872. *The Memories of Fifty Years.* 3rd ed. Philadelphia: Claxton, Remsen and Haffelfinger.

Spencer, A. P. 1937. *Centennial History of Highland, Illinois, 1837–1937.* Highland: Highland Centennial Association.

Steckel, Richard H. 1983. "The Economic Foundations of East-West Migration During the 19th Century." *Explorations in Economic History* 20:14–36.

Stephenson, George M. 1969. "Religion." In *Swedes in America, 1638–1938,* edited by Adolph B. Benson and Naboth Hedin, 126–139. 1938. Reprint, New York: Haskell House.

Stilwell, Lewis D. 1948. *Migration from Vermont.* Montpelier: Vermont Historical Society.

Stock, Harry T. 1919. "Protestantism in Illinois Before 1835." *Journal of the Illinois State Historical Society* 12:1–31.

Strawn, H. J. 1910. "The English Settlement in Edwards County, Illinois." *Transactions, Illinois State Historical Society* 15:51–54.

Stroble, Paul E., Jr. 1987. "Ferdinand Ernst and the German Colony at Vandalia." *Illinois Historical Journal* 80:101–10.

Stuart, James. 1833. *Three Years in North America.* 3rd ed., rev. 2 vols. Edinburgh, Scotland: Cadell.

Sutton, Robert M. 1965. "Illinois' Year of Decision, 1837." *Journal of the Illinois State Historical Society* 58:34–53.

Swierenga, Robert P. 1981. "The New Rural History: Defining the Parameters." *Great Plains Quarterly* 1:211–23.

———. 1989. "The Settlement of the Old Northwest: Ethnic Pluralism in a Featureless Plain." *Journal of the Early Republic* 9:73–105.

Taaffe, Edward J., and Howard L. Gauthier, Jr. 1973. *Geography of Transportation.* Englewood Cliffs, NJ: Prentice-Hall.

Taylor, George R. 1931. "Agrarian Discontent in the Mississippi Valley Preceding the War of 1812." *Journal of Political Economy* 39:471–505.

———. 1951. *The Transportation Revolution, 1815–1860.* New York: Rinehart.

Tevebaugh, John L. 1952. "Frontier Mail: Illinois, 1800–1830." Master's thesis, University of Illinois.

Thrapp, Russell F. 1911. "Early Religious Beginnings in Illinois." *Journal of the Illinois State Historical Society* 4:303–16.

Throne, Mildred. 1949. "Southern Iowa Agriculture, 1833–1890: The Progress from Subsistence to Commercial Corn-Belt Farming." *Agricultural History* 23:124–30.

Turner, Frederick J. 1897. "Dominant Forces in Western Life." *Atlantic Monthly* 79:433–45.

———. 1906. *Rise of the New West, 1819–1829.* New York: Harper and Brothers.

———. 1920. *The Frontier in American History.* New York: Henry Holt.

———. 1935. *The United States, 1830–1850: The Nation and Its Sections.* New York: Henry Holt.

Turner, Lynn W. 1940. "The United Brethren Church in Illinois." *Papers in Illinois History* n.v.:39–66.

Tyler, Alice Felt. 1942. "A New England Family on the Illinois Frontier." *Papers in Illinois History* n.v.:72–92.

Uppvall, Axel J. 1969. "The Swedish Language in America." In *Swedes in America, 1638–1938,* edited by Adolph B. Benson and Naboth Hedin, 52–74. 1938. Reprint, New York: Haskell House.

Vance, James E., Jr. 1970. *The Merchant's World: The Geography of Wholesaling.* Englewood Cliffs, NJ: Prentice-Hall.

———. 1990. *Capturing the Horizon: The Historical Geography of Transportation since the Sixteenth Century.* Baltimore: Johns Hopkins University Press.

van Ravenswaay, Charles. 1977. *The Arts and Architecture of German Settlement in Missouri: A Survey of a Vanishing Culture.* Columbia: University of Missouri Press.

Van Zandt, Nicholas B. 1818. *A Full Description of the Soil, Water, Timber, and Prairies of Each Lot, or Quarter Section of the Military Lands Between the Mississippi and Illinois Rivers.* Washington City: P. Force.

Vedder, Richard K., and Lowell E. Gallaway. 1975. "Migration and the Old Northwest." In *Essays in Nineteenth Century Economic History,* edited by David C. Klingaman and Richard K. Vedder, 159–76. Athens: Ohio University Press.

Villard, Oswald G. 1942. "The 'Latin Peasants' of Belleville, Illinois." *Journal of the Illinois State Historical Society* 35:7–20.

von Grueningen, John P., ed. 1940. *The Swiss in the United States.* Madison: Swiss-American Historical Society.

Wade, Richard C. 1958. "Urban Life in Western America, 1790–1830." *American Historical Review* 64:14–30.

———. 1959. *The Urban Frontier: The Rise of Western Cities, 1790–1830.* Cambridge: Harvard University Press.

Walker, Mack. 1964. *Germany and the Emigration, 1816–1885.* Cambridge: Harvard University Press.

Wallerstein, Immanuel. 1974. *The Modern World-System: Capitalist Agriculture and the Origins of the European World-Economy in the Sixteenth Century.* New York: Academic Press.

———. 1980. *The Modern World-System II: Mercantilism and the Consolidation of the European World-Economy, 1600–1750.* New York: Academic Press.

———. 1989. *The Modern World-System III: The Second Era of Great Expansion of the Capitalist World-Economy, 1730–1840.* San Diego: Academic Press.

Walsh, Margaret. 1978. "The Spatial Evolution of the Mid-western Pork Industry, 1835–1875." *Journal of Historical Geography* 4:1–22.

———. 1982. *The Rise of the Midwestern Meat Packing Industry.* Lexington: University Press of Kentucky.

Walsh, Mary E. 1947. "Land Routes in Southern Illinois, 1763–1830." Master's thesis, University of Notre Dame.

Walton, Gary M. 1987. "River Transportation and the Old Northwest Territory." In *Essays on the Economy of the Old Northwest,* edited by David C. Klingaman and Richard K. Vedder, 225–42. Athens: Ohio University Press.

Wasson, Donald L. 1973. "The Transformation of a Frontier Kankakee County, 1850–1870." Master's thesis, Eastern Illinois University.

Wilhelm, Hubert G. H. 1982. *The Origin and Distribution of Settlement Groups: Ohio, 1850.* Athens, OH: Cutler Hall Printing Services.

Wilkey, Harry L. 1939. "Infant Industries in Illinois as Illustrated in Quincy, 1836–1856." *Journal of the Illinois State Historical Society* 32:475–97.

Winsor, Roger A. 1987. "Environmental Imagery of the Wet Prairie of East Central Illinois, 1820–1920." *Journal of Historical Geography* 13:375–97.

Wittke, Carl F. 1952. *Refugees of Revolution: The German Forty-Eighters in America.* Philadelphia: University of Pennsylvania Press.

———. 1956. *The Irish in America.* Baton Rouge: Louisiana State University Press.

———. 1967. *The Germans in America.* New York: Teachers College Press.

Wood, Joseph S. 1982. "Village and Community in Early Colonial New England." *Journal of Historical Geography* 8:333–46.

Woods, John. 1822. *Two Years' Residence in the Settlement on the English Prairie, in the Illinois Country, United States.* London: Longman, Hurst, Rees, Orme, and Brown.

Wooten, Hugh H. 1953. "Westward Migration from Iredell County, 1800–1850." *North Carolina Historical Review* 30:61–71.

Wyman, Mark. 1984. *Immigrants in the Valley: Irish, Germans and Americans in the Upper Mississippi Country, 1830–1860.* Chicago: Nelson-Hall.

Young, J. H. 1939. *The Tourist's Pocket Map of the State of Illinois.* Philadelphia: S. Augustus Mitchell.

Young, Richard M. 1836. "Military Bounty Lands." *Western Monthly Magazine* 5:334–45.

Zelinsky, Wilbur. 1973. *The Cultural Geography of the United States.* Englewood Cliffs, NJ: Prentice-Hall.

Index

Abbeville (S.C.), 160, 244

Adams County, 151, 202, 205, 217–18, 220–22, 237

agriculture: and commercial growth, 130; corn-livestock farming, 98–100; livestock farming, 101; mixed-pioneer farming, 100–101; and self-sufficiency to marketplace, 98–103; wheat farming, 101

Alabamians: and destinations in eastern America, 159; and settlement patterns in Illinois, 162–63

Albion, 248–49

Allison's Prairie, 12

Alton, 236, 244, 256; commercial character of, 88–89; and commercial rivalry with St. Louis, 88–89; description of, 89; as gateway, 69; location of, 88

America letters, 245–46, 250, 253, 272

American Bottom, 57, 111, 115; and commercial agriculture growth, 132; description of, 3, 10, 110; and dispersed and clustered settlements, 111–13; and evolution of "siren" status, 53–54; locational advantages of, 117–18; and settlement during late 1700s, 19–22; and settlement 1800–1809, 22–23; and settlement shift north, 60

Andover, 271; as colony, 177, 182; and origin of name, 182

Argyle, 256

Argyllshire (Scotland), 256

Augustana College, 272

Baptists, 148

Beardstown, 237; character of, 71; as quintessential pork packing river town, 93–94

Beck, Lewis C., 5–6

Bellefontaine, 19–20

Belleville: accessibility of, 63–64; as German culture hearth of southwest Illinois, 236; German heritage of, 240–41; location of, 5

Berkeley County (W.Va.), 20

Big Muddy River, 124; as attractive settlement area, 121–22; description and location of, 6

Birkbeck, Morris: as English colony promoter, 249; as image maker, 229

Birkbeck and Flower English colony, 122, 248–49

Bishop Hill colony, 272–73; as Swedish utopian experiment, 271–72

Bluegrass Region: as source of Kentuckians, 145

Boehne, Ferdinand, 236

Bourbonnais, 252–54; and "Petit Canada," 253–54

Bourbonnais, François, 253

Braddock's Road, 44

DOUGLAS K. MEYER, a professor of geography at Eastern Illinois University since 1970, received his doctorate from Michigan State University. His previous books include *Common Houses in America's Small Towns: The Atlantic Seaboard to the Mississippi Valley* (coauthored with John A. Jakle and Robert W. Bastian) and *A Pictorial Landscape History of Charleston, Illinois* (coauthored with Nancy Easter Shick).